LAFAYETTE AND THE CLOSE OF THE
AMERICAN REVOLUTION

LAFAYETTE

AND THE
CLOSE OF THE AMERICAN
REVOLUTION

By

LOUIS GOTTSCHALK

THE UNIVERSITY OF CHICAGO PRESS
CHICAGO & LONDON

THE UNIVERSITY OF CHICAGO PRESS, CHICAGO & LONDON
The University of Toronto Press, Toronto 5, Canada

TO

STUART W. JACKSON
Collector, bibliographer, collaborator, and friend

PREFACE

THIS volume covers four years of the life of the Marquis de Lafayette. It begins with his return to France in February, 1779, after his first successes in America. It ends with his visit to Chavaniac in March, 1783, after the signing of the general preliminaries of peace by England, France, and the United States.

No other person played so varied a role as Lafayette in the events which brought the American Revolutionary War to a close. Washington and perhaps some others were more important as soldiers. Franklin and perhaps some others were more important as diplomats. But Washington was a soldier only in America, while Lafayette campaigned in America, France, and Spain; and Franklin was a diplomat only in France, while Lafayette carried on negotiations in Spain as well. He was at Le Havre when an invasion of England was contemplated; at Yorktown, when the serious fighting in America ended; and at Cadiz, when the final effort to end the war was being made. He played a part in securing armies, supplies, and loans for America from France, in maintaining co-operation between the French and American armies, in negotiating peace with England, in winning a friendly attitude toward the United States in Spain. Before the war was over he had begun to think of American problems of peace—union, trade, slavery, and soldiers' grievances. Though in all these starts (to borrow racing language) he rarely if ever took first place, no other participant won as many seconds in as many separate events.

It is not astonishing, therefore, that this part of Lafayette's career has received a large share of historians' attention. Over three hundred bibliographical items are cited in these pages, several hundred others being regarded as either negligible or involving a duplication of effort; and that does not include the numerous unpublished sources that have been exploited. Tower and Doniol have each given these years of Lafayette's career about the same amount of space as is here assigned to them, and subsequent biographers have been content to lean heavily on them. It has proved necessary, however, to re-examine Tower and Doniol, not only because they were overly imbued with the spirit of Franco-American solidarity but also because they allowed themselves to be misled too often by Lafayette's *Mémoires*. Though both historians deserve great credit for discovering and publishing many documents that supplemented those published by the editors of the *Mémoires*, they missed some sources which would have been highly productive, and many more have been made available since they wrote. Even of those which they presented, a more critical examination would have been possible. It has, therefore, been necessary not only to complete and to correct their portrayals in many details, both minute and significant, but also to view them in clearer perspective.

The important departures from the interpretations of other authors are indicated below—usually in the "Bibliographical notes." The first eight chapters are significant not so much because of any new theses that they maintain as because they represent an effort to tell more completely and more accurately than previously the story of Lafayette's part in the proposed invasion of England, in the communications with the French expeditionary force in America, in the discovery of Arnold's treason, and in the mutinies of 1781. The next five chapters, dealing with the Virginia campaign of 1781, present a reinterpretation of Lafayette's generalship, maintaining that his merit lay less in his strategical achievements or in his influence upon De Grasse than in his ability to win the co-operation of the military and civil authorities of Virginia. The last four chapters are largely new since they deal with a phase of Lafayette's career which, coming chronologically after the close of Tower's book and receiving only a casual attention from Doniol, has been largely neglected by earlier biographers. Throughout the volume and particularly in the appendixes it has been necessary to examine some of the traditional anecdotes about Lafayette;

many of them have been repudiated as entirely incredible or as lacking in confirmation. The relations of Lafayette with Washington, Franklin, Hamilton, Wayne, Steuben, Arnold, Rochambeau, Vergennes, Greene, Adams, Cornwallis, and many other eighteenth-century luminaries have also been set forth with details, and sometimes with interpretations, that are new.

This volume is the last of three on the youth of Lafayette. A fitting subtitle for all three volumes would be "The making of a liberal." This volume bears out the contention of the earlier ones that Lafayette acquired his interest in freedom and reform from his American associations. For there is a striking crescendo of attention to such questions as Irish liberty, parliaments, rights of man, emancipation of Negroes, and freedom of trade throughout these years, until they stand forth quite clearly as a major interest in 1783. It also bears out the contention of earlier volumes that Lafayette was officious and *intrigant*, though always with good intentions and often with good results. Having developed the character of a liberal and well-intentioned *intrigant*, he passes from youth to manhood, from the American Revolution and success to the French Revolution and disaster. Subsequent volumes will tell the story of the disaster.

The travel and investigation necessary to prepare these studies could not have been undertaken without stipends from research foundations. For their kindness in supporting my efforts or in providing me with assistants I express my deep appreciation to the John Simon Guggenheim Memorial Foundation, the Social Science Research Committee of the University of Chicago, and the National Youth Administration.

It would be futile to try to mention everyone who has aided me in the preparation of these volumes. I can name only those who have been the most helpful, trusting that if the others do not find my indebtedness expressed in the footnotes, they will, nevertheless, recognize my gratitude. After fourteen years of investigation of the same subject one is likely to forget names more readily than services rendered. I must first acknowledge my debt to the staffs of several libraries in Paris, hoping that some day, in a future brighter for Paris than the present seems to promise, that acknowledgment will reach them. Foremost among those libraries are the Archives du Ministère des Affaires Étrangères, the Archives du Ministère de la Guerre, the Archives Nationales, and the Bibliothèque Nationale. In England the British Museum and the Public Record Office have been especially co-operative, and I wish to express my gratefulness to their staffs. In this country many libraries have opened their manuscript collections and rare books to me, often providing me with photostats of priceless documents and entrusting irreplaceable volumes to the post on my request. Foremost among these were the Alderman Library, the John Carter Brown Library, the University of Chicago Libraries, the William L. Clements Library, the Library of Congress, the Harvard College Library, the Henry E. Huntington Library and Art Gallery, the Pierpont Morgan Library, the National Archives, the New York Public Library, the University of Pennsylvania Library, the University of Rochester Library, the Library of the Supreme Council 33°, the William and Mary College Library, and the Yale University Library. To the librarians and staffs of those institutions I wish to proffer my thanks. Several learned and historical societies have also been most generous with books and photostats. Among these are the American Philosophical Society, the Massachusetts Historical Society, the New Jersey Historical Society, the New York Historical Society, the Historical Society of Pennsylvania, the South Carolina Historical Society, the Virginia State Historical Society, and Colonial Williamsburg, Inc. To the officers, librarians, and staffs of those societies I also wish to express my gratitude. Many collectors of autographs have sent me copies and photostats of their most precious possessions. Some have allowed me to work in their homes. Some have assisted me in deciphering and understanding the documents in their collections. To all of them I am greatly in debt. Foremost among them are George Alexander Ball, Walter Burges Beals, William Bell Clark, the Essex County Country Club, Allyn K. Ford, Walter P. Gardner, Sidney P. Hessel, Stuart W. Jackson (to whom this book is dedicated), Comte Louis de Lasteyrie, and Lloyd W. Smith. For help in the examination of the Morristown National Park and the Colonial National Historical Park, as well as for historical information and documentary assistance, I owe much to Elbert Cox, Melvin J. Weig, and Thomas M. Pitkin, and their staffs. Among students and research assistants who have labored hard and loyally with me I must mention particularly Frances Dorothy Acomb, Jane Lohrer Cates, Donald F. Lach, Melvin Dow Kennedy, Katharine Moser Burks, Gordon H. McNeil, and Gordon Stewart. Many of my colleagues and friends have sent me notes and given me useful bits of information. Among these are Pauline Relyea Anderson, Gilbert Chinard, Bernard Faÿ, Frances E. Gillespie, John Gough, and Georgia Robison. And for seeing this volume as well as earlier ones through the several painful stages by which a manuscript becomes a full-blown book I have to thank my friends Fruma Gottschalk, William Thomas Hutchinson, Marshall Mason Knappen, and Hill Shine.

LOUIS GOTTSCHALK

CHICAGO, ILLINOIS
January 21, 1942

Note to the second printing: The collections that formerly belonged to Judge Walter P. Gardner and to Mr. George Alexander Ball have passed into the possession of the Indiana University Library, and references to them below have been changed to "Gardner-Ball Collection." The collection that formerly belonged to Mr. Stuart W. Jackson has passed into the possession of the Yale University Library, and references to it below have been changed to "Jackson Collection."

L. G.

CHICAGO, ILLINOIS
June 7, 1965

TABLE OF CONTENTS

CHAPTER I

Plotting against England

ANOTHER year had rolled around to the carnival season. Among the young aristocrats at Versailles that meant parties, dances and shows, new clothes, and fresh adventures. There was a war going on somewhere, and far across the ocean sailors were drowning and soldiers were bleeding for the glory of France and the freedom of America. But the winter air of Versailles did not carry their cries. The wonted sedateness was varied now only by the merry shouts of young people in silks and satins as they greeted friends or gave instructions to chair-carriers and coachmen in livery.

Many of the best young men and women were on their way to the home of the Prince de Poix.[1] The prince was giving a ball for his numerous friends at court, and it was an honor to be invited, for the prince was a member of the glorious Noailles family. If he and his friends stopped to think at all that evening, they might have remembered that just two years ago that very February night of 1779 their young crony, the Marquis de Lafayette, had completed his plans to go to America. On that occasion it had been the queen's ball that they had attended.[2]

Few of them had seen Lafayette since. He and Poix had gone to London shortly afterward, not even Poix realizing what was in his younger cousin's mind. Poix had returned to Paris without the marquis, who had meanwhile fled to America. Lafayette was a great man now—a major-general and a hero, far different from the reserved, awkward, inexperienced captain of cavalry

[1] Mrs. Paget Toynbee (ed.), *Lettres de la Marquise du Deffand à Horace Walpole* (*1776–1780*) (3 vols.; London, 1912), III, 496–97.

[2] Cf. Louis Gottschalk, *Lafayette comes to America* (Chicago, 1935), pp. 88–89.

whom they had known. Now that France was herself at war with England and needed her sons for her own army, would he be coming back, as had so many French officers who had gone to volunteer their services to America?

At two o'clock in the morning the prince's ball was still in full swing. Suddenly—as if from nowhere—there appeared in the ballroom the Marquis de Lafayette himself.[3] He had come home, as some had felt sure he would. He had landed five days earlier (February 6) at Brest. After spending two days in the port, he had hastened to present himself at Versailles. Sending an aide on toward Paris to deliver to the American commissioners the instructions he carried for them, he had himself alighted at the home of his cousin and former colonel, the Prince de Poix. Everyone was delighted.

The marquis stayed that night at Poix's house, for he wished to remain in Versailles to see the ministers. The next morning Poix introduced him to Prime Minister Maurepas. Lafayette had been requested by the Continental Congress to submit to the French government a scheme for a joint invasion of Canada. For two hours the prime minister and the marquis remained closeted, discussing the situation in the country from which Lafayette had just come.

That afternoon, without being allowed to pay his respects to the king, Lafayette left for Paris. He was under orders to see no one but relatives. That was not only a precautionary measure, it was required by the dignity of the king as well. For, after all, in going to America in 1777, despite the king's apparent wish, the young soldier had committed an offense that must bear a penalty. The home of his wife's grandfather, where he had lived before he went to America, was to be his jail, and her grandfather, the Duc de Noailles, was to be his jailer.

Adrienne de Lafayette, his wife, learned from her gentle mother that her Gilbert had at last returned.[4] The young wife had not been happy during his absence. He had left without

[3] *Lettres de la Marquise du Deffand*, III, 496.

[4] Virginie de Lasteyrie, *La vie de Madame de Lafayette précédée d'une notice sur la vie de sa mère Mme la Duchesse d'Ayen* (Paris, 1869), pp. 62–63 and 200.

saying goodbye to her. His first-born child, Henriette, had died shortly after he had left; the second, Anastasie, had been born when he had been gone only a few months. Reports that he had been wounded, captured, imprisoned, that he had led great expeditions into trackless wildernesses, that he had returned, came quick upon one anothers' heels. They were not always without foundation. Adrienne's mother had managed to keep from her the worst of the rumors. She had even sent her off to visit relatives and friends in the hope of taking the young mother's mind from her misery. And here at last was her husband, sound in health and famous! Adrienne had not yet learned, as she was one day to do, how to restrain her joy at beholding him. She made no effort to conceal her emotions, but so hard and successfully had she struggled while he was gone not to be unworthy of the dignity of her twenty years that only her mother fully understood how much his safe return really meant to her.

The Duc de Noailles proved to be, as everyone knew he would, a very lenient jailer. Since nearly every member of court society was a sister or a cousin or an aunt by blood or marriage of nearly everyone else, Lafayette did not lack company merely because he was permitted to see only relatives. The Comtesse Marie de Boufflers, who, despite her fifty-five years, was still celebrated as a beauty, was his mother's cousin, hence an aunt *à la mode de Bretagne.* So he was permitted to have supper with her on Sunday.[5] At least one of the illustrious Americans in Paris, Ralph Izard, also called on him.[6]

Lafayette soon made plans to visit John Adams at Passy and to meet Benjamin Franklin in Versailles;[7] but, being confined to Paris and having no way of claiming kinship to them, the king's prisoner was obliged to cancel his appointments. He gave as his

[5] February 14; see *Lettres de la Marquise du Deffand,* III, 496.

[6] Izard to Laurens, February 18, 1779, "Izard-Laurens correspondence," *South Carolina historical and genealogical magazine,* XXII (1921), 81–82.

[7] Adams to Committee on Foreign Affairs, February 13, 1779, C. F. Adams (ed.), *Works of John Adams* (10 vols.; Boston, 1850–56), VII, 82; Lafayette to Franklin, February [13 or 14], 1779, American Philosophical Society (hereafter referred to as APS), Franklin papers, Vol. XLII, no. 134.

excuse that the king wished him to remain secluded in order not to add to the "thousand absurd discourses about the American affairs."[8] He sought permission to have Franklin come to see him instead.[9]

The request gave the neophyte diplomat an opportunity to speak of the proposed Canadian expedition. It was already the subject of common gossip, he warned. He flattered himself, he wrote to the Comte de Vergennes,[10] minister of foreign affairs, that it was through no indiscretion on his part that matters of state had not been treated with appropriate secrecy. Several members of the American Congress were, however, less discreet than himself, he said, and the large number of French officers returning from America made it difficult to keep the truth from being known. It was bound to be detected unless confused with the great number of false rumors that were encountered everywhere. "That," wrote the youthful aristocrat just returned from the transatlantic republic, "is the only means available for saving our secret from all the inconveniences that result in America both from the form of government and from the character of some of the people who have charge of things."

Vergennes had no great love for the Canadian plan. He could see no advantage to France in the conquest of Canada for the United States. And so Lafayette did not get to see Franklin for a while. Franklin, besides, had a bad attack of gout and for over a month did not even go to Versailles to present his new credentials as minister plenipotentiary.

The marquis' week of confinement soon was over. On February 19 he wrote to the king to express his regret that he had

[8] Lafayette to Franklin, February [13 or 14], 1779, *loc. cit.*

[9] Lafayette to Vergennes, February 14, 1779, Archives des Affaires Étrangères (Paris), correspondance politique, États-Unis (hereafter referred to as AAE, corr. pol., É.-U.), Vol. VII, fols. 212–13; B. F. Stevens, *Facsimiles of manuscripts in European archives relating to America, 1773–1783* (25 vols.; London, 1889–98), XVII, no. 1601; Henri Doniol, *Histoire de la participation de la France à l'établissement des États-Unis d'Amérique* (5 vols. and a supplement; Paris, 1886–99), IV, 230 n.; and several other places. (Hereafter when a document is to be found *inter alia* in Stevens' *Facsimiles*, reference will be made only to Stevens' work.)

[10] February 14, 1779, *loc. cit.*

done anything of which His Majesty disapproved.[11] "My love for my country, my desire to witness the humiliation of her enemies, a political instinct which the recent treaty [of France with the United States] would seem to justify . . . . are, Sire, the reasons which determined the part I took in the American cause." He said nothing here, as he so often had in America, of his willingness to sacrifice himself for the American cause. Undoubtedly such sentiments would have sounded strange to Louis XVI's ears. Instead he wrote: "When I received Your Majesty's orders, I attributed them even more to the tender solicitude of my family than to any formula of conduct considered proper toward England. The emotions of my heart overcame my reason. I thought I could foresee that my departure would not be disapproved, just as surely as I saw the impossibility of permitting it; and, if I added to my disobedience behavior which rendered me still more guilty, it is, Sire, because every Frenchman ought to risk his fortune, his hopes, and even public esteem, rather than harm the interests of his country in compromising the government by his conduct." He explained that he would have returned to France sooner if the commandant of the king's fleet in America, Admiral d'Estaing, had not persuaded him to stay longer. "I am very far, Sire," he concluded, "from daring to justify myself before Your Majesty for an act of disobedience of which you disapprove and which I ought to regret. I am even farther from assigning value to a few services much below the reward I found in the very happiness of being useful. But it is important for my peace of mind that Your Majesty attribute to its true motive the conduct which brings upon me your disfavor. The nature of my errors gives me the right to hope that I may efface them. It is to Your Majesty's kindness that I shall owe the happiness of ridding myself of them by the opportunity that you will deign to give me to serve you in whatever country and in whatever manner it may be." The American friends of His Majesty's "very humble and very obedient servant and faithful subject," who had some-

---

[11] Bibliothèque Nationale (Paris), nouvelles acquisitions françaises (hereafter referred to as BN, n.a.f.) 22738, fols. 6–7.

times heard him talk like a republican, might have been surprised by the tone of that petition. *Autres temps, autres mœurs!* Lafayette was once more the soldier of his king and not of General Washington. He found no difficulty in changing into the new character. On the whole, the part of "faithful subject" was still a more natural one for him to play in France than any other, no matter how used he had become to another role on a faraway stage.

Relieved from his "imprisonment" and his week of inactivity, Lafayette resumed the life of a courtier. Those who had once thought of him as a negligible young man, important only because he had money and had made a good marriage, now were forced to admit that they had been mistaken. Lafayette received the attention of ministers and, "what was still more important"[12] (the phrase is his own), the kisses of the ladies. One lady who had once been indifferent to him and whose indifference was commonly supposed to have been among the reasons for his sudden departure for America—the beautiful Aglaé de Hunolstein—now was proud to be able to say that she saw him often. "I consider myself lucky," she confessed, "to have some place in his esteem."[13] He went to the theater one night and found that the play contained a few lines in his honor, which the audience loudly applauded. "It is the first time," commented one of the observers, "that a living person has heard himself praised upon the stage."[14] While Lafayette called on the author to thank him for the compliment, the Duc de Chartres, who was believed to have a proprietary interest in Mme de Hunolstein, was reported to have done everything in his power to discredit the play.[15]

---

[12] *Mémoires, correspondance et manuscrits du Général Lafayette* (hereafter called *Mémoires*) (6 vols.; Paris, 1837–38), I, 65.

[13] Mme de Hunolstein to Shuvalov, March 20, 1779, Louis Gottschalk, *Lady-in-waiting* (Baltimore, 1939), pp. 54 and 120.

[14] [Louis Bachaumont and continuators], *Mémoires secrets pour servir à l'histoire de la république des lettres en France depuis MDCCLXII jusqu'à nos jours* (36 vols.; London, 1783–89), XIV, 29–30 and 51. The play was *L'amour françois* by Rochon de Chabannes.

[15] *Ibid.*; cf. Gottschalk, *Lady-in-waiting*, pp. 58–60, and François Métra *et al.*, *Correspondance secrète, politique et littéraire* (18 vols.; London, 1787–90), VIII, 63.

Queen Marie Antoinette, who had once considered Lafayette an awkward lout, now wished him signally honored. Through the queen's intercession,[16] he received a promotion in the French army. Despite his exalted rank in the American service, in France on his return he was still, as he had been on his departure, a *capitaine réformé*. The chance to take him off the reserve list and to give him a higher rank than captain occurred opportunely with the resignation of the Marquis de Créquy as lieutenant-commander of the regiment of the King's Dragoons. The king named Lafayette to that post, which was to carry with it the rank of *mestre de camp* (about equivalent to the rank of colonel in the cavalry). There was some jealousy and resentment among men who were older than he in the service,[17] but it was generally admitted that it was not an undeserved honor—and it was certainly not unpaid for. Lafayette had to deliver 80,000 livres for the rank. His commission was dated as of March 3, 1779, though the formal details of the transaction were not completed until April.[18]

Meanwhile, the great young man had not been idle in the realm of politics. To be sure, unfortunate circumstances interfered with his meeting Franklin. There was always Franklin's gout, and Lafayette at one time had a sudden fever.[19] In good time he found an opportunity to visit the Americans at Passy. Adams urged upon him the necessity of aid for America—particularly naval aid.[20] Franklin, in accord with the instructions delivered to him by Lafayette, besought the reduction of Halifax and Quebec and stressed the lamentable need of war materials.[21] Between the hoary sage from Pennsylvania and the dashing young soldier from Auvergne was hatched a plan to

[16] *Mémoires*, I, 65.   [17] Cf. below, p. 350 and n. 12.

[18] Archives du Ministère de la Guerre (Paris) (hereafter referred to as AMG), Lafayette, dossier 1261.

[19] Lafayette to Franklin, [February 19], 1779, APS, Franklin papers, Vol. XLII, no. 136.

[20] Adams to Lafayette, February 21, 1779, Adams, VII, 84–86.

[21] Franklin to the Committee of Foreign Affairs, May 26, 1779, A. H. Smyth (ed.), *The writings of Benjamin Franklin* (10 vols.; London, 1905–7), VII, 320; cf. Lafayette to Franklin, [February 22 ?], 1779, APS, Franklin papers, Vol. XLII, no. 143.

bring forcefully to the ministry the necessity for greater vigor in the prosecution of the war in America.

Lafayette readily fell under Franklin's unassuming charm. He intended to return to Passy the next day to see the man whom he now styled "my good friend."[22] He was prevented by an order to attend the king's levee. "In our kingly country," explained the "faithful subject" of Louis XVI,[23] in a manner quite appropriate to a republican philosopher's prejudices, "we have a foolish law called *etiquette* that any one tho' a sensible man, must absolutely follow." Yet that senseless etiquette signified that he was restored to royal favor and enabled him at last to see the king and the king's ministers. The letters of praise which he had brought home from influential Americans, the unstinted commendation which Congress had especially indicted for Louis XVI's eyes had the'desired effect. The king reprimanded him gently for the disobedience to orders of which he had been formally guilty and restored him to liberty, urging him only to avoid public places where he might be too generously lauded for his defiance.[24] His Majesty then invited the young "rebel" to go hunting with him; and the "rebel" soon tried to persuade the king's ministers to believe that the prosperity of the several states of America was in direct proportion to the amount of freedom to be found there.[25]

That was the beginning of a series of visits to Versailles. Lafayette now ran from door to door of the ministers in order to further his and Franklin's plan. They waited eagerly for news from America which might induce the government to take some decisive action, but nothing reliable came. Disturbing reports arrived of British success in Georgia and South Carolina. The only cause for joy was the fall of Senegal to a French expedition. Lafayette wrote to the great champion of humanity in Passy that he rejoiced not only for the victory to the allied cause but

[22] Lafayette to Franklin, [February 21 ?], 1779, APS, Franklin papers, Vol. XLII, no. 142.

[23] *Ibid.*   [24] *Mémoires*, I, 65.

[25] Lafayette to Franklin, [March 20 ?], 1779, APS, Franklin papers, Vol. XIII, no. 3; Harvard College Library, Sparks Manuscripts (hereafter referred to as Sparks MSS) XXXII, pp. 127–28; *Mémoires*, III, 197.

also because he knew that "the Southern gentlemen of America" would be pleased to get Negro slaves once more from that area.[26]

The fall of Senegal was a great balm to French pride. It did not cause the ministry to throw all discretion to the wind, however. For not all avowed champions of liberty in France were as susceptible to Franklin as was Lafayette. There was, for example, the director of finances, Jacques Necker. He knew that the French government, if it were to avoid eventual financial ruin, must economize. Expenditures in the American war were already too large to please him, and he set his face sternly against any new demands. That attitude fitted well with the purposes of Vergennes, who continued to look upon the conquest of Nova Scotia and Canada for the United States as of dubious advantage to France and France's ally, Spain. Lafayette soon discovered that his scheme for a large, generously armed expedition of conquest in America was considered "impossible for the present."[27] Maurepas informed him that other plans were already afoot (and, in fact, France was secretly beginning the preparations of a large-scale invasion of England). "We shall have to wait and see what will result from the operations already determined upon," said the prime minister.[28]

While hoping for a reluctant ministry to come to a decision, Franklin's new friend jumped to another outlet for his restless ambition. Again he went the rounds of the ministers and between interviews wrote them long memoranda. Maurepas, Vergennes, Minister of Marine Sartine, Minister of War Montbarey among Frenchmen, Franklin and Captain John Paul Jones among Americans, soon found themselves enmeshed in his friendly conspiracy. In fact, the new idea was probably first suggested to Lafayette by Jones's confidants, while Lafayette was still at Brest.[29] All Lafayette wanted was permission to

---

[26] Lafayette to Franklin, [March 20 ?], 1779, *loc. cit.*

[27] Lafayette to Congress, June 12, 1779, Library of Congress, papers of the Continental Congress (hereafter referred to as PCC), no. 156, fol. 90.

[28] Quoted in Lafayette to Maurepas, January 25, 1780, Charlemagne Tower, *The Marquis de La Fayette in the American Revolution* (2 vols.; Philadelphia, 1901), II, 500.

[29] Cf. Fourniez to Jones, February 7, 1779, C. H. Lincoln (ed.), *Calendar of John Paul Jones manuscripts in the Library of Congress* (Washington, 1903), p. 72.

take fifteen hundred or two thousand men into the Irish Sea on a few vessels commanded by Jones. They would burn some cities, place others under ransom, drive a wholesome fear into the hearts of Englishmen, add to the prestige of France's name in America, and offset the bad effect on the public mind which news of English successes in Georgia and South Carolina was creating. "Favorable or unfavorable exertion, finance, conduct and views in America depend entirely upon public opinion," the American major-general explained to Maurepas. "It is important to attach it to our side, and anything that has an appearance of boldness and of superiority in relation to England will assure us that advantage. Moreover, the individuals who make up the whole republican administration have private passions, views and prejudices. I believe that I have had the time to learn what strikes them most, and that is why I dare to submit to you some ideas regarding my favorite expedition."[30] He even hoped to create internal disorders in Ireland by encouraging the Protestant counties, which were more friendly to the Americans than the rest. "Every day that defers the news of a success which can be flaunted in America," he argued, "is a day which does us great harm in that country."[31]

Maurepas yielded to Lafayette's importunity. He gave the eager soldier permission to sound out the American plenipotentiary. Franklin thought well of the scheme—had, in fact, thought well of it long before it dawned upon Lafayette.[32] For the English coast was defenseless, the enemy would be taken by surprise, and huge sums of money could be extracted from captured cities for ransom. He offered to put at his young friend's disposal Captain John Paul Jones, who had recently returned from a successful raid in English waters, as well as the vessel "Duc de Duras" and perhaps also the "Alliance," on

[30] March 14, 1779, Archives Nationales (Paris) (hereafter referred to as AN), Marine B⁴ 172, fols. 103–4v.

[31] Ibid.

[32] Franklin to Lafayette, March 22, 1779, Smyth, VII, 269–71; cf. Lafayette to Maurepas, March 23, 1779, AN, Marine B⁴ 172, fols. 99–100. See also Valentine Thomson, Knight of the seas: the adventurous life of John Paul Jones (New York, 1939), pp. 209–12.

which Lafayette had just returned. Lafayette had only to find the men and the means.

The marquis counted on the French government to provide for his expedition. He went to see Maurepas, who referred him to Vergennes. Lafayette submitted to that gentleman a detailed report of his needs and his intentions.[33] If properly equipped, he had little doubt that he would be able to attack Liverpool, White Haven, Lancaster, and Cork, make them pay the costs of their humiliation, and get away before his victims could gather a force large enough to capture him.

Vergennes did not discourage the breathless schemer. He let him go to see the minister of marine. Nor did Sartine discourage him. On the contrary, he was quite receptive. For some time now he had been planning with Captain Jones some such measure, though on a more modest scale. He indicated his willingness to talk to Jones, and Lafayette took it upon himself to summon the sailor to Versailles.[34] Within a few days Jones was in Paris and learned from Franklin and Sartine that he had been chosen to command the sea forces in an expedition which was altogether to his liking and was far more ambitious than he had dared to hope.[35]

One of the principal obstacles was the lack of money. Someone had estimated that an expedition like that which Lafayette had in mind would cost over a million francs.[36] But even that obstacle was soon surmounted. M. Leray de Chaumont, one of the king's commissary agents and a close friend of Franklin, had been initiated by Sartine into Lafayette's secret.[37] He proved willing to place his abilities as a businessman and organizer at the marquis' disposal. Those abilities were very respectable, even though Jones, who had already picked another

[33] Lafayette to Vergennes, March 26, 1779, AN, Marine B⁴ 172, fols. 101–2v.

[34] Lafayette to Franklin, [ca. March 31, 1779], APS, Franklin papers, Vol. XIII, no. 2.

[35] Mrs. Reginald De Koven, The life and letters of John Paul Jones (2 vols.; New York, 1913), I, 402–3.

[36] "Projet d'expédition contre l'Angleterre" (MS), BN, n.a.f. 9428, fols. 344–45.

[37] Lafayette to Vergennes, April 1, 1779, Stevens, Facsimiles, XVII, no. 1602.

commissary agent, never reposed full confidence in Chaumont.[38] With Chaumont's aid in equipping him, Lafayette hoped to be able to start off sometime in April, adequately prepared for any emergency. By the end of the month, however, nothing had yet been done.

Lafayette, meanwhile, had hit upon another way to be helpful to America and to win the war. He had sounded out the Swedish ambassador in a proposal that the king of Sweden lend vessels to the United States. The ambassador thought it could be arranged if France would guarantee payment for them in case they were lost. Lafayette wrote to Vergennes urging his approval and stating that he would put up his own fortune as security for payment, should it prove necessary. "If, while we are negotiating with Sweden," he added, "contributions from England bring us some profit, I might again remind you of my favorite project."[39]

The incessant goings and comings of Lafayette could not fail to excite interest in a public for which he had long ceased to have a private life. The journalists reported his activity in frequent bulletins, guessing (as Lafayette wanted them to guess) that he was preparing an expedition to America.[40] A number of young men offered to volunteer their services for the campaign.[41] "All Paris," Franklin informed Chaumont, "now talks of the Marquis de la Fayette's going to America with troops, etc."[42] That was what Lafayette wanted. It would preserve the element of surprise in his expedition and keep the English from preparing countermeasures.

At the homes of the illustrious whom the marquis visited they tried to pump him for information. Even sedate and fastidious persons like the old-fashioned Duc de Croÿ could not contain

[38] *Ibid.;* De Koven, I, 405–13; [R. C. Sands (ed.)], *Life and correspondence of John Paul Jones* (New York, 1830), p. 255.

[39] April 26, 1779, Stevens, *Facsimiles*, XVII, no. 1603.

[40] Cf. *Gazette de Leyde*, May 11, 1779, p. 2; May 14, supplément, p. 3; May 18, p. 2; May 25, supplément, p. 1.

[41] Cf. AAE, corr. pol., É.-U., Vol. VIII, fols. 136–37; APS, W. T. Franklin papers, Vol. CVIII, no. 36; and Franklin papers, Vol. III, no. 189; Adams, VII, 90–91.

[42] May 10, 1779, Smyth, VII, 313.

their curiosity. One night at a dinner, where Croÿ and Lafayette were both guests, they talked about America for half an hour or more. The young man listened with a politeness which, thought the duke,[43] did him credit and was very rare indeed among young people in those days but refused to state whether he was to sail from the port of Lorient for America or elsewhere, if at all. The duke was impressed with Lafayette's show of modesty, simplicity, and discretion. Strangely enough (for almost no other contemporary shared this opinion), he thought that the young general had a handsome face. But Croÿ was an older man than most of the other observers and perhaps had other standards of beauty.

Even Queen Marie Antoinette was not permitted to know the secret of the expedition preparing at Lorient. She saw Lafayette one day at Versailles and asked him about it. Lafayette replied that he was under orders from M. de Maurepas not to discuss the matter. The queen was greatly annoyed, taking the incident as a deliberate affront by a minister who counted on her husband's support against her. She spoke at great length about it to her trusted Austrian adviser, Comte de Mercy-Argenteau. Mercy consulted the Empress Maria Theresa of Austria, the queen's mother.[44] Thus Lafayette became again a subject of imperial and international conversation, but his plan remained a mystery.

Lafayette's discretion and his constant runnings back and forth to Versailles had meanwhile effected wonders. At the end of April Franklin dispatched formal orders to Jones and added a word of homely advice: "As this is understood to be an American expedition, under the Congress' commission and colours, the Marquis, who is a major-general in that service, has of course the step in point of rank, and he must have the command of the land forces, which are committed by the king to his care. . . . . I am persuaded, that, whatever authority his rank might in strictness give him, he will not have the least desire to

[43] *Journal inédit du Duc de Croÿ, 1718–1784* (4 vols.; Paris, 1906–7), IV, 176–77.

[44] Alfred Arneth and M.-A. Geoffroy (eds.), *Correspondance secrète entre Marie Thérèse et le Cte de Mercy-Argenteau* (3 vols.; Paris, 1874), III, 315.

interfere with you. There is honour enough to be got for both of you, if the expedition is conducted with prudent unanimity. The circumstance is indeed a little unusual; for there is not only a junction of land and sea forces, but there is also a junction of Frenchmen and American, which increases the difficulty of maintaining a good understanding. A cool, prudent, conduct in the chiefs is, therefore, the more necessary; and I trust neither of you will in that respect be deficient."[45] Jones replied that Franklin's "liberal and noble-minded instructions would make a coward brave. . . . . It shall be my pride and ambition in the strict pursuit of your instructions to deserve success."[46] Lafayette also wrote to the captain to assure him, "although this command is not equal to my military rank," of his readiness to co-operate in the common cause. "Be certain, my dear sir, that I shall be happy to divide with you whatever share of glory may await us."[47] Jones answered: "Where men of fine feeling are concerned there is seldom misunderstanding; and I am sure I should do violence to my sensibility if I were capable of giving you a moment's pain by any part of my conduct."[48] To Sartine the elated sailor repeated his assurance: "No misunderstanding will arise between the other commander and myself because we like and esteem each other."[49]

Despite those noble sentiments, it was not until the second week in May that anything was done to give substance to the plan for Captain Jones's armada.[50] Then at last boats began to arrive at Lorient with orders to join his forces. Soon the "Bonhomme Richard" (the erstwhile "Duc de Duras"), the "Alliance," the "Pallas," the "Surf," and the "Vengeance" were at Lorient, and others were expected. Jones put his men to work night and day to make them ready. Pontgibaud and Gimat, two of the marquis' numerous aides, watched their efforts in idle

---

[45] April 27, 1779, Smyth, VII, 296–98.

[46] May 1, 1779, *ibid.*, pp. 299–300 n.

[47] April 27, 1779, De Koven, I, 405.   [48] May 1, 1779, *ibid.*, pp. 406–7.

[49] May 1, 1779, photostat in the Gardner-Ball Collection, Indiana University Library.

[50] Jones to Franklin, May 26, 1779, APS, Franklin papers, Vol. XIV, Part 1, no. 141; incorrectly dated May 22 in De Koven, I, 413–14.

curiosity while waiting for their chief.[51] Jones himself soon found his hands full with a mutiny led by Captain Landais, but the work of collecting and arming the vessels and recruiting the men continued under the capable eye of Chaumont, who had also come to Lorient to assist.[52]

Lafayette in Paris, meanwhile, arranged his affairs against a new departure. This time he was as deliberate as he had earlier béen precipitate. Lafayette's former lawyer, Jean Gerard, had died while his wealthy client was in America, and the courts had designated Jean Grattepain to take his place provisionally until Lafayette's return.[53] To assure the careful management of numerous properties in Auvergne, Touraine, Brittany, and Paris, the major-general reconfirmed the appointment of Jean Grattepain and Jacques-Philippe Grattepain-Morizot as stewards for his estate. On May 12 the Grattepains came to the Noailles home in Paris and formally drew up a power of attorney to buy and sell and otherwise manage his property in his name. The act specified that the delegation of power was made necessary because the marquis was "on the point of boarding ship to go to foreign countries."[54]

Within a week the electric atmosphere which surrounded Lafayette and instilled in most of those who drew near him expectations of great things to come suddenly changed into one of dull defeat and resignation. Exactly what happened is not made clear by the cries of protest that escaped the disillusioned warrior. Montbarey, the minister of war, was probably responsible. He seems to have been the only minister at Versailles who refused to share the prevailing enthusiasm for the youthful general.[55] The minister of war appears to have de-

[51] *Mémoires du Comte de Moré (1758-1837)* (Paris, 1898), p. 97.

[52] Cf. Lafayette to Chaumont, [April 16, 1779], collection of George Dumont, New York City; Jones to Brown, March 13, 1781, Francis Wharton (ed.), *The Revolutionary diplomatic correspondance of the United States* (6 vols.; Washington, 1889), IV, 288-97.

[53] Decree of the Châtelet, January 13, 1779, AN, T 1051⁶³.

[54] "Procuration généralle, M. le Mis. Dela Fayette à MM. Grattepain et Morizot" (MS), Charles A. Brown Collection, University of Rochester Library.

[55] Cf. *Mémoires autographes de M. le Prince de Montbarey* (3 vols.; Paris, 1826-27), II, 261-63 and *passim;* cf. Lafayette to Vergennes, [May 17, 1779 ?], Stevens, *Facsimiles*, XVII, no. 1612; see n. 56 below.

cided—perhaps because Spain had secretly joined the alliance
in April and was expected at any moment to break with England openly—that a major effort might be attempted against the
British Isles. All Jones's vessels would then be needed, and
Lafayette's raiders would have to be assigned to more important tasks. Whatever the explanation, Lafayette soon learned
that he was required to proceed to his post as commander of his
own regiment of King's Dragoons.

The marquis suddenly saw himself deprived of the leading
role in his long-wished-for humiliation of England and obliged
to serve at home under men whom he considered less experienced in the art of war. He protested vigorously in person and
in writing, first to Vergennes.[56] Couldn't the government spare
at least a small force, six hundred men and a couple of ships?
Vergennes was sympathetic, but he must see Prime Minister
Maurepas. Knowing more about future plans for an invasion of
England than he could tell his visitor, Maurepas tried to dissuade the unhappy petitioner.[57] A small force would be beneath
Lafayette's dignity, he said. Besides, Lafayette would be unwise to risk the certainty of the command of his own regiment
for the uncertainty of the newly proposed expedition. Lafayette
was not to be dissuaded, however. Public opinion had been so
kind to him, he answered, that even his setting-out with six
hundred men would be attributed to its real motive and pardoned. Furthermore, to suspect him of being capable of bar-
gaining with his country and of despising any opportunity to
serve her was to be lacking either in judgment or in memory.
Maurepas would do nothing at the moment. He asked the ve-
hement young man to return in two days.

On leaving Maurepas, Lafayette again appealed to Vergennes. Perhaps, he wrote,[58] the government would consider
letting him have a force of fifteen hundred or two thousand

---

[56] Cf. Lafayette to Vergennes, [May 17, 1779 ?], Stevens, *Facsimiles*, XVII,
no. 1612. Another hand has marked the original of this letter (AAE, corr. pol., É.-U.,
Vol. IX, fols. 366–67) "s. d. mais d'août 1779." The letter clearly belongs, however,
to the middle of May. Because of this incorrect dating it has never been properly
understood.

[57] *Ibid.*   [58] *Ibid.*

grenadiers and dragoons to act as an independent advance guard of a larger army destined to invade England. In that case, he would be perfectly willing to serve under some worthy *maréchal-de-camp*. "I want to be chosen in accordance with my place in the army and not at court," he declared. "I am not of the court, still less a courtier, and I beg the king's ministers to look upon me as a soldier fresh from the barracks."[59] Frankly, he said, there were not many lieutenant-generals, fewer *maréchaux-de-camp*, and no brigadiers who had had as important commands as chance had given him. Besides, he knew the English and the English knew him. Wouldn't Vergennes as his friend use his influence with Maurepas in his favor—and that soon, for if he got word from Lorient that his ships were ready, he intended to go off immediately without waiting for a decision.

Whether or not Vergennes did intervene on behalf of his disappointed young friend, Maurepas remained adamant. When Lafayette returned to see him for a second interview, he was no more friendly to the armada of six hundred men than before.[60] Lafayette felt that it would appear immodest to propose the alternative plan he had in mind—a separate advance corps of fifteen hundred or two thousand grenadiers and chasseurs. So he left Maurepas's office disconsolate. In a forlorn note to Vergennes, with whom he felt less timid, he again begged for his separate command. "Bear in mind, Monsieur le Comte," he pleaded,[61] "that after my luck, which I owe to my good star, in making my name known a little in America and to some friends in Europe, it would be desirable for me to have it mentioned from time to time in England."

Nothing came of all the marquis' expostulations. In wrath and despair he poured out his heart to Franklin. Resentment made his English worse than usual. "I could indeed make out

---

[59] *Ibid.*

[60] Lafayette to Vergennes, [May 19, 1779 ?], Stevens, *Facsimiles*, XVII, no. 1613. The misdating of the original of this letter in AAE (*loc. cit.*, fol. 368) has had the same result as that indicated in n. 56 above for the preceding document.

[61] *Ibid.*

an immense book upon so rich a matter," he wrote.[62] "But, my dear doctor, tho' I hate the British nation, I however am obliged to confess that those ministers and theyr executors are unhappily of the same nature (whatever corrupted it might be) as the rest of mankind. Don't you feel any shame in thinking those people are by theyr features some thing like men?"

Protest as vehemently as he might, the deflated marquis had to admit that he was defeated. He sadly penned a long farewell to Jones: "I dare say you will be very sorry to hear that the King's disposition concerning our plan has been quite altered, and that instead of meeting you, I am now going to take the command of the King's Regiment at Saints. . . . . Political and military reasons have occasioned that alteration of things, and I am only to tell you, my good friend, how sorry I feel not to be a witness of your success, ability and glory. . . . . Be convinced, Sir, that nothing could please me more than the pleasure of having again something of the kind to undertake with such an officer as Captain Jones."[63]

Jones was dumbfounded. He explained his disappointment to Franklin in a restrained letter in which he asked for further instructions.[64] When they finally came, they proved to be orders to act as a convoy and to chase the enemy's vessels from the Bay of Biscay. They involved dangerous enough work, but how unlike the "liberal and noble minded instructions" of an earlier day! Jones soon began to blame Chaumont for his disappointment. Chaumont had blabbed so freely about the expedition that now it had to be abandoned![65] Yet Jones was less than just to the well-intentioned and hard-working commissary, who had been in no way to blame for the decisions of his superiors.

Lafayette, meanwhile, made several other gestures as chief protagonist of America and adviser of the ministers on the

[62] May 19, 1779, APS, Franklin papers, Vol. XIV, no. 125.

[63] May 22, 1779, Library of Congress (hereafter referred to as LC), John Paul Jones MSS.

[64] May 26, 1779, APS, Franklin papers, Vol. XIV, Part 1, no. 141; cf. above, n. 50.

[65] Jones to Franklin, July 4, 1779, APS, Franklin papers, Vol. XV, Part 1, no. 15; *Mémoirs of Rear-Admiral Paul Jones* (2 vols.; Edinburgh, 1830), I, 148–49. Cf. De Koven, I, 420–30; [Sands (ed.)], *Correspondence of John Paul Jones*, p. 255.

affairs of England. He suggested, among other things, that Dr. Edward Bancroft, Franklin's secretary, should be sent to Ireland to stir up rebellion there.[66] The idea of a flank attack upon England by exciting rebellion in Ireland naturally suggested itself to her enemies whenever she was at war. Vergennes had first broached the subject to Lafayette,[67] but the minister was cautious where the soldier was vigorous. To the American major-general, Ireland became not merely an avenue of attack upon England; interest in her freedom was the first offshoot in Europe of his career as champion of liberty in America. "I, *in confidence*, tell you," he soon wrote to Washington,[68] "that the scheme of my heart would be to make her [Ireland] as free and independent as America."

Here too—as in America—the cause of liberty was no worse served because merely a by-product of a hatred toward England. Lafayette talked to Vergennes and wrote to Franklin about Ireland. Largely on his insistence Bancroft was sent to Ireland. Bancroft's role as a double spy somehow escaped the notice of nearly all his French and American employers.[69] Franklin and Vergennes, as well as Lafayette, waited for Bancroft to return, little suspecting that his report, though it might contain much that was true, would not be the whole truth. Lafayette was not content to wait for one man's decision, however. He formed secret associations in Ireland and enlisted every disaffected Irishman[70] he met in an effort to foment trouble.

Meanwhile the time arrived for Lafayette to join his regiment. Just before leaving Paris he learned that an English effort to borrow a large sum of money from some Dutch bankers had been frustrated. The lenders, it appeared, were asking for

[66] Lafayette to Vergennes, May 23, 1779, Stevens, *Facsimiles*, XVII, no. 1604.

[67] *Ibid.*; cf. Doniol, IV, 232–33.

[68] June 12, 1779, *Mémoires*, I, 301 (Amer. ed. [New York, 1837], pp. 291–92). See below, pp. 26. n. 9, and 55.

[69] S. F. Bemis, "British secret service and the French-American alliance," *American historical review*, XXIX (1924), 474–95; cf. Gottschalk, *Lafayette comes to America*, p. 92.

[70] Lafayette to Washington, June 12, 1779, *loc. cit.*

1 per cent more interest than the borrowers were willing to pay. None too successful attempts to negotiate a loan in Holland had already been made by American agents. The hesitation of the English negotiators on this occasion seemed like a windfall to the American cause. The marquis immediately took steps to inform Vergennes[71] in the hope that the money could be secured for the Americans. He correctly guessed, however, that M. Necker would not share his eagerness. Nothing came of his agitation. It was not until 1782 that a loan from Dutch sources was to be arranged for the ever penurious Continental Congress.

Without waiting to discover the outcome of his financial proposal, Lafayette set out to take command of his regiment.[72] Just before he left Paris, he and Franklin learned, by the first dispatches which they had received since his arrival from America, that the Continental Congress had changed its views on the conquest of Canada and did not expect French aid for such an enterprise. He could console himself, then, that he had done no harm in failing to overcome Vergennes' indifference to that proposal. Consolation for his failure to carry off his plot against England's coastal towns was not so readily found.

BIBLIOGRAPHICAL NOTES[73]

Lafayette's *Mémoires* contain three separate accounts of events following his return in 1779. That on pp. 64–66 of Vol. I is probably the most reliable, having been written around 1783–84 (cf. *Mémoires*, I, 3). That on pp. 255–57 of the same volume was composed under the consulate of Napoleon Bonaparte. It supplements and confirms the first account. The third account is contained in *Mémoires*, III, 196–97. This was written around 1799, apparently for the purpose of showing what an excellent republican Lafayette had been even in his youth. I have used only one anecdote he tells there (see above, p. 8); the rest sound too anachronistic. A fourth autobiographical record is to be found in the notes taken by Jared Sparks on his visit with Lafayette on November 25, 1828. They are contained in Vol. XXXII of the Sparks MSS. On pp. 192–93 of this volume there are a few details that

[71] Cf. Lafayette to Vergennes, June 1, 1779, Stevens, *Facsimiles*, XVII, no. 1605.

[72] Doniol says (IV, 232) that the date of Lafayette's departure was May 23. I have found no verification of that date. It seems to me more likely that Lafayette left on May 27; cf. Lafayette to Franklin, [May 26 ?], 1779, APS, Franklin papers, Vol. XLII, no. 141.

[73] These bibliographies are intended only to supplement the notes, which should also be consulted.

sound apocryphal and that I have not repeated. Otherwise the story which Sparks heard was in conformity with that given above.

The best studies of Lafayette's career from 1779 to 1782 have been those of Doniol and Tower. The best study of John Paul Jones is that by Mrs. De Koven. None of the biographers of Franklin have given much attention to the episodes narrated in the present chapter. Carl Van Doren's *Benjamin Franklin* (New York, 1938) has given a little, however. My article entitled "Franklin and Lafayette" in the *Bulletin de l'Institut Français de Washington*, no. 12 (1939 [1940]), 7–24, is based largely on the above chapter. In some regards the relations of Jones, Franklin, and Lafayette are best described in Valentine Thomson's biography of Jones; it is, however, unfortunately marred by several inventions and numerous errors.

CHAPTER II

Invasion of England Frustrated

TO COMMAND the King's Dragoons at twenty-one years of age was a distinction of which any young nobleman might feel proud. Two years earlier Lafayette too might have considered it an honor to which he could hardly have dared to aspire. But so much had happened in the interval that now he thought he had been rebuked by the order to proceed to Saintes and take command of his regiment. He who had been a major-general in two hard-fought campaigns, who had led six thousand men against a worthy enemy, who had hoped to be placed at the head of one expeditionary force against Canada and of another against England itself, now had to go to a sleepy provincial town and engage in the routine administration of an inactive cavalry regiment while perhaps, by exploiting his plans, a less worthy officer stole the glory of invading England.

If Lafayette had but known, he could have saved himself all anguish over the exploitation of his schemes by others. The plans of the French ministers were now in the process of reformulation, and in the new strategy there was no room for small operations such as Lafayette had had in mind. Ever since the humiliation of the Treaty of Paris in 1763, the details of a large-scale invasion of England had been elaborated by the French government. One of the most carefully worked-out projects was that of Lafayette's old friend, the Comte de Broglie. Broglie had of late grown insistent that the moment had arrived for putting his plan into operation. England's control of the Channel had been weakened, large parts of her fleet being engaged in the effort to subdue the American colonies. It would be easy to transport a sufficient force to England to carry out the attacks upon vital spots whose weakness Broglie's spies had enabled him to discover.[1]

By the close of 1778 Broglie had won the ear of the government. Even before Lafayette had returned from America more soldiers than were necessary for defense had been stationed on the coast near England, and two large camps, one in Normandy and the other in Brittany, were established under the command of the experienced Maréchal de Broglie, brother of the count. Though many—among them Lafayette—believed the purpose of these troops was to lie idly on the defensive, in reality the government awaited only an opportune moment to embark upon Broglie's daring plot to humiliate the British.

The opportune moment seemed to have come in the spring of 1779. France's freedom of action against England had been hampered by her alliances. Austria, with whom she was associated by the marriage of Louis XVI with Marie Antoinette, was at war with Prussia over their conflicting interests in the Holy Roman Empire; and Spain, to which the traditional Bourbon policy bound her, was reluctant to become involved in a colonial struggle that might result in an independent Protestant empire in America strong enough to rival Spain's own. Thus, while the government at Madrid refused to join her against England, France was being called upon to join Austria against Prussia. The atmosphere cleared rapidly in April and May. Spain consented to renew the Family Compact of the Bourbons and to make war against England; Austria made peace with Prussia. Without having to fear involvement in other European hostilities, France could now count on Spanish support. The combined naval forces of the two Bourbon nations could easily count on superiority in the Channel over the weakened British fleet. All that now delayed decisive action was an open declaration of war by Spain.

Lafayette would have been elated if he had been allowed to

[1] Cf. "Plan de guerre contre l'Angleterre redigé en 1763–1766 par le Comte de Broglie, adopté aux circonstances actuelles," AAE, Mémoires et documents, Angleterre, Vol. LIII.

guess that his sentence to exile in Saintes was part of a vast scheme for the invasion of England. Rumor had it that his journey to Saintes was only a blind to cover his real purpose of stealing off with an expeditionary force to America.[2] His denial of that rumor—his statement that he was joining his regiment for the time prescribed for colonels during summer maneuvers— was not believed. Yet it was the truth, as far as Lafayette himself knew and feared, although he had no intention that his purpose should remain unchanged.

The trip from Paris to Saintes was uneventful. Saintes was the traditional headquarters of the King's Dragoons, but hardly had Lafayette arrived when the Marquis de Voyer, under whom Lafayette was to serve, moved him to the neighboring town of St. Jean d'Angély. It was smaller than Saintes but had the advantage of being several miles closer to Paris. Even so, Lafayette reflected, if the ministers were to change their minds and let him set off for England at the head of his marauders, it would require about two weeks for him to get the orders, return to Versailles, and reach his point of embarkation.[3] That added difficulty only made him the more anxious for their new deci- sion. He began another series of letters to Vergennes, taking ad- vantage of nearly every safe opportunity to write to Versailles. His letters talked of many subjects, personal and official, but each included somewhere a reminder that, while St. Jean d'Angély had its attractions and while his regiment needed his direct supervision because he had found it in an unsatisfactory state, the writer would much prefer to spend the summer in the neighborhood of England. "I should be lacking in candor," he confessed,[4] "if I did not admit that my blood boils a little in my veins. My imagination often advances into enemy country at the head of an advance guard or a separate corps of grenadiers, dragoons and chasseurs. . . . . Don't forget that I love the trade

[2] *Gazette de Leyde*, June 11, 1779, supplément, p. 3.

[3] Lafayette to Vergennes, June 1, 1779, Stevens, *Facsimiles*, XVII, no. 1605. The confusion of the Marquis de Voyer with the Comte de Vaux led Doniol (IV, 234 and 237) into a curious error, where Tower (II, 78) follows him.

[4] Lafayette to Vergennes, June 10, 1779, AAE, corr. pol., É.-U., supplément, Vol. I, fols. 311–13; Doniol, IV, 291–93; Tower, II, 64–66.

of war passionately, that I consider myself born especially to play that game, that I have been spoiled for two years by the habit of having been in command and of winning great confidence. Don't forget that I need to justify the kindnesses with which my country has loaded me. Don't forget that I adore that country and that the thought of seeing England humiliated, crushed makes me thrill with joy. Don't forget that I have been especially honored by the interest of my countrymen and the hatred of our enemies. After all that, Monsieur le Comte (since I do not speak to you as the king's minister), judge whether I have the right to be impatient to know if I am destined to be the first to reach that shore and the first to plant the French flag in the midst of that insolent nation." He would be willing to undertake to do so with only fifty picked men, if that were all the ministry would spare.

The distance between St. Jean d'Angély and Versailles dictated patience. Yet Lafayette could not remain idle. He had found his regiment of cavalry in a state of unpreparedness which shocked him.[5] He devoted himself to improving its equipment and raising its spirit. Shortly after his arrival he found himself also in command of the infantry at St. Jean d'Angély because the Marquis de Voyer was called off to Versailles.[6] This summons of Voyer gave Lafayette reason to hope that great plans were afoot.

Time hung more heavily on the young man's hands than it had in Versailles and Paris. His thoughts turned to his good friends in America and the glorious adventures they had all lived through together. Perhaps he would return to them if the only alternative were to remain in idleness in the provinces of France. A splendid opportunity to remind his American friends that he had not passed out of their existence forever was afforded by the departure of the Chevalier de La Luzerne for Philadelphia. The bad health of Conrad-Alexandre Gérard, Louis XVI's first minister in America, had caused him to ask for his recall, and La Luzerne was being sent out to take his place.

[5] Lafayette to Vergennes, June 3, 1779, Stevens, *Facsimiles*, XVII, no. 1606.
[6] *Ibid.*

By the new minister Lafayette wrote to his old friend, Dr. John Cochran,[7] to Henry Laurens,[8] former president of Congress, to General George Washington,[9] and to Congress,[10] and would have written to many others if an unexpected turn of events had not prevented. The letter to Dr. Cochran was less political in tone and content than the others. Cochran's grateful patient, remembering that the doctor had had to borrow his watch to take his pulse when he was sick, also sent to his "Dr. Bones" a watch adorned with a picture of Washington.

The other letters which La Luzerne was asked to deliver were lengthy and carried nearly the same messages. Lafayette described how well he had been received by the king and the people. He did not exaggerate when he said that he had met "with such an honorable reception, with such kind sentiments" as by far exceeded any wishes he had dared conceive. The returning aristocrat, perhaps better than most observers, sensed the change that had come in public opinion and more strikingly in governmental policy since the time, two years earlier, that he had felt obliged to sneak out of France against the ostensible opposition of his king. He understood that public opinion was more interested in American ideals than was the king, whose motives were diplomatic. He explained to the president of Congress: "That unexpressable satisfaction, which the good will of my countrymen toward me affords to my heart, I am indebted for to theyr ardent love for America, for the cause of freedom and its defenders theyr new allies, and to the idea they entertain that I had the happiness to serve the United States."[11] His popularity, he declared, he had used and would continue

[7] June 10, 1779, *New Jersey Historical Society proceedings*, 4th ser., V (1920), 117–18.

[8] June 11, 1779, *South Carolina historical and genealogical magazine*, IX (1908), 112–14.

[9] June 12–13, 1779. The best published text is in the American edition of Lafayette's *Mémoires:* A. Duer (ed.), *Memoirs, correspondence, and manuscripts of General Lafayette* (New York, 1837), pp. 290–96. The quotations below are from the copy in Sparks MSS LXXXVII.

[10] June 12–13, 1779. The best published text is in the American edition of the *Mémoires*, pp. 286–90. The quotations given below are from the original in PCC, no. 156, fols. 89–94.

[11] PCC. no. 156, fol. 92.

to use to promote the greatest advantage of America. There were certain obstacles to be overcome, like the indifference of some ministers and the positive hostility of Necker, but the disposition of the king's government was friendly, and Monsieur de Vergennes could be especially counted upon to aid the allied cause.

As for himself, Lafayette declared, he wished to return to America upon the earliest opportunity. His "ardent zeal"[12] for America was too well known to need expatiation, he thought. He expatiated, nevertheless, in great detail upon his "unbounded affection and gratitude" for the United States, of which he would ever consider himself a citizen. "There is no pleasure to be enjoy'd which might equal this of finding myself among that free liberal nation by whose affection and confidence I am so highly honor'd, to fight again with those brother soldiers of mine to whom I am so much indebted."[13]

There was one thing that, as the principal champion of America in France, Lafayette felt he must especially insist upon. He described it very pointedly in his letters. It was the tendency of Americans to quarrel, whether at home or abroad. Every day he ran into such disputes—that of Franklin and Lee, that of Jones and Landais. They created a general impression in France that the inhabitants of the United States were divided against themselves. "For God's sake, my good friend," he exhorted Laurens,[14] "tell to the people you keep at home, to those you send abroad that they should at least hold the appearance of union." To Washington he wrote even more emphatically: "For God's sake, prevent theyr disputing loudly together. Nothing hurts so much the interests and reputation of America as to hear of intestine quarrels."[15] He touched upon the same problem in his letter to Congress[16]—but more briefly, for, as he explained to Washington, "there are so many people in it that one can't safely unbosom himself as he does to his best friend."[17]

[12] *Ibid.*, fol. 90.

[13] *Ibid.*, fol. 89.

[14] See n. 8 above.

[15] See n. 9 above.

[16] See n. 10 above.

[17] See n. 9 above.

Each of the personal letters recalled intimate associations and contained sentimental touches. But that to Washington was more than Gallic in its effusiveness and must have been somewhat amusing and embarrassing to the uneffusive American. "There never was a friend, my dear general, so much, so tenderly beloved as I do love & respect you," the young devotee wrote. "Happy in our union, in the pleasure of living with you, in that so charming satisfaction of partaking any sentiments of your heart, any want of your life, I had taken such a habit of being inseparable from you that . . . . I am more and more afflicted of that distance which keeps me so far from my dearest friend. I am the more concerned in this particular time, my dear general, as I think the campaign is opened, you are in the field, & I ardently wish that I might be there next by you, know any interesting event, and if possible contribute to your success and glory." He urged Washington not to expose himself to unnecessary danger, for "in case General Washington was killed—nay, was seriously wounded, there is no officer in the army who might fill his place, that battle or action whatsoever would most certainly be lost, & the American army, the American cause itself would perhaps be entirely ruined." Washington, if he wished, might possibly laugh at his friend's fears and call them "womanlike considerations," but Lafayette insisted that he could not and did not want to conceal them. He made it plain, too, that he had talked about his idol to his wife and that she shared in his devotion. Interspersed among comments on American and European affairs, there was much else in that vein. After many more pages of scribbling than even the verbose Lafayette usually wrote, the letter ended, "Don't forget me, my dear general, be ever as affectionate for me as you have been. Those sentiments I deserve by the ardent one which fill my heart. With the highest respect, the most sincere & tender friendship that ever human heart has felt, I have the honor to be your Excellency's most Obt Humble Svt, LAFA-YETTE." And, as if that were not assurance enough of his affection, he added a postscript: "For God's sake, write me frequent & long letters & speak most chiefly about yourself & your private circumstances."[18] He had some reason for his insistence. Being at least as busy as Lafayette and less given to display of affection, Washington had, nevertheless, written to him more than once since their last meeting.[19] Those letters had, however, never reached Lafayette, probably because of the effectiveness of the British blockade.

Lafayette had intended to write to several other friends in the American army and Congress in order to relieve the weary days in St. Jean d'Angély. But sooner than he expected, great news reached him from Versailles. The invasion of England had been decided upon, and he must return to the capital to take an honorable part in it! He had time only to add postscripts to the letters already written, explaining what had happened, and to dash off a single additional note. That was to another old friend, Richard Henry Lee,[20] whom perhaps even at this time Lafayette recognized as the leader of one of the important factions in Congress[21] and whom, in any event, he knew to be a chief advocate of the scheme to invade Canada that Washington opposed.[22] It was symptomatic of Lafayette's canny ability to be friendly to all parties in America and yet committed to none that in this letter to Lee he did not mention the disputes among the Americans in Paris and had no words of censure for Lee's brother Arthur, Franklin's colleague and opponent.

Lafayette's orders were to repair immediately to Versailles. There he was to meet the Comte de Vaux, newly appointed lieutenant-general of the king's forces in Brittany and Normandy. Lafayette was to serve on his staff as lieutenant (*aide-maréchal-général des logis*) to Monsieur de Jaucourt, one of the

---

[18] See n. 9 above.

[19] March 8 [-10], 1779, John C. Fitzpatrick (ed.), *The writings of George Washington* (26 vols. to date; Washington, 1933——), XIV, 218–22; March 27, 1779, *ibid.*, p. 298 n.

[20] June 13, 1779, APS, Lee papers, no. 43.

[21] Cf. Gottschalk, *Lafayette joins the American army* (Chicago, 1937), pp. 77, 291, 302–3.

[22] Cf. Lafayette to Lee, October 7, 1779, APS, Lee papers, no. 37 (of which a garbled version is to be found in *Memoir of the life of Richard Henry Lee and his correspondence* [2 vols.; Philadelphia, 1825], II, 108).

three quartermaster-generals.[23] That appointment had in fact been made only a few days after the dejected young soldier had left Paris to join his regiment. It had been known in the city several days before news of it had been brought to him.[24] That made it none the less unexpected and welcome. The open declaration of war by Spain was momentarily awaited (and in fact took place on June 16, 1779). The meticulously prepared attack upon England must soon follow.

Lafayette spent about ten days in Paris and Versailles. He made the acquaintance of the Comte de Vaux and discussed the new phase of the war with Vergennes and Maurepas. Thirty thousand men in Vaux's army, assisted by smaller bodies in Flanders and at Brest, were to await the establishment of French predominance in the English Channel by a combined French and Spanish fleet under the Comte d'Orvilliers. Then they were to cross and carry out the long-planned subjection of England. Lafayette was to be in the vanguard with the grenadiers. His own regiment of dragoons was to go to Brest and join him only after the landing.[25] Vergennes proved still willing to send a French force to the United States, if the war lasted until 1780. Lafayette brought him maps of Rhode Island, which appeared to be the best point of attack, and promised in his first leisure hours to prepare a memoir on the advisability of such an expedition.[26]

Lafayette also saw Franklin. They talked about the prospects of his returning to America with a French expeditionary force.[27] It was probably at this meeting, too, that they first

[23] AMG, Lafayette, dossier 1261; cf. M. C. Hippeau, *Le gouvernement de Normandie au XVIIe et au XVIIIe siècle* (9 vols.; Caen, 1863–69), I, 450.

[24] *Gazette de Leyde*, June 18, 1779, supplément, p. 4.

[25] Cf. Lafayette to Vergennes, August 17, 1779, Stevens, *Facsimiles*, XVII, no. 1614; Lafayette to Washington, October 7, 1779, *Mémoires*, I, 324.

[26] Tower, II, 79. Cf. Lafayette to Vergennes, [June 24 ?], 1779, Stevens, *Facsimiles*, XVII, no. 1611. Someone has written on the original of this letter (AAE, corr. pol., É.-U., Vol. IX, fol. 370) "s. d. mais d'août 1779." That error has resulted in the letter's being misunderstood in the past. It seems to belong in the ten days which Lafayette spent in Paris in June, 1779. Since it is dated by Lafayette "jeudi," it probably is of June 24, 1779.

[27] Cf. Lafayette to Franklin, July 12, 1779, APS, Franklin papers, Vol. XV, no. 38; Lafayette to Vergennes, July 18, 1779, Stevens, *Facsimiles*, XVII, no. 1609.

agreed to prepare a "little book"[28] dealing with British misdeeds in America. Propaganda agents, even in those days, had learned to disregard the truth if a lie proved more convenient.[29] Franklin was a publicist by trade and Lafayette by inclination. Both recognized the value of counteracting the spread of British propaganda in Europe and America. To combat British contentions that he was unfriendly to Congress and that the French were not loyal to America, Lafayette requested his American correspondents to publish those parts of his letters which were especially friendly and optimistic.[30] Now he and Franklin proposed to put out their "little book" to rouse humanitarian feelings against British cruelty. With an eye upon public effect Lafayette also arranged the exhibition of a new portrait of Washington at the celebration of Independence Day at Franklin's quarters.[31] Washington was pictured holding the Franco-American Treaty of Alliance and the Declaration of Independence while trampling upon the proclamations of His Britannic Majesty. The portrait made the expected stir at Franklin's reception. Mme de Lafayette was, however, the only person of note who attended. A scribbler of the day wrote a quatrain, describing her as a model of love, virtue, and kindness.[32]

By the time his wife was so honored Lafayette had already reached his new post at Le Havre. Just before leaving Paris again, Lafayette had had a hasty conversation with Dr. Bancroft, who had just returned from Ireland. Having written to many of his French and American friends about his hopes for a new triumph of liberty in Ireland, Lafayette was disappointed in Bancroft's report. Though the doctor had found growing dis-

[28] Lafayette to Franklin, July 12, 1779, *loc. cit.*, p. 4; cf. *List of the Benjamin Franklin papers in the Library of Congress* (Washington, 1905), p. 218.

[29] Cf. Walpole to Mann, March 22, 1779, Horace Walpole, *Letters on the American War of Independence* (London, 1908), p. 101 (on alleged quarrels of Lafayette with Congress).

[30] Cf. Lafayette to Laurens, June 11, 1779, *loc. cit.*

[31] Métra, VIII, 137-38; Bachaumont, XV, 92; *Journal de Paris*, March 29, 1780, p. 368; cf. "Original portraits of Washington," *Putnam's monthly*, VI (1855), 337-38.

[32] Métra, VIII, 139.

satisfaction with the British government, he had concluded that "the fruit was not yet ripe."[33] Lafayette contented himself with reporting Bancroft's opinions to Vergennes without comment.

The first days of July found Lafayette at Le Havre. The presence of the king's armies had converted the usually quiet shipping town into "a little Paris, alive, active and worth seeing."[34] The post of aide-maréchal-général des logis was, Lafayette had told Washington, "a very important and agreeable place."[35] He found a great exhilaration in his new prospects. His quarters faced on the harbor, from which he could see the vessels that, he boasted, "will carry us to England."[36] He liked his commanding officer, whom he considered an intelligent and good disciplinarian. "I am charmed with him," the twenty-one-year-old quartermaster informed Vergennes, "for I, who was also a general in my youth, have always felt that without discipline it was always difficult to lead a large number of troops."[37] Yet he was impatient. "I can be calm only on the English shore," he announced, "and we are not there yet."[38]

Until the combined fleets of France and Spain reached the Channel and wrested control of the Straits from the English, there was nothing to do but wait. Lafayette did not remain idle, however. His duties as a member of the staff kept him sufficiently busy to prevent his writing the memoir regarding an American expedition which he had promised Vergennes. Furthermore, his recommendations upon that expedition would be dependent upon the outcome of the plan to invade England, and he needed to see whether it would mature. For nearly three weeks after his arrival in Le Havre, tireless epistolizer though he was, he had, therefore, written only a few hasty notes to

[33] Cf. Lafayette to Vergennes, July 1, 1779, AAE, corr. pol., É.-U., supplément, Vol. I, fols. 315–16; Doniol, IV, 293–94; Tower, II, 77–78.

[34] Intercepted letter, March 31, 1781, F. E. Chadwick (ed.), *The Graves papers and other documents relating to the naval operations of the Yorktown campaign, July to October, 1781* (New York, 1916), pp. 54–56.

[35] June 13, 1779, *Mémoires* (Amer. ed.), p. 296.

[36] Lafayette to Vergennes, July 1, 1779, *loc. cit.*

[37] *Ibid.*   [38] *Ibid.*

Vergennes[39] and to the chief of Vergennes' staff[40] and a longer one to Franklin.[41] All were in an optimistic spirit; all inquired anxiously about America, where British successes were a cause of uneasiness. The one to Franklin, though it stated Lafayette's preference to be in America rather than where he was, showed that he felt certain of being useful to the common cause at Le Havre. For "the army is about thirty thousand strong, all in good spirits and will I am sure, behave in the most glorious manner. . . . . What I believe to be certain is that the ministry are in earnest, and want if possible to give the enemy some stroke or other before the end of the campaign."

It was not until the month of July had more than half passed that Lafayette began to feel discouraged. D'Orvilliers did not appear, and the British fleet in the Channel was meanwhile growing more formidable. Lafayette now found that he had "only too much time to spare."[42] He resorted to his favorite pastime of scribbling letters. In view of "the incertitude of our embarkation," he sought once more to call Vergennes' attention to "a project which I believe under any circumstances to be very advantageous."[43] A French expeditionary force would assure the allies of great military preponderance in America, "if [and he underlined these words] *it were well led*." France must make plans not only to win over the Americans and gain a present victory but also to prevent a future war of *revanche*. For that purpose it was necessary to capture Halifax, "the storehouse and bulwark of the English navy in the new world."

Lafayette had not forgotten, however, that the most recent advices from Congress had indicated a desire that no joint expedition against Nova Scotia and Canada be undertaken, and he guessed that one of the reasons for American hesitation was their suspicion of French designs on Halifax. He realized that

[39] *Ibid.*; July 3, Stevens, *Facsimiles*, XVII, no. 1607; July 9, *ibid.*, no. 1608; and July 9, AAE, corr. pol., É.-U., Vol. IX, fol. 52.

[40] Lafayette [to Rayneval], July 10, 1779, S. W. Jackson Collection, Yale University Library.

[41] July 12, 1779, *loc. cit.*

[42] Lafayette to Maurepas, January 25, 1780, Tower, II, 500.

[43] July 18, 1779, Stevens, *Facsimiles*, XVII, no. 1609.

without American aid an expedition against Halifax would be foolhardy. Nevertheless, he felt that American reluctance could be overcome by skilful manipulation. "This enterprise," he urged,[44] "should be preceded by services rendered in different parts of the continent. Then we should receive help, and under pretext of having designs on Canada, we should try to capture Halifax. . . . . "

The document gave particular attention to the personnel of the proposed expeditionary force. Knowing that too large a demand would not receive favorable consideration, the marquis went on to propose a contingent of only 4,300 men, led by officers "who could bear fatigue, live on little, put on no airs—especially not a haughty and cutting tone—do without pleasures, women, and letters from Paris for a year"—in short by men of the rank below colonel and from outside court society, "where habits are in no wise American." And he added, "Since I am not writing *to the minister*, allow me, for the sake of argument, to suppose for a moment that I am the acting commander of that detachment. You are sufficiently acquainted with my principles to know that I shall not court selection by the King." Although he had commanded with success a larger body of troops than he now proposed and frankly believed himself capable of leading the expeditionary force, his present purpose was not to push his own claims but to avoid having to speak for the actions of some unknown person. "Since, setting talents aside, the judicious conduct of the commander, the confidence of the people and of the American army would assure half our success, I am obliged, despite my repugnance, to put forward a character that I know in order to build my suppositions upon some sort of foundation." The excuse would hardly have been subtle enough to fool Vergennes, even if the minister had not been thoroughly familiar with Lafayette's *amour de la gloire*.

Knowing the American scene quite well, as a result of having campaigned or traveled on horseback in every state between South Carolina and Massachusetts, Lafayette proceeded to detail a plan for the recapture of Rhode Island, New York, Vir-

[44] *Ibid.*

ginia, and other areas. In any case, no later than the end of June, 1780, he expected to have won signal victories in America and to be ready to act against Halifax. "With the claims that the other expeditions would give us," he assured Vergennes, "I can answer for it that we should be assisted in this by the Americans." With their aid and with the support of discontented elements in Nova Scotia, of whose existence he had been assured, he expected to conquer Halifax. Then he would prepare a revolution in Canada. He recognized the validity of Vergennes' objections to turning over Canada to the Americans, but, he argued, political considerations did violence to Frenchmen's emotions. "Is it better," he asked, "to leave to the Americans an object of fear and jealousy in having an English colony as a neighbor, or to give liberty to our repressed brethren, and recover at the same time the fur trade, the commerce with the Indians, and all the profits of our former establishment without the expenses and depredations involved? Shall we throw into the balance with the new world a fourteenth state that will always be attached to us and by its situation will have a great preponderance in the troubles that will someday divide America?" He knew that opinions differed greatly on that point. "I know yours, Monsieur le Comte," he said, "and my own preference is not unknown to you." Whether or not Canada were to be attacked, the Newfoundland Bank might be tried. Thereafter circumstances would dictate new spheres of activity.

To detail these ideas, Lafayette had taken twelve pages of foolscap paper. He took three pages more to elaborate upon his personal attitude. "I am thoroughly convinced, Monsieur le Comte," he declared, "and I cannot without violating my conscience refrain from repeating that it is very important for us to send a body of troops to America. If the United States should not desire it, I think we could create the desire, and should even seek for pretext. But on this subject we shall be anticipated, for Dr. Franklin is waiting for a favorable moment to make his proposal. . . . . It will certainly be said, Monsieur le Comte, that the French will be coldly received in that country, and regarded with a jealous eye in its army. I cannot deny that the

Americans are somewhat difficult to deal with, especially for Frenchmen; but if I were entrusted with this duty, or if the commander chosen by the King should act with tolerable judgment, I would pledge my life that all difficulties would be avoided, and that our troops would be cordially received." His primary motive in all this, he repeated, was to aid his country. If he were to be considered too young to command, he was willing to take a lesser post, needing no high honors to induce him to serve zealously under other officers.

When completed, Lafayette's document consisted of fifteen long pages. Even the margins had been extensively used for insertions. Though dated simply July 18, it had probably taken more than one day to compose. Despite the rather clumsy effort to hide its official nature, it had nevertheless been drawn up with the consent and probably at the suggestion of one minister for discussion with other ministers. It was the first formal memorandum that Lafayette ever submitted to the French government. It was not to have all the results that he wished, but it was to receive careful attention. It certainly did not determine the French government to follow a policy toward America which it might not otherwise have adopted,[45] for it had been written only after friendly and favorable discussion with Vergennes and apparently also with Franklin; and those two gentlemen were astute enough to have come to their own conclusions. Quite independently of Lafayette, Vergennes had about the same time ventured the statement that "perhaps we shall decide that the great blows should be struck in America rather than in Europe."[46] Still, the young major-general was the most experienced and highest-ranking American soldier in France, and it was proper to consult him. Aside from the wishful passages dictated by his youthfulness and ambition, his report was a sober and well-balanced document, worthy of any government's serious consideration. It played its part in the ultimate decision of the French government to devote its major

[45] Most biographers of Lafayette follow Tower (II, 80) in this mistaken belief.

[46] Vergennes to Montmorin, July, 1779, Doniol, IV, 276.

efforts to the warfare in America rather than in Europe; and that decision was a big factor in the ultimate victory.

After the memorandum was dispatched to Versailles, Lafayette found time again lying heavily on his hands. The next twelve days were filled with idle rumors regarding M. d'Orvilliers' whereabouts. He was reported to have sailed to the Azores, the West Indies, the States. Lafayette began to wonder whether he ought not to buy himself a frigate and sail to America on his own initiative, as he had done once before. There at least he might be "less useless" than at Le Havre.[47] Some excitement and activity was created by a visit of inspection by the minister of war.[48] The receipt of a packet of letters and newspapers from America also relieved the monotony, though they contained bad news—Fort Lafayette in the Hudson fallen, Georgia invaded, West Point threatened, inflation and high prices rampant. He sent off to Franklin[49] to learn whether the ministers had further details and waited for some sign from Versailles of approval of his project to aid America.

When at last acknowledgment came, it was not encouraging. Vergennes had read the document and promised to take it up with Maurepas. It seemed unlikely, however, that anything would be done that year.[50] Vergennes would write again, however, after his consultation with Maurepas.

Convinced that time was getting short, Lafayette did not wait for Vergennes' second letter. He replied to the first without delay. "My love for my country perhaps makes me impatient to the point of importunity," he apologized.[51] Yet he wished to urge that if the full force he had recommended could not be sent in the near future, a smaller one—say two or three thousand men—ought, nevertheless, to be dispatched immediately. Such a contingent-would help to restore the diminishing credit of the United States and check the inflation, would be able to

[47] Lafayette to Vergennes, July 30, 1779, Stevens, *Facsimiles*, XVII, no. 1610.

[48] Montbarey, II, 361–64.

[49] Lafayette to Franklin, July 28, 1779, APS, Franklin papers, Vol. XV, no. 81.

[50] Cf. Lafayette to Vergennes, July 30, 1779, *loc. cit.*   [51] *Ibid.*

take the initial steps for the capture of Halifax, and would bolster the morale of the American army. He closed his letter with a solemn assurance: "I give you my word of honor, that, if half of my fortune were spent in sending troops to aid the Americans, I should feel that I was rendering my country a service that would be worth more than the sacrifice involved."

Nor was that an idle boast. Lafayette was still ignorant of the meaning of money except as something to spend freely in order to get results. His liberality distressed his stewards and lawyers, and they complained to his aunt, Mlle du Motier, who still supervised his property in Auvergne. His intendant, Grattepain-Morizot, was a cautious man, who hesitated to force the peasantry on Lafayette's estates to make advance payments. "It is not necessary to eat Monday's bread on Sunday," he believed.[52] Yet if the marquis continued to make exorbitant demands on him, he trembled for the future. Before leaving Paris Lafayette had taken 9,600 livres with him; more recently he had asked for 1,000 écus, or about 3,000 livres, more. That made a sum of around $12,600 in modern values which Lafayette had demanded in a little over a month. Lafayette had no training in the handling of money. He probably did not even know how much half of his fortune was worth, but he was prodigal where his loyalties and ambitions were involved. Nowhere were both as deeply merged as in America—so deeply, in fact, that he had begun to identify his personal glory with the welfare of those who had his affection and could no longer tell them apart.

Another interval of inactivity passed awaiting a reply from Vergennes. Lafayette busied himself with some details about the King's Dragoons,[53] wrote to Franklin for news,[54] and gathered information about the Franco-Spanish fleet and the Americas—much of it false and discouraging except the report of Estaing's glorious capture of St. Vincent and Grenada in the West Indies. A letter from Vergennes finally announced that

[52] Morizot to Mlle du Motier, July 30, 1779, University of Chicago Libraries, Rare Book Room, DC 146f, L2A3, Vol. I (hereafter referred to as Morizot papers).

[53] Lafayette to unknown, August 2, 1779, Jackson Collection.

[54] August 3, 1779, APS, Franklin papers, Vol. XV, no. 99.

nothing could be done to send an army to America until the spring; and Maurepas soon confirmed that decision, stating that, while he approved of the proposal and "would take all possible care that nothing should be done which could obstruct the plan,"[55] he, nevertheless, felt obliged to wait until Estaing should return from America and give his opinion.

That outcome would have been a severe blow to Lafayette's pride had it not happened at almost the same time that the fleet was reported to have reached the Channel. Wind, fog, and the hazards of the sea had yielded neither to Lafayette's impatience nor to the stoicism of the fleet's commander. The Comte d'Orvilliers had been dogged by adversity from the day he had sailed from Brest early in June. He had had to anchor in a tropical sea for six precious weeks waiting for the Spanish squadron. Insufficient food, water, and medicine led to an outbreak of smallpox. It was August 6 before D'Orvilliers at the head of sixty-six vessels reached the Channel with food and water low, epidemic still raging, and hundreds of men on the sick list. He was over a month late.[56]

Only on August 13 did Lafayette announce to Vergennes that the fleet had arrived in the Channel.[57] Always elastic, his spirit rebounded once more. "The very thought that the French flag is at present moored in English roadsteads is a delightful lift for my pride," he declared. He hoped that now the English navy would be ruined. "I should be quite unhappy if this fuss ended in an operation too far beneath our preparations." Orders had arrived for the Comte de Vaux to go to St. Malo, and Lafayette was afraid only a part of the army would be embarked, leaving his force at Le Havre behind. He begged Vergennes to see that he be included in the invading army. "Ambition, as you know, does not torment me," he asserted (and Vergennes must have smiled), "but if to be useful to my country

[55] Quoted in Lafayette to Maurepas, January 25, 1780, Tower, II, 500 and 504.

[56] E. Chevalier, *Histoire de la marine française pendant la Guerre de l'Indépendance Américaine* (Paris, 1877), pp. 159–66.

[57] AAE, corr. pol., É.-U., supplément, Vol. I, fols. 374–76; Tower, II, 85–86. See also a note giving details on the "formation du détachement" in AAE, corr. pol., É.-U., Vol. IX, fol. 297.

is the chief factor in my happiness, if to lead troops myself into war is a game I love with passion, the pleasure at least of seeing others act is altogether necessary for my peace of mind."

Despite the danger of being left behind by the conquerors of England, Lafayette devoted most of this letter to his favorite project. He commented on the minister's lack of enthusiasm for the American expedition. He repeated his confidence in the American army. "The better part of American virtue is in that army." Vergennes seemed to doubt that a French force would be welcomed in America. Lafayette agreed that that was a touchy problem. It was important, he felt, that any French contingent should appear to be sent only as a reinforcement of the Continental Army and not for any independent objective. If the French ambassador were to make the offer, it would immediately be suspected. "Those who love us least would create obstacles and drag the weaker ones along. Besides, it is in the American character to hope that in three months they will need nothing. I know even some good patriots who in the event of such a request would be afraid to increase their country's obligations to France."

But tactful diplomacy would solve that ticklish situation. Franklin, Lafayette knew, was ready to ask for such a reinforcement, if properly encouraged. "If tomorrow the King ordered me to leave with a French detachment (which, of course, would not exceed a third of the American army), I would pledge to him all that I hold dearest not only that that corps would be well received but that by joining the Continental Army, it would render important services." The only condition he would make was that two weeks before his embarkation he be permitted to send some letters to Congress in a fast boat. Chance had recently brought him into contact with some British officers (probably prisoners of war) who had been stationed at New York and Halifax. After drinking a little too much, those officers let it be known that Halifax contained very many malcontents and that New York was untenable. "All these comments, Monsieur le Comte," Lafayette concluded, "give me a liking for my plan by confirming my original ideas."

Hardly had this daring war project started on its way when Lafayette hit upon an equally daring peace project. Rumors of peace were in the air. Since the truce between Prussia and Austria had been arranged, it had been widely reported that Russia and Austria were going to arrange a treaty between England and France likewise. Lafayette felt sure that the English, fearful of the brilliant preparations that he joyfully witnessed every day in Normandy and Brittany, would welcome mediation. "Do you think, my dear doctor," he asked Franklin,[58] "our British friends will let the blow fall so heavily upon them, and don't you rather believe they'll try to set up a negotiation, and will if necessary consent to a peace?"

With that thought in mind, he made a new proposal to Vergennes.[59] Franklin, he knew, had been instructed to make no treaties without the consent of Congress. When peace overtures were made, therefore, someone would have to be sent to America with the proposals. If some emissary of Franklin brought them, Franklin's enemies in Congress would attack them in order to embarrass him. "But if he were a man whose very arrival would assure the people that the treaty must be advantageous, if he had received the friendship of the different parties, if he knew the leaders and had had the good fortune to win the favor and the very great confidence of the nation, if he had been with the army, whose different units with particular points of view are dispersed among all the states, his journey to America would be useful to our country." While he did not believe he had all those qualifications, it was possible that after the cordial way in which he had been treated in America, his friends might think so. He was therefore ready to go without any compensation, if chosen. "Seasickness is very good for my health, and the moment it is over, I feel very much better. I shall leave tomorrow if you wish in the uniform and with the simple title of an American general officer." To avoid embarrassing M. de La Luzerne, he would be willing to place himself under the ambassador's orders. But he would act in the

[58] August 17, 1779, APS, Franklin papers, Vol. XV, no. 130.

[59] August 16, 1779, AAE, corr. pol., É.-U., Vol. I, supplément, fols. 378–79.

capacity of an American. "I would have of a Frenchman only the name, the heart, and the pleasure that only a Frenchman can feel in serving his country." He preferred a military career, to be sure; "but if by chance," he confessed, "I have the means and the talents to serve my country otherwise than with arms in my hands, I would believe myself quite happy to profit by them."

Neither the proposal for war nor the proposal for peace brought immediate results. Franklin philosophically found the reason for the failure of the English to sue for peace in the perversity of "those people." He had, he informed Lafayette,[60] only one rule to go by in judging their actions: "Whatever is prudent for them to do they will omit; and what is most imprudent to be done, they will do it." Lafayette continued to suspect that even in war he might be obliged to watch while others acted. New orders brought about renewed bustling at Le Havre. The city soon was deserted by most of the senior officers; St. Malo became the center of activity; the King's Dragoons were ordered to Brest; but Lafayette stayed behind, fearful that the forces with which he was stationed would be used merely to make a diversion but would not share directly in the glory of humiliating England.[61]

What had in fact occurred was that orders had been received for an attack upon the English coast. While D'Orvilliers' main body blockaded the port of Plymouth, the units of Vaux's army, which were at St. Malo, were to be convoyed to the attack of Falmouth. Those at Le Havre were to follow later. D'Orvilliers, sick over the loss of his son, discouraged by the epidemic among his men, and aware of the inadequacy of his preparations, felt the plan was impractical and said so. Nevertheless, he proceeded to blockade Plymouth for three days, while the English, unprepared to resist, wondered why he did not attack. Finally, a storm blew his boats out of the Channel, and the expedition against Falmouth had to be abandoned. A few days later Sir Charles Hardy, at the head of an inferior

[60] August 19, 1779, Smyth, VII, 366–67.

[61] Lafayette to Vergennes, August 17, 1779, Stevens, *Facsimiles*, XVII, no. 1614.

British fleet, moved into the Channel. D'Orvilliers sailed forth to meet him and to bring about a decisive action.[62]

As reports of D'Orvilliers' latest maneuvers floated back to Le Havre, Lafayette once more became cheerful over the humiliation in store for England. Permission to move to St. Malo and take part in the glorious invasion had not yet arrived, but glory and recognition came, not wholly unexpectedly, from another quarter. Among the orders which Lafayette had brought to Franklin from Congress had been one to procure and present to Lafayette in the name of the United States of America "an elegant sword with proper devices."[63] Franklin had hired "the best artists in Paris"[64] to make such a sword—at the cost of 200 guineas, which it is possible he secured from French secret funds.[65] The sword was a highly ornate one. The knob on the handle was of gold. On one side of it were engraved Lafayette's coat of arms with its motto, *Cur Non*, and on the other a rising moon reflecting the rays of its light on a stretch of land which was partly covered with trees and partly under cultivation. Franklin, always with an eye to the propaganda value of his public actions, meant to designate the United States by that symbol. Underneath the symbol was the motto: *Crescam ut prosim* ("Let me wax to benefit mankind"). Franklin hoped to express by this device that, as the United States grew, they would become more useful to humanity and that in their present weakness "what light they spread they owed to the King of France." One side of the sword guard bore the legend "From the American Congress to the Marquis de La Fayette 1779." Two medals adorned the handle. One pictured a woman (America) presenting a laurel branch to a Frenchman (Lafayette), the other a Frenchman striking down a lion. On the four surfaces provided by the bow of the guard were represented four of the battles in America in which Lafayette had seen action. They

[62] Cf. Hippeau, II, 42–54; *Gazette de Leyde*, August 24, 1779; J. W. Fortescue, *History of the British army* (13 vols. in 20; London, 1899–1930), III, 289.

[63] Gottschalk, *Lafayette joins the American army*, p. 298.

[64] Franklin to Jay, October 4, 1779, Smyth, VII, 387.

[65] Métra, VIII, 413–14.

were the Gloucester affair, the retreat from Barren Hill, the Battle of Monmouth, and the retreat from Rhode Island.[66]

When at length the sword was completed, Franklin sent it to Lafayette by his grandson, William Temple Franklin. In a letter which accompanied the sword Franklin explained: "By the help of the exquisite artists France affords I find it easy to express everything but the sense we have of your worth and our obligations to you. For this, figures and even words are found insufficient."[67]

Franklin's efforts to make certain that the sword would receive great public notice were not in vain. The papers and the correspondents gave it great space. For the most part they were impressed by the lavishness of the decorations. There was amusement in one quarter at least, where the extravagant description of the sword in the public press was compared to Homer's lines on Achilles' buckler—to which Franklin, who had been largely responsible for putting the description in the reporters' heads, is said to have replied, "Each to his own taste."[68]

The "noble present," Lafayette reported, had "an immense effect" upon the army at Le Havre; and Franklin himself admitted that "some of the circumstances" were "agreeable to the nation."[69] Lafayette freely acknowledged his pleasure at the honor which had been done him. To Arthur Lee, who was still at Lorient preparing to depart for America, he wrote that he would be proud to carry the sword "into the heart of England."[70] It would serve "as a new bond" for "one of the most zealous servants of the United States."

William Franklin remained in Le Havre as Lafayette's guest for several days. The two young men became fast friends. While

[66] APS, Franklin papers, Vol. L, Part 1, no. 19; Part 2, no. 17; *Gazette de Leyde*, September 3, 1779, supplément, pp. 2–3; *Mercure de France*, September 18, 1779, pp. 132–33. Cf. Jules Cloquet, *Recollections of the private life of General Lafayette* (London, 1835), pp. 197–209.

[67] Franklin to Lafayette, August 24, 1779, Smyth, VII, 370.

[68] Métra, VIII, 335.

[69] Lafayette to Franklin, August 29, 1777, APS, Franklin papers, Vol. XV, no. 153, p. 3; Franklin to Jay, October 4, 1779, Smyth, VII, 387.

[70] August 28, 1779, Jackson Collection.

they were still together, reports of several minor successes of D'Orvilliers and of an imminent major engagement between his main fleet and an inferior English force were received. Prompted by Lafayette's certainty of a great victory at sea, young Franklin expressed the desire to accompany the invading army. Lafayette gladly consented to make him an aide if his grandfather and the French authorities would agree.

When William Franklin returned to Passy, he carried two letters from his friend to his grandfather.[71] One was a formal expression of thanks for the sword. The other dealt more with young Franklin's military ambition. In the more formal letter, while declaring that the honor done him exceeded any expectations he might have had, Lafayette protested: "Some of the devices I can't help finding too honorable a reward for those slight services which in concert with my fellow soldiers, and under the God like American hero's orders, I had the good luck to render." The less formal letter also expressed to Franklin, not as the minister of the United States, but as "my friend Doctor Franklin," Lafayette's "particular and private" thanks. In the awkward and involved English which the marquis used when he became excited, he wrote: "The noble present I have the honor of receiving from Congress has been adorned by you with so many flattering attributes that I have no idea of such a glorious reward being ever conferr'd by a nation upon any soldier, and that nothing may be added to it, but a much greater share of merit on my part, which might render me a more proper object for so great an honor."

The larger part of the more personal letter was devoted to a request that Franklin use his influence to have his grandson appointed to the French army as Lafayette's aide. It was not long before Franklin sent an enthusiastic approval of William's wishes,[72] and the minister of war gave his consent.[73] The ques-

[71] Both dated August 29, 1779; the more formal one has been frequently published and is to be found *inter alia* in Smyth, VII, 371; it is no. 154 in APS, Franklin papers, Vol. XV. The other, apparently unpublished, is no. 153.

[72] Franklin to Lafayette, October 1, 1779, Smyth, VII, 380–81.

[73] Montbarey to Vaux, September 2, 1779, Hippeau, II, 80; cf. Association des amis du vieux Havre, *La Fayette au Havre: hommage à sa mémoire* (Le Havre, 1921), p. 5.

tion of young Franklin's rank then arose, and Lafayette thought that he and the American minister could arrange to make the new aide a captain in the American army. "If there is some thing against the rules of Congress in the appointement," he said,[74] "I take it upon myself and know General Washington will not disapprove any thing I have done, because friendship between my respected, belov'd general and myself gives me the right of taking his name whenever I please, and I am sure Congress has not the least objection to that undertaking of mine on the occasion."

William never became either aide or captain. For neither he nor Lafayette was destined to reach the English coast in the invading army. Since the fleet of D'Orvilliers greatly outnumbered that of Sir Charles Hardy, British strategy was directed at avoiding battle. For three days D'Orvilliers managed to keep Hardy in sight but could not come close enough to force battle. Finally, Sir Charles eluded D'Orvilliers entirely and fled into Plymouth Harbor. D'Orvilliers returned to Brest early in September. It soon became known in Paris to such unmilitary figures as Lafayette's lawyer, Morizot, that the danger of equinoctial storms on the Channel would make the invasion impossible.[75] Yet Lafayette refused to give up hope. "To grieve in silence," he declared,[76] "is the role that I have assigned myself. At the moment, it is less difficult than to hope for an invasion this autumn, but having been one of the first to hope, I want to be the last to give up faith in it." He, nevertheless, sent word to young Franklin that there was no need for him to come to Le Havre.[77]

More than ever the plan to send an expeditionary force to America loomed as a possibility. Vergennes now informed Lafayette that his proposal to lead a small army across the Atlantic

[74] Lafayette to W. T. Franklin, September 7, 1779, APS, Franklin papers, Vol. XV, no. 176.

[75] Morizot to Mlle du Motier, September 4, 1779, Morizot papers.

[76] Lafayette to Vergennes, September 11, 1779, Stevens, *Facsimiles*, XVII, no. 1615.

[77] September 14, 1779, APS, William T. Franklin papers, Vol. CI, no. 127.

had met with the ministers' friendly consideration.[78] The eager soldier begged Vergennes to recall him to discuss the matter. "There are a thousand things that can be said and can not be written," he argued.[79] But no orders came for him to leave Le Havre.

For weeks Lafayette did, in fact, grieve in a silence and inactivity which were entirely uncharacteristic. News of the dramatic exploits of Captain John Paul Jones in Scottish waters caused him to write to Jones an enthusiastic letter of congratulations.[80] He also wrote to Franklin[81] to felicitate him upon the achievements "of the little squadron in which you know I have been greatly concerned." This gave him an opportunity to express his grief. He apologized for the waste of an entire campaign season. "You had certainly yourself a firm idea that my services would be more actively employ'd," he pleaded. ". . . . I hope Congress will be sensible of it, and approve the reasons I had of serving them on this side of the Atlantic."

News that Estaing had returned to the Continent and was engaged in an effort to recapture Savannah, lost to the British the preceding winter, made him feel that he could have been especially useful in Estaing's force. "Had I thought his operations would turn that way, nothing could have hindered me from joining G[al] Washington's army," he declared.[82] Since he knew that there was a packet leaving for America, he sent similar apologies to Congress,[83] requesting his friends Henry Laurens[84] and Richard Henry Lee[85] to be present when it was read, in order to shield him from possible censure for not having re-

[78] This is inferred from Lafayette's comments in his reply, September 11, 1779, *loc. cit.*

[79] *Ibid.*

[80] Cf. Jones to Bancroft, October 26, 1779, LC, John Paul Jones MSS; Jones to Lafayette, October 28, 1779, *ibid.*

[81] October 6, 1779, APS, Franklin papers, Vol. XVI, no. 7.

[82] *Ibid.*

[83] October 7, 1779, *Mémoires* (Amer. ed.), pp. 456–58; PCC, no. 156, fols. 95-100.

[84] October 7, 1779, Massachusetts Historical Society.

[85] October 7, 1779; see n. 22 above.

turned to his post in the American army. "How thoroughly concern'd," he wrote,[86] "how truly unhappy I am in being confin'd to mere wishes, Congress, from the knowledge they have of my sentiments, will better feel for me than I might myself express. . . . . The sense I have of the favors conferr'd on me by Congress and the marks of confidence which I have obtain'd on many occasions, give me the freedom of reminding them that the moments where I may find myself under American colours, among my fellow soldiers, and take orders from our great and heroic general will ever be considered as the happiest ones in my life."

But Lafayette revealed his deepest chagrin only to Washington. Though he had received no letters from the general since he had left America, he persisted in believing that Washington must have written to him often[87] and that only the hazards of war had kept those letters from him. He felt confident that Washington would agree with him that circumstances had required him to remain in Europe. Yet "nothing," he announced,[88] "could make me so delighted as the happiness of finishing the war under your orders. . . . . Be certain, my dear General, that in any case, let me act as a French or as an American officer, my first wish, my first pleasure, will be to serve again with you. However happy I am in France, however well treated by my country and King, I have taken such an habit of being with you and am tied to you, to America, to my fellow soldiers, by such an affection that the moment where I shall sail for your country will be one of the most wished for, the happiest of my life." He closed his letter with assurrances of "such an affection as is above all expressions any language may furnish."

[86] See n. 83 above.

[87] See n. 19 above; since March, 1779, Washington had written to Lafayette on July 4, 1779 (Fitzpatrick, XV, 369–70), September 12, 1779 (*ibid.*, pp. 267–69), and September 30, 1779 (*ibid.*, XVI, 368–76); and was to write again on October 20, 1779 (*ibid.*, pp. 491–94).

[88] Lafayette to Washington, October 7, 1779, Sparks MSS LXVII. This letter has been published in several places, including Lafayette's *Mémoires*, I, 322–26. These versions are, however, taken from that in Jared Sparks, *The writings of George Washington* (12 vols.; Boston, 1834–37), VI, 555–56, where it has been badly garbled.

No one in America knew that Lafayette had himself taken a leading part in bringing about those circumstances which had made it impossible for him to go to America. It had been largely on his own insistence that he had first been expected to join Captain Jones and had finally found himself at Le Havre awaiting the order, which he had more than once described as his most cherished desire, to assault the tight little island. No one in America could therefore question whether he was entirely sincere in his statement that his "first wish" was to serve in America under Washington. And, indeed, it would have been ungenerous to raise the question. Lafayette was a young man of many enthusiasms. That of the moment was the most important to him, the one which he marshaled all the superlatives at his command to describe. No matter how inconsistent, such a man was not insincere.

Hardly had Lafayette written the letters telling Washington and Congress how anxious he was to go to America, when he took another step which would have kept him in Europe if it had proved successful. Again, though it was neither a modest nor an unambitious program, it was a patriotic step, intended to promote the interests of both France and America. The rumors that there would be an arrangement of peace had not abated. Lafayette, still preferring the profession of arms but willing to become a diplomat if there was to be no war, thought again that he was particularly qualified to be one of the negotiators. Having already approached Vergennes on that subject without effect, he now addressed himself to Franklin.[89] Wouldn't Franklin, as if on his own initiative, suggest that Lafayette be named to represent France in any forthcoming congress? The advantages to America, he pointed out, would be several. Lafayette was committed to American independence; he knew more about America than the regular French diplomats; he would be less likely to compromise on important matters because of ignorance that they were important. In that way he had of seeming to laugh at the aristocracy while never forgetting that he was himself an aristocrat, he pointed out,

[89] October 11, 1779, APS, Franklin papers, Vol. XVI, no. 30.

"As for our European prejudices, birth is a thing much thought off [*sic*] on such occasions. I am the only one of my rank (tho' I can't help laughing in mentionning these chance-ranks before an American citizen) who is acquainted with American affairs." Somehow he felt that whole thing must be handled as a deep conspiracy. "Don't answer my letter by the post," he concluded, "and indeed it needs no answer at all. You know my offer, my zeal, my means of serving America, and you will do what you think consistent with the interests of America and your friendship for me. I beg the strictest secrecy, and expect you will be so kind as to burn immediately this confidential letter." He did not sign the letter, though anyone might have recognized the handwriting and the style; nor did Franklin burn it. Since, in fact, there had been no peace overtures, he simply filed Lafayette's letter away among his papers.

Up until this time a faint hope had survived that an invasion of England might yet be undertaken. But it was soon reported that D'Orvilliers had gone out of his mind, and shortly afterward he was removed and another officer appointed to take his place. On October 14 it was decided that the plan which had been so carefully developed for nearly two decades could not be executed. A few days later orders to disband the army of invasion were received from Paris.[90] Even after that date Lafayette asked young Franklin[91] to procure some English or Dutch maps of England, since there were no good ones in France, as well as maps of some Irish towns. Evidently he was not only still thinking of a possible future invasion of England but also still recurring to his notion that Ireland was ripe for revolution.

Of late Lafayette had been giving some thought to such matters as revolution and its corollary—the rights of man. They entered his mind, however, not as abstract principles but as concrete problems. The king had recently freed all the serfs upon the royal domains, hoping that the landowners of France would follow his example. Lafayette, with estates in Brittany,

[90] October 17, 1779, Doniol, IV, 276.
[91] October 29, 1779, APS, Franklin papers, Vol. LXI, no. 108.

Touraine, and Auvergne, was one of the wealthiest among them, but he knew little about his own estates. He did not even know whether there were any serfs upon them. Up to this time social inequalities had affected him little; as we have seen,[92] his chief reason for being pleased at the capture of Senegal, aside from the prestige it gave, was that it furnished a new source of slaves. Now, however, he wished to play the part that his reputation as a friend of liberty entailed. He wrote to Morizot to find out about his serfs.[93] There were none on his estates in Brittany and Touraine, Morizot knew, but whether there were any in Auvergne Morizot did not himself know and had to write to Lafayette's aunt to find out.[94]

At the same time, Morizot, not wishing to surrender any sources of income no matter how small, took steps that would have marred his client's growing reputation as a liberal if they had become known. He urged upon Mlle du Motier to send him Lafayette's baptismal record, duly notarized, since the king was re-examining all pensions and required a birth record of all beneficiaries.[95] Lafayette received a pension of 600 livres because his father had been killed in action, and Morizot had no intention of letting it lapse. Like many intendants of the aristocracy at this time of feudal reaction, Morizot was anxious to make as much profit for his employer as he could. Lafayette's constant demands for more and more money made him frantic. Morizot complained of having had to send more than he had received; and, since the estates in Brittany and Touraine had furnished all he could expect, he begged Lafayette's aunt "to put a little pressure on debtors" in Auvergne.[96] "They should not forget that when there is a war going on, there is need for money." The baptismal record was duly sent. When it was delivered to Lafayette in Le Havre for signature, he signed with his full name: Marie-Joseph-Paul-Yves-Roch-Gilbert du Motier M[is] de Lafayette.[97] The pension was resumed.

---

[92] See above, pp. 8–9.

[93] Cf. Morizot to Mlle du Motier, September 4, 1779, Morizot papers.

[94] *Ibid.*   [95] *Ibid.*   [96] *Ibid.*   [97] AMG, Lafayette, dossier 1261.

Perhaps the curious contrast of Morizot's efficiency in regard to pensions and his ignorance in regard to serfs caused Lafayette to ponder over the question of why some people were born to toil and others to enjoy the royal bounty. If that did not, his apologetic claim to a diplomatic mission because he held the highest title among the friends of America in France, lamely put forth in the recent letter to Franklin, perhaps had done so. Still more recently, having been called upon to recommend to Congress a Dutch savant named Noemer,[98] who wished to settle in America, he had been obliged to give the subject still more thought. To Congress he wrote: "From my professed principles on the blessings of a free constitution and the rights of mankind, from the particular feelings of my ardent love for America, I will ever encourage any one who wishes to become a citizen to the United States."[99] Though that was fairly liberal language, it indicated no more profound conviction than similar stock phrases in past letters to Americans—phrases which he had almost immediately counteracted in addressing Frenchmen in clichés about the shortcomings of free governments. His letter[100] asking Franklin also to recommend the Dutch gentleman was somewhat along the same lines. Dr. Noemer, he wrote, in a semihumorous vein, "has from his calculations found out that men were born to be free, and that freedom was to be perfectly enjoy'd but upon American shores. In consequence thereof he wants immediately to embark for and settle in a country where one may be bless'd with the healthy air of liberty."

Such liberal catchwords might have been a mere concession to the preferences of Drs. Franklin and Noemer. But when, in November, 1779, he turned once more to the prospects of revolution in Ireland, he seems to have given the questions of liberty and privilege more serious thought than on any previous occasion. "With a true satisfaction," he announced to Franklin,[101]

---

[98] This may be Johann Samuel van Noemer, author of *De lochiorum fluxu naturali atque praeternaturali* (1805).

[99] October 14, 1779, PCC, no. 156, fols. 101–2.

[100] October 14, 1779, APS, Franklin papers, Vol. XVI, no. 42; cf. *ibid.*, no. 80.

[101] November 2, 1779, *ibid.*, no. 87.

"I have seen that the royal influence in the Irish parliament fell very short of ministrial expectations, and that some patriots begin to speack [*sic*] a bold language, and mention the blessed words of independency and the Rights of Mankind. In the eyes of the people that would be strangers to parliamentary barking, such speeches would be mistaken for a certain signal of what they call at St. James a rebellion." He denounced the sufferings of Ireland "under the blundering tyrannical measures of our friend George the Third." Then he went on to say, "I want very much, my dear Sir, to know your opinion upon a point which from my zeal to the common cause, and my principles on the Rights of Mankind, you may judge very interesting to me. Do you believe that a firm Reconciliation will take place between these two parts of the British Empire? Do you on the contrary entertain hopes that the Revolution will be ripe enough? . . . . I am not very found [*sic*] of seeing dukes and other lords at the head of the business. Nobility is but an insignificant kind of people for revolutions. They have no notions of equality between men, they want to govern, they have too much to loose [*sic*]. Good Prebiterian [*sic*] farmers would go on with more spirit than all the noblemen of Ireland. Don't you think I am right in this opinion?"

That is the first unreserved denunciation of aristocrats that has been traced to Lafayette's pen. He had previously indicated a polite doubt that they had any greater merit than commoner men, as behooved an American officer when speaking to Americans. In this declaration, however, there was something more than courteous concession to another's opinion on a matter not worth disputing. To be sure, Ireland was now, as America had once been, only a tool to use in the war against the feared and envied English. But America had come to mean to him much more than that. It had become a cause worthy of effort for its own sake. He had gradually acquired a genuine sympathy for American ideals—for liberty and the rights of men—things about which he had given little thought before touching American soil. And now he transferred those words, those symbols to which he was beginning to react emotionally, to another country where there might be revolution against a common enemy. He earnestly hoped that the new revolution would be like the one in America—a revolution of the people who really cared for equality among men, not merely a revolt of one group of noblemen against another. In this anxiety he used more sweeping language, more liberal thought than he had ever pronounced before. He really believed he had hit upon an original and radical idea when he described it to Franklin and asked, "Don't you think I am right in this opinion?"

Meanwhile, as nothing further seemed to be required of the army at Le Havre, its generals began to prepare for winter quarters. Unexpectedly there came a special courier with orders to be ready to march at a moment's notice. None of the officers knew what was in the wind. Conflicting rumors were tossed about: they were going to make a show to keep the English guessing; Hardy's fleet had been sent to Gibraltar, and it would be safe to cross the Channel; they would be sent to winter in Brittany. Lafayette himself immediately thought of the possibility of an invasion of Ireland to support the independence party there. Hastily he wrote to Franklin[102] again to request details and to indicate his fears that the Irish situation might be mismanaged. "My military countrymen don't know how to manage republican interests," he said, "and I am of opinion that this must be treated with a great delicacy. I think it very important, my good friend, that your ideas on that head be followed by our Ministry." This was a new Lafayette speaking —a Lafayette who was interested in the success of republics somewhat for their own sake and not merely as tools for the building of French prestige. The old Lafayette, aristocrat and chauvinist (before the word was invented and the phenomenon itself became common), would have rushed in blindly, certain that the French ministry could manage any situation well so long as they had French soldiers to carry out their orders.

Lafayette sent off his letter to Franklin by a private courier, who brought back an immediate reply.[103] Franklin knew noth-

---

[102] November 9, 1779, *ibid.*, no. 98.

[103] November 10, 1779, E. E. Hale and E. E. Hale, Jr., *Franklin in France* (2 vols.; Boston, 1887–88), I, 304–5; Wharton, III, 405–6.

ing of the new orders and so had no opinions. And, indeed, it proved that Lafayette was needlessly perturbed. The orders led to nothing. The marquis was soon permitted to return to Paris.

BIBLIOGRAPHICAL NOTES

Despite its age Hippeau's *Gouvernement de Normandie* continues to be the best collection of documents dealing with the proposed invasion of England in 1779 (I, 439–76; II, 1–182). For the naval operations which resulted from that proposal the work of Chevalier on *La marine française pendant la Guerre de l'Indépendance Américaine* is still standard, though there have been several more general studies of the French navy since Chevalier's time. For the English tactics of defense the brief discussion in Fortescue's *History of the British army* (III, 289–90) has been most helpful. Doniol (Vol. IV, chap. v) also gives a well-documented account, with greater attention to Lafayette's part in it than other writers with the exception of Tower, who drew largely on Doniol for his materials.

Lafayette's *Mémoires* borrowed from Sparks's *Writings of Washington* its versions of the correspondence of Washington to Lafayette. Sparks frequently revised those letters, sometimes omitting whole passages. Fortunately, the editor of the American edition of the *Mémoires* went to the originals. Hence the texts are quite often more fully and reliably presented in that edition than in the French. Whenever possible Sparks's own notes, now preserved in the Harvard College Library, have been used, for it has been found that on occasion even the American editor misread the texts. Sparks's copies often indicate the changes and omissions which he wished made in his published versions.

CHAPTER III

To America's Rescue

THERE are few periods in Lafayette's life when he cannot be followed almost day by day and from place to place. The interval between November 10 and December 9, 1779, is such a period. Exactly when Lafayette left Le Havre and returned is not known. He was in Paris, however, by December 9.[1] Shortly after his arrival he learned that disaster had overtaken the French fleet under Estaing.[2] Estaing's forces, supported by an American army under General Benjamin Lincoln, had been defeated in an attack upon Savannah, had retreated, and sailed off. Estaing himself had been badly wounded.

The prospect of a new outburst of American dissatisfaction with the French alliance readily rose in the marquis' mind. He had witnessed several anti-French demonstrations during Estaing's earlier sojourn in America. Though this time the relations between the French admiral and the American general had been more cordial, Lafayette could suspect only the worst. He begged Vergennes for details on the Savannah affair, fearing that it would have "a bad effect on America."[3]

More than ever Lafayette became convinced that his place was in America. He informed Vergennes that he was ready to drop everything else and start off alone immediately.[4] Hungrily he pressed the foreign minister and the staff of the American envoy for news. "No intelligence must be looked upon as

[1] Lafayette to Harcourt, December 9, 1779, Hippeau, II, 398–99.
[2] Lafayette to Vergennes, December 10, 1779, Stevens, *Facsimiles*, XVII, no. 1617.
[3] *Ibid.*   [4] *Ibid.*

56

trifling for me," he charged young Franklin.[5] ". . . . What is become of the Confederacy?"

There was good reason to feel concern over the Confederacy. Never had its plight been worse than it was now to become. The army suffered in its winter quarters at Morristown, New Jersey, worse hardships than those which Lafayette had witnessed at Valley Forge in 1777. Washington complained to Congress of "the absolute emptiness of our magazines every where and the total want of money or credit to replenish them."[6] Quartermaster-General Nathanael Greene declared: "Our army is without meat or bread; and have been for two or three days past. Poor fellows! They exhibit a picture truly distressing. More than half naked, and above two-thirds starved."[7] American currency reached a lower point, and there was greater intrigue and despair in Congress than ever. Greene blamed the suffering of the army on the legislature. "A country, once overflowing with plenty," he said, "are now suffering an army, employed for the defense of every thing that is dear and valuable, to perish for want of food. . . . . Legislatures are guarding against little trespasses, while they suffer the great barriers of political security to be thrown down, and the country over-run."[8] In the preceding fall the British had withdrawn from Rhode Island, to be sure, but only the better to lay siege to Charleston, which they were to capture in the spring. The best that Washington proved able to do was to stand stoically on the defensive, hoping for that aid which it was doubted in Versailles he would welcome. The American cause was more dependent on France than ever before.

It was at this moment that Lafayette by a simple gesture showed his unquestioning faith in his friend George Washington. On the day before Christmas in 1779 Adrienne de Lafayette gave birth to a son. She was at Passy; her husband, occupied

[5] December 21, 1779, APS, W. T. Franklin papers, Vol. CI, no. 154.

[6] December 15, 1779, Fitzpatrick, XVII, 272.

[7] Greene to Furman, January 4, 1780, collection of Lloyd W. Smith, Florham Park, Madison, N.J.

[8] *Ibid.*

with political affairs, was in Paris. With her own hand, though she had been ill most of the preceding months, she scrawled an affectionate letter to him. There was good cause for rejoicing, because the new child was the first boy in Adrienne's family. "Accept my compliment, Monsieur le Marquis," she wrote.[9] "It is very sincere, it is very live. America will put up illuminations, and I claim that Paris should put some up also. The number of those who resemble you is so small that an increase in their number is a public benefaction." At any rate her grandfather, the Duc de Noailles, would no longer have reason to say that "they were always giving him girls."[10] The faithful Desplaces, who had been Lafayette's servant for years, brought him Adrienne's letter.[11] Though it was two o'clock in the morning, the proud father immediately informed Franklin.[12] The boy would be called George, he said, "as a tribute of respect and love for my dear friend G[al] Washington." And he wished Dr. Franklin, young Franklin, and Dr. Bancroft as Americans to be the first to know.

Adrienne urged him to surrender himself for a while to the joys of paternity. They are "so sweet, nothing else is so good," she said.[13] And that he did—but not for long. Shortly after the new year began, he was again in Paris, directing the officers of the King's Dragoons by correspondence[14] and again pulling wires in order to get assistance for the United States.

In January, 1780, the French government began to show an inclination to undertake a major military effort in America. Up to that point they had had several reasons to hesitate. In some quarters it was felt that Europe was the better battleground; the Spanish were especially anxious to push the attack upon Gibraltar. Moreover, it was not altogether clear, notwith-

[9] December 24, 1779, Henry E. Huntington Library and Art Gallery, San Marino, Calif., HM 9426.

[10] *Ibid.;* cf. *Mémoires,* I, 125 and 146.

[11] Morizot to Mlle du Motier, December 24, 1779, Morizot papers.

[12] December 24, 1779, APS, Franklin papers, Vol. XVI, no. 172.

[13] December 24, 1779, *loc. cit.*

[14] Cf. Lafayette to Villeneuve, January 5, 1780, Gardner-Ball Collection.

standing Lafayette's confidence to the contrary, that the Americans would welcome a large French force. Despite the marquis' assurances that Franklin was ready to ask for an army if he were properly encouraged, Franklin was exceedingly cautious. When sounded out regarding a project to raise an army in France for service in America,[15] he would promise only to lay the matter before Congress and did so. He knew nothing, he said,[16] "of the sentiments of Congress on the subject of introducing foreign troops among them, and therefore could give no expectation that the plan would be adopted." The reluctance of both of France's allies (who were not yet allies of each other) left the French ministers unconvinced that their young friend's proposals were practical.

And yet both the French and Spanish governments felt that America was an important, if not the most important, theater of the war.[17] They proved ready to heed Lafayette's requests to send arms and supplies to Washington. On that score Franklin had been active for several months and had won friendly consideration at Versailles.[18] The American minister had already received three million livres as a loan for the purchase of badly needed supplies, but at the last moment had decided that because of numerous outstanding debts he could use only about a quarter of that sum for such purchases.[19] That would provide altogether too small a supply.

Lafayette volunteered to secure more. He made appointments with Montbarey, Maurepas, and Vergennes in turn. He urged that fifteen thousand stands of arms and a large quantity of powder be sent from the royal magazines to America.[20] He also expected the king to furnish money with which to buy clothing. Being on a less formal footing with the foreign minister than with the others, he again dared to bring up his dearer

[15] Franklin to Jay, October 4, 1779, Smyth, VII, 388.

[16] *Ibid.*, p. 389.   [17] Cf. Doniol, IV, 352-55.

[18] Cf. Franklin to Jay, October 28, 1779, Smyth, VII, 392-93; Franklin to Lovell, October 17, 1779, *ibid.*, pp. 402-3.

[19] Lafayette to Congress, December 16, 1780, PCC, no. 78, fols. 481-84.

[20] Lafayette to Franklin, January 9, 1780, APS, Franklin papers, Vol. XVII, no. 25.

project. He reminded Vergennes of the damage a British force sent from New York to the French West Indies might do. America, "whose independence is so important for the honor and welfare of our country," must not be overlooked in preparing the next campaign, he insisted.[21] Though "a violent cold"[22] kept him from some of his appointments, he succeeded in getting the supplies that he asked.

Letters finally arrived that made it plain that Washington and his fellow-countrymen were anxious for men as well as supplies. They were from George Washington and Alexander Hamilton. The one from Washington had been written the preceding September.[23] It was in answer to the letter that Lafayette had sent Washington by La Luzerne. In replying to Lafayette's unrestrained assurances of devotion of himself and his wife, Washington—probably to cover his own confusion—indulged in a little bantering regarding "the Marchioness." "Tell her," he wrote, "(if you have not made a mistake and offered your own love instead of *hers* to me) that I have a heart susceptible of the tenderest passion, and that it is already so strongly impressed with the most favorable ideas of her, that she must be cautious of putting love's torch to it, as you must be in fanning the flame."[24] But there was no banter in the words addressed to Lafayette himself: "Your forward zeal in the name of liberty; your singular attachment to this infant world; your ardent and persevering efforts, not only in America, but since your return to France, to serve the United States; your polite attention to Americans, and your strict and uniform friendship for *me*, has ripened the first impressions of the esteem and attachment, which I imbibed for you, into such perfect love and gratitude, that neither time nor absence can impair. Which will warrant my assuring you, that whether in the character of an officer at the head of a corps of gallant French (if circumstances should require this), whether as a major-genl. command-

[21] Lafayette to Vergennes, January 9, 1780, Stevens, *Facsimiles*, XVII, no. 1618.

[22] Lafayette to Franklin, January 10, 1780, APS, Franklin papers, Vol. XVII, no. 28.

[23] September 30, 1779, Fitzpatrick, XVI, 368–76.   [24] *Ibid.*, p. 375.

ing a division of the American army; or whether, after our swords and spears have given place to the plowshare and pruning-hook, I see you as a private gentleman, a friend and companion, I shall welcome you in all of the warmth of friendship to Columbia's shores."[25]

Pleasing though the words of affection from his "beloved general" must have been to Lafayette, what struck him the most forcibly in Washington's letter was the implication that he would be welcome "in the character of an officer at the head of a corps of gallant French."[26] The letter from Alexander Hamilton contained a similar implication,[27] and Lafayette felt certain that Hamilton would not have written without Washington's approval. At about the same time one of the French volunteers who had distinguished himself on American battlefields and whom Lafayette knew well—Colonel de Fleury—came to call upon him.[28] The marquis cross-examined him on conditions in America and found that they were indeed discouraging. Upon his return to France Fleury had prepared for Lafayette a report on American affairs. After examining political and military conditions state by state, Fleury had come to the conclusion that, if France were to prevent some sort of arrangement between England and her revolted colonies, she must send them "clothes, arms, money, or even still more effective support."[29]

Lafayette sent Fleury with a letter of introduction[30] to deliver his report in person to Vergennes. He himself, meanwhile, had gone after bigger game—the prime minister. Maurepas had hitherto given as the reason for his indecision that he wished to consult with Admiral d'Estaing, who had recently returned to

[25] *Ibid.*, pp. 369–70.   [26] *Ibid.*, p. 369.

[27] This letter has not been found. It is known only through the references to it contained in Lafayette to Maurepas, January 25, 1780, AAE, corr. pol., É.-U., supplément, Vol. I, fols. 413–16; Tower, II, 499–504; Doniol, IV, 308–12.

[28] Lafayette to Vergennes, January 25, 1780, Stevens, *Facsimiles*, XVII, no. 1619.

[29] "Sommaire de l'état politique et militaire de l'Amérique," Stevens, *Facsimiles*, XVII, no. 1616; cf. Fleury to Lafayette, November 16, 1779, AAE, France et divers états, Vol. 463, fol. 188.

[30] January 25, 1780, AAE, mémoires et documents, É.-U., Vol. I, fol. 296.

France with his honorable wounds. But Maurepas by this time had seen Estaing, and Lafayette felt certain that the admiral would say nothing to oppose the expedition. He succeeded in getting a short interview with Maurepas and showed him his American letters. Maurepas granted that they were interesting but refused to commit himself to anything.[31]

Lafayette tried to see Maurepas again. He went back twice,[32] only to find the prime minister too busy to be interrupted. After several days he decided to resort to his favorite device— a letter which should be written not to the minister but to his friend the Comte de Maurepas and thus talk on ministerial affairs all the more frankly. He quoted Washington's letter to prove the point that he had been making since his return from America—that an expeditionary force would be welcome. Now, in fact, since American affairs were going badly, it was needed more than ever. If it were to arrive in time for the next campaign, there was not a moment to lose. "We ought to be ready," he exhorted,[33] "by the *end of February;* we ought to write to America within a *fortnight;* and within *four days* I should like to see actively begun the preparations for which there is no need for an answer from Madrid." He could see only two objections to immediate action: the Americans were now too discouraged to fight, and French co-operation would produce jealousy and disputes among them. To the first he answered that he knew from personal experience with the American army that "it is judged with far too great severity in this country." To the second he replied in words similar to those he had once addressed to Vergennes: "If the French commander should not know how to deal with the sentiments in Congress and the different sentiments in each state, if he should understand neither the prejudices of the people nor the parties formed in the government, nor the way in which to please the army, nor the proper mode of dealing with the civil authorities—if he should talk to an officer from Boston as he would to one from New York, to a member of the Assembly of Pookepsie [*sic*] as to one from the

[31] Cf. Lafayette to Maurepas, January 25, 1780, *loc. cit.*
[32] *Ibid.*   [33] *Ibid.*

self-styled State of Vermont—he would be absolutely sure to give offence, absolutely sure to defeat the purposes of his voyage. But, without considering, Monsieur le Comte, whether my intimate friendship with the general, or the confidence of the army and the people, in short my *popularity*, to use the English expression, justify my boldness, yet in the event of my having command of the land detachment I *will answer for it, upon my head*, that I shall avoid even a shadow of jealousy or of dispute."

The young general realized that he would be accused of being ambitious, but he denied the accusation: "Forgive me, Monsieur le Comte, if I refer to myself in this connection; but should I not be singularly unwise to answer for some other whom I do not know? I love glory deeply, it is true, and for the past year it has been an unlucky passion; but, for all that, if I were impelled merely by a desire to command men, they would give me more in America than I am now asking for here." So little in fact was a higher rank in the French army among his desires that he intended to use no other title or uniform when he set out than those he had won in America. In fact, if the minister wished, he was willing to act merely as a volunteer, putting his knowledge and his personal prestige in America at the disposal of any other commander who might be selected—"not for his sake, nor even for the ministry, but for the good of my country."

This appeal produced almost immediate results. It was soon decided to send an expeditionary force to America.[34] But who was to command it? Vergennes asked Lafayette to give his opinions on two alternatives that the ministry was considering—an expedition to be commanded by himself and an expedition to be commanded by another while he resumed his rank in the American army. Lafayette's answer was: "This appointment is not only a military and political matter but also a social matter, and in view of my circumstances, I give you my word of honor that I believe the first choice very much better for the public service and the interests of France in relation to her allies."[35] He repeated his offer to serve merely in his quality of American general

34 Cf. Vergennes to Montmorin, January 29, 1779, Doniol, IV, 352 and n. 2.

35 February 2, 1780, Stevens, *Facsimiles*, XVII, no. 1620.

officer and to hold no French rank whatsoever, adding that he was also willing to take a French title valid in America alone or to accept any other arrangement which would place him only temporarily ahead of older men in the French service.

In considering the alternative, he argued in exactly the same way: "We must first anticipate the bad effect in America that the arrival of another commander would have. The idea that I cannot lead this detachment would be the last to strike anyone there. I shall therefore say that I preferred an American division." But he would have to be informed of all secret plans in order better to ward off the suspicion of Washington and Congress. "A secret that I should not share would appear decidedly suspicious at Philadelphia." If he were not to have command of the expeditionary force, he would rejoin his division in America, keeping in touch with the French ambassador. But in that event, care must be taken not to give the command to an officer who would outrank American generals like Gates, Sullivan, and St. Clair, for they would be displeased. The French commander must also be instructed to think of himself as an American major-general under Washington's orders.

Everyone knew that the marquis really had the popularity and prestige in America of which he boasted. Having an established rank in the American army, he would have presented no new problems of rank or seniority; he had the confidence of the army and Congress; he knew American manners and sensibilities; he would have been able to bring about cordial co-operation between the American army and a French auxiliary. But in the French army he was only a recently appointed colonel of cavalry without experience in leading European troops in battle. The command of thousands of Frenchmen could not be entrusted to one so young and inexperienced even if he had once captained thousands of Americans.

Shortly after Lafayette's last request a decision was reached. The ministers chose to send him back to America to resume his command in the Continental Army and to name an older soldier to command the French expeditionary force. In general they adopted Lafayette's proposals regarding the course to follow in the event that some other officer were chosen to command the auxiliary force. In that way they hoped to exploit all Lafayette's popularity in America without having to risk a French corps to his independent judgment. Vergennes so informed La Luzerne on February 5.[36]

Lafayette did not learn of this decision until over two weeks later. Since he did not feel free to disclose his own suggestions, his correspondence with Franklin and others still dealt largely with the supplies that he had at length secured for America.[37] In his anxiety to expedite shipments to America he issued orders which differed from those of Congress regarding the making of uniforms, and brought about only delay.[38] The goods never reached America, in part because Lafayette's officiousness undid what his steadfastness and devotion had accomplished, in part because of the quarrels between Jones and Landais.[39]

At length Lafayette was allowed to know the ministry's decision. Without being given direct and decisive orders, he gathered that he would be expected to leave for Boston on March 4. Command of the expeditionary force, Lafayette soon learned, was to go to the Comte de Rochambeau. Rochambeau was an older man and a superior officer in the French service. He had been a brigadier-general before Lafayette was born. For nineteen years he had had a rank in France equivalent to that which Lafayette had held in America for less than three. During those nineteen years he had usually commanded the vanguard of the French army. He had fought and bled in the Seven Years' War and had been the colonel of that Chevalier d'Assas whose courageous death had already made of him a legendary figure.

[36] AAE, corr. pol., É.-U., Vol. XVII, fol. 165v.

[37] Cf. Lafayette to Franklin, February 7, 1780, Hale and Hale, I, 305–7; Lafayette to unknown, February 15, 1780, in Noel Charavay's catalogue no. 485 (sale of June 8, 1929), item 79; Lafayette to Adams, February 19, 1780, Adams, VII, 125–26; Lafayette to Franklin, February 24 and 29, 1780, APS, Franklin papers, Vol. XIII, no. 139, and Vol. XVII, no. 98.

[38] Lafayette to [Leray de Chaumont ?], February 12, 1780, APS, Franklin papers, Vol. XVII, no. 65; Williams to Franklin, February 19, 1780, University of Pennsylvania Library; Franklin to Lafayette, March 2, 1780, Smyth, VIII, 20–21.

[39] Lafayette to Congress, December 16, 1780, loc. cit.

Lafayette had known Rochambeau since he was a child[40] and had probably met him again when both were stationed with the Comte de Vaux's army. He did not have that qualification which Lafayette had set forth as most important (with either Rochambeau or the Comte de Broglie in mind) when he wrote to Vergennes: "There is a certain excellent officer, who would give much satisfaction here, but whom, from my intimate acquaintance with our allies, I should be sorry to see sent among them. . . . . A knowledge of the language would be an immense advantage."[41] Despite Rochambeau's inability to speak English, Montbarey, who several times before had interfered with Lafayette's ambition, had chosen him for the place that Lafayette had hoped to have.[42] By the choice of Rochambeau, the aspirations of Lafayette, Broglie, and several other candidates were definitely frustrated. Though Lafayette was disappointed, he had already guessed that he would be considered too young to command a large corps of French soldiers. And so he was obliged to be content to go back to America as an American major-general returning from a furlough, carrying the news that another would lead the expeditionary force which, more than any one other person, he had influenced the French government to dispatch.

The next few weeks were filled with errands, interviews, letters, and instructions, which again carried Lafayette in and out of the offices of various ministers. One of the first things he had to assure was his safe passage to America. That gave him an opportunity to write to Minister Sartine[43] a set of suggestions regarding the role of the navy in the proposed expedition. Sartine was urged to see to it that the squadron sent to America was large enough not to be stopped by a small enemy force, that

[40] Lafayette to Rochambeau, August 18, 1780, LC, Rochambeau letter book, fols. 129–30; see also below, p. 116.

[41] July 18, 1779, Tower, II, 498.

[42] Montbarey, II, 337–40; cf. Jean-Edmond Weelen, *Rochambeau* (Paris, 1934), pp. 110–11.

[43] February 21, 1780, AN, Marine B4 172, fols. 105–6; cf. *ibid.*, B4 153, fol. 65, and B4 172, fols. 117–23; and BN, n.a.f. 9427, fols. 164–65.

it was sufficiently well equipped not to have to depend upon renewing its stores in America, and that it carry a large quantity of presents for the Indians. Lafayette suggested that the commander of the fleet be placed entirely under Washington's orders to avoid any disputes and misunderstandings. He emphasized that the Americans were sensitive regarding prestige and that "more honor should be shown to the uniform of an American general or the dignity of a state governor than would be shown to Imperial or Prussian officers of like rank." It was important to be polite to private citizens and on all occasions to show great respect for civil authorities. Sartine showed an extraordinary willingness to follow Lafayette's suggestion.

The next thing for Lafayette to do was to take care of his private affairs. This he did by confirming the power of attorney (*procuration*) of the Morizots, allowing them to borrow large sums (as high as 115,000 livres) on the advice and with the consent of Mme de Lafayette and Lafayette's uncle, the Comte de Lusignem. He also authorized the Morizots to accept Mme Lafayette's decisions in place of his own whenever necessary.[44] No longer being obliged to act secretively, he took better care of his growing family in this way than he had upon his previous departure for America.

Direct and precise orders soon reached Lafayette.[45] He was instructed to proceed to rejoin General Washington and to announce the coming of six ships of the line and a corps of men. They were to sail in the spring to Rhode Island, which the English had recently evacuated. Lafayette was to get permission from Washington to send officers to the outermost points of the island in order to signal whether it would be safe for the king's vessels to approach. If it were not, the fleet was to proceed to Boston. Emphasis was laid upon the point that the French troops were to be purely auxiliary to the American army and to act under Washington's orders.

Care was taken, however, to provide that the French general

[44] "Procuration généralle," February 23, 1780, University of Rochester Library.

[45] February 24, 1780, AAE, corr. pol., É.-U., Vol. XVII, fols. 219–22.

should be second to no other than Washington. For that purpose Rochambeau was promoted to the rank of lieutenant-general, a rank which did not exist in the American army and was higher than that held by Lafayette and the other major-generals in the Continental service. The plan of campaign was to be determined by Washington in collaboration with Lafayette, who was also to remain in close touch with La Luzerne.

The political significance of those instructions could hardly have escaped anyone who read them. They not only added a great corps of well-equipped men to Washington's army—sufficient nearly to double the army he commanded directly—but they also placed him in a position to dispose of that force independent of any authority but his own. He need not consult Congress except so far as he saw fit, and he need not answer to the king's representative in America. It appeared that, for the first time in his career as commander-in-chief, Washington was to have a force at his disposal with which no political arm could interfere. Lafayette's arguments and entreaties had been largely responsible for this personal triumph of Washington.

On the morning of February 29, Lafayette, dressed in the blue, white, and gold uniform of an American major-general, went to Versailles to take formal leave of the king and queen.[46] He was received graciously. Marie Antoinette was particularly kind, expressing her confidence that he would be able to advance the common cause.[47] That afternoon he attended a gathering of notables at the home of the Duc de Choiseul, once prime minister of Louis XV. He still wore the American uniform. Among those present (since in eighteenth-century society it was not considered improper to entertain guests from a country with which one's own was at war) there was a certain Thomas Walpole, grand-nephew of a former English prime minister. Walpole was indiscreet enough to express surprise at Lafayette's uniform and to comment upon the nakedness of the American

[46] *Gazette de Leyde*, March 7, 1780, supplément, p. 4; *ibid.*, March 14, 1780; Franklin to Carmichael, March 31, 1780, Smyth VIII, 51–55; A. B. Gardner, "Uniforms of the American army," *Magazine of American history*, I (1877), 481.

[47] Lafayette to Poix, August 24, 1781, private collection.

army. Lafayette replied, "with the coolness of a Socrates,"[48] that the Americans had various uniforms. He described them and admitted that not all American troops were equally well dressed. But, he concluded, those who had captured Burgoyne's army were also almost naked. Everyone laughed but Walpole, who was too confused, and Lafayette, who was too intent.

In the few days that remained before his departure Lafayette saw much of the Americans in Paris. Philip Mazzei, who had recently been appointed the special emissary of the state of Virginia, called on him frequently.[49] John Adams, who had just returned to Paris, wrote letters for him to present in America.[50] Franklin was bombarded with questions regarding the shipment of clothing.[51]

Lafayette also saw Rochambeau.[52] He impressed upon the newly appointed lieutenant-general that the Americans were poor in everything. Rochambeau had therefore better take with him from France such things as a printing press, mortars, flints, flour, biscuits, wool, cloth, leather, tenting, tools, and bricks. Lafayette was particularly insistent upon the necessity of transporting numerous and well-equipped cavalry. Moreover, no success could be counted upon, he contended, unless the allies controlled American waters. Rochambeau reported this conversation to Montbarey and Sartine.[53] Lafayette himself suggested to the ministers that a *fournisseur*, or commissary agent, be sent along with him to attend to the provisioning of the aux-

[48] Mazzei to Jefferson, March 2, 1780, Howard R. Marraro (ed.), *Philip Mazzei, Virginia's agent in Europe* (New York, 1935), p. 31.

[49] *Ibid.*; and Mazzei to Jefferson, April 21 and May 3, 1780, *ibid.*, pp. 46 and 47.

[50] Adams to Warren, February 28, 1780, *Warren-Adams letters* ("Massachusetts Historical Society collections," Vol. LXXIII [Boston, 1925]), p. 126; Adams to Knox, February 28, 1780, Adams, VII, 124–30; Adams to Gerry, February 29, 1780, J. T. Austin, *Life of Elbridge Gerry* (2 vols.; Boston, 1828), I, 333–34.

[51] See above, n. 37; also Lafayette to Franklin, March [4], 1780, APS, Franklin papers, Vol. XLII, no. 145.

[52] "Résultat de la conversation de M. le Comte de Rochambeau avec M. de Lafayette pour M. le Prince de Montbarey," [*ca*. March 1, 1780], Doniol, V, 315.

[53] *Ibid.*; and "Résultat de la conversation de M. le Comte de Rochambeau avec M. de Lafayette pour M. de Sartine," [*ca*. March 1, 1780], *ibid.*, pp. 315–16.

iliary force in advance. On his suggestion they designated M. de Corny.[54]

Despite Lafayette's anxiety to be off, bureaucratic entanglements held up his preparations, and he was obliged to return to Versailles to visit the ministers again. At Montbarey's office precise orders for Rochambeau and Corny were elaborated so that the returning major-general might have exact details to give to Washington.[55] To avoid disputes regarding rank, it was made clear that, in all joint enterprises, generals of the two forces were to be independent of one another, though all were to take the orders of Washington. Lafayette further insisted that Rochambeau be instructed to regard him and other Frenchmen in the American service only as American officers. With M. de St. Paul, the *premier commis* of the war office, he arranged for the leave of his aides Gimat and Capitaine.[56] At the ministry of marine he secured precise instructions for Admiral de Ternay,[57] who was to command the promised fleet, so that Washington might be correctly informed regarding them. Those instructions, he insisted, must make it perfectly plain that Ternay was also under Washington's command, that the supplies destined for the American army were to be delivered only on Washington's or Lafayette's orders, and that Lafayette was to be conveyed from port to port if circumstances required it. Exact details were also arranged regarding signals to be used to indicate whether or not the coast of Rhode Island was clear. It was provided further that, if the winds blew the fleet south, they were to be signaled from Cape Henry in a similar fashion.

[54] Claude Blanchard, *Guerre d'Amérique, 1780–1783; journal de campagne* (Paris, 1881), p. 36. Marquis de Chastellux (*Travels in North America in the years 1780, 1781, and 1782* [2 vols.; Dublin, 1787], I, 32) is mistaken regarding this appointment.

[55] Cf. two memoranda of Lafayette to Montbarey, [March 4, 1780], AMG, archives historiques, carton XLVIII, Lafayette, folder marked "1780, Amérique, etc.," nos. 42 and 44; and *ibid.*, folder marked "Analyse des principales pièces concernant la campagne de 1780," no. 9.

[56] Lafayette to Montbarey, [March 4, 1780], *loc. cit.*, no. 425; Fleurieu to [Sartine], March 6, 1780, AN, Marine B⁴ 172, fol. 119.

[57] BN, n.a.f. 9427, fols. 122–27; cf. memoranda to and from Sartine, March, 1780, AN, Marine B⁴ 172, fols. 116–18.

Lafayette spent the last two days before his departure at Versailles (March 4–5). There he learned that the frigate "Hermione," which had just returned to France, had been designated to take him to America. Resolved to lose no further time, he called upon M. de Vergennes for final instructions. They had been carefully written out for him in two parts. Though both parts were secret, presumably one might be shown to all those who were entitled to see it; the other was intended for himself alone. The first part[58] indicated that he was to announce to Washington, in addition to six ships of the line, the coming of an army of 6,000 men—or (on Rochambeau's special request) 2,000 more than Lafayette had suggested. They were to be under Washington's orders except for details of internal policy, which were to be governed by their own laws. Lafayette was enjoined to report to Congress only after agreeing with Washington and consulting with La Luzerne. "All the King desires," declared the French government, "is that the troops that he is sending to the support of his allies the United States will cooperate effectively in delivering them once and for all from the yoke and the tyranny of the English. His Majesty expects that out of the mutual regard that friends owe each other, General Washington and the higher American officers will show the French officers and men every consideration that is compatible with the good of the service."

These instructions largely coincided with Lafayette's proposals. The special orders[59] contradicted them somewhat. They placed a restriction upon Washington's complete freedom by suggesting that, out of deference to Spain's probable wishes as well as the advantage of the United States, the auxiliary force should be employed to challenge the English control of Florida. Two plans of campaign might achieve that end. The first was to use the auxiliary force in the states that were closest to Florida. The other was to attack New York, thus obliging the English to recall to the defense of their capital in America the armies

---

[58] "Instructions remises à M. de La Fayette le 5 mars 1780," Doniol, IV, 314–18.

[59] "Projet particulier remis à M. de La Fayette le 5 mars 1780," *ibid.*, pp. 318–20.

which held Savannah and threatened Charleston. The greater part of the special instructions was devoted to suggestions for such an attack. But they were not made binding. "The discretion, the capacity of the generals, and their local information" were in the end to indicate whether to accept or to reject the proposals of the king's ministers. Lafayette's favorite arena —Canada and Nova Scotia—was mentioned only once, and nothing was said in favor of using the king's troops there. Lafayette was to sound out General Washington regarding these proposals and to report to the French generals the commander-in-chief's reaction. The king counted on the "well-known humanity of General Washington" not to risk needlessly "a corps of brave men sent more than a thousand leagues to the aid of his country." Ready though they were "to dare all for the welfare of America, they ought not to be sacrificed lightly or rashly."

These instructions had been in preparation for two weeks. They had been examined by the minister of the marine as well as Vergennes. To make sure that they would be carried out even if some mischance kept Lafayette from delivering them, copies were sent to La Luzerne[60] by Captain Jones's cruiser, the "Alliance," which was expected to sail shortly after the "Hermione." La Luzerne was enjoined to execute them if Lafayette failed to arrive in time.

With his orders in his pocket, Lafayette returned to Paris. He went to see Franklin for final instructions and letters for America.[61] He picked up packets and trunks that others had prepared to be carried by the "Hermione."[62] He also called on Morizot for some money. Morizot was worried by an old debt of one hundred thousand livres and a new one of one hundred and twenty thousand now incurred for the proposed return to America. He warned his client that "he was buying his glory

[60] Vergennes to La Luzerne, March 5, 1780, AAE, corr. pol., É.-U., Vol. XI, fol. 239.

[61] Cf. Lafayette to Franklin, March 5, 1780, APS, Franklin papers, Vol. XLII, no. 139; Franklin to Gates, March 5, 1780, Smyth, VIII, 27; Franklin to Washington, March 5, 1780, *ibid.*, pp. 27–29; Franklin to Lovell, March 16, 1780, *ibid.*, pp. 35–37.

[62] Cf. Marquis de Clonard to Holker, March 4, 1780, LC, Holker papers, IX, 1628; Bancroft to Holker, March 13, 1780, *ibid.*, pp. 1659–60; Lafayette to Fleurieu, March 5, 1780, AN, Marine B⁴ 172, fol. 115.

at the expense of his fortune."[63] Morizot might have added, too, "at the expense of the peasantry on Lafayette's estates," because he was obliged immediately to write to his intendants for "all the help they could possibly furnish."[64] But, Morizot found, "it is impossible to induce him to vary his principles in this regard."[65]

On Monday, March 6, Lafayette left Paris for Rochefort.[66] Adrienne was once more left alone, a prey to that fear for her husband's safety which was to be her regular companion throughout life. But she soon regained composure. "Madame la Marquise," Monsieur Morizot reported to Lafayette's aunt within a few days,[67] "has become somewhat calmer. She hopes that Providence will keep him from all harm. Everybody shares that hope. There is probably not a single man in Paris who would not consider himself happy to make some sacrifice for your nephew. It is very much to his credit that at so tender an age he has earned everyone's confidence." Morizot could only wish that his young patron's success had been won at less expense in hard cash.

The marquis' party reached Rochefort three days after their departure from Paris.[68] He boarded the "Hermione" the next morning with Gimat and Capitaine, a secretary, and six servants.[69] That afternoon the delighted Captain Latouche, who "regarded as a favor the opportunity to show the great esteem"[70] which he had for Lafayette, lifted anchor and sailed into the roadstead close by the Isle d'Aix. On the thirteenth they were in the roadstead of La Rochelle, awaiting some other pas-

---

[63] Morizot to Mlle du Motier, March 25, 1780, Morizot papers.

[64] *Ibid.*   [65] *Ibid.*

[66] *Gazette de Leyde*, March 14, 1780, supplément, p. 1; Mme du Deffand to Walpole, March 6, 1780, *Lettres de la Marquise du Deffand*, III, 585.

[67] Morizot to Mlle du Motier, March 25, 1780, *loc. cit.*

[68] Latouche to [Sartine ?], March 11, 1780, BN, n.a.f. 9419, fol. 154.

[69] Logbook of the "Hermione" under date of March 10, 1780, Stevens, *Facsimiles*, XVII, no. 162. I have been unable to identify the secretary. A M. Poirey became Lafayette's secretary later, but he did not go to America at this time (see below, p. 144).

[70] Latouche to [Sartine ?], March 4, 1780, BN, n.a.f. 9419, fol. 149.

sengers. Among them were the commissary Corny, and, interestingly enough, Rousseau de Fayolle, who had been one of those who had sailed with Lafayette on the "Victoire" when he had left France for America the first time.[71] Early the next morning they turned their prow toward America.

They did not get very far. Two days out at sea a strong wind roared upon them and broke their mainyard. Captain Latouche put back to port. Three English cutters chased the "Hermione," and she had to fire a broadside at one of them. Being under orders to convey Lafayette to America as rapidly as possible, Latouche did not try to capture the cutter but hastened back to the Isle d'Aix as rapidly as his crippled rigging would permit. Lafayette had missed the fun. He was seasick.[72]

Three days later, on March 20, with mainyard repaired, they again set sail for America.[73] By that time Lafayette had been in France a little over a year since his return from America. During that year he had made himself as well beloved in France as he was in America. Before his American venture, those who had known him had noticed a certain reticence in him and had labeled it timidity. Now that he was famous the same quality was called modesty. Yet Lafayette was not modest. His frequent insistence that he was betrays him. Anyone who had read his letters to Vergennes and Maurepas setting forth his claims to the leadership of the French auxiliary force would have felt that here was a man who did not hide his light though he felt called upon to apologize for letting it be seen. He was not modest so much as anxious to appear modest. Not without cause, he had a high opinion of himself, though he had since childhood learned to be reticent. Fortunately, that reticence disappeared as soon as he picked up a pen. Otherwise, we should never have learned that fundamentally he was reluctant

[71] Rousseau de Fayolle, "Journal d'une campagne en Amerique 1777–1779," *Bulletin et mémoires de la Société des Antiquaires de l'Ouest* (Poitiers), XXV (1901), 45; cf. logbook of the "Hermione," *loc. cit.*

[72] Rousseau de Fayolle, *loc. cit.*; Latouche to [Sartine ?], March 17, 1780, BN, n.a.f. 9419, fol. 169.

[73] Lafayette to Franklin, March 20, 1780, APS, Franklin papers, Vol. XVII, no. 143.

to talk about himself in the presence of others rather than truly modest. Yet several of his friends, impressed by the good manners and the extraordinary achievements of one so young, found him modest because he was not outwardly boastful.

The Americans in France were especially enchanted by their "marquis." Franklin expressed their view when in a letter which Lafayette was himself to deliver, he wrote to Washington, praising the young soldier's "modesty" and "his zeal for the honour of our country, his activity in our affairs here, and his firm attachment to our cause and to you."[74] Franklin had good reason to be grateful. Without Lafayette's support he might not have obtained the supplies which he was now daily expecting to send to his impecunious country; and without Franklin's open support Lafayette had induced the French government to send that army to America which was to be a most decisive factor in winning the war. The year had not been wasted, even if it had witnessed no invasion of England.

BIBLIOGRAPHICAL NOTES

Weelen's biography, though brief and partisan, is the best available study of Rochambeau. Rochambeau's *Mémoires militaires, historiques, et politiques* (2 vols.; Paris, 1809) were written so long after the American Revolution as to be undependable for the study of that period. Marraro's *Mazzei* is more complete than R. C. Garlick's *Philip Mazzei, friend of Jefferson: his life and letters* ("Johns Hopkins studies in Romance literatures and languages," Vol. VII [Baltimore, 1933]), which, however, is also helpful.

An English translation of Blanchard's *Journal* by William Duane (Albany, 1876) appeared before the French text was published. References in the present volume are always to the French edition.

Lafayette's *Mémoires* (I, 28–29 n.) has caused several biographers to believe that Maurepas said it was lucky for the king that Lafayette did not ask

---

[74] Franklin to Washington, March 5, 1780, Smyth, VIII, 28. Franklin credited Lafayette with "modesty" because he "detained long in his own hands" a letter from Washington praising him. But Lafayette had earlier delivered an even more laudatory letter from Samuel Cooper (cf. Franklin to Cooper, April 22, 1779, *ibid.*, VII, 292, and Gottschalk, *Lafayette joins the American army*, pp. 316–17). It is possible that, if Washington's letter had been delivered to Franklin earlier, the battle of Monmouth Courthouse would not have figured on the sword which Franklin presented to Lafayette (cf. Gottschalk, *op. cit.*, pp. 230 and 313). It would be unfair, however, to insist that that was why Lafayette had delayed in delivering it, since there are many other possible explanations. Mazzei also called Lafayette "modest": Mazzei to Jefferson, March 2, 1780, Marraro, p. 31. And cf. p. 13 above.

for the furniture in the Versailles palace for his Americans, because His Majesty would have been unable to refuse it: cf., among others, Edward Everett, *Eulogy on Lafayette* (Boston, 1834). Since the ministers frequently refused Lafayette's requests and he almost always had to work hard in order to get what he did get, Maurepas' remark must be discounted, if, indeed, he ever made it. General H. L. V. Ducoudray-Holstein, *Memoirs of Gilbert M. Lafayette* (Geneva, N.Y., 1835) tells a highly colored story of the friendship of Lafayette and Marie Antoinette. At least one later biographer, Joseph Delteil, in his *Lafayette* (New York, 1928) falls into the same error. The relations of Lafayette and Marie Antoinette were proper, though friendly, in 1779–83.

The arrangements for signals to the fleet that was to make harbor at Rhode Island have led D. B. Sanger, in "General La Fayette—some notes on his contribution to signal communications" (*Signal Corps bulletin*, no. 78 [1934], pp. 41–49) to believe that Lafayette brought from France "a novel scheme for transmitting messages" (p. 47). The signals, however, were nothing more than a display of French and American flags, which arranged in one order were to mean that the coast was clear and in another that the English held the island (cf. Doniol, IV, 315).

CHAPTER IV

Lafayette Rejoins Washington

THE "Hermione" entered the port of Marblehead, Massachusetts, on April 27, 1780. The next day it took on a pilot and sailed to Boston.[1] Thirteen salutes boomed from the vessel's guns as it greeted the fort in the harbor, and thirteen guns barked again as the fort returned the courtesy. It had been an uneventful crossing. In thirty-eight days the "Hermione" had met with no enemy, had encountered only occasional contrary winds, and had had no other mishaps than the death of one of its crew from fever.[2]

The noise of the guns roused the town from its ordinary afternoon pursuits. Word spread from mouth to mouth that "the Marquis" had returned. When the passengers landed at Hancock's wharf, they were greeted with undisguised pleasure. The leading citizens of the town and a number of Continental officers surrounded Lafayette and, amid the ringing of bells and the blare of bands, escorted their honored guest to his lodgings. After being officially greeted by a committee of both houses of the Massachusetts legislature, Lafayette in his turn visited the State House and paid his respects amid another demonstration of joy. That night there were cheers, fireworks, and bonfires in front of his lodgings, and he was obliged to appear on the balcony and make a speech. Plans were soon afoot for a round of banquets both on shore and on board the "Hermione."[3] Rous-

[1] Rousseau de Fayolle, "Journal d'une campagne en Amérique," p. 48.

[2] Journal of the "Hermione," January 23, 1780—February 26, 1782, AN, Marine B⁴ 153, fols. 40–197.

[3] Latouche to [Sartine ?], April 30, 1780, BN, n.a.f. 9419, fol. 110; *Boston Independent Chronicle*, May 4, 1780, and *Continental Journal*, May 4, 1780, quoted in Allan Forbes and P. F. Cadman, *France and New England* (3 vols.; Boston, 1925–29), I, 12–13; R. R. Wilson (ed.), *Heath's memoirs of the American war* (New York, 1904), p. 248.

seau de Fayolle could not help remarking that Frenchmen seemed more welcome in Boston than they had been two years earlier.[4]

There was good reason why they should be. The winter of 1780 had been the most trying that patriots in America had yet had to endure. Taxes were high; prices had advanced. Paper money, Lafayette found, had dropped "in an unbelievable fashion."[5] Congress had lost prestige. As the individual states acquired the habit of independent action, the national assembly had become only the representative of the states in foreign affairs without power to act in domestic crises.[6] The English blockade, furthermore, was so effective that, of seven letters which Washington had written to Lafayette during his absence, only three seem ever to have reached him.[7] The very reports that Lafayette now sent off to Vergennes got to Versailles only by the mouths of the sailors who carried them, for they had to be thrown overboard, sometimes to be fished up again by the British who had pursued.[8]

The oldest people in the country could not remember so hard a winter, Washington reported.[9] The Continental Army had fallen to a "very small number."[10] It had been "without bread or meat" a large part of the time and "almost perishing for want."[11] Some soldiers occasionally took to plunder and, to avoid greater depredations, Washington resorted to requisitions.

[4] *Loc. cit.*, p. 48.

[5] Lafayette to Vergennes, May 2, 1780, Stevens, *Facsimiles*, XVII, no. 1623.

[6] Cf. Doniol, IV, 348–49.

[7] Those of September 12, September 30, and October 20, 1779, seem to have been delivered by La Colombe. Those of March 8–10, March 27, and July 24, 1779, and March 18, 1780, probably were never delivered. They are known from the copies retained by Washington; all are to be found in Fitzpatrick's *Writings of Washington*.

[8] Cf. Vergennes to Lafayette, August 7, 1780, *American historical review* (hereafter designated as *AHR*), VIII (1903), 507–8; the British Museum (London), additional MSS 24321, fols. 62–107.

[9] Washington to Lafayette, March 18, 1780, Fitzpatrick, XVIII, 125.

[10] Lafayette to Vergennes, May 2, 1780, *loc. cit.*

[11] Washington to the magistrates of New Jersey, January 8, 1780, Fitzpatrick, XVII, 363.

The depreciation in paper money, the great indifference of some states to the needs of their enlisted men, the inequality in terms of enlistment and in personal resources among the officers created discontented elements and "seditious combinations."[12] By spring Washington was forced to confess that never had dissatisfaction been so "general or alarming."[13]

Washington insisted that a committee of Congress be named to remodel the army. Until that was done he could not go himself to direct the defense of South Carolina[14] (where Charleston was to surrender within a few days). Such a committee finally was appointed. It described the shocking conditions which it found in words that made Washington's rebukes appear restrained. "The patience of the soldiery who have endured every degree of conceivable hardship, and borne it with fortitude and perseverance, beyond the expectation of the most sanguine," they bluntly announced, "is on the point of being exhausted."[15] When Lafayette discovered how hopeless had been the patriotic cause in America while he was telling the ministers in France of its great prospects, he refused to write home a full report of what he had learned. To those who were equally pained by the desperate situation, the marquis confessed: "Pride did not permit my entering into those details, and I avoid'd them entirely trusting on the future exertions of America."[16]

While the people of Boston did not know the full extent of the difficulties that the American commander-in-chief had to cope with, they knew that all was far from well. Lafayette's personal amiability was therefore not the sole cause of his joyful welcome. In him and Captain Latouche they gratefully recog-

[12] Washington to the president of Congress, April 3, 1780, *ibid.*, XVIII, 210.

[13] *Ibid.*, p. 209; cf. James Thacher, *A military journal during the American Revolutionary War* (Boston, 1823), p. 228.

[14] Washington to John Laurens, April 26, 1780, Fitzpatrick, XVIII, 300.

[15] Committee at headquarters to the several states, May 25, 1780, E. C. Burnett (ed.), *Letters of members of the Continental Congress* (8 vols.; Washington, 1921–36), V, 166.

[16] Lafayette to Bowdoin, May 30, 1780, Massachusetts Historical Society; cf. Lafayette to Reed, May 31, 1780, W. B. Reed, *Life and correspondence of Joseph Reed* (2 vols.; Philadelphia, 1847), II, 207–8.

nized assurances that, despite Estaing's departure, the alliance with France was not yet dead. Though Lafayette kept his secret from all but one or two of them,[17] they sensed that there were favors yet to come.

Lafayette did not stop for the festivities at Boston that were to celebrate his arrival. He was a very conscientious young man and had a duty to perform. From Marblehead, on the day before the "Hermione" reached Boston, he had informed his "beloved and respected friend and general" of his arrival, indicating that he had "affairs of the utmost importance" to communicate.[18] He stayed in Boston only long enough to pay his respects to most of the celebrities—John Hancock, William Heath, Samuel Adams, Samuel Cooper, among others—and to send to Vergennes and Adrienne optimistic reports of the conditions that he found.[19] On May 2, after expressing his thanks[20] to the Massachusetts legislature for the kindnesses shown him, he started out for Washington's camp at Morristown, New Jersey.

On May 5 it was known at Morristown that Lafayette was coming.[21] Washington did not attempt to hide the delight which the announcement brought him. During Lafayette's absence his affection for his young friend had conspicuously grown. To very few persons had the severe Virginian given his friendship as warmly and freely as to the young French nobleman. Every letter had made it plain that he had missed Lafayette's companionship and frank devotion. His replies to the candid out-

[17] Cf. Lafayette to Samuel Adams, May 30, 1780, Frederick Butler, *Memoirs of the Marquis de la Fayette* (Wetherfield, Conn., 1825), p. 36.

[18] April 27, 1780, *Mémoires* (Amer. ed.), p. 318; Tower, II, 106.

[19] Lafayette to Vergennes, May 1, 1780, AAE, corr. pol., É.-U., Vol. XII, fol. 10; cf. Vergennes to Lafayette, August 17, 1780, *AHR*, VIII (1903), 507-8; Mme de Lafayette to unknown, August 11, 1780, Brand Whitlock, *Lafayette* (2 vols.; New York, 1929), I, facsimile facing 204; Latouche to [Sartine ?], May 8, 1780, BN, n.a.f. 9419, fol. 111; Cooper to Franklin, May 23, 1780, John Bigelow (ed.), *Complete works of Benjamin Franklin* (10 vols.; New York, 1887–88), VII, 60; *Gazette de Leyde*, September 29, 1780, supplément, p. 1.

[20] *Boston Independent Chronicle*, May 4, 1780, quoted in Forbes and Cadman, I, 13.

[21] Washington to president of Congress and to La Luzerne, May 5, 1780, Fitzpatrick, XVIII, 331 and 335.

bursts of his much less reticent correspondent had been couched in a tone which was very different from the unbending and business-like style that he usually employed. They were intimate, affectionate, and humorous, and they never failed to confirm the sentimental tie that existed between them. Washington had not even tried to hide from others the depth of his affection for Lafayette. When the French ambassador La Luzerne and his secretary Barbé-Marbois had visited Washington at camp the preceding summer, Washington had asked with unconcealed tenderness after Lafayette and, deeply moved when the Frenchmen praised his young friend, declared, "I do not know a nobler, finer soul, and I love him as my own son."[22]

And now that "son" was returning. Washington and his wife made ready a room in the Ford mansion, which was their home and headquarters, to receive their guest. He sent Major Caleb Gibbs, of his own bodyguard, to meet Lafayette on the road and to escort him into camp. Gibbs carried with him a letter of greeting from the commander-in-chief, assuring Lafayette that the news of his arrival had been received "with all the joy that the sincerest friendship could dictate and with that impatience which an ardent desire to see you could not fail to inspire."[23]

Lafayette's progress through New England and New York was slow. The roads were bad and horses hard to get. On the first day he reached Watertown, Massachusetts, from which he wrote Vergennes a report of his reception.[24] Four days later he wrote again from Waterbury, Connecticut.[25] On May 8 he was at Fishkill, New York, where, on encountering English reports that a French fleet was coming to America, he publicly declared he knew nothing about it.[26] At one point between New York

[22] E. P. Chase (ed.), *Our revolutionary forefathers, the letters of François, Marquis de Barbé-Marbois* (New York, 1929), p. 116; Percy Noël (tr.), "Our revolutionary forefathers: the journal of François, Marquis de Barbé-Marbois," *Atlantic monthly,* CXLII (1928), 156.

[23] May 8, 1780, Fitzpatrick, XVIII, 341.   [24] May 2, 1780, *loc. cit.*

[25] May 6, 1780, Stevens, *Facsimiles,* XVII, no. 1624.

[26] Colonel Udny Hay to Governor Clinton, May 8, 1780, Hugh Hastings (ed.), *Public papers of George Clinton, first governor of New York* (10 vols.; New York, :899–1914), V, 692–94.

and New Jersey he had to pass through well-known Tory territory. General Knyphausen, of the Hessian forces in the British army, who knew of his approach, had planned to surprise him at the Clove. Lafayette nearly fell into Knyphausen's hands, but somehow, probably without ever learning how narrow his escape had been, went on unmolested.[27]

There was great joy at Morristown when finally, on the morning of May 10, the marquis and the escorting cavalcade rode into camp. After the enthusiastic greeting by officers and men was over, Washington and Lafayette retired to a private room, and there the young general imparted to his chief the good news that he had been sent by his king to deliver.[28] He presented the instructions suggesting a continued effort in the South or against New York. In addition, of his own accord, he emphasized the desirability of an attack upon Halifax.[29] Since the excellent English spy system had already informed the enemy that a French auxiliary force was on its way and the Tory newspapers were soon to spread the report throughout the land,[30] Washington and Lafayette also talked of ways to divert the English. A proclamation addressed to the Canadians giving the impression that the French troops were destined for a major effort in their behalf and another addressed to the savages pretending that New York was to be the chief objective would, it was hoped, confuse the enemy regarding the true intentions of the allied effort.[31] And, indeed, if conditions warranted, an attack upon Canada might well be made in the winter.[32]

[27] Robertson to Germain, May 18, 1780, E. B. O'Callaghan (ed.), *Documents relative to the Colonial history of the State of New York* (15 vols.; Albany, 1853–57), VIII, 792.

[28] Lafayette to Vergennes, May 20, 1780, Stevens, *Facsimiles*, XVII, no. 1625; cf. Washington to La Luzerne, May 11, 1780, Fitzpatrick, XVIII, 348.

[29] Cf. Washington to Heath, May 15, 1780, Fitzpatrick, XVIII, 360–62.

[30] *Rivington's Royal Gazette* (New York), May 17, 1780, cited by J. A. Stevens, "The French in Rhode Island," *Magazine of American history*, III (1879), 395; cf. Sidney Everett, "The Chevalier de Ternay," *New England historical and genealogical register*, XXVII (1873), 409; Rupert Hughes, *George Washington; the rebel and the patriot* (3 vols. to date; New York, 1927–30), III, 516; Bernard Faÿ, *Revolutionary spirit in France and America*, tr. Ramon Guthrie (New York, 1927), p. 111.

[31] Washington to Lafayette, May 19, 1780, Fitzpatrick, XVIII, 386–88.

[32] Lafayette to Vergennes, May 20, 1780, *loc. cit.*

Washington immediately understood the importance of vigorous action. If the United States could prepare a big army to co-operate with Rochambeau (somewhere near the 25,000 that Congress had once promised La Luzerne),[33] the ensuing campaign might be decisive. But Washington could not himself lawfully take the measures to recruit a bigger army, and he refused even to make plans for co-operation with the expected French forces without the consent of a jealous Congress. Yet he recognized that that assembly was far too numerous for quick or secret action. He therefore preferred that it name a small committee which should be empowered to make the necessary decisions. He counted on La Luzerne to induce Congress to take such a step. Lafayette must go to Philadelphia, he determined, and secure the co-operation of La Luzerne.[34] If Rochambeau's army arrived in time and if it were not deprived of maritime supremacy by a reinforcement of the British fleet in the waters around the Hudson, he hoped the combined forces might succeed in an attack upon New York.

Lafayette stayed four days at Morristown recovering from a cold contracted from backbreaking days on horseback in the raw spring weather of the northern states. Meanwhile he communicated the news that he carried to the congressional committee which was at camp, to La Luzerne, to his old friend, Alexander Hamilton, and to several others.[35] He and Hamilton together drew up a memorandum of the things that had to be done to prepare for the French expeditionary force.[36]

Recovered from his cold, the young general once more mounted his horse. On May 15 he was in Philadelphia. He carried

[33] J. C. Fitzpatrick, "The significance to the historian of the new bicentennial edition of the writings of George Washington," *Annual report of the American Historical Association for the year 1932* (Washington, 1934), I, 115.

[34] Washington to La Luzerne, May 11, 1780, Fitzpatrick, XVIII, 348; cf. Washington to Lafayette, May 16, 1780, *ibid.*, p. 369.

[35] Schuyler to Clinton, May 15, 1780, *Papers of Clinton*, V, 708–10; minute of the committee at headquarters, May 15, 1780, Burnett, V, 141–42; Hamilton to Duane, May 14, 1780, J. C. Hamilton (ed.), *Works of Alexander Hamilton* (7 vols.; New York, 1850–51), I, 137–38; Washington to Joseph Jones, May 14, 1780, Fitzpatrick, XVIII, 356–58; Washington to Duane, May 14, 1780, *ibid.*, p. 358.

[36] Cf. Washington to Lafayette, May 19, 1780, Fitzpatrick, XVIII, 387.

with him letters from Washington to several members of Congress, all of which urged the formation of a "plenipotentiary" committee that should make it simple for Washington to collaborate with Congress. In accordance with Vergennes' instructions and Washington's preferences, he first interviewed La Luzerne and agreed with him on the proper way to approach Congress.[37] Then he presented his respects to Congress in a letter informing them of his return,[38] but carefully avoiding any mention of the aid which was being sent by His Most Christian Majesty Louis XVI. Congress drew up a resolution commending the marquis' "disinterested zeal and persevering attachment" in returning from his furlough.[39]

Meanwhile, Washington had had a chance to think of the proposals that Lafayette had brought. The longer he thought, the more convinced he became that an immediate attack upon New York was the most desirable of the three plans that Lafayette had placed before him.[40] Sir Henry Clinton and the major part of the British forces were engaged before Charleston. The garrison of New York was considerably reduced, and its naval force was inferior to the expected French fleet. If Rochambeau and Ternay were to sail directly to New York, the chances of a successful attack were very good. They would be better yet if the French West Indies fleet, now under the Comte de Guichen, could also come to the continent. Washington urged Lafayette to send such a message to Guichen. Meanwhile, Washington busied himself in writing the governors of the states and other influential citizens, beseeching them to co-operate in improving the country's military resources.

Lafayette had been kept busy in Philadelphia communicating with La Luzerne and clearing the way for the numerous transactions of M. de Corny, who had remained behind at Morris-

---

[37] Cf. La Luzerne to Congress, May 16, 1780, Wharton, III, 683; La Luzerne to Vergennes, May 20, 1780, AAE, corr. pol., É.-U., Vol. XII, fol. 101.

[38] May 16, 1780, PCC, no. 156, fols. 105–6.

[39] May 16, 1780, W. C. Ford et al. (eds.), Journals of the Continental Congress, 1774–1787 (34 vols.; Washington, 1904–37), XVII, 432.

[40] Washington to Lafayette, May 16, 1780, loc. cit.

town.[41] Now he gladly added to his duties the honorific burden of acting as interpreter of Washington's wishes. He sent to Rochambeau and Ternay[42] a detailed account of Washington's plan for an attack on New York, translating almost literally the comments that Washington had made to him on that subject. Copies of this letter were sent to each of the two French commanders at the various points where the fleet might land. To Guichen[43] he sent the first letter he had ever written in code, urging him to come to the support of the projected attack upon New York.

Meanwhile La Luzerne had communicated to Congress His Most Christian Majesty's generous plans.[44] The great news succeeded in rousing a lethargic Congress into action. Lafayette personally visited the delegates of the more important states like Massachusetts,[45] while La Luzerne busied himself through diplomatic channels. In a burst of new energy Congress resolved to call on the states for more money. A quota for each state was decreed, and the president empowered to demand that sum in addition to the amount required for provisioning the troops. Congress also instructed the committee at headquarters to assist the commander-in-chief in securing supplies and militia, urging more efficient co-operation on the states in that regard as well. Lafayette was enjoined to give Washington all possible information on the French fleet, and Washington was authorized to take such measures as seemed to him most effective toward increasing the Continental forces. A congressional com-

---

[41] Cf. Holker to Trumbull, May 17, 1780, *The Trumbull papers, part IV* ("Collections of the Massachusetts Historical Society," 7th ser., Vol. III [Boston, 1902]), p. 45; Lafayette to La Luzerne, May 17, 1780, W. G. Leland, "Letters from Lafayette to Luzerne (1780–1782)," *AHR*, XX (1914–15), 342–44.

[42] May 19, 1780, LC, Rochambeau letter book; a signed copy of this letter intended for Ternay if he sailed to Cape Henry is in the Huntington Library, DE 78; another is in AAE, corr. pol., É.-U., supplément, Vol. XIV, fols. 87–90. It is published, *inter alia*, in *Mémoires*, I, 335–42.

[43] Incorrectly dated May 10, 1780, but actually of May 19 or 20, 1780, AN, Marine B⁴ 183, fols. 284–89.

[44] La Luzerne to Congress, May 16, 1780, *loc. cit.*

[45] "Journal of Doctor Samuel Holten," *Historical collections of the Danvers Historical Society*, VIII (1920), 126; cf. Burnett, V, 156, n. 2.

mittee was to confer with the French ambassador regarding the best way of supplying the expected French force.[46] Congress thus sanctioned what Lafayette and Washington had, in fact, already largely done. When Lafayette returned to camp, bearing the resolutions of Congress, he had good reason to hope that Washington might soon have an army of 15,000 men, not counting militia.[47]

Before leaving Philadelphia, Lafayette again reported his success to Vergennes. Without hiding how difficult it would be to get effective American co-operation (chiefly because of the inflation of Continental currency), he remained optimistic. He had confidence in Washington. "I can answer for it," he wrote, "that the French generals and troops will have nothing but praise for his uprightness, for his delicacy, for that noble and easy courtesy which characterizes him, and at the same time they will have to admire his great qualities. Although I repeated to him that our land generals were under his orders as much as the generals of his own army, you will see by what he charged me to write them that he does not intend to make his command hard or arbitrary. The same love of liberty, a greater union in Congress, a very much greater conviction of their need of France to win their independence, more readiness to receive any aid whatsoever—those, Sir, are the sentiments which I have had the pleasure of finding among my American friends; and Paris may be assured that they will not abandon us."[48] Leaving this report to be coded and sent off by La Luzerne, Lafayette hastened "home"—as Washington had requested him to call headquarters.[49]

At camp everyone was now counting the minutes until the French fleet should arrive. Lafayette continued to co-ordinate the work of Quartermaster-General Greene with that of La Luzerne and other French agents in providing provisions for

[46] *Journals of Congress*, XVII, 433 (May 17), 436 (May 18), 437 (May 19), and 442–43 (May 20). Cf. president of Congress to the governors of several states, May 19, 1780, Burnett, V, 155–56.

[47] Lafayette to Vergennes, May 20, 1780, *loc. cit.*   [48] *Ibid.*

[49] Washington to Lafayette, May 20, 1780, Fitzpatrick, XVIII, 397.

Rochambeau's army.[50] He collaborated with the congressional committee in the preparation of a circular to the states detailing the penury of the army and urging greater co-operation in the forthcoming campaign. In suppliant letters to several influential leaders, he made a personal appeal to their pride and patriotism.[51]

Meanwhile, the effort to beguile the enemy regarding the objective of Rochambeau's force was further developed. Lafayette prepared a proclamation to the Canadians which was intended to make the British believe that the destination of the French fleet was Canada. Five hundred copies of that proclamation were printed, and a few of them were allowed to pass into English hands.[52] It had the desired effect of confusing the enemy and making them take added precautions in Canada against local disaffection.[53] At the same time, since the British were not themselves innocent of deceit, the marquis was obliged to send

[50] Lafayette to La Luzerne, May 24, 1780 (three letters), *AHR*, XX (1915), 344-46, 346-48, and 348-49; May 25, 1780 (two letters), *ibid.*, pp. 349 and 350; May 27, 1780, *ibid.*, pp. 350-51. Replies to these letters and others from La Luzerne to Lafayette are to be found in AAE, corr. pol., É.-U., Vol. XII, fols. 164-68 and supplément, Vol. XIV, fols. 106-74.

[51] Lafayette to Samuel Adams, May 30, Butler, pp. 34-36; to Bowdoin, May 30, *Massachusetts Historical Society proceedings*, V (1860-62), 348-50; to Reed, May 31, *loc. cit.*; to Heath, June 11, *Heath papers, part III (Jan. 1780-1783)* ("Massachusetts Historical Society collections," 7th ser., Vol. V [Boston, 1905]), pp. 66-70. Cf. Samuel Adams to Lafayette, June, 1780, H. A. Cushing (ed.), *Writings of Samuel Adams* (4 vols.; New York, 1904-8), IV, 197-99; Heath to Lafayette, June 20, *Heath papers, part III*, pp. 73-74; Gerry to president of the council of Massachusetts, July 3, J. T. Austin, *Life of Elbridge Gerry* (2 vols.; Boston, 1828-29), I, 351-52; and Bowdoin to Lafayette, June 12, July 10 and 29, *Massachusetts Historical Society proceedings*, V, 350-53.

[52] Washington to Lafayette, May 19, 1780, Fitzpatrick, XVIII, 386-88; Lafayette to Vergennes, May 25, AAE, corr. pol., É.-U., supplément, Vol. XIV, fol. 97; Washington to Arnold, June 4, Fitzpatrick, XVIII, 476; Arnold to Claypole (printer), June 8, described in Parke-Bernet Galleries catalogue of the sale of the John Gribbel collection, no. 34, part I, October 30–November 1, 1940, p. 7. A manuscript copy of the proclamation is to be found in AAE, corr. pol., É.-U., supplément, Vol. XIV, fols. 98-101, and printed copies in the Yale University Library and the John Carter Brown Library. Cf. Carl Van Doren, *Secret history of the American Revolution* (New York, 1941), pp. 263-64.

[53] Clinton to [Eden], August 18–September 1, 1780, Stevens, *Facsimiles*, VII, no. 730 and note; Clinton to Germain, August 31, 1780, W. C. Ford (ed.), *Writings of George Washington* (14 vols.; New York, 1889-93), VIII, 281 n. Cf. J. M. McIlwraith, *Sir Frederick Haldimand* (Toronto, 1910), pp. 128 and 278.

French officers to test reports that the French fleet had appeared outside New York.[54]

No step that Washington, La Luzerne, or Lafayette could take was overlooked in order that the French auxiliary force might be properly guarded, welcomed, and placed in readiness for the campaign. A council of war called together by the commander-in-chief approved of making New York the principal objective of the allied effort when the fleet should come.[55] Since it was uncertain, however, whether Rochambeau would arrive at Rhode Island or at Cape Henry, precautions had to be taken to provide for him at either destination. Lafayette for a second time sent off instructions to meet the fleet in both harbors, repeating Washington's wish that the French sail for New York at the first opportunity. He dispatched his letters by French officers who were ordered to put themselves at the disposal of the French generals on their arrival.[56] Dr. James Craik, assistant general-director of hospitals, was sent to Rhode Island to prepare for the care of Rochambeau's sick if they should land there.[57] General Heath was instructed to proceed to Providence and place himself at the disposal of the French commander.[58] Since a proper signal corps and a regular system of communications did not exist in the American army, Lafayette saw to it that, with money provided by La Luzerne, there was established a regular chain of express couriers from Cape Henry through Philadelphia to Morristown and thence north to Providence.[59] In that way, it was hoped, Ternay's fleet would be greeted with the prearranged signals whether it took the southern or the northern route across the Atlantic; and news of its arrival would speedily be brought to Washington, who could then provide for its co-operation in the attack upon New York.

[54] Lafayette to La Luzerne, May 24, 1780, *AHR*, XX (1915), 346–47.

[55] June 6, 1780, Fitzpatrick, XVIII, 482–85.

[56] Lafayette to Rochambeau and Ternay, May 23, 1780, LC, Rochambeau letter book; Galvan to Ternay, June 13, 1780, AN, Marine B⁴ 183, fols. 234–35.

[57] Washington to Craik, May 24, 1780, Fitzpatrick, XVIII, 410–11.

[58] June 2, 1780, *ibid.*, pp. 467–68.

[59] Lafayette to La Luzerne, May 24, 1780, *loc. cit.*; June 3, 1780, *ibid.*, p. 352.

New York, indeed, did not wait idly to be attacked but assumed the offensive. Early in June the British under General Knyphausen moved into New Jersey and encamped close to Elizabethtown. Washington's army moved in the direction of Springfield to meet them. Lafayette commanded the left wing made up of the Connecticut division. He was outranked only by Greene, who commanded the right.[60] Headquarters were established on the heights near Springfield. The two armies thus drew close together and watched each other cautiously. Washington was anxious to avoid a fight, since his army was in "weak, diminished condition"[61] and he wished to keep it intact, if possible, against the coming of the French.

It was while these maneuvers were taking place that Washington and his generals were definitely informed that Charleston had fallen to Sir Henry Clinton. General Lincoln had, in fact, surrendered with his entire army shortly after Lafayette first arrived at Morristown, but the rumors of the defeat reached the North only at the beginning of June. At first Lafayette refused to believe them,[62] but eventually the full extent of the disaster could no longer be denied. It immediately became clear that the attack on New York must not be delayed much longer, since the British forces that had besieged Charleston would soon return to reinforce the garrison there. Washington sent express riders to Rhode Island and Cape Henry to urge Rochambeau's speedy attack on New York or the prompt interception of Sir Henry on his way from Charleston.[63] No Rochambeau appeared, however. And while Knyphausen was worrying Washington around Springfield, Sir Henry sailed into New York. Lafayette immediately sent new dispatches to Rhode Island and Cape Henry to inform Rochambeau of that fact.[64] The commander-in-chief now felt that it would be wisest for Rocham-

---

[60] General orders, June 7, 1780, Fitzpatrick, XVIII, 486–87.

[61] Washington to Bowdoin, June 14, 1780, *ibid.*, XIX, 10.

[62] Cf. Lafayette to La Luzerne, June 3, 1780, *AHR*, XX (1915), 352.

[63] Hamilton to Ternay, June 13, 1780, *Works of Hamilton*, I, 140.

[64] June 20, 1780, LC, Rochambeau letter book.

beau, after landing at Rhode Island, to rest and await further orders.

It was not at all clear to Washington and his generals what Knyphausen's purpose was in marching into New Jersey. Some thought it might be to cover Washington's army while West Point was attacked by another British force. In actual fact Knyphausen was simply engaged in harassing his enemy. When Clinton returned, he ordered the British to evacuate, which they did only after pushing General Greene's men out of Springfield and burning the town. Lafayette had not engaged in the fighting. The American army then moved through Whippany and Ramapo to Preakness (Paterson), where it could be ready to go to the relief of West Point, if necessary, while also protecting New Jersey.

In all this marching and countermarching, Lafayette had not lost sight of his major purpose. Not for a moment did he forget or allow anyone else to forget Rochambeau and Ternay. His bulletins to La Luzerne and the French consul-general, John Holker, were frequent and spoke always of the need for money, clothing, and supplies; and La Luzerne nearly always was able to be helpful.[65] If pressure had to be brought to bear on tardy legislatures and lax governors, Lafayette wrote to them to exhort or to shame them, and he called upon La Luzerne to do likewise. He took up with Washington at great length the simple matter of clothing.[66] As he had done when he first joined the American army, he lamented as a source of bad discipline the lack of distinctive uniforms and the inadequate markings of the separate ranks. He hoped to be able to remedy that shortcoming by the new supplies from France. He warned his fellow-generals not to speak to French officers of uniforms as if they were "a novelty in our army."[67] He felt certain that "in the fighting way they shall see that we are equal to anything; but for what concerns dress, appearance, &c., we must cheat a

---

[65] Cf. *AHR*, XX (1915), 353–62; A. Koszul, "Lettres inédites de Lafayette," *L'Alsace française*, XXVII (1934), 386–87.

[66] July 4, 1780, *Mémoires* (Amer. ed.), pp. 325–27.

[67] Lafayette to Heath, June 11, 1780, *loc. cit.*, p. 68.

little."[68] Learning that the women of Philadelphia were raising a fund to clothe soldiers, he sent a contribution of one hundred guineas in the name of his wife, "who heartly [sic] wishing for a personal acquaintance with the ladies of America would feel particularly happy to be admitted among them on the present occasion."[69] Nor did that gesture misrepresent Adrienne in any way. At about that time Adrienne described herself as "a good American" in begging Franklin for confirmation of all-too-favorable rumors in Paris that Clinton had been killed and Charleston saved.[70]

Clinton was far from dead. And as the American army once more found itself free to observe him at leisure, its strategists again began to speculate on how best to embarrass him. The disappointed marquis' thoughts turned once more to Canada. On La Luzerne's suggestion he sounded out Washington's attitude regarding that objective. Washington could not exclude it as a possibility, but he refused to think of it as an immediate aim.[71] Meanwhile, Lafayette sent off French-Canadian officers to spy upon Quebec and Montreal.[72]

The more Washington and Lafayette thought of it, the less disastrous Clinton's return to New York appeared and the more logical the scheme suggested by the French ministry seemed. New York was the center of British strength in the United States. It was not only the headquarters of the army but the fountainhead of its propaganda, the center of its Tory activities. If New York could be taken, the British offensive might collapse. Four days and almost four nights spent in cross-examining the ablest pilots he could find and studying the best maps led Lafayette to the conclusion that naval supremacy could easily be established in the harbor while a land force reduced

[68] *Ibid.*, p. 70.

[69] Lafayette to Mrs. Reed, June 25, 1780, *Correspondence of Joseph Reed*, II, 263; cf. *Mémoires*, I, 374.

[70] June 20, 1780, APS, Franklin papers, Vol. XVIII, part 2, no. 154½.

[71] Cf. Lafayette to La Luzerne, June 20 and July 4, 1780, *AHR*, XX (1915), 358–62; La Luzerne to Vergennes, July 1, 1780, AAE, corr. pol., É.-U., Vol. XIII, fols. 22–25.

[72] AAE, corr. pol., É.-U., supplément, Vol. XIV, fols. 175–77.

the Brooklyn fortifications and made New York untenable.[73] Meanwhile, he and Washington had also become convinced that by the beginning of August they could count on double the 7,000 men then in the Continental Army and about 6,000 militia besides. These together with the French auxiliary force would more than outnumber Clinton's combined forces in New York, who, at most, would total 15,000. Therefore, Washington reverted again to his preference for an attack on New York and instructed Lafayette to explain his proposal in detail to Rochambeau and Ternay.

Lafayette gladly complied.[74] His explanation made it quite clear that he was speaking as an American officer to trusted allies: "We are now, Gentlemen, not with the reserve which is proper with strangers, but with that friendly confidence which is justified by alliance, ... going to take you entirely into the secret of our situation. Among the advantages of popular government are to be found certain inconveniences which make themselves felt in time of war, and the fear of giving too great power to a small number of men necessarily occasions more tardiness in operation." Nevertheless—and despite inflation and recent military setbacks—"the virtue of private citizens remains always the same." In consequence of measures taken by the states, the Americans would be able to count on soldiers who would be "equal at least to the best troops that will be sent against them." In view of this increasing confidence in the American forces ("based," Lafayette stated, "not on promises which have been made us but upon the particular examination of those promises and the discounting of them that we believe we ought to make in order to avoid giving any hope which we could not fulfill") Washington was again willing for the attack on New York to begin just as soon as the French commanders thought they would be ready. A careful plan was outlined and maps provided. Copies of Lafayette's letter were

---

[73] Lafayette to Rochambeau and Ternay, July 9, 1789, LC, Rochambeau letter book.

[74] *Ibid.*; cf. La Luzerne to Vergennes, July 15, 1780, AAE, corr. pol., È.-U., Vol. XIII, fols. 58–67.

sent to Rhode Island, Black Point (at the entrance of New York Bay), and Cape Henry to await the French, who were still expected any day at one of those points.

BIBLIOGRAPHICAL NOTES

The latest biography of Washington is by N. W. Stephenson and W. H. Dunn (2 vols.; New York, 1940). Though it is useful, J. C. Fitzpatrick's *George Washington himself* (Indianapolis, 1933) remains the best interpretation of the commander-in-chief. Rupert Hughes's as yet incomplete biography contains much documentary material that is difficult to obtain otherwise. Étienne Charavay's *Le Général Lafayette, 1757-1834* (Paris, 1898) is still the most scholarly brief presentation of that subject, and Brand Whitlock's two-volume work the best in English, despite its inaccuracies.

Forbes and Cadman, *France and New England*, quote contemporary newspapers freely. J. Bennett Nolan's *Lafayette in America day by day* (Baltimore, 1934) is a helpful compendium, though mistaken regarding the date of Lafayette's arrival in Boston (which was April 28, not 26).

The letters of Lafayette to Rochambeau and Ternay have been incompletely published by Doniol in his "Correspondance du Comte de Rochambeau," which is an appendix to his Volume V (pp. 308–590). Contemporary copies of the original letters are to be found in Archives du Ministère de la Guerre, AH 3733, but I have preferred above to rely on Rochambeau's own letter book in the Rochambeau papers in the Library of Congress.

E. C. Burnett's *Continental Congress* (New York, 1941) is by the outstanding student of that subject.

CHAPTER V

Liaison Officer

THE French reached American waters nearly two months later than expected. Bringing together, despite the British blockade, a force of 6,000 men, eight ships of the line, five smaller men-of-war with their crews and marine, and a convoy of about thirty-six transports had proved to be a feat that had taxed the waggoners and storekeepers on all the roads leading to Brest and all the shipyards on France's Atlantic coast. Loading the warships and their convoy with men and supplies, with tens of thousands of the many articles that an army might need in a land where they could count on finding very little was another time-consuming accomplishment. The Comte de Guichen, who had just led a fleet to the West Indies, had already combed the same area for stores, and what little was left was hard to find.

It was the middle of April before the last regiment that had been assigned to Rochambeau arrived in the neighborhood of Brest. Among the officers were several whom Lafayette called friends. Of those the Chevalier de Chastellux, the only one among them who had a reputation as a writer and a dealer in ideas, held a general's rank. The others were no more than colonels. There was his brother-in-law, the Vicomte de Noailles, whom he had once held in awe. There was Charles de Lameth, nephew of the Comte de Broglie, who had been a fellow-subaltern in Broglie's army in those faraway days before Lafayette had become a champion of liberty. There were young blades like the Comte Mathieu Dumas, the Comte de Charlus, and the Swedish Comte de Fersen, said even now to be the lover of

France's queen. There was the Chevalier de Mauduit-Duplessis, with whom Lafayette had campaigned in America.

These men did not think of themselves as crusaders of liberty. They were soldiers fighting the inveterate enemy of their country—noblemen and officers doing their traditional duty and going where the fortunes of war had determined that their superiors should send them. Chastellux had given some thought to the subject of public welfare—had even written a book upon it. But the future Revolutionary leaders—Lameth, Noailles, Dumas—if they had thought of reform at all at this stage, had not strained at the thought. Their experience in America, like that of Lafayette and several of his aides, was to give them a different set of values.

When the last soldier finally arrived, Ternay found that he did not have room for all of them and their baggage. A painful decision had to be made. Rochambeau must either wait for more ships or leave some of his men behind. Since a British fleet under Admiral Thomas Graves was known to be preparing to leave Plymouth, the French ministry decided that Rochambeau must get to America first, even if with only part of his forces. So he divided his men into two sections and, begging the king to send the second division after him, determined to sail with only 5,000 men.

It was May before favorable winds permitted Ternay to give the order to hoist anchor. He took the southern route. Storms, calms, and fog delayed his ships; and twice they encountered contingents of British war vessels, which Ternay, for the sake of his convoy's safety, preferred to run away from rather than to pursue.

At length, after nine weeks' sailing, they beheld the coast of Virginia. From an English sloop which they had captured on the way, the Frenchmen already knew that Charleston had fallen. From another prize taken off the shore of Virginia, they learned that Clinton had returned to New York. It was obvious that they could be of no use in the South and that they would be safest at Rhode Island. After another week of skirting the coast, they reached the waters around Newport. It had taken them seventy days to make the crossing that Lafayette had made in thirty-eight. On each shore of the harbor they beheld a French flag, the prearranged signal, which Lafayette's aides had set up weeks earlier and which for many days had idly waved that the coast was clear of Englishmen.[1]

Ternay's fleet dropped anchor off Newport early in the morning of July 11, 1780, only two days before Admiral Graves, close on their heels, reached New York. General Heath, Captain Latouche, M. de Corny, Dr. Craik, and several other officers and agents whom Washington and Lafayette had sent to Rhode Island to prepare for their coming hastened to welcome them. The people of Newport at first seemed disappointed at the size of the auxiliary force, which they had so long hoped would prove to be an invincible armada. No one turned out to cheer Rochambeau and his staff when they landed. But by evening Rochambeau had succeeded in spreading the impression that he had come with what was only an advance guard of a larger army, and then the townsfolk publicly celebrated. They rang their church bells, placed candles in their windows, shot off their fireworks, and poured out into the streets to cheer.[2] A few more days elapsed before preparations were sufficiently advanced on shore to allow the entire French auxiliary force, with its six or seven hundred invalids, to get off the boats. Among Ternay's sailors there were thirteen hundred sick.[3] On landing, Rochambeau found copies of only the first three of the four letters which Lafayette had sent to Rhode Island for him. The last of those three had been written just after Clinton's return to New York; it urged Rochambeau to stay at Rhode Island until further orders.

Rochambeau dutifully hastened to inform Washington of his arrival and his readiness to carry out Washington's commands. In fact, before landing, Rochambeau had issued instructions

[1] *Journal de Blanchard*, p. 35.

[2] Rochambeau to Washington, July 12, 1780, Doniol, V, 348–49; Rochambeau to Montbarey, July 16, 1780, *ibid.*, p. 344; letter of an officer in Rochambeau's army, August 8, 1780, *Gazette de Leyde*, October 10, 1780.

[3] Ternay to Lafayette, July 16, 1780, Ford, *Writings of Washington*, VIII, 352 n.; entry for July 22, 1780, LC, Rochambeau letter book, p. 46.

that the president of Congress and General Washington were to be accorded the honors due to a marshal of France and that the governors of the states as well as American major-generals were to be treated like *maréchaux-de-camp.*[4] In that way Rochambeau, as the only lieutenant-general in the allied forces, stood second only to the president of Congress and the commander-in-chief.

At Washington's headquarters in New Jersey the arrival of the French fleet was known even before Rochambeau's letter was delivered. Lafayette's chain of express riders had brought word from Heath and Corny that Ternay's armada had been sighted off the coast of Rhode Island.[5] It was reported to include twelve ships of the line. Without waiting for the courier who was to bring confirmation of Rochambeau's actual landing and more reliable statistics, Lafayette drafted a new letter for Rochambeau.[6] Though informing him of Admiral Graves's arrival in New York, he urged the French general, nevertheless, to continue with the plans for an attack upon New York. Graves's fleet presented an additional obstacle, the proposed letter admitted, but it "also affords us an opportunity to win greater glory and to inflict greater harm on the British nation." Therefore, the draft continued, Washington wished Ternay's fleet to sail to Sandy Hook as soon as possible.

Colonel Hamilton wrote out Lafayette's draft in French and consulted General Washington upon it.[7] Washington disapproved of it. It was much too bold. His own preparations for an attack on New York were far from complete. It was not at all clear that Ternay's force was sufficient to give the allies decisive maritime supremacy, which, in Washington's opinion, must be considered "as a fundamental principle, and the basis upon which every hope of success must ultimately depend."[8] He

[4] Orders of July 8, 1780, BN, n.a.f. 9427, fol. 264.

[5] Fitzpatrick, XIX, 176–78, and 211, n. 66; cf. Lafayette to La Luzerne, July 14, 1780, *AHR*, XX (1915), 363.

[6] July 15, 1780, LC, Hamilton papers (in Hamilton's handwriting).

[7] Cf. *ibid.*; also Washington to Lafayette, July 16, 1780, Fitzpatrick, XIX, 183–84.

[8] Memorandum of July 15, 1780, *ibid.*, p. 174.

therefore proposed another letter. It would merely announce the arrival of Admiral Graves's fleet, leaving it to the French general to determine whether he ought to proceed against New York and promising no relaxation in American efforts to that end.[9] At the same time Washington sent Lafayette a memorandum outlining fuller instructions for Rochambeau and Ternay.[10] They described how, provided Ternay's forces were superior to the British navy in and around New York harbor, a joint attack by French and American land forces might be carried out sometime in August.

When Lafayette found that Washington had repudiated his own bold course, he was disappointed. He obediently sent Rochambeau the more prosaic letter which Washington called for.[11] Yet he could not keep from protesting his disappointment. From his quarters at Samuel Van Saun's house he hastened to see Washington, who lived at Colonel Theunis Dey's, a mile away,[12] in order to present the case for attacking New York rather than starving it out. Lafayette, still under the impression that there were twelve ships of the line in Ternay's fleet, felt that daring was sure to succeed. Even if the French fleet were inferior, he contended,[13] some offensive stroke must be tried during that campaign. This was probably one of the occasions (which Lafayette later described)[14] when the young soldier felt obliged to tell his chief that he pushed the fear of taking risks to an extreme and received the reply that the king's confidence required a double carefulness and prudence. In the end Washington asked him to put his ideas in writing. Lafayette did so the next day.[15] After examining his friend's remarks, Washing-

[9] Washington to Lafayette, July 16, 1780, *loc. cit.*

[10] Memorandum of July 15, 1780, *loc. cit.*

[11] July 15, 1780, LC, Rochambeau letter book, pp. 102–3.

[12] Cf. William Nelson, "Washington's headquarters at Preakness," *Magazine of American history*, III (1879), 490; cf. Lafayette to Washington, July 16, 1780, LC, Washington papers, Ser. F, Vol. II, Part II, fol. 191.

[13] Lafayette to Washington, July 16, 1780, *loc. cit.*

[14] Lafayette to Vergennes, July 19, 1780, Stevens, *Facsimiles*, XVII, no. 1626.

[15] Lafayette to Washington, July 16, 1780, *loc. cit.*

ton repeated that he had no idea of abandoning the attack on New York unless it should appear "obviously impractical."[16] He had discouraged the first draft of Lafayette's letter, he said, only "because I never wish to promise more than I have a moral certainty of performing." It was a gentle rebuke for youthful temerity.

Almost at the very moment that Lafayette was expressing his belief that his commander was too cautious, the French generals received the last of the four letters that Lafayette had sent before their arrival. That letter had likewise urged an attack upon New York. The next day Rochambeau and Ternay wrote to Lafayette[17] that they could not carry out altogether the part that he had said was expected of them. The great number of sick, the problem of getting supplies, the obvious English naval predominance in American waters, and the difficulty of clearing New York harbor with large vessels would make necessary certain changes in the plan of campaign. Rochambeau could not expect to be ready to take the offensive until August 15; and Ternay would not go to Sandy Hook but would take his post somewhere near Long Island. Rochambeau begged that Washington meet him and Ternay halfway between their two camps. "In an hour of conversation we shall come to a better understanding than in volumes of writing."[18]

Even before that request reached Preakness, Washington had himself decided that only in a personal interview could a plan of campaign quickly and secretly be arranged. Yet he also felt that he could not go away and leave his army in command of subordinates. To have absented himself at the moment when he was most needed to collaborate with the congressional committee at camp in securing men, money, and munitions would have been to check or destroy the preparations that were already under way. Someone else must be sent in his place. No one could better act as Washington's representative than Lafayette,

[16] Washington to Lafayette, July 16, 1780, *loc. cit.*

[17] Rochambeau to Lafayette, July 16, 1780, Doniol, V, 350; Ternay to Lafayette, July 16, 1780, *loc. cit.*

[18] Rochambeau to Lafayette, July 16, 1780, *loc. cit.*

and he requested Lafayette to go. In a letter of explanation which he sent to Rochambeau,[19] he lauded his proxy: "As a general officer I have the greatest confidence in him; as a friend he is perfectly acquainted with my sentiments and opinions; he knows all the circumstances of our army and the country at large; all the information he gives and all the propositions he makes, I entreat you will consider as coming from me." A letter to Ternay,[20] though briefer, was in the same vein, describing Lafayette as a "friend from whom I conceal nothing" and from whom Ternay might "receive whatever he shall tell you as coming from me."

Everything Washington said in those letters was well deserved. And yet Washington nodded in that appointment. It is probable that he did not know that Lafayette was not as highly esteemed in the French army as in the American. It is even more probable that he did not know that there was a certain personal rivalry between Rochambeau and Lafayette. Yet not to have sent his ranking officer was an error, which was only made worse by his sending one who was particularly difficult for some French officers to regard as an equal.

As yet no communication had been received at Preakness from Rochambeau or Ternay. Washington would not permit Lafayette to leave camp until some formal statement from Rochambeau should arrive indicating that he considered himself under Washington's orders. Rochambeau's first letter to Washington, though written on July 12, arrived only on July 18.[21] That day Lafayette borrowed from Holker against the account of Leray de Chaumont a large sum of money for his expenses.[22] The next morning, after dashing off a letter to Vergennes[23] speaking optimistically of American efforts and emphasizing the necessity of maritime supremacy, he started out for Rhode Island. The effect of the young man's optimism, when Vergennes finally received his letter, was somewhat dimin-

[19] July 16, 1780, Fitzpatrick, XIX, 185–87.   [20] *Ibid.*, pp. 187–88.

[21] Washington to Rochambeau, July 19, 1780, *ibid.*, p. 215.

[22] Statement of debts "pour compte de M. Leray de Chaumont," November 23, 1781, Gardner-Ball Collection.

[23] July 19, 1781, *loc. cit.*

ished by some comments of La Luzerne,[24] who, as requested by Lafayette, had put it in cipher and sent it to Vergennes in his own pouch. La Luzerne, though he praised Washington's and Lafayette's efforts and granted that they might have 20,000 men by August, doubted whether the men would be sufficiently well trained to carry out a successful siege.

Meanwhile, Lafayette hastened toward Rhode Island. The first day out he met an express carrying Rochambeau's and Ternay's last messages to camp.[25] He opened those addressed to Washington as well as to himself. One of them proved to be the letter in which Rochambeau asked for a personal interview with Washington. That Rochambeau was not altogether pleased with the way Lafayette had handled the correspondence which had already passed between New Jersey and Rhode Island might have been guessed from the closing sentence: "I embrace you, my dear Marquis, most heartily, and don't make me any more compliments, I beg of you."[26] But perhaps that was meant for a jest. Lafayette learned, too, that the clothing and munitions which he had wrung from the French ministry before he left had not come with the French convoy.

Another man might have been discouraged. Lafayette was not. He saw in the desire of the generals to speak to Washington personally only an additional reason for hastening to meet them. "In case (what however I don't believe) they would wish to speak to yourself," he wrote Washington,[27] "I shall immediately send an express to inform you of it, but I dare say they will be satisfied with my coming." The failure of Captain Jones to join the French convoy with the supplies that had been so earnestly sought was harder to bear smilingly. Lafayette had based his expectations of success during the ensuing campaign largely on

[24] July 23, 1780, AAE, corr. pol., É.-U., Vol. XIII, fols. 128–36; cf. Doniol, IV, 372, n. 1.

[25] Lafayette to Washington, July 20, 1780 (from Peekskill, N.Y.), *Mémoires* (Amer. ed.), pp. 459–60. A more complete version of this letter is in Sparks MSS LXXXVII, fols. 137–40.

[26] Rochambeau to Lafayette, July 16, 1780, LC, Rochambeau letter book, p. 46. This line is omitted from the version printed in Doniol, V, 350. The original of this letter, partly in the handwriting of Rochambeau, is in the Pierpont Morgan Library, Lafayette, Vol. II.

[27] July 20, 1780, *loc. cit.*

the assumption that the American forces would be well equipped through his efforts. Not knowing that there had been a mutiny on board the "Alliance," Lafayette was inclined to feel bitter about "Captain Jones's delays."[28] But his active mind soon thought of remedies. He would borrow all the powder and arms that he could from the French forces, and he would urge the governments of the states through which he passed to send as much as they could manufacture or purchase.

Having already passed through New York by the time that resolution was made, the young general fell immediately to work upon the Connecticut authorities. Brigadier-General Samuel H. Parsons, whom Washington had sent to Connecticut to supervise recruitments, Colonel Jeremiah Wadsworth, who performed in Connecticut the duties of commissary-general for the Continental Army, and finally Governor Jonathan Trumbull received visits from the importunate major-general as he passed through Danbury, Hartford, and Lebanon. He exacted from them promises to furnish as large a quantity of men, powder, balls, shells, arms, and money as the state could by special exertions afford. Though Trumbull had the uneasy feeling that he had promised more than he could do, he gave the persistent general permission to relay his promises to Washington.[29]

By making free with horses that belonged to the French government, Lafayette completed in four days the journey from Preakness to Newport, which usually took his couriers five or six. There was genuine pleasure among many officers at Newport when the marquis galloped into camp in the evening of July 24.[30] Others who did not yet know him fell quickly under the influence of his studied efforts to make himself well liked.

[28] Lafayette to Washington, July 21, 1780 (from Danbury, Conn.), *Mémoires* (Amer. ed.), p. 462.

[29] *Ibid.*; Lafayette to Washington, July 22, 1780 (from Hartford, Conn.), *ibid.*, pp. 462–63; July 23, 1780 (from Lebanon, Conn.), *ibid.*, pp. 464–66; *Calendar of the correspondence of George Washington with the officers* (4 vols.; Washington, 1915), II, 1412; I. W. Stuart, *Life of Jonathan Trumbull* (Boston, 1859), p. 482.

[30] Heath to Washington, July 25, 1780, Jared Sparks (ed.), *Correspondence of the American Revolution, being letters of eminent men to George Washington* (4 vols.; Boston, 1853), III, 41; extract from letter of one of Rochambeau's officers, August 3, 1780, *Gazette de Leyde*, October 10, 1780, supplément, p. 2.

Lafayette soon found, however, that he would have to postpone all discussion of plans to attack New York. A British fleet had been cruising in Long Island Sound for several days. This gave rise to the supposition that Clinton proposed to attack Rhode Island. Messengers had been sent posthaste from headquarters, shortly after Lafayette had left, to inform him and the French generals that New York was advancing against them.[31] Rochambeau immediately issued orders to hasten the fortifications on both Conanicut and Rhode Island; Heath called up the Continental troops in the neighborhood and requested the state to send a body of militia. Lafayette was inclined to doubt the reports of an English attack but put himself under Heath as second officer.[32]

The first day in camp the marquis spent in examining the fortifications along with his senior officers.[33] On the next, he busied himself with the gathering of a force of six hundred Continentals and militia, who, together with a French force under his brother-in-law Noailles, were to defend Conanicut.[34] Expresses were sent off with letters from Lafayette and Heath asking Washington to make some sort of diversion with his troops. At a council of French general officers later that morning, Lafayette, who had campaigned in Rhode Island before, advocated concentration of forces, and it was decided not to try to hold Conanicut. That day Rochambeau, Chastellux, and Lafayette met again at lunch with Admiral de Ternay, and they agreed on a plan of action. So many French soldiers were sick that only thirty-six hundred were fit for active duty, and several of the ships were undermanned. Rochambeau, nevertheless, favored defending the island to the last man. Lafayette's experiences on Rhode Island two years earlier caused him to advocate that a

[31] Hamilton to Lafayette, July 21, 1780, LC, Washington papers, Ser. B, Vol. XII, Part I, fol. 199; Washington to Rochambeau, July 21, 1780, Fitzpatrick, XIX, 223.

[32] Lafayette to Washington, July 26, 1780 (from Newport, R.I.), *Mémoires* (Amer. ed.), p. 466.

[33] Lafayette to Washington, July 26, 1780, *ibid.*, and another of same date, *ibid.*, pp. 468–70.

[34] Cf. Lafayette to Colonel [Christopher] Greene, July 26, 1780, Rhode Island Historical Society.

line of retreat to the continent be held open. Rochambeau made it clear that, though he did not wish to ask it directly, he hoped Washington would aid him by sending a corps of Continental troops to attack the English in the rear. Lafayette took it upon himself to send the request to Washington, meanwhile taking precautions to keep open communications with the mainland, should such a Continental force arrive.[35]

Washington had not waited for requests from Rochambeau and Lafayette to take such measures as would be most helpful to his allies. He placed his men in a position to attack New York if Clinton moved in force on Rhode Island. "There are only two things," he wrote Lafayette,[36] "that would hinder us from taking New York before you return" if its garrison were sufficiently weakened in favor of operations against the French. Those were, he said dryly, "the want of men and arms to do it with." Lafayette could give him small consolation on the score of arms. He found and took good care of the small shipment of American supplies that had come with the French convoy. His supplications to the French admiral for additional provisions produced a promise of not more than fifty tons of powder. He kept spurring on the authorities in Connecticut and, at Washington's own suggestion, added the governments of Rhode Island and Massachusetts to his list of those who were to be dunned for aid. But a disquieting dearth of matériel remained.[37]

General Clinton, in the meantime, made no offensive move, realizing, no doubt, as well as the generals who faced him that to do so would expose him to an attack on front and rear. While waiting to determine what Clinton would do, Lafayette wasted no time in concerting the plans for which he had come to Newport. He was disappointed to learn that Rochambeau's forces were smaller than he had had every reason to hope and that the French generals preferred not to act until they heard from the second division.[38] He found it difficult to hide his displeasure.

[35] See n. 33, above.
[36] July 27, 1780, Fitzpatrick, XIX, 269–70.
[37] Lafayette to Washington, July 29, 1780, *Mémoires* (Amer. ed.), pp. 470–71.
[38] *Ibid.*, pp. 471–72.

"Don't fear by any means their acting *rashly*," he informed Washington,[39] "and be assured that you may very far depend on their *caution*." An interview with Rochambeau elicited only the opinion that, if the French dominated the water or if Ternay thought he could secure passage into the harbor with his batteries and each attacking force were equal to the whole of the enemy, an assault upon New York might be risked. That left the decision largely to Ternay, and Lafayette arranged to see him and Rochambeau together.[40]

The interview between Lafayette as Washington's proxy and the French generals took place on the evening of July 30. Lafayette began the conversation by describing how bad had been the situation of the Continental Army before he had returned to America and the heroic efforts that had recently been made to improve it. Those efforts had resulted from a patriotic desire to co-operate with the French immediately upon their arrival. The militia could be expected to serve for only three months; the main army would itself dwindle by the new year. A similar burst of energy could not be expected again from an impoverished and exhausted people. It would therefore be necessary to act that summer. "All that, my dear General," he reported to Washington,[41] "was said in my own name, and therefore in a less delicate way than when I am your interpreter."

Only after he had thus unburdened his own mind did Lafayette begin to speak in Washington's name. He began with "assurances of confidence"[42] and finally got to the plans for an attack upon New York which Washington had contemplated if maritime supremacy were assured. Those he described at some length. He could not resist the temptation, however, to depart from Washington's instructions in order to propose his own plan. Even without maritime supremacy, he felt, the allies, by skilful operations on land, could keep the British navy from interfering with the landing of the French on Long Island. While Rochambeau's transports brought him from Rhode Island to Long Island, Washington could take up a position at

<hr />

39 *Ibid.*, p. 472. 41 Lafayette to Rochambeau, July 31, 1780, *ibid.*, p. 475.
40 *Ibid.*, pp. 472–73. 42 *Ibid.*

some strategic point which would command the straits between New York Harbor and Long Island Sound. Thus, he argued,[43] the English fleet could be held in the harbor while Rochambeau landed his forces on the shores of the Sound.

Neither Rochambeau nor Ternay liked that proposal. They insisted upon supremacy in New York waters. Ternay believed his ships were too big to enter the harbor, but, whenever he became satisfied he controlled the sea, he would blockade it. In brief, as Lafayette wrote his commander,[44] "Both were of opinion that nothing could be undertaken unless we had a naval superiority, and as I know it is your opinion also (tho' it is not mine), I durst not insist on that article." Remembering, moreover, that the American army had neither arms nor powder (though he thought it better not to mention that point at this juncture), he felt obliged to assent to their decision, contenting himself with urging on his own responsibility that they must somehow "act before the winter and get rid of a shameful defensive."[45]

Before breaking up, the three officers agreed upon a certain course of action. They would write to the French government to speed the second division on its way and to make it larger than originally planned. They would also request Guichen to send them five ships of the line from his fleet. As soon as Ternay's force became equal to the enemy's, he promised to challenge the British. Whenever it became clear that the French were superior, they would immediately proceed to carry out their part of the plan for an attack upon New York. Ternay even promised to mull over the desirability of entering New York Harbor rather than blockading it from the outside.[46]

And so Lafayette had perforce to wait for the second division. The generals were quite content with the outcome of the meeting, though they still hoped for a personal interview with Washington. Rochambeau, in sending an account of the conference

[43] *Ibid.*, pp. 475–77; Lafayette to Rochambeau and Ternay, August 9, 1780, LC, Rochambeau letter book, pp. 115–21; La Luzerne to Vergennes, August 21, 1780, AAE, corr. pol., É.–U., Vol. XIII, fols. 348–53.

[44] July 31, 1780, *loc. cit.*, pp. 475–76.   [45] *Ibid.*, p. 476.   [46] *Ibid.*, pp. 476–77.

to La Luzerne, spoke approvingly of Lafayette's "ardor and courage,"[47] though he did not hide that he was somewhat disturbed by his impatience. Ternay informed Washington[48] that Lafayette deserved his confidence "for his talents, his patriotic zeal, and above all for his attachment to you."

Lafayette was less content. Ternay he believed to be disappointingly and unnecessarily cautious. Rochambeau, in whom he had greater faith, he felt, nevertheless, was too much under Ternay's influence.[49] He could not understand (nor for that matter could Washington) why Rochambeau insisted upon defending Rhode Island, forgetting that it was desirable for Rochambeau not to move from the place where the second division expected him to be when they arrived and where he could help defend Ternay's fleet as long as it was blockaded in Newport harbor. Both Washington and Lafayette would have preferred the French to retire to the mainland, where they would be in a better position to join or to co-operate with the Continental Army.[50]

The interview had not ended as Lafayette had wished, but his spirits rebounded immediately. All that was needed to inspire his canny countrymen to take risks was the assurance that the risks would be small. The second division would give that assurance, and it could not be far off. Lafayette began at once to send requests and orders to those who might hasten its debarkation and welcome. Counting upon La Luzerne to cajole the French generals into greater activity, he waited only for a good opportunity to complain about the lack of enterprise he had found in Rhode Island.[51] He was still hopeful that the campaign might begin in September.

By the time Lafayette sent to headquarters an account of his interview, excitement was once more rife on Rhode Island. Clinton was expected to attack at any moment. Some of the

---

[47] Quoted in La Luzerne to Vergennes, August 21, 1780, *loc. cit.*

[48] July 31, 1780, LC, Washington papers, no. 39, fol. 341.

[49] Lafayette to La Luzerne, August 11, 1780, *AHR*, XX (1915), 368.

[50] *Ibid.*, p. 367.

[51] Cf. Lafayette to La Luzerne, August 8 and 11, 1780, *ibid.*, pp. 365–68.

militia who had been sent home because it was thought they would not be needed were now recalled. Lafayette was given command of Heath's vanguard, which was intended to oppose an enemy landing and to assure communication with the mainland. This assignment with militia seemed to him less glorious than his post with the Continental Army if Washington were to attack New York, but he dared not risk returning to headquarters lest action on both fronts take place while he was hastening between the two.[52] He was, nevertheless, greatly pleased with the militia. They had turned out in goodly numbers, though inadequately equipped. One Connecticut contingent, which was without provisions or tents, was taken in by the French troops, who shared their beds and their supper with them. The patience and sobriety of the American citizen-soldier so impressed one French colonel that, Lafayette was pleased to learn, he had called all his officers together and held the American troops up to them as good examples. "On the other hand," he added, in describing these friendly gestures to Washington,[53] "the French discipline is such, that chiken [sic] and pigs walk between the lines without being disturbed, and that there is in the camp a cornfield, from which not one leaf has been touched. The Tories don't know what to say to it."

The good will of the two armies toward each other was gladdening to the young Frenchman who could remember how Estaing's men had been insulted on Rhode Island two years before. Yet good will was not sufficient when one army lacked discipline, organization, and uniforms. To Lafayette those things were important. For he had made some boasts about the Americans when he was in France and hoped not to be exposed now. His post was with General Heath and the militia at Butt's Hill at the north of the island, some distance from Newport. While visiting Rochambeau one day, he found that the French general, as ranking officer on Rhode Island, was going to inspect the fortifications at Butt's Hill. Lafayette knew that they were not ready. Making the excuse that Heath had intended to go to

[52] Lafayette to Washington, August 1, 1780, *Mémoires* (Amer. ed.), pp. 479–80.
[53] July 31, 1780, *ibid.*, pp. 478–79.

Bristol, Lafayette induced Rochambeau to postpone the inspection until the next day. Meanwhile, he dispatched a letter to Heath,[54] urging him to put a thousand men to work on the fortifications early in the morning. "I think we ought to learn our men how to present properly theyr arms to Count de Rochambeau," he added, in the bad English which he frequently fell into when he was under stress. Not being sure that Heath himself knew how, he described what a sentry must say and do. Lafayette planned to remain in Newport and go up with the inspecting party. He hoped to be able to dissuade Rochambeau from making a tour of the camp and cautioned Heath to meet them at Butt's Hill Fort. Lafayette promised to let Heath know exactly when to expect him. "Look as if you was not sure of the time of his coming, or if you like it better meet him on the road." No record indicates whether Heath was amused, annoyed, or thankful; but, if Rochambeau made the tour of inspection, he was probably pleased, because he long afterward remembered the "truly patriotic zeal" of the American militia.[55]

The British had their troubles, too. The leaders of their land and sea forces likewise disagreed regarding the plan of campaign. Admiral Marriot Arbuthnot, who commanded the British fleet, had an exaggerated notion of the allied preparations on Rhode Island and refused to encourage or effectively to cooperate with Clinton's maneuvers.[56] He was content to blockade the French fleet without attempting to attack their land supports. Clinton was obliged to reland his army on Long Island, feeling safe to be on the defensive as long as the English controlled the waters.[57] At the same time, Washington began to move his men (who were nowhere nearly so numerous as was reported to Clinton) toward the east bank of the Hudson in order to be in a better position either to march to Rochambeau's relief or to attack New York if it were sufficiently deprived of defenders.

[54] August 2, 1780, Massachusetts Historical Society.

[55] Rochambeau, I, 245.

[56] Cf. Fitzpatrick, XIX, 293–94, n. 93.

[57] Clinton to Eden, August 18, 1780, Stevens, *Facsimiles*, VII, no. 730.

Washington soon wrote Lafayette from his new position, permitting him to decide for himself whether to stay with Heath or to return to headquarters.[58] Lafayette, who had continually doubted whether Clinton would attack, determined that in any event he preferred to be with the troops near New York. Before he had left headquarters a corps of picked troops had been promised him for the campaign.[59] No defensive post on Rhode Island could bring as great honor as to lead that corps against New York. In a message which Lafayette now sent to Heath,[60] informing him that Rochambeau would arrive at Butt's Hill in the late afternoon for the proposed inspection, Lafayette also asked for permission to rejoin his division in the main army. Heath gave the permission immediately,[61] but hours were lost in the exchange of messages between Ternay's flagship, where Lafayette waited, and Howland's Ferry, where Heath's headquarters were. Having delayed as long as he dared, Lafayette started off without receiving leave, counting on Heath's friendly understanding of his fear that he might be deprived "of the happiness to serve our noble cause and sharing a part of the common glory."[62] Promising to "ride day and night to regain the precious hours" he had lost, he expected to join the Grand Army at the Highlands in New York. But even before all the army had crossed the Hudson, Washington had at last satisfied himself that Clinton had returned to New York[63] and immediately recrossed to the west bank. He was at Orangetown (Tappan, New York) when Lafayette caught up with him after a little over three days of hard riding.

On the way Lafayette had tried to find out how the American people felt regarding the French auxiliary force. He had become convinced that they would be discouraged if nothing happened in the ensuing campaign. The Tories had spread the report that

[58] July 31, 1780, Fitzpatrick, XIX, 284.

[59] See below, pp. 121–22.

[60] August 3, 1780, *Heath papers, part III*, pp. 97–98.

[61] August 3, 1780, *ibid.*, pp. 99–100.

[62] August 3, 1780, "at six o'clock," *ibid.*, pp. 98–99.

[63] Washington to Lafayette, August 1, 1780, Fitzpatrick, XIX, 293–94.

there would be no second division and that the French government had sent over only enough men in the first to make trouble
and prevent reconciliation with England but insufficient to end
the war.[64] On arriving in camp, Lafayette was in his turn disappointed to find that there would be no immediate attack upon
New York.

It began to look as if the Tories were right. While the marquis
had been away from headquarters, Washington had had occasion to think over the part that he expected the French to play.
The frequent bulletins from his indefatigable liaison officer had
caused him to write often in reply. Washington could not hide
from his loyal subordinate that he feared his own inability to co-
operate with the French even if they should acquire complete
control of the seas. The failure of the expected arms, ammunition, and clothing to arrive from France was "serious,"[65] but
even more serious was the improbability that the quotas of men
required of the various states would ever be filled.[66] The commander-in-chief was therefore all the more unwilling to urge the
French to undertake any line of action for which they showed
no readiness. "Only inform them," he instructed the absent Lafayette, "what we can do, what we are willing to undertake, and
let them intirely consult their own inclination for the rest. Our
prospects are not so flattering as to justify our being very pressing to engage them in our views."[67] He too felt inclined to wait
till the second division should arrive. Meanwhile, he proposed
to resort to the long and wearying process of a siege. The great
disadvantage of a siege to the American forces was that so many
soldiers had enrolled for short terms. The three-month militia
would depart with the summer, and many of the rest with the
new year. In fact, they would be needed only if an attack were
made. In a siege they would simply use up what little provisions
there were and would render no useful service. "We shall ex-

[64] Lafayette to La Luzerne, August 11, 1780, *AHR*, XX (1915), 367; Lafayette to
Rochambeau, August 18, 1708, LC, Rochambeau letter book, pp. 129–30.

[65] Washington to Lafayette, August 3, 1780, Fitzpatrick, XIX, 313; cf. letter of
July 22, *ibid.*, pp. 236–37.

[66] July 27, 1780, *ibid.*, pp. 269–70.   [67] August 3, 1780, *ibid.*, p. 314.

haust ourselves to no purpose," Washington feared,[68] "and every day will add to the impressions that relinquishing the enterprise will make on the mind of the people." But he saw no other course until naval reinforcements should arrive either from France or from the West Indies. All this Washington had patiently explained in his letters to Lafayette at Rhode Island.

When Lafayette returned to camp, he gave to Washington a long account of his conference at Newport. Not content with an oral report, Washington wished to have a written statement of what had been said on both sides. Accordingly, two days after his arrival, Lafayette wrote to Rochambeau and Ternay,[69] submitting for approval the minutes of their conference and detailing Washington's comments upon their decisions. It was not an uncolored report. Lafayette was no more able to share Washington's desire for objectivity than to sympathize with Rochambeau's cautious patience. Washington had twitted him with the remark that he was "determined at all events to take New York," and obstacles only increased his zeal.[70] The youthful zealot was, moreover, convinced that the French officers at Newport did not understand American ways, depending too much upon the six or seven inhabitants of Newport who dined with them for their estimate of American sentiment.[71] His letter to Rochambeau and Ternay thus became a curious intermixture of reporting and persuading. He implicitly—occasionally explicitly—criticized both Rochambeau's decisions and Washington's agreement with them. He concluded with an unfortunate paragraph, which a cooler head would have obliged him to delete: "From an intimate knowledge of our situation, I assure you, Sirs (as an individual and in my own name), that it is important for us to act during the present campaign, and that all the troops which you may expect from France next year, as well as all plans with which you may fondly foster, will not repair the fatal consequences of our inaction now. Without the resources

[68] August 5, 1780, ibid., p. 329.

[69] August 9, 1780, loc. cit.

[70] Washington to Lafayette, July 27, 1780, loc. cit.

[71] Lafayette to La Luzerne, August 11, 1780, AHR, XX (1915), 367.

of America, all foreign assistance will accomplish nothing in this country; and although, under any circumstances, you may count upon us unconditionally, I consider it very urgent to take advantage of the [present] opportunities, whereby you find at hand a cooperating force, without which you will be able to accomplish nothing in America for the common good."[72] If anyone else had condemned French inaction in such tones, Lafayette's hand would have reached indignantly for his sword.

Rochambeau did not look upon Lafayette's tactless epistle as the minutes of a meeting. His patience with the marquis was exhausted by the scolding tone which the young man, only a little older than his own son, had adopted. He replied immediately to Lafayette's long letter with one that was pointedly brief.[73] For his opinion on the military details which Lafayette had asked, Rochambeau curtly referred him to a letter which he had recently sent to Washington and again begged for a personal interview with "our general." He then proceeded to argue that the presence of the French in Rhode Island had brought distinct advantages to the Americans. If it was true that Washington had recently been obliged to move to his protection, it was no less true that he would have been able to give the British a warm reception during which Washington might have taken New York. Moreover, it was possible that Clinton had confined himself to New York and Long Island out of fear of the French. At any rate, the concentration of the British fleet at Rhode Island to blockade Ternay left the rest of the American coast free for American commerce. Under those circumstances, Rochambeau thought, "we can afford to await the naval and military reinforcement which the King assured me." As he had freely acknowledged in his letter to Washington,[74] he feared a repetition of Estaing's defeat at Savannah "and other events of that nature of which I have seen so many in my lifetime." The rebuke was no less severe because Rochambeau ended with a polite "I embrace you, my dear Marquis, most heartily."[75]

[72] Lafayette to Rochambeau and Ternay, August 9, 1780, *loc. cit.*, p. 181.

[73] August 12, 1780, LC, Rochambeau letter book, pp. 122–23.

[74] August 10, 1780, Doniol, V, 362.   [75] August 12, 1780, *loc. cit.*, p. 123.

Having thus answered the charge of uselessness and inaction contained in Lafayette's dispatch, Rochambeau felt that he must, nevertheless, make clear, if not to Lafayette, at least to his superiors, why he preferred not to attack Long Island without predominant naval force. That he undertook to do in letters which he sent to Washington[76] and La Luzerne.[77] The proposal, he said, seemed risky. Even if Washington's batteries at some strategic land point could keep the English fleet out of Long Island Sound, that would only protect his right flank, as he disembarked his army at Long Island. It would still leave his left exposed to Arbuthnot's fleet; and besides, his abandoning Rhode Island for Long Island would make it hard for Ternay's ships cooped up in Newport harbor.

If he had thought that Washington approved of Lafayette's stand, Rochambeau explained to La Luzerne, he would have been somewhat less vexed. But several recent letters from Washington had convinced him that the commander-in-chief did not endorse their young friend's proposals.[78] Rochambeau therefore suspected that Lafayette was influenced by "some wrong-headed people" to propose "extravagant things" and that there was a "cabal" of "young and ardent people" who surrounded Washington but whom he was too wise to heed. He decided not to reply any longer to the "pieces of writing" which "these go-betweens" would send but to correspond directly with "my chief" (as he called Washington). "The admiral and I are infinitely pleased," he told La Luzerne,[79] "with the dispatches of that general, and it is impossible to be more grateful for them." At the same time he requested Washington[80] to "continue to give me your orders directly, to feel certain of my zeal and my obedience," repeating that he and the admiral would like a personal conference.

Lafayette in his turn was astonished and hurt when he re-

[76] August 14, 1780, Doniol, V, 365.

[77] August 14, 1780, *ibid.*, pp. 364–65.

[78] Cf., however, Rochambeau, I, 248–49, where he says that Lafayette expressed "substantially" the opinions of Washington.

[79] August 14, 1780, *loc. cit.*   [80] August 14, 1780, *loc. cit.*

ceived Rochambeau's letter. The most convenient explanation
he could find for the misunderstanding of his intention was, he
thought, that he must have expressed himself awkwardly. The
implication that he had acted without proper regard for the
wishes of his commander seemed to him especially unjust and in
need of correction. He tried to justify himself in two separate
communications. One he formally addressed to both French officers.[81] All that he had said regarding Rhode Island and New
York, he insisted, had been on Washington's "reiterated orders." The only thing he could reproach himself with in that
regard was that he had urged immediate action but that had its
excuse in the widespread disappointment of Americans because
nothing was being done. "As for my political opinions, which I
will avoid in the future because they ought to come from M. le
Chevalier de La Luzerne," he continued, "I assure you that,
though, as your compatriot, it was more considerate of me to
give them on my own responsibility, they are no less in conformity with the ideas of General Washington." He indignantly
repudiated the imputation that he thought the French occupa-
tion of Rhode Island harmful. It had never occurred to him to
say so. In fact for nearly two years he had urged such an occu-
pation—first on Estaing and then on the French government—
and he now never lost an opportunity to make its advantages
known throughout America. He apologized for the awkwardness of sóme remarks in his last letter. But he assured Rochambeau and Ternay of his devotion under any circumstances to his
country ("the foremost of all feelings in his heart") and his
respectful affection for them.

That letter might have sufficed if Lafayette had been content
merely with explaining and apologizing for his error. He had,
however, not yet developed in his early twenties that toughness
to others' opinions that he was one day to acquire. Rochambeau, as an old friend whom he had long admired, was one
whose good opinion he especially wished to have. It was quite
clear too that, as Lafayette had himself frequently warned, an
altercation between French and American generals would be

[81] August 18, 1780, LC, Rochambeau letter book, pp. 127–29.

easy to incite. Sensitive as he was to Tory accusations of French
idleness and meddling, he was even more concerned that the
quarrels which he had witnessed and participated in during
Estaing's expedition to Rhode Island should not be renewed by
his own tactlessness.[82] Letters from his personal friends in the
French army led him to understand that he was suspected in
high places of a certain unpatriotic contempt for the value of the
French alliance.[83] As he hastened to explain to La Luzerne,[84]
all this was "extraordinary," but he proposed, he said, "to get
down on my knees if they like" and "let them beat me" rather
than bring harm to the common cause. Though he had been
angry at first, "in the end," he declared, "I shall laugh, and I
shall always say that it is I who am at fault but that I shall
never do it again." He only hoped that La Luzerne, taking on
where he would be obliged to leave off, would urge upon the
French generals the same policy.

And so Lafayette also addressed to Rochambeau alone a brief
letter,[85] protesting "that affectionate friendship, that veneration for you which I have felt and I have tried to express since
my tenderest childhood." After his sincere exertions to secure a
favorable reception of Rochambeau on Rhode Island, he explained, he could not help being pained by the unfavorable and
certainly unexpected interpretation which Rochambeau had
put upon his remarks. He had done what he had done out of a
sense of duty, a desire to clear the French of Tory accusations,
and mortification at the sight of French helplessness before the
English blockade. "If I have offended you," he pled, "I ask
your pardon for two reasons: first, because I am earnestly attached to you; and secondly because my purpose is to do everything here that I can to please you. Wherever I am only a private citizen, your orders will be laws for me; and I shall make
any sacrifice for the most humble of the Frenchmen who are

[82] Lafayette to Mme de Lafayette, October 7, 1780, *Mémoires*, I, 374–75.

[83] Lafayette to La Luzerne, August 18, 1780, *AHR*, XX (1915), 369.

[84] *Ibid.*, pp. 369–70.

[85] August 18, 1780, LC, Rochambeau letter book, pp. 129–30. This letter has been
translated somewhat too freely in Tower, II, 153–55.

here, rather than not contribute to their glory, their pleasure, and their union with the Americans." Lest Rochambeau or anyone else think, however, that he had receded from his position that daring action was immediately called for, he added in a postscript: "I am entirely convinced, and no one here can deny it, that if you had not come, it would have gone badly with American affairs during the present campaign. But, in our condition at this moment, that is not enough; we need to have victory. Believe me, although I urged this upon you *in my own name*, that is not my opinion alone. My mistake was that I wrote with warmth and officially what you would have pardoned on account of my youth if I had written to you as a friend and privately. But I was acting with such perfect good faith that your reply has astonished as much as it has distressed me, and that is saying a great deal."

Lafayette did not trust to his own judgment alone in writing his apologies to Rochambeau. He sent them to his brother-in-law the Vicomte de Noailles. "I beg Charlus and you," he wrote, "to examine the two letters inclosed and if you find them all right, to deliver them to their address after sealing them and trying to fix up these two things as well as you can."[86] Lafayette's friends allowed the letters to reach Rochambeau.

As the young penitent had hoped, his soft answer turned away Rochambeau's wrath. Moreover, Washington had assured Rochambeau shortly before Lafayette's letters arrived in Rhode Island, that "our ideas are substantially the same, and I hope a further explanation will obviate whatever little differences there may be."[87] Yet Rochambeau waited to reply to Lafayette's abject apology and, as he waited, there came still another letter from Washington.[88] Though indicating that he felt more optimistic than Rochambeau about the practicability of a successful debarkation on Long Island of unassisted land

---

[86] August 18, 1780, Jean Patou (ed.), *Lettres inédites du Général de La Fayette au Vicomte de Noailles écrites des camps de l'armée américaine durant la Guerre de l'Indépendance des États-Unis (1780–81)* (Paris, 1924), pp. 11–12.

[87] August 16, 1780, Fitzpatrick, XIX, 383.

[88] August 21, 1780, *ibid.*, p. 420.

forces, Washington, nevertheless, stated definitely, "I entirely agree in opinion with you for several reasons that it will be best to defer the commencement of the enterprise till we get a superiority at sea."

So Rochambeau could well afford to be generous to his exuberant compatriot. He replied to Lafayette's apologies only after they had been in his hands several days.[89] "Permit an old father, my dear Marquis," he began, "to answer you as he would an affectionate son whom he loves and prizes very much." Lafayette's errors, he pointed out, had been several. In the first place, he had thought he could persuade Rochambeau to take a step which for military reasons—as their commander, except on some minor details, agreed—would have been inadvisable. Then he had felt humiliated that the French were blockaded at Newport. "But," Rochambeau added, not without irony, "console yourself, my dear Marquis. The port of Brest has been blockaded for two months. . . . . If you had fought the last two wars, you would have heard of nothing but these blockades." Lafayette had also thought the French could not be beaten. "That is always right, my dear Marquis," Rochambeau continued in the same tone, ". . . . but I am going to tell you a big secret derived from forty years' experience. There are no troops more easily beaten when they have once lost confidence in their leader; and they lose it immediately when they have been exposed to danger through private and personal ambition. If I have been fortunate enough to retain their confidence until now, I owe it to the most scrupulous examination of my conscience that, of the 15,000 men or thereabouts who have been either killed or wounded under me in the different grades and in the most bloody engagements, I have not to reproach myself with having caused the death of a single man for my own personal advantage." That would have been severe language indeed, had it not been followed by a few sentences that removed the sting: "Be assured of my most affectionate friendship, and

[89] August 27, 1780, Tower, II, 155–56 (among others). I have in some minor details departed from Tower's translation on the basis of the original in AMG, correspondance de Rochambeau.

that when I called your attention very gently to the things which displeased me in your last dispatch, I decided immediately that the warmth of your heart and mind had somewhat overheated the evenness and wisdom of your judgment. Preserve the latter quality for the council, and keep all of the former for the moment of execution. This is still old Papa Rochambeau talking to his dear son La Fayette, whom he loves, and will continue to love and to esteem until his last breath."

The blow was somewhat softened, too, by letters from La Luzerne in the same kindly vein. "Public comments," he said,[90] "regardless of the attention which they deserve in a republican government, ought never to force a general to take steps which he believes dangerous. . . . . Although I am very anxious that this campaign should not pass without some enterprise worthy of the efforts which have been made, I nevertheless think that it is better to wait than to run too great risks." He approved of Lafayette's letter of apology to Rochambeau: "Rest assured," he stated,[91] "that no one will accuse you seriously of having antipatriotic sentiments." At the same time La Luzerne wrote to Rochambeau,[92] approving of his intention to communicate with Washington only directly. He solemnly declared that the young men who surrounded the American commander were not sufficiently influential to determine Washington's plans. Most of them besides were well meaning and reasonable officers. "I am therefore inclined to believe," he concluded, "that what M. de La Fayette has written to you is purely the result of his zeal and of a courage that experience will moderate."

A few days later the king's minister praised Lafayette's "good spirit" during the entire episode.[93] And it was, indeed, well deserving of praise. A less conciliatory stand by the rebuked soldier could easily have persisted until ill will had been created on both sides and the intervention of the commander-in-chief would have become inevitable. For as ambitious and sensitive a

[90] August 19, 1780, AAE, corr. pol., É.-U. supplément, Vol. XIV, fols. 168–69.

[91] August 23, 1780, ibid., fols. 169–69v.

[92] August 24, 1780, ibid., supplément, Vol. XV, fols. 50–51v.

[93] Ibid., fol. 62.

character as Lafayette to agree to accept the blame, even though he felt he was not altogether at fault, was an act both of generosity and of political good sense. Thus he gave another example of his ability to win the friendliness of all parties—all the more laudable because this was the first time in his life that he was placed in a position where all sides would have agreed he had not been entirely justified. Stubbornness or pride would not have saved his beloved cause from the blunder which his impatience and audacity might have brought to it.

BIBLIOGRAPHICAL NOTES

The above account of Rochambeau's army leans heavily upon the *Mémoires* of Rochambeau, the *Journal de Blanchard*, and the manuscript copy of the "Journal of Jean-Christophe-Louis-Fréderic-Ignace, Baron von Closen" in the Library of Congress. The first, written many years after the events with which they deal, are especially guilty of that lack of accuracy which is so characteristic of memoirs. Blanchard's and Closen's works, though also memoirs, are less sinful in that regard. Blanchard was Rochambeau's chief commissioner of war, and Closen was one of his officers.

The best secondary account of Rochambeau's part in the American Revolution is Doniol's. Weelen's biography of Rochambeau is too thin and too partisan. The Vicomte de Noailles' *Marins et soldats français en Amérique pendant la Guerre de l'Indépendance des États-Unis (1778–1783)* (Paris, 1903), Thomas Balch's *Les Français en Amérique pendant la Guerre de l'Indépendance des États-Unis* (Paris, 1872; English tr., Philadelphia, 1895), and D. R. Keim's *Rochambeau* (Washington, 1907) are still helpful though now out of date.

CHAPTER VI

Benedict Arnold's Treason

UPON returning from Rhode Island to the main army, Lafayette took command of the corps of light infantry. It was a *corps d'élite*, made up of picked companies from the New Hampshire, New York, Connecticut, Massachusetts, and Pennsylvania lines. Among the officers were Lafayette's first aide-de-camp, Jean-Joseph Gimat, now a colonel. The corps was divided into two brigades commanded by Generals Enoch Poor and Edward Hand. The Tories soon hit upon the obvious pun that Lafayette would make a "poor hand" of it.[1] Since the "corps" contained only 1,850 men,[2] the pun seemed not altogether inappropriate. Nevertheless, with its four cannon, 100 riflemen, and the 300 men in the Light Horse Corps of Major Henry Lee (about half of whom actually had horses),[3] it had its good points, and Lafayette tried to be philosophical about the bad ones. "This corps, which is always kept at full strength," he told Noailles,[4] "is distinguished by a red and black feather. I should prefer that it be a uniform, or a good pair of shoes, but our skin is visible, and we are sometimes barefoot, not to mention that often the inside is no better garnished than the out; but in such cases we send them to sleep."

The Light Division had actually been created while Washington was expecting to attack New York upon Clinton's move against Rhode Island. Since Lafayette was absent at that time,

[1] Sparks MSS XXXII, p. 135.

[2] "Return of the infantry division commanded by Maj. Gen. the Marquis La Fayette," August 10, 1780, Gardner-Ball Collection.

[3] Lafayette to Noailles, September 2, 1780, Patou, pp. 13–14.

[4] *Ibid.*; cf. Lafayette to Washington, July 4, 1780, *Mémoires* (Amer. ed.), pp. 325–27.

Major-General Benedict Arnold first,[5] and then, when Arnold showed reluctance, Major-General Arthur St. Clair,[6] had been invited to take charge of the division temporarily. Washington indicated to St. Clair that the command for the ensuing campaign had been promised to Lafayette "for reasons which I dare say will be to you obvious and satisfactory." St. Clair accepted temporary command of the Light Division. Upon Lafayette's return the command passed to him, and St. Clair took charge of the Pennsylvania division.

Lafayette soon devoted a part of his inexhaustible energy to making the Light Division the best-spirited corps of the army. He himself gave each regiment an "elegant standard."[7] One standard carried the emblem of a cannon with the device *ultima ratio* ("the final argument"), the word *regum* ("of kings"), which usually was included in that motto, having been omitted as unbecoming a republican cannon. Another was decorated with a laurel crown linked with a civic crown and bore the motto *No other*.[8] Those were strange sentiments for a leading member of the court nobility in an absolute monarchy to select, but they were directed at the British king and crown and not at Louis XVI. In keeping with his new dignity as commander of the select corps of the Continental Army, Lafayette asked John Holker, the French consul at Philadelphia, to find for him a horse "of a perfect whiteness and the greatest beauty."[9] Holker found a magnificent animal for which Lafayette estimated he had paid one hundred louis d'or and embarrassed the marquis by refusing to be reimbursed for his expenditures.[10]

The Light Division took up its post as the vanguard of Washington's army about three miles south of the main camp. At the "Light Camp," as Lafayette called the various posts which his

[5] Cf. Fitzpatrick, XIX, 302, n. 8; Hughes, III, 542.

[6] Washington to St. Clair, August 1, 1780, Fitzpatrick, XIX, 295.

[7] "Diary of events in the army of the Revolution . . . . from the journal of Capt. Joseph McClellan," *Pennsylvania archives*, 2d ser., XI (1895), 601.

[8] *Mémoires*, I, 261 and n. 1.

[9] August 14, 1780, Koszul, "Lettres inédites de Lafayette," p. 387.

[10] Lafayette to Poix, January 30, 1781, private collection.

van thereafter took, he presented each man with his red and black feather and each officer besides with a sword, in addition to a cockade, epaulets, and other decorations for uniform and caps.[11] He also arranged for his officers to procure uniforms at cost from a friendly merchant in France.[12] The *esprit de corps* of Lafayette's unit soon became renowned. One of its officers who sold Lafayette's sword because he already had one was made so uncomfortable that he felt called upon to resign.[13] Eventually, the commander-in-chief gave to the Light Division the exclusive right to wear red and black feathers.[14]

Shortly after taking command of the vanguard of the Continental Army, Lafayette came to the conclusion that the best way to assure a successful campaign that summer would be to entice General Clinton to divide his forces. That would deplete the garrison of New York, and the French generals at Rhode Island had agreed that under such circumstances they might concert with Washington in an attack upon that city. Lafayette hoped that, since Washington refused to attack New York until he could count on naval superiority, the enemy might be induced by some strategem to cross the Hudson and attack the Continental Army on its own ground[15] or that some expedition against the constantly victorious British troops in the South might be undertaken or that an invasion of Canada might be risked—anything rather than stay in idleness watching the

[11] "Diary of Capt. Joseph McClellan," pp. 602 and 604; Lafayette to Ogden, September 16, 1780, Morristown (N.J.) National Park; Ogden to unknown, May 6, 1835, Jackson Collection; *New Jersey Historical Society proceedings*, 3d ser., I (1867–69), 11–12; Captain Roger Welles to his father, September 22, 1780, H. R. Stiles, *History of ancient Wethersfield, Connecticut* (New York, 1904), p. 470.

[12] Lafayette to Ogden, September 15, 1780, "Unpublished Revolutionary manuscripts," *New Jersey Historical Society proceedings*, 2d ser., XIII (1895), 158; "Diary of Captain Joseph McClellan," p. 605; LC, Holker papers, XII, 2235–2435 and XIII, 2396–2420.

[13] J. R. Trumbull, *History of Northampton, Massachusetts, from its settlement in 1654* (2 vols.; Northampton, 1902), II, 392; F. M. Thompson, *History of Greenfield Shire Town of Franklin County, Massachusetts, 1682–1900* (2 vols.; Greenfield, 1904), I, 274, n. 1.

[14] General orders, August 29, 1780, Fitzpatrick, XIX, 466.

[15] Lafayette to Washington, August 10, 1780, LC, Washington papers, Ser. F, Vol. II, Part II, fol. 327.

campaign pass and the militia go home without having tried their mettle. He did not give up hope that Rochambeau's second division or M. de Guichen would yet appear at some American port and sent urgent letters to Guichen through La Luzerne. He resumed his correspondence with American political authorities ("as one who has many reasons for wishing for the eternity of this alliance"[16]), urging upon them, just as he had urged upon his own countrymen, that they must make greater efforts for the welfare of the alliance. At one moment his heart leaped when he heard that the second division had come with eight ships of the line. Exultantly he sent a dispatch rider to La Luzerne with the report[17]—only to have to send another rider after him to deny it.[18]

As the summer wore on, the idea of enticing the enemy across the Hudson seemed more and more attractive. Lafayette had reconnoitered the English outpost at captured Fort Washington[19] and had concluded that it would be easy to recapture. His scheme was finally adopted by the commander-in-chief. General Greene was ordered to take the Light Division and four additional brigades upon a foraging expedition.[20] That would spread out his men in a long line which might appear inviting to the enemy. The right wing of the main army would, however, be ready to support Greene. If the English fell into the trap, the French could attack New York while its defenders were engaged elsewhere. If nothing came of the maneuver (and Lafayette doubted that the enemy would accept the challenge),[21] at least the Light Division could do some foraging in the neighborhood of Bergen and Paulus Hook (Jersey City). The food shortage

[16] Lafayette to Bowdoin, August 20, 1780, *Massachusetts Historical Society proceedings*, V (1860–62), 353–55. Cf. Lafayette to Clinton, August 29, 1780, New York Public Library (hereafter referred to as NYPL), Bancroft transcripts, America 1780, II, 252.

[17] August 24, 1780, *AHR*, XX (1915), 370.

[18] August 24, 1780, *ibid.*, p. 371.

[19] Lafayette to La Luzerne, August 15, 1780, *ibid.*, p. 369; Lafayette to Washington, August 14, 1780, Sparks MSS LXXXVII, pp. 186–89.

[20] Fitzpatrick, XIX, 431–32.

[21] Lafayette to La Luzerne, August 24, 1780, *loc. cit.*, p. 371.

was getting serious, largely, Lafayette thought, because of the high prices that the French commissaries were paying in gold in all the neighboring markets. "We are entirely without meat and for three days the army has suffered greatly," he informed La Luzerne.[22]

On August 24, the plan was put into operation. The main army moved south to the neighborhood of Liberty Pole Tavern in Teaneck (Englewood), New Jersey. The Light Division took up a post about four miles away, near Fort Lee, almost immediately opposite Fort Washington. Major Henry Lee was sent off with his Light Horse to raid in a northerly direction, and Lafayette with his Light Division went south. For nearly three days the right wing of the Continental Army was spread out from Fort Lee to Staten Island in a thin line that overlapped the extremities of the English lines on New York Island. Lafayette's men came within range of English muskets at Paulus Hook. They found very little but took what they could find— some oxen and some fodder.[23] The English had refused to fall into the trap, and Lafayette was frankly disappointed. Their refusal, he felt, "put them under the same disgrace as that of a man who refuses a challenge."[24]

The expedition had one indirect result, however, that Lafayette did not know. It was the occasion (barring some casual references earlier) of his first passing into American verse:

> Seest thou, my good sister, where you are, these rogues
> Who fight us to death without stockings or brogues?
> They say a French marquis commands, my dear girl.
> Is not the same would have cudgeled an earl?[25]

[22] *Ibid.*

[23] *New Jersey Gazette*, September 6, 1780, quoted in C. H. Winfield, *History of the County of Hudson, New Jersey, from its earliest settlement to the present time* (New York, 1874), pp. 183–84; *New York Mercury*, August 28, 1780, quoted *ibid.*, p. 192; *Gazette de Leyde*, October 24, 1780, supplément, p. 4; Robertson to Germain, September 1, 1780, O'Callaghan, VIII, 800; "Diary of Capt. McClellan," p. 602; Lafayette to La Luzerne, August 27, 1780, *AHR*, XX (1920), 371–72.

[24] Lafayette to Clinton, August 29, 1780, *loc. cit.*

[25] By Susannah Livingston of New York, quoted in Winfield, pp. 186–87. The reference to the "earl" is to Lafayette's challenge of Lord Carlisle to a duel, which Carlisle rejected (see Gottschalk, *Lafayette joins the American army*, pp. 277–79, 286–87, and 293–94).

And the Tory poet Joseph Stanbury, who was incensed that nothing had been done to stop Lafayette, composed an even poorer rhyme, which ran:

> "Has the Marquis La Fayette
> Taken off all our hay yet?"
> Says Clinton to the wise heads around him:
> "Yes, faith, Sir Harry,
> Each stack he did carry,
> And likewise the cattle—confound him."

And there were several more verses in the same vein.[26]

Stockings, brogues, cattle, and hay were sad problems for the rogues whom the French marquis commanded. But they were not the only ones. As if it were not enough to be forced to spend in inaction a summer that had been looked forward to as the last and decisive campaign of the war, Lafayette and his friends now had to assume a philosophical patience, which Lafayette at least did not really have, as blow after blow fell upon them. Late in August it was known at headquarters that the "Alliance" had arrived, and it was hoped that she carried the supplies of powder, arms, and clothing which Lafayette had been expecting ever since he had returned. It soon became known, however, that she had run away from her moorings in defiance of Captain Jones with only a small part of the cargo she had been intended to carry and that her officers had been obliged to put Captain Landais under arrest before they landed. The remainder of the supplies would have to await the second division or Captain Jones and his "Ariel." Since Jones was then being lionized in Paris, there was no likelihood, Lafayette thought, that he would hurry.[27] A French marine officer informed him that the second division was being blockaded at Brest by a strong English fleet; and a letter from Vergennes made it clear that it would be unlikely to leave before the fall.[28] That meant

---

[26] Quoted by M. C. Tyler, *Literary history of the American Revolution 1763–1783* (2 vols.; New York, 1897), II, 92.

[27] Lafayette to La Luzerne, September 10, 1780, *AHR*, XX (1915), 374; cf. Gottschalk, *Lady-in-waiting*, pp. 63–73.

[28] Lafayette to La Luzerne, August 24, 1780 and September 10, 1780, *loc. cit.*, pp. 371–73.

that the supplies they counted on to make Washington's army effective would not arrive for this campaign and that they might as well give up any hope of maritime supremacy unless Guichen should send reinforcements.

At that juncture it began to look, too, as if the South were going to be completely lost to the Americans. Early in September it was learned in the North that General Horatio Gates had been badly beaten in the Battle of Camden the preceding August and had retreated, leaving mortally wounded on the field General Dekalb, who had come to America with Lafayette and unlike him had never returned to France. About the same time one of Lafayette's brigadiers, General Enoch Poor, died of a fever—though the rumor soon spread that he had been killed in a duel with a French officer.[29] Frustration, death, defeat all about. The situation was rapidly approaching disaster, and a drastic solution seemed called for.

To Lafayette the solution was simple. A famished army unable to move against inferior numbers because it had no supplies or supporting men-of-war and obliged to sit idly while it learned of disasters to comrades in arms was not likely to feel that the cure of its ills was greater democracy. There were many outside of the army who believed that the remedy was a more closely knit confederation with a Congress that had greater authority. Lafayette's correspondence had made him aware of that movement. He approved of it but felt it was not enough. Faced with a crisis in the cause to which he had devoted the last three years and with which he had become completely identified, he had been forced to do much more serious thinking along political lines than ever before; and his political penchant proved not to be democratic. He had several times before been called upon to note that the republican way was not an efficient way when rapid decisions and energetic action were called for. This was certainly such a moment. There was only one person who could meet the crisis successfully. That was Washington.

[29] S. C. Beane, "General Enoch Poor," *Proceedings of the New Hampshire Historical Society*, III (1895–99), 462–66; cf. Lafayette to Noailles, September 10, 1780, Patou, pp. 19–20.

Some other persons, he had heard, thought that Washington ought to be made dictator. He certainly approved. The French generals, too, he knew, would approve; and so would the French ambassador. He felt that only if Washington were made dictator would the French government have enough confidence in the fate of America to lend it the money without which its cause was lost.

Yet, as Washington's friend and as a member of the military, he hesitated to act as his inclinations dictated. He communicated his mixed feelings to La Luzerne: "Some people say, M. le Chevalier, that they are going to make General Washington dictator. I do not know whether as his friend I ought to wish it for him, but I most certainly do know that I ought neither to mention that proposal nor to give the impression of desiring it, though it nevertheless seems to me to be extremely important. . . . . My republican, and, I might say, altogether democratic principles should lead me to oppose such a step, and so I would not approve of it if I did not know the man and if I did not believe his dictatorship necessary to the public welfare."[30]

For the leading French soldier in the American army to make such a suggestion to the most important French civil authority in America was not a mere academic gesture. Nothing ever came of it, but it nevertheless constitutes a most significant indication of Lafayette's political theory at this juncture. It was the first time that he had spoken to a Frenchman about his republican leanings without an apologetic or ironical note. It was the first time that he had mentioned to anyone that he had democratic principles. And yet, as even this declaration shows, he had small confidence that a republic could weather a storm. If he had read the outstanding French political literature of his day (which he had not yet done), he would have learned that even more liberal-minded, theoretical gentlemen had much the same point of view that he had acquired by actual contact with a republic in a crisis. It was a point of view which conformed with eighteenth-century historical scholarship and experience.

Washington, however, was neither a French nobleman nor a

[30] September 10, 1780, *loc. cit.*, p. 374.

philosophe. If the solution that others thought inescapable ever struck him, it was only to be repudiated. In a crisis he found that the only way to proceed was to redouble one's precautions and wait all the more patiently for fortune to smile or for enemies to make mistakes. The one thing that he had not so far done that obviously ought to have been done was to confer personally with Rochambeau and Ternay. The demands of Rochambeau for a meeting with "our general" had become even more persistent of late.[31] Washington, now convinced that the English would not cross the Hudson to attack his army and having given up all hope of an offensive and dismissed most of his three-month militia,[32] felt that he could afford to leave his men for a few days. Consequently, on September 8 he requested the French generals[33] to meet him secretly at Hartford. "Our plans," he confided in them, "can only turn upon possibilities; which is the more unfortunate, as the affairs of this country absolutely require activity, upon whichever side they are viewed." Lafayette and Brigadier-General Henry Knox, commandant of the artillery, and Lieutenant-Colonel Jean-Baptiste Gouvion, commandant of the engineers, would accompany him.

Before Washington actually set out for the rendezvous, hope was once more buoyed by the report that Guichen was heading from the Indies toward the Continent. If he went north, perhaps that maritime supremacy which alone was awaited before the allied armies attacked New York would at last be obtained. If he reached some southern point, perhaps an attack on the victorious British forces under Lord Cornwallis might be risked in that quarter. Washington immediately sent off to him a letter supporting the ones which Ternay and Lafayette had already forwarded.[34] It gave a pathetic account of the dire straits in

[31] Cf. Rochambeau to Lafayette, August 14, 1780, Doniol, V, 365; August 25, 1780, *ibid.*, p. 370.

[32] Lafayette to Rochambeau, August 28, 1780, LC, Rochambeau letter book, p. 141; Washington to Rochambeau, September 3, 1780, Fitzpatrick, XIX, 495.

[33] Fitzpatrick, XX, 16; cf. Lafayette to Rochambeau, September 8, 1780, LC, Rochambeau letter book, pp. 150–51.

[34] September 12, 1780, Fitzpatrick, pp. 39–42.

which the American cause lay: "The Government without finances; its paper credit sunk, and no expedients it can adopt
capable of retrieving it; the resources of the country much diminished by a five years war, in which it has made efforts beyond
its ability; Clinton . . . . in possession of one of our capital
towns and a large part of the state to which it belongs; the
savages desolating the other frontiers; . . . . Lord Cornwallis
. . . . in complete possession of two states, Georgia and South
Carolina; a third, North Carolina, by recent misfortunes at his
mercy. . . . ." He begged Guichen to come to the rescue.

Guichen did not come, but, as they waited, the disheartening
rumor spread that Sir George Rodney had reinforced the English fleet at New York with thirteen vessels. That news came
the night before Washington was to leave for Hartford. Lafayette lost a whole night's sleep but in the morning found that
the rumor was believed to be baseless.[35] "Though a little more
tranquil since morning," he wrote to La Luzerne,[36] "I am still
quite worried about that report on Rodney." It eventually
proved to be a fact, however, and not even Guichen's arrival
would have given the allies the coveted superiority on the seas
at that moment. Yet when Washington and his companions
finally started out for Hartford, they were not sure whether
Guichen would come or whether Rodney had come.

Washington, Lafayette, Knox, Gouvion, Lieutenant-Colonel
Alexander Hamilton as Washington's aide, Dr. James McHenry
as Lafayette's aide, Major Samuel Shaw as Knox's aide, three
other aides, and an escort of twenty-two dragoons set out for
Connecticut by coach and horseback on September 17. At noon
of the same day they dined at the home of Joshua Hett Smith
between Stony Point and Haverstraw, New York. Major-General Benedict Arnold, in proper accord with military etiquette,
had come down to meet them. As commander at West Point,
Arnold had one of the most strategic posts in America under his
control. In fact, at one time Lafayette had feared that Arnold
might prefer to take the Light Division, but the wound which

[35] Lafayette to La Luzerne, September 17, 1780, *AHR*, XX (1915), 374.
[36] *Ibid.*, p. 375.

Arnold had suffered at the Battle of Saratoga had permanently crippled him, and he had used that as a pretext to claim the no less crucial, though much less active, post at the fortress up the river.[37] Lafayette had seen little of Arnold since their first meeting at Albany in 1778, but they had remained good friends, and Lafayette, as he later admitted, "had always been fond" of Arnold's attractive wife.[38] Recently Lafayette had had a slight disagreement with Arnold over a question of spies. Lafayette was known to spend large sums of money for intelligence of the British army. Arnold had asked to know the names of spies employed in New York. The marquis, feeling that he was honor bound to keep their secret, refused to reveal them even to a friend.[39] The episode passed unremembered until a later day.

After the midday dinner at Smith's house, the commander-in-chief's party was ferried across the Hudson in Arnold's barge. Lafayette sat close to Arnold. He was still wishfully speculating upon the possibility of Guichen's arrival. Since Arnold as commandant at West Point was known to send occasional flags to New York on quite routine matters, Lafayette wondered whether Arnold could not learn from the British whether they had any better information than the Americans had. As nearly as he could afterward remember it,[40] Lafayette said to Arnold, "Since you have communication with the enemy, you must ascertain as soon as possible what has become of Guichen." "What do you mean?" cried Arnold, obviously flustered. But the boat by that time scraped the shore. They all got out and immediately forgot the incident.

General Arnold accompanied them as far as Peekskill, where they passed the night. Spies (and perhaps General Arnold) kept the British informed (not always accurately) of what went on at

---

[37] Sparks MSS XXXII, p. 97; Ogden to unknown, May 6, 1835, Jackson Collection.

[38] Lafayette to La Luzerne, September 26, 1780, Baron Ernouf, "Complot d'Arnold (1780) raconté par Lafayette," *Revue de la Révolution*, V (1885), 173. (Ernouf mistakenly gives this letter the date of September 25.)

[39] Sparks MSS XXXII, pp. 97–98; Ogden to unknown, May 6, 1835, *loc. cit; Mémoires*, I, 262.

[40] Sparks MSS XXXII, pp. 98–99. See also p. 142 below.

Washington's various visits.[41] It was soon believed in New York that, if Washington did not get the support he needed from the French, he would resign. "I have not since the year 1777 seen so fair a prospect of winning back the people, and putting an end to the revolt," wrote Lieutenant-General James Robertson,[42] who had been the last British governor of New York.

On September 21, the party reached Hartford. The Governor's Guards and a company of artillery were drawn up to honor them. A salute of thirteen guns boomed forth and mingled with the cheers of the loyal citizens who had turned out to see the generals. They went to the home of Colonel Jeremiah Wadsworth. Somewhat later Count Axel de Fersen, Rochambeau's aide, arrived to pay the respects of the French generals. Fersen had been sent ahead to explain that, because of accidents to their coach, the Frenchmen would arrive late. There were just six of them.[43] They had no need of an escort, since unlike Washington's party, they had traveled only through friendly territory. Fersen was impressed with the "handsome and majestic, but at the same time gentle and frank face" of the American commander. "There is an air of sadness about him," he wrote to his father.[44]

[41] Cf. Robertson to Eden, September 22, 1780, Jackson Collection, where, however, Washington is said to have "called on Genl Howe at Fishkill" on his way to Hartford. I can find no evidence that Howe was at Fishkill at this time. Moreover, Washington went to Hartford by way of Peekskill, N.Y., and Waterbury, Conn.; cf. Fitzpatrick, XX, 66, n. 8.

[42] Robertson to Eden, September 22, 1780, loc. cit.

[43] Rochambeau, Ternay, Desandrouin (chief of engineers), the Vicomte de Rochambeau, Damas, and Fersen. Cf. Fersen to his father, October 16, 1780, F. W. Wrangel (ed.), Lettres d'Axel de Fersen à son père pendant la Guerre d'Indépendance d'Amérique (Paris, 1929), p. 82; Rochambeau, I, 250; Lafayette to Mme de Lafayette, October 7, 1780, Mémoires, I, 373; Stuart, pp. 484–88. There has been a great deal of confusion regarding the dates of the conference at Hartford. I have followed W. S. Baker's Itinerary of General Washington from June 15, 1775, to December 23, 1783 (Philadelphia, 1892), which agrees with the itinerary for Lafayette given by Nolan and the program of Governor Trumbull given by Stuart. Cf. Connecticut Courant, September 26, 1780, quoted in G. H. Hollister, History of Connecticut from the first settlement of the colony to the adoption of the present constitution (2 vols., 2d ed.; Hartford, 1857), II, 387, n. 1. Mathieu Dumas, Mémoirs of his own time (2 vols.; Philadelphia, 1839) includes Providence in the itinerary (I, 29–30), but he obviously confuses the conference at Hartford in 1780 with the meeting at Newport in 1781.

[44] October 16, 1780, loc. cit.

Washington and his suite had not long to wait. The sound of gun salutes and cheering soon indicated that the distinguished Frenchmen had crossed the ferry. Washington went forth to meet them. The two generals clasped hands in front of the Connecticut capital. Rochambeau and Ternay, Washington and Lafayette shortly withdrew and remained closeted the whole day in a room in Wadsworth's house.[45] Lafayette as the only one among them who spoke both French and English acted as interpreter and secretary.

The certainty of Rodney's arrival had been established by the French generals as they were on their way to Hartford. Consequently, a prominent part of their conference centered around the question of naval superiority. It was agreed that only if Guichen came and could establish control of the sea would New York be the object of combined operations. If Guichen could not command New York Harbor, however, then a joint expedition was to be tried in the South. Washington proposed that, whenever it could be done with safety, the French army join him while the French fleet sailed to Boston, but the French generals insisted that their orders required them not to separate. The possibility of a winter's attack on Canada was also broached, but Rochambeau and Ternay (quite rightly) suspected that there might be political objections to such an enterprise. They agreed most decidedly that the French government should be urgently requested to increase their forces in America.[46]

After many hours of interpreting for both parties on that day and the next,[47] Lafayette was called upon to put into writing an account of the matters upon which the conference had led to

[45] Stuart, pp. 487–88.

[46] The sources for what happened during the interview are: "Summary of a conversation between His Excellency General Washington, the Count de Rochambeau, and the Chevalier de Ternay," September 22, 1780, Fitzpatrick, XX, 79–81; "Conférence de Hartford," September 22, 1780, Doniol, IV, 404–7 (of which Fitzpatrick [XX, 76–78] publishes only the queries of Rochambeau and Ternay, mistakenly calling them Washington's answers to their queries); and Lafayette to Vergennes, October 4, 1780, Stevens, *Facsimiles*, XVII, no. 1627.

[47] On the basis of Fersen's letter to his father (October 16, 1780, *loc. cit.*) and Stuart (p. 488), many historians assume that the conference took place only on Thursday,

marked agreement. He did so in a document of two columns, in one of which he stated the French generals' point of view and in the other Washington's rejoinders. The document was in French. After repeating that New York was the most important enemy stronghold in America and that it could be prudently attacked only if the French controlled the harbor, both parties pointed out the absolute necessity for an increase of French land and naval forces and of the moneys at their disposal. Rochambeau and Ternay signed their side of the document and Washington his.[48] It was agreed that the French generals should send a representative to Versailles in order to present the need of men, boats, and money most forcibly to His Majesty.[49] When the generals finally emerged from their conference, they all openly expressed themselves as well content with the results of their meeting.[50] Washington, nevertheless, carried away the distinct conviction that his command over the French troops stood "upon a very limited basis."[51]

Since the generals could not afford to remain away from their camps any longer in the face of the recent arrival of Rodney, they parted. The French officers left shortly after the conference was over. The Americans began their journey back the next morning. One day of jogging over bad roads brought Washington's party to Litchfield, and another morning's ride took them to the town of Fishkill near the banks of the Hudson. On the afternoon of September 24 they started down the river to Arnold's quarters when they ran into another distinguished group headed in the opposite direction. It was the French minister La Luzerne and his escort, going to Rhode Island in order also to have an interview with Rochambeau and Ternay. It seemed a fortunate encounter that would save much

---

September 21. The minutes of the conference in the handwriting of Lafayette and of Hamilton show, however, that the important documents were drawn up on September 22; cf. Fitzpatrick, XX, 76, n. 21; 78, n. 22; 79, n. 23, and 81, n. 24.

[48] "Conférence de Hartford," September 22, 1780, *loc. cit.*

[49] Lafayette to Vergennes, October 4, 1780, *loc. cit.*

[50] Fersen to his father, October 16, 1780, *loc. cit.*, p. 83.

[51] Washington to Lafayette, December 14, 1780, Fitzpatrick, XX, 474.

correspondence and afford a full explanation of what had happened at Hartford. So both parties went to the nearest tavern, and Lafayette spent another day in a conference intended to promote the co-operation of the French with their allies. Colonel Hamilton went ahead with the baggage the next morning to tell the Arnolds that the commander-in-chief's party would have breakfast with them.[52]

Early the next day the Americans again started out for Arnold's house, expecting to stop there for breakfast. On the way Washington determined to turn aside in order to examine some redoubts that were located between Fishkill and Arnold's headquarters at Robinson's House opposite West Point. When Lafayette remarked that they would be late for breakfast, Washington smiled and said, "I know that you young men are in love with Mrs. Arnold."[53] Yet he felt that he must postpone the honor of breakfast with her that morning, though they might go forward if they pleased. Since the young men, thus challenged, would do no less than accompany their chief, Lafayette's aide McHenry and Knox's aide Shaw[54] were sent to ask Mrs. Arnold not to expect them until later.

The two aides found General and Mrs. Arnold at table and were invited to join them. While they were eating, two letters were brought to Arnold. They later proved to be reports from his subordinates that Major John André, adjutant-general of the English army, had been captured and that the papers found on him were being forwarded to General Washington. The news was a cruel blow to Arnold. Only three days previously he and André had had a treasonable conversation, and André carried

[52] "Mr. Col. Tobias Lear's diary" (reporting a conversation with Washington under date of October 23, 1786), quoted in Richard Rush, *Occasional productions, political, diplomatic, and miscellaneous* (Philadelphia, 1860), p. 82; cf. Lafayette to Vergennes, October 4, 1780, *loc. cit.* Lafayette says McHenry accompanied Hamilton (*Mémoires*, I, 263), but this is contradicted by earlier testimony (see n. 54 below).

[53] Sparks MSS XXXII, p. 119; cf. Lafayette to Mme de Lafayette, October 8, 1780, *Mémoires*, I, 375.

[54] Letter from an officer at Robinson's House, September 26, 1780, *Pennsylvania Packet*, October 3, 1780, quoted in Frank Moore, *Diary of the American Revolution from newspapers and original documents* (2 vols.; New York, 1860), II, 324–25. This officer is obviously McHenry. Cf. Lafayette to La Luzerne, September 26, 1780, *loc. cit.*

papers that proved Arnold's treachery. Despairing of the American cause and hoping for greater prestige and reward than he had received in the American army, Arnold had agreed, after several months of negotiations, to make it possible for the British to capture West Point. It had apparently not entered into his calculations to arrange the capture when Washington and Lafayette should be in his power, and yet, had luck been on his side, that might have happened. The fall of West Point, by cutting the American confederation in two and separating the French forces from the Continental Army, might alone have brought an end to the Revolution. The capture of Washington, Lafayette, Knox, and Gouvion, along with West Point, probably would have done so. But the very accident that would have made that awesome result possible, if all had gone well, was likewise the factor that now made discovery of the plot inevitable. If Washington had not met La Luzerne, he would not now have been in the neighborhood; André might have been released by Arnold's orders; the conspiracy might have come to a head before it could be hindered. With the commander-in-chief known to be near, Arnold's suspicious subordinates communicated directly with the higher authority; their mere suspicion might now result in Arnold's arrest.

Arnold read his letters with an embarrassment that McHenry did not understand,[55] sat a moment in thought, and then, ordering a horse to be saddled, went to his wife's room. When she followed, he told her that all was lost. She fainted. Leaving her unattended, he mounted his horse, charging his aide to inform Washington, when he came, that he had been called to West Point and would return in an hour. When Washington and his party rode up, he was well on his way to the British vessel "Vulture," which had recently brought André up the river.

The aide gave Arnold's message to Washington. Suspecting nothing, Washington, Lafayette, and Knox breakfasted and then crossed the river to join Arnold, whom they expected to find at the fortifications on the other side.[56] On the way over,

[55] Moore, p. 325; Lafayette to La Luzerne, September 26, 1780, *loc. cit.*

[56] "Mr. Col. Tobias Lear's diary," p. 83; LC, MSS Division, [Lafayette], "Observations sur quelques parties de l'histoire américaine par un ami du Gal Lafayette," p. 42.

Washington remarked that he was glad that Arnold had gone ahead of them because, as they would now have a salute, Lafayette would hear the fine roaring that the cannon made among the palisades of the Hudson.[57] There was no salute as they landed, nor could the surprised officers tell him where to find Arnold. Somewhat puzzled by the impropriety of Arnold's conduct, they recrossed the river.

Colonel Hamilton had, meanwhile, received some papers that had been sent to Washington by Arnold's subordinates. The commander-in-chief and his aide withdrew to a private corner, and Lafayette went to his room. When Washington read the papers Hamilton had given him, he learned that a spy had been arrested and had proved to be none other than the adjutant-general of the British army; among the documents on him were the report of a council of war recently held in Washington's headquarters and plans for an attack on West Point written in Arnold's hand.[58] Washington could hardly believe it. He immediately sent Hamilton and McHenry to pursue the fleeing Arnold.

The first inkling Lafayette had that something was amiss came when McHenry rushed into the room in which he was dressing for dinner and, without explanation, started to look for his pistols.[59] When Lafayette rejoined Washington, Hamilton and McHenry were already in full chase after their man. Sadly Washington told Lafayette and Knox what he had just learned. "Whom can we trust now?" he asked them.[60] Lafayette and Knox were no less dumbfounded than their chief. All, however, made a heroic effort not to seem unduly disturbed. By this time the afternoon dinner was ready, and Washington decided that, as Mrs. Arnold was not well and as the general was absent, they would sit down without ceremony.[61]

Meanwhile, the absconding general made good his head start. Hamilton could show for his pains only two letters to Washing-

[57] Sparks MSS XXXII, p. 121.

[58] Lafayette to La Luzerne, September 26, 1780, *loc. cit.*

[59] J. F. Cooper, *Notions of the Americans picked up by a travelling bachelor* (2 vols.; London, 1828), I, 286.

[60] Sparks MSS XXXII, p. 123.   [61] *Ibid.*, pp. 122–23.

ton written from the "Vulture." One was from Arnold demanding good treatment of his wife and the other from the Loyalist Colonel Beverly Robinson demanding the release of André. When dinner was over those letters were delivered to Washington. For a moment he lost his composure on reading them. They removed all possibility of considering Arnold guiltless or his plans unpremeditated. Rapid steps were now taken to concentrate at West Point the troops that Arnold had dispersed upon one pretext or another. The outposts were placed in readiness against attack, and orders were dispatched to General Greene to be prepared to move the main army to the defense of West Point on a moment's notice.[62]

Meanwhile Mrs. Arnold had had medical attention. Her head now seemed clear. Between fits of hysteria she asked to see Washington. The commander-in-chief went to her room. Amid tears and storms she accused him of wishing to murder her child. He left without saying a word. When it was definitely known that Arnold was safe on the "Vulture," Washington sent her assurances that, despite all he could do, her husband was safe.[63]

The next morning cross-examination of possible accomplices was begun. For Mrs. Arnold, Lafayette felt nothing but compassion. He believed, as did everyone else (though there was good reason to doubt it), that she had not known a word of the conspiracy, that she was no less a victim of her husband's treachery than any other, and that her convulsions and loss of reason of the night before had been genuine.[64] That morning she was calmer and sent for Lafayette and Hamilton. They did what they could to reassure her. She told them that she would return to her family in Philadelphia. General Washington gave his consent, and Lafayette wrote to La Luzerne[65] asking him,

[62] Lafayette to La Luzerne, September 26, 1780, *loc. cit.;* cf. Fitzpatrick, XX, 84–88.

[63] Lafayette to La Luzerne, September 26, 1780, *loc. cit.;* Sparks MSS XXXII, 122–23; *Mémoires,* I, 264.

[64] Lafayette to La Luzerne, September 26, 1780, *loc. cit.;* and Hamilton to Miss Schuyler, September 25 [26?], 1780, *Works of Hamilton,* I, 186–87; but cf. Hughes, III, 539 and 555–57; and Van Doren, *Secret history,* pp. 346–51.

[65] September 26, 1780, *loc. cit.*

when he returned to Philadelphia, to befriend her. "It would be exceedingly painful to General Washington if she were not treated with the greatest kindness," he declared.

The young man's resentment against Arnold's male accomplices was somewhat less gallant. Lafayette took part in the inquisition of both Mr. Joshua Hett Smith and André.[66] The cross-examination of Smith, who had been their host but a few days before and who seemed also to have served as intermediary between Arnold and André, was still going on and Major André had not yet been delivered to Robinson's House when Lafayette wrote, "I hope both of them will be hanged, but especially the latter, who is a man of influence in the English army and whose very distinguished social rank will act as a warning to spies of less degree."[67] He sent an account of the astonishing event to Newport to catch up with La Luzerne.[68] "Our struggles," he said, "have revealed some heroes (General Washington, for example) who would otherwise have been merely honorable private citizens. They have also developed some great scoundrels who otherwise would have remained merely obscure rogues. But that an Arnold, that a man who, although not so highly esteemed as has been supposed in Europe, had nevertheless given proof of talent, of patriotism, and, especially, of the most brilliant courage, should by a single stroke destroy his very existence and sell his country to the tyrants whom he has fought against with glory, is an event, M. le Chevalier, which confounds and distresses me, and, if I must confess it, humiliates me, to a degree that I cannot express. I would give anything in the world if Arnold had not shared our labors with us, and if this man, whom it still pains me to call a scoundrel, had not shed his blood for the American cause." He begged La Luzerne to soften the bad impression that "the incredible story" must make upon the French soldiers at Newport: "Unaccustomed as they are to

[66] J. H. Smith, *An authentic narrative of the causes which led to the death of Major André* (London, 1808), pp. 51 and 92.

[67] Lafayette to La Luzerne, September 26, 1780, *loc. cit.*

[68] *Ibid.* I have borrowed freely from Tower's translation of this document (II, 164–68), without accepting it entirely.

the convulsions of a revolution, what will the officers of the French army say when they see a general abandon and basely sell his country after having defended it so well!" And to Rochambeau he wrote at the same time, "This is the first example of treason in our armies—an extraordinary thing in this kind of revolution, but the example pains us all as much as it disgusts us."[69]

West Point having been secured against immediate attack, Washington and his escort started for camp, leaving Gouvion behind to aid in the defense of the threatened fortress. André and Smith had been sent ahead as prisoners under escort. On September 29 they were again at Orangetown (Tappan). Immediately, fourteen general officers with the main army were constituted a court martial to try André. There were six major-generals and eight brigadiers. Only Greene, Stirling, and St. Clair were Lafayette's seniors. The trial was quickly over; André was found guilty of spying and sentenced to death. Lafayette signed the report with the rest.[70] He afterward spoke of his part in the court martial as "one of the most painful duties he had to perform."[71] The unfortunate Englishman was sentenced to be executed on October 1. That day Washington postponed the execution until the next—perhaps in the expectation that a last-minute exchange of André for Arnold might take place. At any rate, with Washington's approval, Lafayette sent Captain Aaron Ogden to the British lines with a flag of truce to make such a proposal.[72] Since Clinton would not listen, André was executed at noon on October 2. He had "conducted himself in so candid, noble, and delicate a fashion," Lafayette wrote to his wife shortly after the execution, "that I could not help feeling extremely sorry for him."[73]

[69] September 26, 1780, LC, Rochambeau letter book, pp. 172–73.

[70] A facsimile of the proceedings is given in Fitzpatrick, XX, frontispiece.

[71] A. A. Parker, *Recollections of General Lafayette on his visit to the United States in 1824 and 1825* (Keene, N.H., 1879), p. 64.

[72] "Autobiography of Col. Aaron Ogden, of Elizabethtown," *Proceedings of the New Jersey Historical Society*, 2d. ser., XII (1892), 23–24.

[73] October 8, 1780, *loc. cit.*, p. 376.

Joshua Smith's trial dragged on through most of the month of October. The marquis was one of the principal witnesses to appear against him, and Smith complained that his testimony was delivered "with acrimonious severity and malignant bitterness."[74] In the end, however, Smith was acquitted by the court martial, only to be rearrested by the civil authorities and forced to flee to the enemy.

The summer by this time had passed. There had been no campaign, though the French had sent a large force to America and the states had made exhaustive efforts to inflict a final blow. But Lafayette still hoped for Guichen, the second division, or an error on the part of the English to enable his friends to win New York and the war. Obviously "a most providential interposition"[75] (as Washington put it)—or a "miraculous chain of accidents and circumstances,"[76] an "almost unbelievable combination of chance events"[77] (as the more skeptical Lafayette put it) —had not saved them from Arnold's machinations for nothing.

BIBLIOGRAPHICAL NOTES

One of the best discussions of the Light Division is by Col. John W. Wright in "The corps of light infantry in the Continental Army," *AHR*, XXXI (1926), 454–61; see also the same author's "Some notes on the Continental Army," *William and Mary College quarterly historical magazine*, 2d ser., XI (1931), 188, and XIII (1933), 92.

Lafayette left several accounts of the events leading to and from the detection of Arnold's treachery. The best of them is the one he rendered to La Luzerne on September 26, 1780; it was published by Ernouf in the *Revue de la Révolution*, V (1885), 168–73. Ernouf, apparently by his own error in reading the text of Lafayette's letter, makes Washington sit down to breakfast with Arnold (cf. Tower, II, 164–65, n. 3). A comparison of Ernouf's text with a contemporary copy of Lafayette's letter in the Archives des Affaires Étrangères (corr. pol., É.-U., Vol. XIII, fols. 545–46) makes this error clear.

Lafayette's account of September 26 is bolstered in many details by the letter of Hamilton to Miss Schuyler of the same date (erroneously dated in Hamilton's *Works*, I, 186–87, as of September 25) and by McHenry's account, likewise of that date, in the *Pennsylvania Packet* for October 3, 1780. The

[74] Smith, p. 134.

[75] Washington to Heath, September 26, 1780, Fitzpatrick, XX, 88–89.

[76] Lafayette to La Luzerne, September 26, 1780, *loc. cit.*

[77] Lafayette to Vergennes, October 4, 1780, *loc. cit.*

failure of earlier historians to recognize that the last account was by McHenry explains the misundertanding of his role in the Arnold affair (see n. 54, above). Washington's testimony regarding the events of September 25 was not recorded until 1786 and then became available only at second hand. It, nevertheless, confirmed the testimony of the other eyewitnesses in important regards and furnished no supplementary details that did violence to their credibility. Thus the testimony of four of the principal actors in that day's drama became available within a few years. The four accounts agree to a remarkable extent.

Difficulties in piecing events together and fitting anecdotes and episodes into their proper chronological order arise from the several subsequent accounts which Lafayette wrote or was instrumental in getting written. Probably the earliest of these were two narratives by Lafayette himself. The first, which was given in a memoir entitled *Observations sur quelques parties de l'histoire américaine* (probably written between 1800 and 1814), is the *Manuscrit No. 2* of the *Mémoires* (see I, 3). A contemporary copy of these *Observations* is now in the Library of Congress. The second of Lafayette's narratives, which is given in the text of the *Mémoires* (I, 261–65), dates from approximately the same period. In 1824–25, while making his tour of the United States, Lafayette told James Fenimore Cooper the story that Cooper related in *Notions of the Americans*, pp. 278–97. And in 1828 he told Jared Sparks the story that Sparks wrote on pages 119–26 of the notebook which is now Vol. XXXII of the Sparks MSS.

These four accounts are more confused and less reliable than the earlier four. Unfortunately, the earlier ones were either not available or, if available, not carefully exploited by the first historians of the Arnold affair, among whom the best were Jared Sparks with *The life and treason of Benedict Arnold* (New York, 1851) and Winthrop Sargent with *The life and career of Major John André* (Boston, 1861; 2d ed., New York, 1902). Though the main outline of the story they tell is correct, it is necessary to depart from their stories in certain details. William Abbott, *The crisis of the Revolution, being the story of Arnold and André*, etc. (New York, 1899) has been superseded as the best monograph on the subject by Van Doren's *Secret history*. The story that Lafayette played a leading part in an effort to kidnap Arnold from New York (cf., e.g., Colonel Bryan Conrad, "Lafayette and Cornwallis in Virginia, 1781," *William and Mary College quarterly historical magazine*, 2d ser., XIV [1934], 101) seems to be legend; at least I can find no firsthand testimony for it, though such a plot did exist (cf. Henry Lee, *Memoirs of the war in the southern department of the United States* [2 vols.; Philadelphia, 1812], pp. 159–87; Fitzpatrick, XX, 233–34 and n. 34).

CHAPTER VII

"Dull as a European War"

TWO summers had gone by since Lafayette had breathed the smoke of battle. In the days before warfare became national and democratic, war was fine sport. A soldier had a good chance of coming out unscatched from the hottest contest and finding himself a hero. Lafayette, having been wounded once, knew what pain was like. Yet it had done him no permanent harm, he had won glory by it, and he felt ashamed of inaction. Idleness was disgraceful to him particularly. He had boasted of American perseverance in France and of French daring in America. He had been responsible—perhaps more than any other person—for the sending of Rochambeau's army to America. Yet Rochambeau proved to be everything but daring, and at any moment it looked as if the Americans would cease to persevere. Lafayette was personally affronted by this state of affairs. When Admiral Ternay died suddenly in December, 1780, Lafayette believed or pretended to believe (for the greater effect it might have in France) that he had died of mortification at being held in disgraceful idleness at Newport,[1] though Ternay's death was in fact caused by nothing more glamorous than fever and high blood pressure. Lafayette was probably closer to the truth when he maintained that the younger officers in the French army were growing impatient and apologetic.[2]

Yet there seemed to be only one thing that could be done while waiting. La Luzerne had sent a plea for men, money, and

---

[1] Lafayette to Mme de Lafayette, February 2, 1781, *Mémoires*, I, 406; cf. Rochambeau to Lafayette, January 18, 1781, Doniol, IV, 570 n.

[2] Cf. Fersen to his father, October 16, 1780, *loc. cit.*

ships to the king. Rochambeau was to send his own son the Vicomte de Rochambeau, with the minutes of the Hartford meeting signed by Washington and Ternay as well as himself. Lafayette could do no less than add his voice to theirs. With André safely out of the way, he gave his whole attention once more to the problems that had so long filled his mind and heart. At any cost to France (and, knowing little of French finances, he could not conceive of any cost as being too high), the alliance with America must secure its end. Not much more could be hoped for this year, but, if anything was to be done for the next campaign, it must be begun now—the fall of 1780.

The Light Camp at this time was situated at Harrington, New Jersey (near Orangetown, New York). In a room filled with military noises and interruptions, Lafayette and his secretary Poirey, recently arrived on the "Alliance,"[3] took out their codebook and labored upon a letter in code to Vergennes.[4] With some errors of ciphering, they finally put into a complicated number system a long cryptogram that was both a report and a prayer. Because of Rochambeau's persuasion, Lafayette was now ready to admit that the presence of the French fleet had probably been productive of some good; it had at least kept Clinton on the defensive in New York. And he still insisted that the American soldiers had shown themselves to be long-suffering martyrs in their own cause. "They show a fortitude in misery which is unknown in European armies." Yet the political conditions in America were so bad that another burst of energy such as had just been demanded of them to no purpose could hardly be expected. Congress had lost its prestige and authority, and the states were poor, though some of the northern states seemed pathetically willing to co-operate. The great obstacle was money—money which would be set aside "for the army only." If the army had a goodly sum of hard cash, "three quarters of our troubles" would disappear. And they also needed clothing, guns, and powder.

But money and supplies were not enough. "Situated and dis-

[3] Cf. Lafayette to Noailles, September 2, 1780, *loc. cit.*, p. 15.

[4] Lafayette to Vergennes, October 4, 1780, Stevens, *Facsimiles*, XVII, no. 1627.

posed as America now is," Lafayette pleaded, "it is essential to the interest as well as the honor of France that our flag reign on these seas, that the campaign be decisive, and that it begin next spring." As he had long maintained, vigorous efforts earlier would have rendered it unnecessary to make still more vigorous efforts now. What would have sufficed last spring would be insufficient next spring. "On my return to this country," Lafayette reported, "I found bad feeling greatly diminished. It has continued to diminish for some time now, and I have proposed, not only as something worth while but as something altogether necessary, that you open the next campaign here early in the spring with a corps of ten thousand and an assured naval predominance. The situation of America requires your most serious attention; every year of delay increases the number of vessels, men, and money that you will ultimately have to send."

The plea was vigorous, but Lafayette felt it was not enough. He must bring public pressure, also, to bear upon the ministry. Since no part of the Paris public was more influential than his own friends, he sought to enlist their good will. Within the next few days he penned a letter, long overdue, to his wife,[5] and another to her aunt Mme de Tessé.[6] To her cousin, the Prince de Poix, who since his subaltern days had been one of his closest companions, he had written regularly since his arrival in America, and now he wrote again.[7] And to place the ministry under fire from still another influential quarter he also sent a letter to Benjamin Franklin.[8]

All these letters narrated some part of the young soldier's experiences since his arrival in the United States, but, mingled with the friendly gossip, there was always a political message. Both French and Americans, they said, had been bogged down in shameful inactivity. Recalling the fruitless campaign of 1779 in Normandy and Brittany, he apologized to his "dear cousin," as he called Mme de Tessé, for the waste of another

[5] October 7–10, 1780, *Mémoires*, I, 372–76.

[6] October 4, 1780, *ibid.*, pp. 370–72.

[7] October 9, 1780, private collection.

[8] October 9, 1780, APS, Franklin papers, Vol. XX, no. 16.

year: "All this is as dull as a European war, and to keep up our interest, we need some kind of catastrophe. . . . . The nation will not be satisfied with our tranquillity. But without ships we can expect only blows, and General Clinton appears to be in no hurry to come and inflict them upon us here." Then came again the familiar semiapologetic tone for the weaknesses of the republican form of government: "As for us republicans, we preach to our sovereign master, the people, that they be pleased to recommence their exertions. Meanwhile we live in a frugality, poverty, and nakedness, which, I hope, will be put to our credit in the next world as a sort of purgatory."[9]

The longer dispatch to Franklin not only repeated the need for maritime supremacy but also painted an agitated picture of the army's shabbiness: "We are nack'd, shokingly nack'd and worse off on that respect than we have ever been. For God's sake, my dear friend, let us have any how fifteen or twenty thousand compleat suits (exclusive of what is expected) and let it be done in such a way as will insure theyr timely departure from France. Cloathing for officers is absolutely necessary. No cloth to be got—no money to purchase." The persistent young beggar hoped that the arms and powder which had long ago been procured would at length reach their destination. "How did it happen that nothing is yet come to hand? Expectations were rais'd. The disappointment is of course attended with bad consequences. You have no idea of the shoking situation the army is in."[10]

The letter to Adrienne was written in three instalments as the Light Division moved with the army westward from the Hudson and New York and took up a new post at Totowa Bridge on the Passaic River. It was more personal in tone than the others, but even here a note of political urgency made a modest appearance. "You may rest assured of the health of your friends in America," he told his *cher cœur*,[11] "so long as our maritime inferiority continues." She could judge the extent of American efforts from the contribution he had made in her behalf to the women's fund for soldiers' aid. "The fruit of all these labors has

<hr>

[9] *Mémoires*, I, 370–71.   [10] *Loc. cit.*   [11] October 7, 1780, *Mémoires*, I, 373.

been to prove to the French that the Americans ask nothing better than to second their views; to show the English that the flame of liberty is not put out in America; and to put us for the whole campaign in readiness for battle, which General Clinton, although equal in numbers, judged inappropriate to accept. If we had had some vessels, it would have been possible to do more."[12] He ended his last instalment with a tender message from General Washington. "We often speak of you and our little family"—particularly of little George,[13] he said.

As the Vicomte de Rochambeau was expected to sail soon in a French frigate,[14] Lafayette sent these messages to him, enclosed in a packet to Vergennes. In a little note to the minister, Lafayette again was careful to mention the need for naval superiority in America.[15] Washington, taking the same opportunity, wrote to Franklin.[16] Praising Lafayette for his "zealous attachment to our cause," he spoke feelingly of the marquis' unhappiness: "He came out flushed with expectations of a decisive campaign and fired with hopes of acquiring fresh laurels, but in both he has been disappointed; for we have been condemned to an inactivity as inconsistent with the situation of our affairs as with the ardor of his temper." He would not, he said, speak on political questions, since Congress must have kept Franklin fully informed. "If I were to speak on topics of the kind," he added, nevertheless, "it would be to show that our present situation makes one of two things essential to us—a Peace—or the most vigorous aid of our allies particularly in the article of money."

Though Washington—always more realistic than Lafayette— saw that keeping the Continental Army together constituted a more pressing need than winning a victory, both men recognized that without the concrete aid of America's ally the war would soon end in a peace of compromise. The choice between American independence or defeat turned more than ever before

[12] *Ibid.*, p. 374.   [13] October 10, 1780, *ibid.*, p. 376.

[14] Rochambeau to Lafayette, October 4, 1780, LC, Rochambeau letter book, p. 100.

[15] October 8, 1780, Stevens, *Facsimiles*, XVII, no. 1628.

[16] October 9, 1780, Fitzpatrick, XX, 142–43.

upon Vergennes' judgment. Few judges have ever had to hear pleas from more picturesque advocates than the triumvirate—Washington, Rochambeau, and Lafayette—who now looked toward the hesitant French minister in supplication. The young Vicomte de Rochambeau might well have felt appalled at the responsibility which had been thrust upon him as he set forth to deliver their petitions to the government at Versailles. He learned part of his messages by heart in order to be able to recite them should he be obliged by English pursuers to throw his dispatch bag overboard.[17]

There seemed little left now for Lafayette to do but to sit back and hope. That, however, was not his nature. As he declared to Hamilton, "You know I am not of a desponding, dark temper."[18] The political need for some coup grew more glaring as the days grew shorter. The people of America expected something for their efforts. "Even a defeat (provided it was not fatal) would have its good consequences," wrote Lafayette to Washington.[19] It would also have a desirable effect upon the French, he believed, showing them that the Americans were capable of exertions in their own behalf. Moreover, if peace negotiations were to begin that winter, the English representatives ought not to be able to boast that the Americans were "half conquered." And so he proposed new ventures.

The first was an attack upon the English and Hessians on Staten Island. As the Light Division had moved from below Tappan to its new post near Totowa, "Light Horse Harry" Lee had had a brief skirmish with an enemy party that had given him a taste of blood.[20] He now proposed a raid on enemy shipping on the Passaic River, which would give the Light Division enough boats to carry it to Staten Island. Lafayette, believing that "unless we hunt for enterprises, they will no more come in our way this campaign,"[21] asked Washington to approve of the

[17] Rochambeau, I, 256–57.

[18] October 21, 1780, LC, Hamilton papers, p. 62.

[19] October 30, 1780, *Mémoires* (Amer. ed.), p. 359.

[20] Lafayette to Washington, October 7, 1780, Sparks MSS LXXXVII, pp. 192–93.

[21] October 12, 1780, *ibid.*, pp. 194–96.

enterprise. From numerous agents on the island he had learned that the posts were in no fear of attack and were very badly guarded. Spies were retained to guide the movements of his army. Each understood that he would receive a big reward if the enemy were surprised but stabbed to death if the enterprise were discovered.[22] Though Washington did not approve of Lee's raid, he did not object to the raid of Staten Island. On October 23, the Light Division was ordered by Washington to take post closer to Cranestown (Montclair), New Jersey, "for the more effectual security of our right."[23] There they waited for a night when moon, tide, and fog might co-operate in their enterprise. The night of October 26 was fixed upon for the sally. Lafayette's own officers learned of the plan only at a gala dinner to Washington and La Luzerne on the eve of its execution.[24]

Colonel Timothy Pickering, who had replaced General Nathanael Greene as quartermaster-general, had been ordered to provide all the boats which could be hired, borrowed, or impressed, to add to them the boats which Washington had carried on wheels with his army all during the campaign, and to bring them together at Elizabethtown. It soon became clear that there would be very few boats indeed. Some of the wagons on which the boats were to be carted broke down. Some of the boats proved to lack oars or other essentials.[25]

Lafayette's division reached Elizabethtown, New Jersey, by secret marches. They conducted themselves in a way that made their commander proud, preserving perfect silence, good order, and eagerness for the fight. Major Lee was especially deserving of praise, Lafayette thought.[26] On the way to Elizabethtown Lafayette saw only five boats, and a little later Pickering said he could provide only three. Lafayette was furious and vented his fury upon the quartermaster's department in letters to his sev-

[22] Lafayette to Noailles, October 28, 1780, Patou, p. 28.

[23] General orders, Fitzpatrick, XX, 251.

[24] Lafayette to Noailles, October 28, 1780, *loc. cit.*, pp. 28–29.

[25] Lafayette to Washington, October 27, 1780 (two letters), *Mémoires* (Amer. ed.), pp. 481–85.

[26] Lafayette to La Luzerne, October 28, 1780, *AHR*, XX (1915), 376.

eral friends. Since, however, it was no longer dark and the element of surprise was gone, he was wise enough to give up the enterprise.[27]

Again Lafayette felt disgraced, particularly since La Luzerne had gone off to Philadelphia believing that the campaign was sure to end with at least a slight victory. "I never have been so deeply wounded by any disappointment," the marquis confessed to Washington.[28] Reluctantly he brought his division back through Cranestown to Totowa. His men shared his chagrin. As they passed the waggoners on the road back, they cursed them for having made a fool's errand out of what ought to have been a glorious sally.[29] Once more they took an advanced position seven or eight miles from headquarters. The threatened invasion by "a Frenchman at the head of some of his Majesty's deluded subjects"[30] had caused a momentary excitement among the British on Staten Island, but things soon settled down again to their wonted calm.

Instead of discouraging Lafayette from thinking again of a surprise attack, his experience at Elizabethtown made him all the more anxious for a new attempt. The same personal and political reasons that had induced him to suggest the raid on Staten Island now caused him to mull over an attack upon New York. He had long felt that Fort Washington could easily be retaken. If that were done, Washington could land on New York island more men than the English had there and take the upper posts. Clinton might then have to offer battle. "If he does," Lafayette argued, "and by chance beat us, we retire under Fort Washington; but, if we beat him, his works will be at such a distance that he will be ruined in the retreat." In either case the claims of the United States at any peace conference

[27] *Mémoires* (Amer. ed.), pp. 481–85.

[28] October 27, 1780, *loc. cit.*, p. 484.

[29] Lafayette to Noailles, October 28, 1780, *loc. cit.*, pp. 39–30; cf. J. B. Reeves, "Extracts from the letterbooks of Lieutenant Enos Reeves of the Pennsylvania line," *Pennsylvania magazine of history and biography*, XX (1896), 458.

[30] Proclamation of Lieutenant-Colonel John G. Simcoe, quoted in J. J. Clute, *Annals of Staten Island* (New York, 1877), p. 102. Cf. *Simcoe's military journal* (New York, 1844), p. 156.

that might be held in the winter would be stronger. The defeat at Charleston had brought American stock low in Europe, the marquis feared. "But what the difference," he exclaimed, in his quaint Gallican English, "if France might say, the American army has taken, sword in hand, your best works; they have offered to you the battle upon your own island, and, perhaps may they add (for news increase in travelling), are they now in possession of New York!" Even if the enterprise failed, it would not prove fatal, "for the loss of 2 or 300 men, half of them being enlisted for two months, I don't consider as a ruinous adventure"—especially since fifteen hundred of the enemy would either be killed or isolated.[31]

Washington apparently had a higher regard for the lives of two or three hundred men, even though enlisted for only two months. "It is impossible," he assured his "dear Marquis,"[32] "to desire more ardently than I do to terminate the campaign by a happy stroke; but we must consult our means rather than our wishes; and not endeavor to better our affairs by attempting things which for want of success may make them worse." He, too, had long considered the plan which Lafayette proposed but had concluded that it would be imprudent "to throw an army of ten thousand men upon an island against nine thousand, exclusive of seamen and militia." Until some very good opportunity presented, Washington preferred merely to watch for the enemy's mistakes.

Summer had meanwhile passed, and the commander-in-chief began to think of winter quarters. A council of war on the last day of October considered the problem. In the written statements submitted by the generals, Lafayette's view was clearly different from that of the others.[33] While they favored going into winter quarters without delay, the marquis advocated remaining in the field till December. One reason for his lone opinion he had already made clear: he still hoped for an

[31] Lafayette to Washington, October 30, 1780, *Mémoires* (Amer. ed.), pp. 358–62.

[32] October 30, 1780, Fitzpatrick, XX, 266–67.

[33] Cf. *ibid.*, p. 273, n. 39; Lafayette to Washington, November 1, 1780, LC, Washington papers, Ser. F, Vol. II, fol. 339.

attack on New York island. Another reason was his belief that a contingent of infantry and horse (of whom, he hoped, he might himself be given command)[34] ought to be detached to the southern department, where Greene had recently replaced Gates as commander. Washington tended toward Lafayette's point of view. Likewise wishing to end the campaign with some bold stroke, he had been looking most of the summer for a proper opportunity to attack New York. He, too, preferred to delay going into winter quarters.

Meanwhile, the migration of restless French officers from Rhode Island threatened to become a veritable stream. Lauzun, though Lafayette's superior in the French army, was willing to be placed under Lafayette if his young compatriot went south, where fighting actually was taking place, rather than to watch his horses grow fat in Connecticut pastures. Noailles likewise thought of accompanying Lafayette if he went to join Greene. Lafayette had to discourage both of them, knowing full well that Washington would consent to their transfer only if Rochambeau agreed, and Rochambeau, they knew, would not agree.[35] In fact, when Lauzun actually asked permission to place his legion under Lafayette, he was refused, and several officers of the French army felt he had acted unbecomingly.[36] Major-General Chastellux, asking permission only to see the country and his relative, the Marquis de Lafayette, was more successful. Several of Lafayette's other friends—the Vicomte de Noailles, the Comte de Damas, the Chevalier de Mauduit-Duplessis— also received permission to go.[37]

Chastellux and his two aides, Lynch and Montesquieu, were the first to set out. When they reached West Point, General

[34] Lafayette to Greene, November 10, 1780, William L. Clements Library (Ann Arbor, Mich.); cf. William Johnson, *Sketches of the life and correspondence of Nathanael Greene* (2 vols.; Charleston, 1882), I, 325–26.

[35] Lafayette to Noailles, November 4, 1780, Patou, pp. 33–34.

[36] M. F. Barrière and M. de Lescure (eds.) *Mémoires du Duc de Lauzun* ("Bibliothèque des mémoires relatifs à l'histoire de France pendant le 18ᵉ siècle," Vol. XXV [Paris, 1882]), pp. 189–90.

[37] Cf. Lafayette to Heath, November 13, 1780, *Heath papers, part III*, pp. 128–29; Lafayette to Washington, November 13, 1780, *Mémoires* (Amer. ed.), pp. 363–65.

Heath, whom they had known when he was at Newport, received them cordially. Before Chastellux and his companions left West Point, they were joined by Noailles, Damas, and Mauduit, who were traveling together. But soon the three younger men pushed on to the Light Camp. Chastellux, being older and less anxious to see Lafayette, proceeded by easier stages.[38] Except for fleeting moments, Noailles had not seen Lafayette since the days when they had planned together to go to America with Dekalb. Now Dekalb was dead, Lafayette was a major-general in the American army, and Noailles was a colonel in the French auxiliary force. They and their friends, Damas and Mauduit, had much to say to one another.

The next day the young men went to Washington's quarters to meet Chastellux, who, they thought, would go there first. Chastellux, however, had gone directly to Lafayette's camp, which was seven or eight miles to the left of headquarters. As his horse would go no farther, he stopped to rest. He examined the excellent position in which Lafayette had placed his men, occupying two heights with easy communication between them and taking full strategic advantage of the near-by rivers. He noticed that the men of Lafayette's corps were better equipped and smarter than the rest of the American army and learned that it was largely at Lafayette's expense that this was so.[39] When ready, he was conducted to headquarters by Dr. McHenry, Lafayette's aide.[40] At length they came to Washington's headquarters. In front of a large tent stood Lafayette in conversation with "a tall man . . . . of noble and mild countenance," whom Chastellux immediately recognized as "His Excellency."[41] Greetings were warm but brief. Chastellux stayed at Washington's quarters at Preakness, while Lafayette returned to his camp.

The next day, as Washington took Chastellux, Lynch, and Montesquieu to review his troops, he apologized that there was

[38] Chastellux, I, 95–96.
[39] Ibid., pp. 100–108.
[40] Ibid., p. 110.
[41] Ibid., p. 113.

no salute. The reason was, he explained,[42] that all his troops on the other side of the North River were in motion. They were carrying out the initial steps of the surprise movement which Lafayette had so long contemplated. Despite Washington's coolness to his first proposal, the young man had persisted in believing that a surprise attack upon New York island must be attempted. He had kept a stream of spies running in and out of New York.[43] At last he won over the commander-in-chief. Orders to commanding officers at West Point[44] and elsewhere[45] had gone out, requiring them to play small roles in a major maneuver which would strike hardest at the upper outposts of New York. Washington was afraid that a salute might now give the enemy the alarm.

It rained hard during the review, and Chastellux, upon Washington's asking his preference, chose to visit Lafayette's house rather than to complete the review of the entire army. They were soaked through when, after riding along the Passaic River for about seven miles from Washington's quarters at Colonel Theunis Dey's house, they reached Lafayette's quarters near the Ryerson homestead. Chastellux was glad to sample the bowl of grog which the marquis always had ready on his table for his officers. Lafayette was at the Light Camp. As soon as the rain let up, Chastellux followed Washington there.[46]

Lafayette had taken his post at the head of his troops. They were drawn up in battle array on the height to the left of his house. The marquis seemed happier, Chastellux thought, to receive him after an autumnal rainstorm on a hill near a farmhouse in the New Jersey wilderness than he would have been in his château in the Auvergne mountains. Chastellux was struck not only by the obvious devotion of Lafayette's men to their

[42] *Ibid.*, pp. 119–20.

[43] Cf. Lafayette to Washington, November 8, 1780, Sparks MSS LXXXVII, pp. 213–14; November 11, 1780, *ibid.*, p. 215; November 13, *ibid.*, pp. 216–20; November 14, *ibid.*, p. 223; November 18, *ibid.*, pp. 224–27; November 19, *ibid.*, pp. 228–29. See also Lafayette to Washington, November 13, *Heath papers, part III*, pp. 128–29, and Lafayette to Hamilton, November 22, LC, Hamilton papers.

[44] Cf. Chastellux, I, 77; Fitzpatrick, XX, 350–52.

[45] Cf. Fitzpatrick, XX, 380–96 and 423–28.   [46] Chastellux, I, 120–21.

youthful commander but also by the great influence he had acquired in political spheres. "I do not fear contradiction when I say that private letters from him have frequently produced more effect on some states than the strongest exhortations of the Congress. On seeing him, one is at a loss which most to admire —that so young a man as he should have given such eminent proofs of talents, or that a man so tried should give hopes of so long a career of glory." There was an ominous note in Chastellux's observation: "Fortunate his country if she knows how to avail herself of them; more fortunate still should she stand in no need of calling them into exertion."[47] The day was not very distant when Lafayette's country would need his talents and not know how to use them.

Since the rain began to fall again, the review was brought to an end. Washington set off at a gallop for his quarters with Chastellux. Lafayette was left at his house with Noailles, Damas, and Mauduit. He had arranged to call for Chastellux the next day and take him to visit the other generals, but it rained so hard that day too that Chastellux found it impossible to set foot outside the house.

By the next morning, however, the rain had stopped, and the visitor could be shown around. After breakfast with the commander-in-chief, Chastellux went to Brigadier-General Wayne's quarters where Lafayette joined them. Together they visited other generals of the main army—Howe, Huntington, and Glover. Then (to satisfy Chastellux's scientific curiosity) they went to visit a young victim of elephantiasis in the neighborhood. On the way they fell in with General Knox, who took them to his house to visit with his wife and children. Then back to headquarters for dinner with Washington and several other officers.[48]

The next day Chastellux left camp to go to Philadelphia. Washington's bags, he found, were also packed—to go to winter quarters. While at camp, Chastellux had witnessed the end of a minor tragedy. The two days' downpour and the unexpected maneuvers of some English vessels in the Hudson had spoiled

[47] *Ibid.*, pp. 121–22.   [48] *Ibid.*, pp. 123–36.

the plan that during the whole campaign Washington and Lafayette had carefully considered and worked out to the smallest detail.[49] While entertaining Chastellux, they had kept unobtrusively busy sending out secret orders intended either to hide their real purpose or to take measures that were necessary to assure its success.[50] On the day that Chastellux reviewed the army, Heath's men had been in motion north of New York island, and outposts on the west side of the North River had been gathering materials, stopping shipping on the river, or marching to the points from which they were to row across. The main attack had been scheduled for that very night but had been countermanded at the eleventh hour.[51] Heath's foraging party had been quite successful and had managed to surprise Fort St. George on Long Island, killing a few men and burning some stores.[52] But it was not the great coup that Lafayette had looked for to end the campaign.

On the day that Chastellux left camp, the Light Division was dissolved, and the separate units returned to their former brigades for the winter. Orders of the day announced: "The General presents his thanks to the Marquis de la Fayette and to the officers and men under his command for the excellent order and soldierly disposition which have been conspicuous in the corps. He regrets that opportunities did not offer to avail himself of that zeal and ardor which in this corps and in the army at large afforded the strongest assurance of success."[53] Instructions for marching to winter quarters followed. Dr. James Thacher, a surgeon in the Continental Army, who had long known Lafayette, recorded in his journal how bitterly the young general felt that his corps "formed and modeled according to his wishes" had disbanded without showing its mettle. "They were the pride of his heart, and he was the idol of their regard," said the sympathetic doctor. ". . . . This brilliant corps is now dis-

[49] Cf. *ibid.*, p. 129; Fitzpatrick, XX, 395, n. 81; Ford, IX, 37–38 n.

[50] Cf. Washington to Lafayette, November 23, 1780, Fitzpatrick, XX, 392; Reeves, "Extract from letterbooks," p. 468.

[51] Fitzpatrick, XX, 395–97.

[52] Reeves, "Extracts from letterbooks," p. 469; Fitzpatrick, XX, 416–17 and 420.

[53] November 26, 1780, Fitzpatrick, XX, 401–3.

solved . . . . and we are soon to retire into the wilderness to prepare for winter quarters."[54]

Lafayette did not propose to accompany the main army into
the wilderness. He contemplated going south to join Greene.[55]
The prospects of favorable action in a land which would not be
frozen tight were enticing, particularly since one of Cornwallis'
subordinates had been defeated in a battle at King's Mountain,
South Carolina, and Cornwallis had been obliged to fall back to
Camden. Lafayette, on learning the good news, had sent an
account of it to Franklin[56] in the hope of counteracting any bad
effect on possible peace negotiations that previous discourage-
ments might have had. Having already written to Greene that
he would come with several of his best officers, he now determined to set out. But first he wished to cast a last nostalgic
glance upon New York island, which had been a source of so
much disappointment to him.

Noailles, Damas, Mauduit, and their companions had expected to go to Philadelphia with Chastellux but were easily
persuaded to accompany Lafayette instead. With a small party
of horse they cantered up to the North River to look at the
island and "to try if they could not tempt the enemy to favor
them with a few shots."[57] After having reconnoitered from
across the river as far north as Spuyten Duyvil, Lafayette confessed that he felt better than "when looking at those forts with
an hopefull eye."[58] Without receiving from an unaccommodat-
ing enemy the pleasure of being put under fire even once that
campaign, they went to Paramus for the night and the next day
set off for Morristown.[59]

[54] Thacher, pp. 286–87; cf. Welles to his father, December 4, 1780, Stiles, p. 470.

[55] Cf. Lafayette to Greene, November 10, 1780, loc. cit.

[56] November 19, 1780, Sparks MSS XLIX, pp. 245–47, which is copy no. 1. The
copy in APS, Franklin papers, Vol. XX, no. 75, is the quadruplicate and does not have
a postscript contained in copy no. 1.

[57] Chastellux, I, 145.

[58] Lafayette to Washington, November 28, 1780, Sparks MSS LXXXVII, p. 243.
The version in Mémoires ([Amer. ed.], pp. 365–66) is somewhat "Englished."

[59] This itinerary differs somewhat from Nolan, p. 141. It is based upon Lafayette
to Washington, November 28, 1780, loc. cit., and Lafayette to Hamilton, November
28, 1780, Works of Hamilton, I, 196.

There Lafayette met Washington again. The general urged him to go south only if news from Europe and the South were to indicate that he might be more useful there than in the North because no maritime supremacy could be expected until the spring.[60] Lafayette by this time was fairly certain that no naval reinforcements would be received before spring but was prepared to wait until he got to Philadelphia to make his final decision.

Meanwhile, another matter also disturbed the marquis. His friend Alexander Hamilton was unhappy with the little glory that fell to the lot of an aide-de-camp and hoped for a more responsible post. He had asked for a command in Lafayette's Light Division, but it had been dispersed without heed to his request. Now that an important post had been opened by the resignation of Colonel Alexander Scammel as adjutant-general, Hamilton hoped to be named in Scammel's place. He had appealed to Lafayette to use his celebrated influence with Washington on his behalf. Lafayette, who had lost none of his fine hand in recommending Frenchmen for promotions and rewards,[61] proved no less skilful in advocating his American friend's cause. Since Washington had consulted him on the matter, he had taken the liberty of writing to Washington from Paramus[62] designating Hamilton as "the officer whom I should like to see in that station."

That letter, unfortunately, did not reach the commander-in-chief in time. When the marquis caught up with him at Morristown, Washington had already offered the post to General Hand and had just sent a letter of nomination to Congress.

[60] Cf. Washington to Lafayette, Dec. 8, 1780, Fitzpatrick, XX, 439.

[61] Cf. Lafayette to Vergennes, November 2, 1780, Stevens, *Facsimiles*, XVII, no. 1630, and February 4, 1781, *ibid.*, no. 1634; Washington to Congress, November 1, 1780, Fitzpatrick, XX, 275–76; Lafayette to Sigonier [Segond de Sederon], October 30, 1780, Arna-Janvier catalogue, sale of June 28, 1937, item no. 59; Lafayette to Maurepas, November 2, 1780, AAE, corr. pol., É.–U., Vol. XIV, fol. 207.

[62] Lafayette to Washington, November 28, 1780, *loc. cit;* cf. Lafayette to Hamilton, November 28, 1780, *loc. cit.;* also J. C. Hamilton, *History of the republic of the United States of America* (7 vols.; 3d ed.; Philadelphia, 1868), II, 141–42; and Hamilton to Washington, November 22, 1780, J. C. Hamilton, *Life of Alexander Hamilton* (2 vols.; New York, 1840), I, 318.

Lafayette was all for sending a courier to overtake the messenger and bring him back, but Washington considered that unbecoming. The young general, already fearful that he had perhaps been warmer than either Washington or Hamilton himself would have liked, had to be satisfied with a promise to oblige his friend on some future occasion.[63]

From Morristown, Lafayette and his companions went to Trenton, New Jersey, and finally arrived in Philadelphia on December 1.[64] The first lap of the journey toward General Greene's army and the war in the South was finished. The young men were themselves undecided whether they would ever start on the remaining laps.

BIBLIOGRAPHICAL NOTES

This is perhaps the place to caution the reader once more regarding Lafayette's English (cf. Gottschalk, *Lafayette joins the American army*, pp. xii and 103). He had by this time acquired a more ready command of his adopted country's tongue and wrote it with fewer errors than in previous years. It was, nevertheless, far from perfect as yet. Wherever in the quotations in this volume his English grammar seems correct, the explanation is either that some editor has "doctored" the original text or that it is a translation from the French.

The Dublin (1787) translation of Chastellux's *Voyages* has been used in this and the next chapter. That translation was made by one [George Grieve] who described himself as "an English gentleman who resided in America at that period." This edition is preferable to the earlier French ones because of the numerous helpful notes that the translator has appended.

[63] Lafayette to Hamilton, December 9, 1780, LC, Hamilton papers; also in *Works of Hamilton*, I, 199–200, where, however, some omissions occur.

[64] This itinerary differs somewhat from Nolan, pp. 141–42, but cf. Rendon to Galvez, December 3, 1780, LC, Cunningham transcripts, no. 141, pp. 162–63.

CHAPTER VIII

Signals of Distress

THERE was much to do in Philadelphia. Chastellux, Noailles, and the marquis' other companions wished to see the city's sights, and Philadelphia society wished to fete them in a manner becoming their station. After long months of camp life Lafayette gladly played his part in teas, parties, and receptions in his friends' honor.[1] Then there were members of Congress to cajole into finding food for the army and adopting sensible plans for the next campaign. To his old friends, La Luzerne and Barbé-Marbois of the French embassy, he now added Señor Francisco Rendon, who, without formal title (since Spain had not yet recognized the independence of the United States), represented His Most Catholic Majesty at Philadelphia. Lafayette, who had at first been the guest of La Luzerne, joined Damas and Noailles at Rendon's house after a few days.[2] In fact, Rendon became an object of great attention, because the marquis had learned most confidentially from La Luzerne that the Spanish were contemplating an attack upon Florida. Perhaps they could be induced to take a force of Continentals to attack Charleston at the same time, the resilient young man suggested. Or perhaps they might, after landing in Florida, send a contingent northward to threaten Georgia. To that end he immediately submitted for Washington's approval

[1] Chastellux, I, 226–27; Margaret Armstrong, *Five generations: life and letters of an American family, 1750–1900* (New York, 1930), p. 7.

[2] Rendon to Navarro, December 10, 1780, LC, Cunningham transcripts, no. 135, pp. 120–23.

copies of letters which he proposed to send to the Spanish and French commanders in the West Indies.[3]

That done, Lafayette, feeling he was again on the eve of glorious labor, attended a party at the home of Theodorick Bland, a member of Congress. The next day Lafayette, Mauduit, and Gimat, who had fought in the Battle of Brandy-wine, went with Chastellux, Noailles, Damas, Montesquieu, and Lynch for a tour of that battlefield, thirty miles from Philadelphia.[4] Lieutenant-Colonel Presley Neville, one of Lafayette's aides, who had been captured by the English and released on parole, also accompanied them.[5] Lafayette had not seen the field since he had received his baptism of fire there over three years earlier and, wounded, had been taken care of by Gimat, who was then his aide. Benjamin Ring, the Quaker with whom Lafayette had made his quarters before the battle, was glad to see him again and to accommodate him and some of his friends for the night (the nearest inn not having room enough for all of them). In the morning they united to go over the field once more, guided by a major who lived in the neighborhood and, having fought in the battle himself, knew the ground well.

On the way back, Chastellux, Noailles, and Lafayette separated from the rest. The topic of conversation changed from war to the society of Paris, which they all loved, and the friends they had in common. "This transition was truly French," Chastellux remarked,[6] "but it does not prove that we are less fond of war than other nations, only that we like our friends better." That evening they had a good dinner at Mrs. Withy's inn at Chester. "The people of the house, who saw in this company merely two general officers, one French and the other American, accompanied by their *families*, and not a society of friends joyous to meet together in another hemisphere, could not con-

[3] December 4, 1780, *Mémoires* (Amer. ed.), p. 486; and two letters of December 5, 1780, *ibid.*, pp. 367–70 and 487–88.

[4] Chastellux, I, 234–38.

[5] Cf. Lafayette to Washington, December 9, 1780, Sparks MSS LXXXVII, pp. 259–61; Washington to Lafayette, December 14, 1780, Fitzpatrick, XX, 475.

[6] I, 249.

ceive how it was possible to be so gay without being drunk," Chastellux recorded,[7] "and looked upon us as people descended from the moon."

The next day, in barges sent by the president of Congress, the society of joyous friends went to visit the fortifications on the Delaware River. At Fort Mifflin they saw an excellent military engineering project in process of completion, and at Redbank they were badly received by a Quaker whose barn Mauduit-Duplessis had knocked down in a battle he had fought there in 1777. Finally, after three days' absence, they returned to Philadelphia and a dinner at the home of Samuel Huntington, president of Congress, where Chastellux was surprised to find Mrs. Huntington waiting upon her guests.[8] After dinner Chastellux went off to talk political philosophy with Mr. Samuel Adams; Noailles and Damas to dance at the French embassy with two pretty young Americans;[9] and Lafayette, who cared little for either political philosophy or dancing, presumably to his room at Rendon's house.

The few days of tramping around historic scenes in the neighborhood of Philadelphia had brought no news that made it possible for Lafayette to decide definitely in favor of going south. "I am more than ever puzzled, my dear General, to know what to do," he informed Washington. ". . . . I see that the people in whom you confide the most are a great part for the present far from you. I also candidly confess that private affection for you makes me hate the idea of leaving the man I love the most in the world to seek for uncertainties, at a period when he may want me. On the other hand . . . . there is a possibility of being useful, and the love of glory spurs me on."[10] And so he remained in Philadelphia, torn between the loyalty that bade him return northward and the thirst for fame which drew him to the south.

Meanwhile, Congress had voted to send a representative to France to support the pleas of the Vicomte de Rochambeau for more money, troops, and men-of-war. Lafayette thought imme-

7 *Ibid.*, pp. 251–52.

8 *Ibid.*, pp. 249–50 and 252–68.

9 *Ibid.*, p. 277.   10 Lafayette to Washington, December 9, 1780, *loc. cit.*

diately of his friend Alexander Hamilton as the most proper envoy and wrote to him to be prepared to leave his "amorous occupations" (Hamilton had recently returned to his bride) and set out for Europe. He explained at length his own indecision about going south: "I don't know what to do. The General . . . . is going to be alone. You know how tenderly I love him, and I don't like the idea of abandonning him. . . . . But I don't like to lay still and if I think that, upon the whole, I may be useful I shall go. . . . . Some few days will determine me."[11]

Those few days were spent in further jaunts among the battlefields of Philadelphia and further festivities.[12] With Chastellux, Noailles, and Damas, Lafayette first visited Germantown and the old camp at Whitemarsh. That was followed by dinner at La Luzerne's and tea at Miss Shippen's (Mrs. Arnold's patriotic cousin), where Noailles played the violin and the others danced. After another night's rest they visited Barren Hill, where Lafayette had distinguished himself in 1778 by skilfully extricating his army from a trap. Excitement at dinner at La Luzerne's that evening was enhanced by the arrival of two other notable Frenchmen, the Comte de Custine and the Marquis de Laval-Montmorency. There were also visits with other celebrities.

Lafayette heard and talked more political theory in a few days in Chastellux's company than at any other period in his life. It was a rare intellectual treat to take part in the conversation of Chastellux, the author of *De la félicité publique*, with Thomas Paine, the author of *Common sense*, or James Wilson, the author of the address *To the inhabitants of the United States*.[13] To crown Lafayette's rather sudden rise to philosophical distinction came a signal honor. The American Philosophical Society proposed to elect him a foreign member, the annual elections falling just at the time that the eminent French aristocrats were visiting the city. Chastellux's nomination was unanimous, a rare honor befitting the greatest French literary

[11] December 9, 1780, LC, Hamilton papers. A truncated version of this letter is to be found in *Works of Hamilton*, I, 199–200.

[12] Chastellux, I, 290–305.   [13] *Ibid.*, pp. 304–16.

figure yet to have visited Philadelphia. What was considerably more surprising, however, was that Lafayette, whose literary efforts had so far been entirely epistolary, was also nominated—and formally elected a few weeks later, when he was no longer in Philadelphia. There was but a single blackball against him, and that one, Chastellux was told, only by accident.[14] Lafayette thus became a member of the leading literary and philosophical society of the United States—one which Chastellux looked upon (not without reason) as the academy of the state of Pennsylvania. On the eve of Chastellux's initial attendance at the American Philosophical Society, Lafayette went to a dinner in his honor at the home of the French consul, John Holker, at which the Chevalier de La Luzerne and other French gentlemen foregathered. The next day Chastellux left Philadelphia to visit Washington again and to return to his post in Rhode Island.[15]

Lafayette stayed in Philadelphia. He had finally decided not to join Greene. While at Chester, touring the battlefields of Pennsylvania, he had learned of the appointment of his old friend the Marquis de Castries in the place of the Comte de Sartine as minister of marine. That led him to hope for more vigor in that department than heretofore.[16] Moreover, it began now to look as if he would again be needed as a liaison officer.[17] He and La Luzerne had been working hard on behalf of the scheme to bring about a Spanish diversion. The French envoy had not only written to Washington, pleading with him to consider co-operation in the South with the Spanish, he had also gone with Lafayette to see Rendon. Together they prevailed upon the Spanish "minister" to urge such co-operation upon the ranking Spanish officials of the Western Hemisphere.[18] Lafa-

---

[14] *Ibid.*, p. 318; APS, "Early proceedings of the American Philosophical Society, transcript of minutes," p. 110; J. B. Nolan, "Lafayette and the American Philosophical Society," *Proceedings of the American Philosophical Society*, LXIII (1934), 118-19.

[15] Chastellux, I, 318-23.

[16] Lafayette to Washington, December 9, 1780, *loc. cit.*; Lafayette to Hamilton, December 9, 1780, *loc. cit.*

[17] Lafayette to Washington, December 16, 1780, *Mémoires* (Amer. ed.), pp. 488-89.

[18] Rendon to Navarro, December 15, 1780, LC, Cunningham transcripts, no. 136, pp. 123-26; cf. Washington to La Luzerne, December 14, 1780, Fitzpatrick, XX, 476-77.

yette hoped that the appeal of La Luzerne, reinforced by his own persuasions, would also induce Washington to sound out the French at Newport. In that event he might become more useful in the negotiations between Washington and Rochambeau than as a lieutenant of General Greene.[19] La Luzerne, Rendon, and Lafayette thus took several steps that would have been difficult to retrace even before they learned what Washington might think of their proposal.

The usual slowness of communication between distant points was now enhanced by the absolute poverty of the military treasury. The regular post had become Washington's only means of communication. The chain of couriers that had been established during the summer could no longer be maintained; there was not enough money in the whole army, Washington complained, to bear the expense of an express.[20] A letter which Washington had written to Lafayette on December 8[21] reached him only a week later. Washington seemed to imply in that letter that he opposed Lafayette's joining Greene only for the winter, "as it may contravene a permanent arrangement [in the southern army] to the disgust of those who considering themselves as belonging to the army may be hurt at disappointments." Nevertheless, if in Lafayette's judgment there was to be no action in the North, "your seeking service to the southward where there is a more fruitful field for enterprize is not only an evidence of your zeal but will be supported by every rule of military reasoning: hence it is, I again repeat, that circumstances should alone decide." To make Lafayette's welcome in the South doubly sure he wrote to Greene,[22] urging him to give Lafayette "a temporary command in your army worthy of his acceptance," and "to sundry gentlemen in Virginia,"[23] recommending the marquis and his companions Noailles and Damas

[19] Lafayette to Washington, December 16, 1780, *Mémoires* (Amer. ed.), pp. 488-89.

[20] Washington to Lafayette, December 14, 1780, Fitzpatrick, XX, 473; and Washington to La Luzerne, December 14, 1780, *ibid.*, p. 477.

[21] *Ibid.*, pp. 439-40.

[22] December 8, 1780, *ibid.*, p. 438.   [23] December 8, 1780, *ibid.*, p. 440.

as gentlemen of family, rank, and fortune as well as devotees of the American cause.

By the time Lafayette learned of those letters, he had decided not to go south. He, nevertheless, thanked his chief[24] for the confidence shown in leaving the decision entirely to him. "I am so happy in your friendship that every mark of your affection for me gives me a degree of pleasure which far surpasses all expressions." And Washington's sentiments in turn were no less candid: "It is unnecessary, I trust, on my part to give assurances of mutual regard, because I hope you are convinced of it."[25]

In one respect, however, the American commander believed Lafayette's judgment to have been at fault. He did not fully agree with the French minister and his "dear Marquis" that the projected co-operation with Spain was feasible. He had come away from his conference at Hartford with the distinct impression that his control of the French auxiliary force was more nominal than real. Until Rochambeau and Ternay agreed to such a joint enterprise, he considered it "impoliticly fruitless in me to propose any measure of cooperation to a third power."[26] Nevertheless, he did submit an outline of the plan to Rochambeau, who proved just as cautious as ever; and the Chevalier Destouches, Ternay's senior captain and successor, was no more daring than Ternay had been.[27]

So that venture, like many other creations of Lafayette's mercurial brain, passed into the limbo of pious hopes. Once more he had to content himself with an exhortation to Vergennes[28] to hasten the expedition of shoes, ships, sealing wax, and louis d'ors. Just a few days earlier Vergennes had written to him[29] (in a letter that perhaps he never received), urging him to be somewhat less audacious: "In your first campaigns your reputation was still to be made. You had to take risks in order to ac-

[24] December 16, 1780, *loc. cit.*, p. 488.

[25] December 14, 1780, *loc. cit.*, p. 474.

[26] *Ibid.*   [27] *Ibid.*, p. 481, n. 19.

[28] December 16, 1780, Stevens, *Facsimiles*, XVII, no. 1631.

[29] December 1, 1780, Sparks MSS XLIX, Vol. III, fols. 196–97.

quire one. Now it is made, and your valor will pass for imprudence if you expose yourself unnecessarily." Washington, when he learned of Lafayette's decision not to join Greene, approved,[30] though only by implication. Greene, too, soon wrote in a fashion which Lafayette guessed was to discourage his leaving for the South.[31]

Having at last decided to return to headquarters, Lafayette planned to go with an old companion. Congress had finally designated not Alexander Hamilton, as Lafayette had originally wished, but Colonel John Laurens as special minister to France to plead with His Most Christian Majesty for more vigorous support. Laurens was instructed to confer not only with Lafayette but also with Washington, Rochambeau, and Destouches before sailing to fulfil his mission. Lafayette arranged to travel with Laurens to the commander-in-chief's quarters, now at New Windsor, New York.[32]

The journey nearly ended in imprisonment for both of Washington's brilliant young friends. The new year of 1781 began with ominous rumblings. Soldiers who could remember the miserable winter at Valley Forge in 1777–78 and the even worse one at Morristown in 1779–80 looked to the current winter with foreboding. Money was gone and provisions were disappearing, pay had been in arrears for a year or more, and disputes arose between men and officers regarding terms of enlistment. Everyone who knew the privations that the American soldier had been asked to suffer (Lafayette as much as any other) had admitted their patience. But at last it came to an end.

Mutiny broke out first in the Pennsylvania line, commanded by Brigadier-General Anthony Wayne. On New Year's Day they revolted and shot some of their officers. Organized under their noncommissioned officers, they immediately determined to march to Philadelphia and put their grievances before Congress

[30] Washington to Lafayette, December 16, 1780 Fitzpatrick, XXI, 17–19.

[31] Greene to Lafayette, December 29, 1780, Johnson, I, 340. Cf. Lafayette to McHenry, February 15, 1781, B. C. Steiner, *Life and correspondence of James McHenry* (Cleveland, 1907), pp. 32–35; the original is in the Huntington Library, MH 156.

[32] Lafayette to Washington, December 26, 1780, Sparks MSS LXXXVII, pp. 270–71; cf. *Journals of Congress*, XVIII, 1138, 1141, 1178, 1184, and 1187.

and the government of the state of Pennsylvania. Unable to control them, General Wayne and Colonels Butler and Stewart nevertheless went along with them (more as prisoners than commanders) in the hope of keeping them from violence as they went. They stopped at Princeton, halfway between the enemy at New York and Congress at Philadelphia. They immediately made it clear that, if an attempt were made to send force against them, they would desert to the enemy. A committee of Congress was appointed to investigate. President Joseph Reed of Pennsylvania also undertook to negotiate with the mutineers. Both the committee and President Reed requested General St. Clair, who was then in Philadelphia, to proceed to New Jersey and endeavor to curb the revolt. Knowing Lafayette's popularity with the rank and file of the army, the committee also requested him to stop in New Jersey on his way to headquarters and to use his influence in making peace.[33]

Without having waited for Laurens, the two major-generals arrived in Trenton on January 3.[34] They learned that the mutineers had already made demands which Wayne considered extravagant. They spoke to President Reed, Lord Stirling, and Major Charles Stewart, all of whom had had some dealings with the mutineers. Lord Stirling had tried to parley with the men but had been warned on peril of his life not to come within their lines. St. Clair and Lafayette, nevertheless, decided to run that risk.[35] Major Stewart, who had listened to some of the com-

---

[33] The *Mémoires* (I, 265) state that Lafayette was asked to go by both Reed and Congress; but cf. Lafayette to Washington, January 7, 1781, Sparks MSS LXXXIV, p. 35, and Lafayette to Sullivan, January 7, 1781, O. G. Hammond (ed.), *Letters and papers of Major-General John Sullivan* ("Collections of the New Hampshire Historical Society," Vols. XIII–XV [3 vols.; Concord, N.H., 1930–39]), III, 252. The contemporary letters make clear that Lafayette was asked to go only by the committee of Congress but that St. Clair was asked by both the committee and President Reed. It would appear that St. Clair was expected to play the major role.

[34] St. Clair to Reed, January 4, 1781, W. H. Smith (ed.), *Life and public services of Arthur St. Clair* (2 vols.; Cincinnati, 1882), I, 532.

[35] Lafayette to Washington, January 7, 1781, *loc. cit.*; Lafayette to Sullivan, January 7, 1781, *loc. cit.*; Lafayette to La Luzerne, January 4 and 7, 1781, *AHR*, XX (1915), 578–81; Stewart to Reed, January 4, 1781, *Pennsylvania archives*, 1st ser., VIII (1853), 698–99; St. Clair to Reed, January 7, 1781, *ibid.*, p. 701; St. Clair to Washington, January 7, 1781, Smith, *St. Clair*, I, 533–34. Cf. J. B. Linn (ed.), "Diary of the

plaints, declared that Lafayette was almost the only general they liked (though even he, they thought, was too severe a disciplinarian). The marquis felt that the situation was far from hopeless. Fearful of the effect that the mutiny might have in France, he wrote to beg La Luzerne not to let it be known abroad.[36] The Pennsylvania line, he explained (though not with complete statistical accuracy), was unlike the other regiments. It was made up of foreign-born citizens, and there was no need to feel concern that the mutiny might spread.

The next day St. Clair and Lafayette went to see the mutineers. At first they were well received. Outside Princeton they met some noncommissioned officers and soldiers. What was all the trouble about, they asked. The soldiers answered with such obvious embarrassment that the two generals felt encouraged. They went on to the camp. Challenged by the sentry, they were conducted to the Committee of Sergeants, which had taken command. Quite respectfully the committee showed them the correspondence between themselves and Wayne. They were then permitted to go to Wayne's quarters and there interview several of the chosen leaders among the soldiers.

Just as it was beginning to appear that a peaceful arrangement could be made, Lafayette and St. Clair were asked by the Committee of Sergeants to leave town. They had been joined by Colonel Thomas Proctor, of the Pennsylvania artillery, and shortly afterward by Colonel Laurens. The soldiers became uneasy upon seeing so many officers in Princeton and suspected some trick. Lafayette and his companions were warned that there might be "evil consequences"[37] if they did not leave. When they demurred, another messenger was sent, giving them an hour and a half to get out. Fearing that the mutineers might hold them as hostages,[38] they concluded that it would be wise to

---

revolt in the Pennsylvania line, January 1781," *Pennsylvania archives*, 2d ser., XI (1896), 657–706, and C. J. Stillé, *Major-General Anthony Wayne and the Pennsylvania line in the Continental Army* (Philadelphia, 1893), pp. 241–62.

[36] January 4, 1781, *loc. cit.*, p. 579.

[37] Quoted by Lafayette in letter to La Luzerne, January 7, 1781, *loc. cit.*, p. 580.

[38] Cf. St. Clair to Reed, January 7, 1781, *loc. cit.*

withdraw. They went to Morristown. On their way they met some soldiers whom the marquis persuaded to return to winter quarters.[39]

Lafayette took stock of the situation upon his arrival in Morristown. The committee organization that the mutineers adopted made it impossible to appeal to them as a group, and their careful military discipline would make it impossible to divide them. Moreover, Lafayette was himself easily convinced that their grievances were real and deserved friendly consideration. The only chance he saw of appeasing them was to appeal to the honor of the best of them. That meant Colonel Stewart's battalion, which was made up of select men and had served in Lafayette's Light Division. Some of the soldiers, he reported to La Luzerne,[40] had assured him that they were willing to follow wherever he should lead and to die under his orders, "but that I did not know what they had gone through; that they would get justice from their country. . . . ." Since direct appeal to the men seemed impossible, he addressed Colonel Stewart, apparently hoping that the colonel might have a chance to deliver his message. "Whatever has been said by some on this occasion," he wrote, "I cannot yet believe that the soldiers of your line and particularly those of the Light Infantry have forgot theyr sentiments for one whom they must know to be theyr friend. However dissatisfied I may be with theyr present mode of conduct which makes me more unhappy than any thing I have experienced I shall still try to render them service if it comes within the reach of my power."[41] He appealed to their devotion to the commander-in-chief. Having been mistakenly informed that Washington was coming, he announced: "General Washington is expected here at any minute. What he must feel you will eazely guess. I am sure he will be dispos'd to do any thing that may prove serviceable to the soldiers. But they ought to be sensible of his dispositions and therefore apply to him through your mediation."

[39] Lafayette to La Luzerne, January 7, 1781, *loc. cit.*, p. 581.   [40] *Ibid.*

[41] January 7, 1781, collection of Sidney P. Hessel, Woodmere, N.Y.

Lafayette did not wait to learn what happened at Princeton, or even to fathom the grumblings he heard also in the New Jersey line at Pompton.[42] Laurens had to hasten on to headquarters, and the young major-general, feeling there was little he could do that St. Clair and Wayne could not do,[43] went on with him. They and their companions arrived at New Windsor on January 11.[44]

Conversation with the commander-in-chief soon made clearer what Lafayette already knew—that the situation was desperate. His letters to Vergennes had said just that so often that he feared a repetition would only seem like exaggeration. He turned again to La Luzerne. "We must hope that your voice will appear more impartial" he wrote.[45] Even if France had the odious policy which the Tories had the impudence to attribute to her ("and which the inaction of the past campaigns would seem to confirm," he confessed), it was now time to give effective aid if the advantages of the American Revolution were not to be lost. Who could blame the Pennsylvania line if they mutinied? "When I think that the great majority of the soldiers are misled by a few leaders, that these brave men have suffered with us for four years, have been wounded with us, have shared our triumphs and our misfortune, that they have reason to complain not only of their prolonged misery but also of manifest trickery in their enlistments, I assure you that the necessity of suppressing them seems to me pretty unfortunate." He still feared the effect that the mutiny would have on Rhode Island and in Europe. "But if their troops had suffered for four years as ours have, if for fifteen months they had received not a single sou of their pay, if they had been given neither clothes nor food, if they had been kept in service a year longer than their enlistments stipulated, it is likely that they would not have waited until the thirteenth month to say that it is unjust to keep them any

[42] Lafayette to La Luzerne, January 7, 1781, *loc. cit.*

[43] *Ibid.*, and Lafayette to Stewart, January 7, 1781, *loc. cit.*

[44] Washington to Heath, January 12, 1781, Fitzpatrick, XXI, 90. This itinerary differs from Nolan, p. 150.

[45] January 14, 1781, *AHR*, XX (1915), 582–83.

longer." Nevertheless, he thought that the Pennsylvania line must now be disbanded and re-enlisted by the state of Pennsylvania, "whose bad faith toward some of its soldiers had caused all this disturbance."

To make matters worse, Washington was undecided whether to move against the mutineers. He had at one time considered advancing from the Hudson with enough men to quell the mutiny. In the end, however, he had concluded that he could neither run the risk of stripping West Point of its defenders nor trust his own forces to fire upon comrades whom they knew to be victims of the very neglect which they themselves were experiencing. So he left it to Wayne, St. Clair, and President Reed to handle the situation as well as they could, determined to move only in the last extremity.[46]

Largely because Sir Henry Clinton overplayed his hand and tried to win the mutineers to the British side by a show of force and a promise of all that Congress had so far refused them, the mutiny was on the whole amicably settled by Wayne shortly after Lafayette reached New Windsor. The men received some clothing, back pay, and redress of grievances. Two of Clinton's emissaries were hanged. Lafayette, more American than most Americans, continued to maintain that a goodly part of the trouble was due to English agents, who had found willing ears because the ranks were "almost all composed of foreigners."[47]

For a brief period Washington and Lafayette were permitted to forget mutiny in the excitement of entertaining new visitors from Rhode Island. Lafayette found Comte Guillaume de Deux-Ponts at headquarters when he arrived. He and Deux-Ponts visited General Heath on January 13.[48] A few days later they were joined by Comte Mathieu Dumas (sent by Rochambeau to request Washington to honor him with a visit to Newport) and still later by Comte de Charlus and Comte Robert Dillon on their way to Philadelphia.[49] Another reunion of Paris society was celebrated in the wilderness. Lafayette wrote

---

[46] *Ibid.*, p. 582.

[47] *Ibid.*   [48] *Heath's memoirs*, p. 285.

[49] Washington to Rochambeau, January 20, 1781, Fitzpatrick, XXI, 120–21.

proudly to the Prince de Poix[50] about his friends in America:
"Without wanting to be vain about it, I can not help acknowledging that this society is the most amiable, as well as the most
respectable, that was ever formed." After having been reduced
to one aide at various times, Washington now had Lafayette,
Laurens, and Hamilton to help him entertain his guests. On
January 19 they were all together. Though their fare was plain
and the outlook far from cheerful, few more distinguished gath-
erings had ever sat down to dinner. Dumas remembered particularly, long afterward, the "marks of affection" which Washington showed to Lafayette. "Seated opposite him he looked at
him with pleasure and listened to him with manifest interest."[51]

The serenity of the reunion was short lived. News came on
January 21 that the New Jersey line, the early grumblings of
which Lafayette had heard when he was at Morristown, had
followed the example of the Pennsylvania line and risen in mutiny. Washington determined to deal with this sedition in a
sterner fashion. Nevertheless, he did not postpone a jaunt
which had been planned for the next day. He had business at
West Point and permitted his visitors to accompany him. The
inspection of fortifications and troops fatigued them, and Washington decided that they would not return by horseback but
would take a barge. That was an error, for the wind was strong,
the river filled with ice, the palisaded banks offering no welcome
spot to land. It soon began to snow and to grow dark. The boat
filled with water. The master of the barge was obviously
alarmed. Washington took the helm from him. "It is my duty
to be at the helm," Dumas afterward remembered him to have
said.[52] They finally made a landing, and after another few miles
of trudging, reached New Windsor and Washington's house.

Preparations against the mutineers of the New Jersey line
now went forward. A large part of the unit had refused to join
the revolt. Washington proceeded with severity against the
others. He ordered General Robert Howe to attack the insur-

---

[50] January 30, 1781, private collection.

[51] Dumas, I, 35; cf. Lafayette to Rochambeau, January 20, 1781, *loc. cit.*

[52] Dumas, I, 35–36; cf. *Heath's memoirs*, p. 286.

gents. The outbreak was suppressed by force, and the ring-
leaders executed. On January 29, Washington was able to inform Rochambeau "that the spirit of mutiny is now completely
subdued and will not again show itself."[53]

Lafayette had had little to do with the suppression of the New
Jersey line. Out of fear that the English might make another
effort to aid the mutineers, Washington had gone to Ringwood,
New Jersey, prepared for whatever action might be necessary.
He traveled on horses that were "scarcely able to stand" because they had not had "a mouthful of long or short forage for
three days" and had "eaten up their mangers."[54] Lafayette,
Charlus, and Dillon went with him. As events developed, they
were not called upon to take any action.[55] Washington and Lafayette soon returned to New Windsor, while Charlus and Dillon
went on to Philadelphia, and Dumas made ready to return to
Newport. Thus, by a mixed policy of force and compromise,
sedition was kept from spreading further. The army somehow
held together for the next campaign, though Washington quite
often now used discouraged language, forecasting "the utter
ruin of our cause."[56]

Throughout both mutinies Lafayette's feelings had been the
confused reactions of one who was both a humanitarian and a
military disciplinarian. He felt that the soldiers had been mis-
treated and, if civilians, would have been justified in protesting
vigorously. Yet mutiny in an army at war was unforgivable and
must bear some sort of exemplary penalty. He disapproved of
the generous way in which the Pennsylvania line had been
treated and blamed such unmilitary leniency upon the intervention of the civil authorities.[57] The manner in which, by military
action alone, the mutiny in the New Jersey line had been
crushed, won his unqualified approval.[58] He thus still showed
himself more soldier than humanitarian.

[53] Fitzpatrick, XXI, 151.

[54] Washington to Pickering, January 25, 1781, *ibid.*, p. 141.

[55] Lafayette to La Luzerne, January 26, 1781, *AHR*, XX (1915), 584–85.

[56] Fitzpatrick, XXI, 130, n. 1.

[57] Lafayette to La Luzerne, January 14, 1781, *loc. cit.*, p. 582.

[58] Lafayette to La Luzerne, February 2, 1781, *AHR*, XX (1915), 585.

There now seemed only one way open to prevent the "utter ruin" which Washington feared. That was help from France. No news had come from France since December, but that had held forth a little hope.[59] The Vicomte de Rochambeau must have arrived, meanwhile, and delivered the petitions which he carried. The last desperate chance seemed to be to reinforce his arguments from the American side by one who had witnessed the struggle and exhaustion of the United States from the beginning. That was Laurens, who had all the advantages that Lafayette could have claimed for Hamilton—youth, intelligence, tact, the ability to speak French, the friendship of the commander-in-chief—and a greater prestige as the son of Henry Laurens, former president of Congress and now a prisoner in the Tower of London. Washington had given him a memorandum regarding the needs of the American army and the pleas he was to make.[60] The general frankly confessed that the treasury was exhausted, the army disaffected, the population hesitant. Yet he felt that, adequately supported, the people would rally again. "A large majority," he concluded, "are still firmly attached to the independence of these states, abhor a reunion with Great Britain, and are affectionate to the alliance with France, but this disposition cannot supply the place of means customary and essential in war, nor can we rely on its duration amidst the perplexities, oppression and misfortunes that attend the want of them." In accordance with the instructions of Congress, Laurens soon went to Rhode Island to consult Rochambeau and Destouches likewise.

Shortly afterward, Washington decided that the time had come to accept Rochambeau's invitation to Newport. Lafayette expected to go to him.[61] Since there would be little time to write long dispatches during the ceremonies and reviews that would undoubtedly be staged at Newport, he spent a good part of the intervening period in writing letters to be forwarded to Laurens. They were intended to smooth the colonel's way in

[59] See above, p. 164.

[60] January 15, 1781, Fitzpatrick, XXI, 105–10.

[61] Lafayette to Stewart, January 30, 1781, Hessel collection; Lafayette to La Luzerne, February 2, 1781, *loc. cit.*, p. 586.

France. The members of the American Philosophical Society would have been proud of Lafayette's literary activity in the next few days. One letter alone ran to eleven long pages of eloquent manuscript, and there were three others only somewhat shorter, to say nothing of several that were merely two or three pages in length. After spending the whole of one day at his desk, he apologized for his handwriting to the Prince de Poix, to whom he was writing the last of three long letters penned that day. "It is beginning to be time to say my prayers, my friend," he explained, "for it is so late that my light is almost gone and my hand worn out with scribbling."[62] Nevertheless, he kept at it until he had written to some of the most important ministers, to many of his friends, and to several members of his family. All of them, whether Lafayette's letters were in light friendly mood or in formal official language, were asked to help Colonel Laurens to fulfil his mission.

The first of these many epistles was to the new minister of marine, the Marquis de Castries.[63] Since Lafayette had long known him well, he was able once more to resort to his old trick of separating the official personage from the personal friend. He presented Laurens to Castries "not only as the king's minister but more especially as I would have presented him to you before your nomination." He went on at considerable length to make clear how he felt about the petition which Laurens was to present. His opinion, he said, was "in exact agreement with that of M^r de La Luzerne and Mr de Marbois and particularly with that of General Washington."

The greatest need, Lafayette declared, was for money. "Our Continental soldiers are excellent; our recruits are almost all men who have had more experience with gunfire than three quarters of the soldiers of Europe; our regular troops, as brave as any others, are more hardened, more patient, more acclimated. . . . . Immense sums would be necessary to bring the same number of Frenchmen to the various regions of America, and they would cost very much more to maintain." It was

[62] January 30, 1781, *loc. cit.*
[63] January 30, 1781, AN, Marine B⁴ 192, fols. 163–68.

money rather than men that was needed. "The miracle of a campaign fought without a shilling can not be repeated another year. The methods which we are obliged to use are entirely opposed to republican principles. The discontent which recently burst forth among some troops proved that human patience has its limits. . . . . We have reached the point where our plan to aid the American army by a loan has become not only politically important but, I repeat, absolutely necessary." He begged for clothing, too. "You will appreciate, Monsieur le Marquis, how humiliated officers and men, who often are richer than those of corresponding rank in the French army, must feel to appear before them in their nakedness. You know our fellow countrymen too, and appreciate that an army covered with rags inspires less respect in them. The American army has suffered so much that, in short, it is necessary to clothe them as well as to pay them."

Next to money and supplies the greatest need was for naval reinforcements. With naval superiority "we can do everything, without it we can do nothing—at least with certainty." British propaganda was making headway because nothing had happened in the last campaign. The Tories had spread the report that the French wished merely "to stir up the fire without putting it out." The emphatic promise of a vast French armada "without our receiving a single letter" had shaken American confidence. The next campaign must be decisive, and only naval preponderance would make it victorious.

Men were needed, too, but not so much as money, supplies, and ships. Rochambeau, Lafayette said, seemed to believe that the greatest need was for well-trained French troops. Lafayette admitted that he had himself been the first to suggest sending a large body of Frenchmen to America, but, if sending more men resulted in diminishing the certainty of naval superiority or the amount of money to be sent, the resources of France would not be wisely distributed. "For the same sum we could have double the number of American regulars. . . . . In all the confidence of friendship, Monsieur le Marquis, and setting aside your title of king's minister, I shall say to you that Mr de Rochambeau is mistaken in the estimate that he has, or that is attributed to him, of the American soldier, whom incidentally he has never seen."

Lafayette's devotion led him to speak on a point which Washington would have found impossible and Laurens might have found difficult to broach. His personal relation to Castries made it proper for him to do what in the others would have been tactless. It would be highly desirable, he urged, to repeat to Rochambeau that he was expected to give the most implicit obedience to General Washington. He disapproved of the secret instructions that seemed to have been given to Rochambeau. They made necessary personal consultations between Washington and Rochambeau, and Washington's delicacy, "which it is easy to abuse," made him hesitant to give commands. "Everything ought to be under General Washington's orders alone. . . . . In accordance with the confidence with which you have so kindly honored me, I undertake to advise, definitely and with characteristic candor, that everything be left to the wisdom of the generalissimo in conformance only with those instructions of which I was the bearer." The same orders ought to be issued to the commander of the French fleet. "General Washington's talents, his knowledge of this country, his firmness, and his admirable prudence can not be questioned. He pushes delicacy to excess. He will be adored by the French army, and I think it necessary, for military as well as political reasons, to depend upon him alone without reservation." If his advice were followed, Lafayette promised that, even though Rochambeau seemed to believe New York as hard to take as some highly fortified European stronghold, its capture was certain and a decisive campaign assured.

The letter to Vergennes[64] was even longer than the one to Castries. Lafayette described it as "a big volume."[65] It, too, contained the requests which Lafayette had already made several times to Vergennes and had repeated in his letter to Castries —money and supplies, naval reinforcements, men—as well as a favorable reception for Laurens. It made the same complaints

[64] January 30, 1781, Stevens, *Facsimiles*, XVII, 1632.
[65] Lafayette to La Luzerne, February 2, 1781, *AHR*, XX (1915), 585.

(sometimes in nearly the same words): there had been too few letters from France; the promise of the second division had not been kept; Rochambeau was not sufficiently receptive of Washington's suggestions. It retold the praises of the American soldiers: "If anyone should be surprised, Monsieur le Comte, that it should be looked upon as a great effort to fill the army, I beg to observe that, since hunger, cold, nakedness, hard work, the certainty of receiving neither pay nor the necessary clothes and food are the prospect held out to an American soldier, it is not very inviting to citizens, most of whom live in a state of comfort at home." He again urged that Washington's command over Rochambeau's troops be made real: "The wisdom of the government in putting that corps under the orders of General Washington allows me only to repeat how important it is that his authority be complete and without any restrictions whatsoever. The talents, prudence, delicacy, and knowledge of the country, which are united in him to the highest degree of perfection, are qualities any one of which would have sufficed to assure that the instructions of which I was the bearer would be exactly followed; and the longer I stay here, the clearer it becomes that every article in them is equally important for harmony and the good of the public service." Lest anyone in France lose faith in the American cause because of the recent mutiny, he hastened to point out that the lines of Pennsylvania and New Jersey were made up mostly of foreigners; they had to suffer "extremities which would not be endured in any army"; they had refused to have dealings with the enemy; and many of them, though they had insisted on being discharged, would reenter among the new recruits. The loyalty of the troops that suppressed the rebellion of the New Jersey line was all the more striking because they too had suffered the hardships that had made the others revolt. "This proves, Monsieur le Comte, that human patience has its limits," he repeated, "but that citizen soldiers are much more patient than foreigners. However, we ought to draw from this yet another argument in favor of the necessity of sending money."

By the time he finished the letter to Vergennes, Lafayette had written more than thirty foolscap pages which had to be put into code, but he continued writing until he had letters to send by Laurens to Mme de Tessé, the Comtesse de Hunolstein, the Comtesse de Boufflers, the Princesse d'Hénin, and the Prince de Poix.[66] He complained to Poix that he had received no news recently: "Instead of swearing thirty times a day, my dear prince, even if I were to swear only once a month, my American and French vocabularies would be all used up since I began to feel distressed over this cursed silence of everyone who interests me." When he reflected that, but for Landais' strange behavior, Aglaé de Hunolstein's brother-in-law Vauban would have arrived on the "Alliance" with a packet of letters, he exclaimed, "Good lord, man, when will those letters that we want so much come to us? Unless the devil has turned fashionable and become an Anglomane like the jockeys in the Bois de Boulogne, it is impossible that the volumes I have overwhelmed you with have all been intercepted." Since this message to Poix was not to be put into cipher, he spoke little of politics. He did ask, however, that Poix introduce Laurens to the most influential people in court society. "See that he is well received, especially by the queen."

A sheaf of letters of such length and to such persons would have constituted a sufficient introduction for any envoy, even one on so vital an errand as Laurens. Lafayette did not rest content with them alone, however. After one day of rest he penned an additional note to Vergennes[67]—shorter but more personal in tone, intended to underline the points already made. On the same day he added one to Necker, "whom," he said, "it is not useless to convince of the absolute necessity of giving money to the Americans,"[68] and another to Franklin.[69] Fearful that Franklin might consider the appointment of Laurens as due to a lack of confidence in his own efforts at Versailles, he sought

[66] The letters to Mme de Tessé, the Comtesse de Hunolstein, the Comtesse de Boufflers, and the Princesse d'Hénin have not been found. They are mentioned in the letter to Poix, January 30, 1781, *loc. cit.*

[67] February 1, 1781, Stevens, *Facsimiles*, XVII, no. 1633.

[68] Quoted *ibid.* The letter itself has not been found.

[69] February 1, 1781, APS, Franklin papers, Vol. XXI, no. 45.

to smooth the way for Laurens even with his own countrymen in France. He explained that Laurens was a "flying minister," whose powers were limited to requests for military aid. "That you have enemies in Philadelphia both within and without doors," he tactfully declared, "is a thing to be expected in opposition to the numberless blessings of a popular government..... But I hope I need not mentionning to you that you have in Congress as well as every where many faithfull friends, and that the people at large have a due sense of theyr obligations to, and a proper affectionate respect for the name of Doctor Franklin." He also recalled the treatise upon English atrocities that he and Franklin had planned, suggesting that "the first volume" might go to press with the material that Franklin already had. "As the ennemy are working very fast on this hellish trade, I shall furnish you with further materials."

On the next day Lafayette exhorted La Luzerne to second his efforts.[70] Finally, he introduced Laurens affectionately to his Adrienne.[71] Laurens was, he said, "a man whom I am very fond of and with whom I want you to become intimately acquainted," since he was beloved by Washington and all Americans. "If I were in France, he would live with me and I would take him to the homes of my friends. .... I would give him every opportunity to meet people and to be agreeably received at Versailles." He asked her to do those things in his stead, to take the colonel to see her influential parents, uncles, and grandfather. "Treat him as a friend of the family." He told her also of the many friends who had come to visit them and how charmed they had been with General Washington. Now he expected to go with Washington to Newport, and, he confessed, he looked forward to that journey as a personal triumph. "When you recall what was thought in France of 'those poor rebels' when I went off to get myself hanged with them, and when you think of my tender affection for General Washington, you will understand how pleasant it will be for me to see him received there as the generalissimo of the joint armies of the two na-

[70] February, 2, 1781, *AHR*, XX (1915), 585–86.

[71] February 2, 1781, *Mémoires*, I, 404–9.

tions." Nor did he forget those words of affection for her and his children which were Adrienne's most cherished reward for her lonesomeness and devotion.

Somewhere in the course of his days of scrawling, Lafayette also wrote to the prime minister, the Comte de Ségur, the Duc d'Ayen, Admiral d'Estaing, the minister of war, and the Spanish ambassador at Versailles.[72] By the time his courier set out to deliver his packet to Laurens at Boston, he carried a portfolio of letters that would have opened almost every door worth trying in the French capital. Only if Lafayette had gone to France to represent America himself, as, indeed, some members of Congress had wished,[73] could he have more effectively exerted himself on behalf of his adopted country. Lafayette was none too hopeful that Laurens would succeed in getting the entire sum he was directed to seek. But he assured Laurens that he would find a great willingness to help.[74] "If they do but little, which I think would be a great folly, it will, I believe, be because they won't think themselves able to do better."

Laurens had left for Boston and France before Lafayette's letters were all ready. Eventually, his mission proved successful. Through his prayers, a further liberal loan was made to the United States. Again, as in the case of France's loan a year earlier, it would be difficult to say that the money would have been secured without Lafayette's intercession. And yet too much credit may easily be given to the French nobleman in this instance, for some (perhaps all) of his letters failed to reach Laurens before he sailed[75]—through no fault of either.

Having amply fulfilled his task as sponsor to the American

---

[72] These letters have not been found. They are known only from references to them in the letters that have survived, particularly in that to John Laurens, February 3, 1781, South Carolina Historical Society.

[73] Cf. J. W. Barnwell (ed.), "Letters of John Rutledge," *South Carolina historical and genealogical magazine*, XVIII (1917), 42.

[74] February 3, 1781, *loc. cit.*

[75] Cf. Laurens to Washington, March 24, 1781, Sparks, *Correspondence of the American Revolution*, III, 270; Washington to Laurens, April 9, 1781, Fitzpatrick, XXI, 436–37; Lafayette to Noailles, April 8, 1781, Patou, p. 39; Laurens to Congress, September 2, 1781, Wharton, IV, 685–92.

envoy extraordinary, Major-General Lafayette busily prepared for the conference of Rochambeau and Washington. In the midst of his preparations two incidents occurred which improved his education. The first indicated that Lafayette was becoming increasingly political-minded. He and Dr. McHenry had some months earlier debated whether there was greater liberty in England than in France. Lafayette had maintained that English institutions, despite appearances, were no more free than the French. In a letter to one of his numerous friends, Lafayette had continued that argument. He let Dr. McHenry see it, and the doctor asked for a copy. Lafayette let him have only a part of what he had written. That had been sometime in the fall of 1780, before McHenry went off to the South. From the South the doctor now asked for that part of the letter which he had not copied.[76]

By this time Lafayette had no copy of either part, and so he set forth his ideas in full again for McHenry's benefit.[77] He contended that the French parlements (law courts, of which, in his younger days Lafayette had made fun),[78] though like the English parliament chiefly in name, were a more effectual source of opposition to the royal authorities. They were able to express their opinions "more collectively and more freely." They also had two advantages which the British parliament did not have. They were located in remote provinces and thus became more representative of the people of their provinces and less open to "court influence and corruption"; and they constituted a separate class of the population, drawn usually from families of independent fortune but not from the court and therefore excluded from the army, the navy, and "almost every appointement which in England become means of corruption." Thus they had become a stern group. "They renounce the pleasures of dissipation, their very dress imposes upon them a sober way of living which still renders them more independent, while as a body they become formidable." Lafayette, to be sure, exaggerated the austerity of the French parlementary nobility, but that was unim-

---

[76] Cf. Lafayette to McHenry, February 15, 1781, *loc. cit.*

[77] *Ibid.*   [78] Cf. Gottschalk, *Lafayette comes to America*, pp. 44-45.

portant. What was of real significance was that his hostility to England had now led him to champion the superiority of French institutions. Perhaps his days with Chastellux and with Chastellux's aide Montesquieu, the grandson of the great president of the Bordeaux parlement, had played some part in his political education. It is significant, too, that he was still an apologist, a conservative, where France was concerned. Not only were French soldiers the best (though more costly than good Americans), but French institutions were likewise the best.

From praise of the French parlementary nobility, Lafayette passed to a consideration of French justice. He admitted that he would have preferred the jury system. "It might however be said that French judges must be more enlightened, more used to business, and more stranger to local little cabals." France also had a court of appeals—the Grand Council; and French ideas of justice were superior, requiring capital punishment less frequently and protecting personal liberty more thoroughly than the English. Moreover, the French government was more tolerant. "Tolerance is much commended in English writings, and no where less practiced than in that country." He pointed to the mistreatment of Dissenters and Catholics by the Church of England. "In France there is also a predominant religion, but persecution has long since vanished." He pointed to a special order created for distinguished Protestant army officers, to the high ranks Protestants held in the civil arm, to the large number of generals and soldiers who were Protestant, to the purchase of manors by Jews, to a church in Strasbourg which was used by both Protestants and Catholics, to the greater popular demand for tolerance in France.

Lafayette must have known that some of these arguments were weak. He stated with pride that the Protestant Necker, for example, was minister of finances, though Necker had the title only of director of finances and was shortly to resign, partly because the king would not make him minister since he was a Protestant. He singled out the Regiment de Deux-Ponts, then at Rhode Island, as a good example of a military unit in which many of the officers and men were Protestant, though he knew that it was a German regiment and could not be considered as typical of the French military regime. Nor could the once free Strasbourg be considered a typical French city. Yet better informed and more objectively minded observers would have found it hard to determine whether or not the England of George III was more tolerant than the France of Louis XVI.

That Lafayette should have been pondering the problem at all showed that his political education was proceeding along with his military development. Despite obvious prejudices in favor of France and aristocracy, apparently his education had a distinctly American tinge, for his sympathies were decidedly in favor of justice, tolerance, and an effective parliamentary opposition to royal prerogative. Had he lived in France without ever going to America, he might have developed those sympathies—other young men of his class did. But his political philosophy was, in fact, the result of a merging of traditional Anglophobia, acquired pro-American devotion, and natural French patriotism. As yet it was Catholic, but not devoutly or intolerantly so; aristocratic, but not haughty or insistent upon privilege; and, above all, nationalistic, though not blind to the abuses of his country's institutions. Moreover, it was derived not from book learning or inward speculation but from personal experience. The young soldier from the court of France became a questioner not because of others' observations but because of his own.

McHenry was the cause of his speculations upon the merits of French institutions. Hamilton became the cause of his first inkling that even Washington was not perfect. Except for Washington himself, Hamilton had become Lafayette's closest friend in the American army. The marquis had singled out Hamilton for special mention in his last letter to Adrienne. Washington's aide was, he told her, "a man whom I love very much."[79] Hamilton had failed to receive any of the several distinguished appointments which had been available, though Lafayette had urged him upon both Washington and Congress on several occasions. The young colonel was beginning to resent the personal

[79] February 2, 1781, *loc. cit.*, p. 407.

dependence of an aide-de-camp, and Washington apparently was disturbed by his resentment.

The middle of February was a particularly hard time for both Washington and Hamilton. Never had the course of American independence seemed more desperate. If Laurens failed in his mission, disaster seemed inevitable. As if to add insult to injury, Clinton sent Arnold, now a brigadier-general in the English army, with fifteen hundred troops to Portsmouth, Virginia, from which he was devastating the neighboring area. At first there was nothing that Washington could do to check the renegade, since he could spare no troops. But good fortune was again on the side of the smaller battalions. A storm scattered Arbuthnot's vessels from their position in front of Newport, and, when they gathered together again at Gardiner's Bay, it was found that enough British capital ships had been seriously damaged to give Destouches a momentary naval superiority. Acting on the suggestion of Washington, Destouches immediately prepared to sail to oppose Arnold. On learning that at last the French were prepared to move, Washington determined that naval action alone might not suffice to check Arnold and decided to co-operate with a land force of twelve hundred men. Faced as Washington was with a situation which left him hardly enough troops and provisions to defend West Point, it was a difficult decision for him to reach, and apparently the strain had its effect on his usually smooth temperament. And Hamilton, perhaps, was also more excitable than usual in the hope of going with the force destined for Virginia. A new batch of visitors from Rhode Island added to the tension. Among those that had to be entertained that February were the Duc de Lauzun, Comte de Fersen, Comte de St Maisme, Colonel de Sheldon, and Captain de St. Victor.[80]

On a day when neither the commander-in-chief nor his aide was fully composed, they quarreled, and Lafayette was innocently the cause of their quarrel. It happened that Washington, meeting Hamilton on the stairs, told him that he wished

[80] Cf. Fitzpatrick, XXI, 225–32; Lafayette to [Stewart?], February 19, 1781, NYPL, Colonel Walter Stewart papers.

to see him. Hamilton replied, "Immediately," but went to deliver something to another aide and then returned to go to Washington's rooms. On the way he met Lafayette, and Lafayette, though Hamilton thought it must be obvious that he was impatient to get on, kept him talking on a matter of business. After what appeared "two minutes" to Hamilton and "ten minutes" to Washington, Hamilton left Lafayette in a manner (as Hamilton himself described it)[81] "which, but for our intimacy, would have been more than abrupt." Washington was waiting for him not as usual in his rooms but at the head of the stairs, angry. He accused Hamilton of disrespectful behavior, and thereupon Hamilton offered to resign. Washington accepted, and they separated. Somewhat later Hamilton agreed to stay till Washington could find some other person to fill his place. Both men also consented not to mention their quarrel to others. But Hamilton immediately informed Lafayette, in confidence, of what had happened. He also wrote to his father-in-law, General Schuyler, and to Dr. Mc-Henry[82] of the misunderstanding. Lafayette regretted the rift between his two friends and did what he could to repair it. Though Hamilton was not complimentary in his comments about Washington, the marquis tried to induce the colonel to reconsider his resignation—to no avail. He was obliged to be content with apologizing for Hamilton to Washington when a good opportunity arose.[83] He never undertook to apologize for Washington to Hamilton.

Just before his resignation, Hamilton had written for Washington the proposals that went to Newport regarding the intended co-operation in Virginia. Washington asked that Rochambeau send all of Destouches' fleet and one thousand soldiers besides. If that could be done, he hoped to capture Arnold

---

[81] Hamilton to Schuyler, February 18, 1781, H. C. Lodge (ed.), *The works of Alexander Hamilton* (10 vols.; New York, n.d.), IX, 232–37. The original of this letter is in the collection of Lloyd W. Smith, Madison, N.J. The version in the J. C. Hamilton edition of the *Works of Hamilton* (I, 211–14) is incomplete.

[82] February 18, 1781, Steiner, p. 35.

[83] Lafayette to Washington, April 15, 1781, LC, Washington papers, no. 48, fol. 144a; Washington to Lafayette, April 22, 1781, Fitzpatrick, XXI, 491.

with all his men. The visit to Rhode Island was now postponed. But Lafayette was not at all disappointed. For the twelve hundred soldiers whom Washington now ordered to be ready to start for Virginia by February 19 were to be chiefly light infantry. And Lafayette was to be their commander![84]

BIBLIOGRAPHICAL NOTES

C. J. Stillé's volume on Anthony Wayne is still the best study of "Mad Anthony" for this period. His narrative of the mutiny has been helpful here. J. C. Hamilton's filiopietistic *Life of Alexander Hamilton* much too adroitly justifies his ancestor for his part in the quarrel with Washington; nor was he above suppressing evidence that would have hurt Alexander Hamilton's claim to fairmindedness in telling the story (cf. Lodge, *Works of Hamilton*, IX, 232 n.). Hamilton's letter to Schuyler of February 18, 1781, remains the best narrative of the quarrel, nevertheless; it should be examined, however, in conjunction with the letter to McHenry of the same date (Steiner, p. 35), the account in Lee's *Memoirs of the war* (II, 341–42 n.), given to the author by Hamilton during the siege of Yorktown, and that in George Bancroft and Stephen Salisbury, "Report of council" (*Proceedings of the American Antiquarian Society*, N.S., III [1883–85], 41–50), apparently based upon what Lafayette told Sparks of the incident.

[84] Washington to Lafayette, February 20, 1781, Fitzpatrick, XXI, 253–56.

CHAPTER IX

Lafayette Nearly Bags Arnold

I T WOULD have been a striking example of classic justice if
Lafayette had captured Arnold—if the young soldier who,
though bred in the tradition of French aristocracy, now devoted his life to the American nation, had brought to retribution
the older soldier who, though bred in the traditions of American
nationalism, now devoted his life to the British aristocracy.
That picture of evil confounded was perhaps not far from Washington's mind when he selected Lafayette to lead the expedition
against Arnold's force in Virginia. The reason he openly
avowed, however, was that, since it was an expedition to operate in conjunction with a French force, it was politically wise to
place his senior French officer in command.[1] Moreover, since
speed would be necessary if Arnold were to be taken by surprise,
it was important that the maneuver should be entrusted to fast-
moving, well-trained troops. Parts of the old Light Division
were chosen for the task, and their former commander once
more was designated to lead them,[2] though the contingent was
not made up exclusively of light troops and was not to be
formally known as the Light Division.[3]

On February 19 the light infantry of the Massachusetts,
Connecticut, New Hampshire, and Rhode Island lines and some
other troops began to assemble at Peekskill. The men did not
know where they were going. The hurried preparations had the
air of another sudden raid upon Staten Island, and, to deceive

[1] Washington to Heath, March 21, 1781, Fitzpatrick, XXI, 342–44.

[2] Washington to Lafayette, February 20, 1781, *ibid.*, pp. 253–56.

[3] Cf. Lafayette to Washington, April 8, 1781, *Mémoires* (Amer. ed.), p. 400.

the enemy, that impression was carefully fostered.[4] Even the officers had failed to provide themselves with baggage for a long journey, and they were nearly all penniless. When at last they understood that they would be gone a long time, the officers' baggage was sent for, but most of them were still obliged to travel without the comforting jingle of hard cash in their purses.[5] On February 20, the contingent crossed the river. The next day they marched to Ramapo, New York, and on February 23 they reached Pompton, New Jersey. There Lafayette joined them. He passed out standards to each battalion,[6] and they took on something of the distinguished character of his old Light Division.

The corps was divided into three battalions, numbering about eight hundred men in all. The battalions were commanded by Colonels Joseph Vose, Francis Barber, and Lafayette's former aide Gimat, with Gouvion in charge of the engineers. Lieutenant-Colonel Ebenezer Stevens had gone ahead to Philadelphia to procure some artillery.[7] Despite their gallant appearance, they were poverty stricken. "It's a funny thing to see us making a journey," Lafayette admitted. "We haven't a sou, a horse, a wagon, a whisp of hay." But he expected to find provisions on the way and was not downcast. "The general must be thoroughly convinced of the importance of this expedition to bleed himself so much."[8]

At dawn on February 24 they marched again. Their anxious leader pushed them on. They proceeded to Hanover, New Jersey, three miles from Morristown.[9] Lafayette went on to Morristown that day, but it was not until the next day that his little

[4] *Mémoires*, I, 266.

[5] Cf. Board of War to Congress, February 28, 1781, *Journals of Congress*, XIX, 204.

[6] "The journal of Ebenezer Wild (1776–1781)," *Massachusetts Historical Society proceedings*, 2d ser., VI (1890–91), 130–31; cf. Lafayette to Washington, February 24, 1781, LC, Washington papers, no. 46, fol. 330.

[7] Lafayette to La Luzerne, February 19, 1781, *AHR*, XX (1915), 593; cf. J. A. Stevens, "Ebenezer Stevens, lieutenant-colonel of artillery in the Continental Army," *Magazine of American history*, I (1877), 605.

[8] Lafayette to La Luzerne, February 19, 1781, *loc. cit.*, pp. 593–94.

[9] "Wild's journal," p. 131.

army, with Colonel Vose in command, caught up with him.[10] While they rested and drew their clothing from Continental stores, Lafayette started out for Philadelphia.

At Morristown Lafayette had at last learned that his expedition ought to proceed with all haste. His instructions from Washington[11] before leaving New Windsor had made it clear that his land force was to operate only in conjunction with a naval force that Destouches was expected to send to the Chesapeake. That force was expected to bottle up Arnold's detachment and make possible his capture by an attack on land. Without it Arnold could escape by sea. Washington, therefore, had ordered Lafayette to return if he were to learn that no vessels had been sent from Newport into the Chesapeake. At Morristown Lafayette was relieved to receive intelligence that a small but apparently sufficient naval detachment from Destouches' fleet had already begun to blockade Arnold.[12] On the request of the Virginia delegates in Congress, La Luzerne had urged Destouches to dispatch a few vessels to the Chesapeake in order to check Arnold.[13] Even before receiving Washington's request for vigorous naval co-operation with Lafayette's forces, Destouches had sent Le Gardeur de Tilly with a man-of-war and a few smaller vessels. They had forced Arnold to take a safe position at Portsmouth, Virginia, up the Elizabeth River, where it was too shallow for Tilly to follow.

While Lafayette proceeded to Philadelphia, his contingent marched toward Trenton. Despite a late start, they made twenty-two miles on February 26, being joined by a detachment from the New Jersey line on the way. They reached Somerset at sundown and spent the night there. Sunrise saw them on the march again toward Princeton, where they were quartered in the college and other houses of the town.[14] There the hostility between the soldiers of New Jersey and of New England, which contin-

[10] Cf. Lafayette to Pickering, February 24, 1781, Yale University Library.

[11] Washington to Lafayette, February 20, 1781, *loc. cit.*

[12] Cf. Lafayette to Washington, February 24, 1781, *loc. cit.*

[13] Bland to Jefferson, February 9, 1781, Burnett, V, 566–67; cf. Rochambeau, I, 264.

[14] "Wild's journal," p. 131.

ued to smolder throughout the campaign,[15] flamed into a riot that was quelled only by the intervention of the officers. Off again at sunrise the next day, they reached Trenton early in the afternoon, and there they stayed for several days waiting for boats that were to take them on their way.

The rapidity of his detachment's movement even in his absence proved Lafayette to be an excellent hand at the art of transporting and supplying an army in motion. Though logistics was a form of military activity which he had never before been called upon to employ, he showed a native ability for it. His knack of charming and cajoling those from whom he wished favors served him in good stead. People all along the route aided his diminutive army. He also found to his surprise, "as I know we have not a farthing,"[16] that the Quartermaster's Department had made efficient provision for his detachment's march through New Jersey. Within a week he had moved about one thousand men a distance of about one hundred miles on foot, through rain, and over roads that for the most part oozed with mud. They had had practically two days for rest and provisioning, and were not fatigued when they arrived in Trenton. Only two men had fallen behind, and those two caught up with the rest at Trenton.[17] Lafayette attributed his speed to the "order and alacrity"[18] of his men, but not a little of the credit is due to his own tireless pen. He had spent hour upon hour sending orders and begging supplies from civil and military authorities en route.[19]

[15] Cf. Lafayette to Greene, April 17, 1781, Clements Library.

[16] Lafayette to Pickering, February 27, 1781, NYPL, Ford collection.

[17] Lafayette to Washington, March 2, 1781, LC, Washington papers, no. 47, fol. 68.

[18] Lafayette to Pickering, February 24, 1781, *loc. cit.*

[19] In addition to the letters cited above: several letters of Lafayette to Pickering, February 18–March 4, 1781, National Archives (Washington), Records of the War Department, Revolutionary docs. 31636–41; to Jefferson, February 21, 1781, Gilbert Chinard, *Letters of Lafayette and Jefferson* (Baltimore, 1929), p. 17; to Dayton, February 23, 1781, Historical Society of Pennsylvania; to Washington (two letters), February 23, 1781, LC, Washington papers, no. 46, fols. 324 and 326; to Steuben, February 24, 1781, New York Historical Society, Gates papers (hereafter referred to as Gates papers), box 16, no. 12; to Washington, February 25, 1781, LC, Washington papers, no. 46, fol. 351.

While his contingent was still in Trenton, Lafayette arrived in Philadelphia. The principal reason for going ahead had been to secure a reinforcement from the Pennsylvania line and to arrange for the future needs of his army, particularly in artillery. In Philadelphia he visited La Luzerne, Quartermaster-General Pickering, Major-General St. Clair, Brigadier-General Wayne, the Board of War, and the Navy Board. Pickering made special efforts to provide for Lafayette's needs this time. A steady stream of instructions to his deputies and requests to his superiors went forth from Philadelphia and soon resulted in new instructions and requests from those who received them.[20] Unfortunately, munitions, boats, wagons, and food could not be produced by strokes of the pen, and, despite Pickering's efforts, Lafayette was to encounter a distressing poverty of supplies. But before he left Philadelphia, he had procured fifteen hundred pairs of shoes, in addition to some medicines and tools. La Luzerne, moreover, had given him permission to draw upon the French supplies of flour and salt meat that he might find along the bay.[21] In addition, his men were enabled to buy some provisions of their own, since by special resolution, Congress voted them a month's pay in brand new Pennsylvania currency.[22]

By the industry of Colonel Stevens, a train of artillery, consisting of twelve heavy pieces and six smaller ones, was prepared. On Lafayette's order, this artillery with four companies of artillerymen moved to Head of Elk (Elkton, Md.) to await the arrival of the rest of his detachment.[23] His army thus grew

[20] Cf. Lafayette to Pickering, February 27, 1781, *loc. cit*; Fitzpatrick, XXI, 294–97; J. A. Shriver, *Lafayette in Harford County 1781* (Bel Air, Md., 1931), pp. 45–49; Robert Purviance, *A narrative of events which occurred in Baltimore town during the Revolutionary War* (Baltimore, 1849), pp. 227–28; B. C. Steiner (ed.), *Journal and correspondence of the State Council of Maryland, 1780–81* ("Archives of Maryland," Vol. XLV [Baltimore, 1927]), pp. 330–31; Lafayette to St. Clair, February 27, 1781, LC, U.S. Revolution collection; Lafayette to Vose, February 28, 1781, *Massachusetts Historical Society proceedings*, V (1860–61), 150–51; *Journals of Congress*, XIX, 204; Lafayette to Washington, March 2, 1781, *loc. cit.*

[21] Lafayette to Washington, March 2, 1781, *loc. cit.*

[22] "Wild's journal," p. 132; *Journals of Congress*, XIX, 204.

[23] Stevens, "Ebenezer Stevens," pp. 605–6; Lafayette to Washington, March 2, 1781, *loc. cit.*

to twelve hundred strong. The disruption that still prevailed in the Pennsylvania line made it impossible to add to his contingent immediately the several hundred men whom he had hoped to get from the Pennsylvania line, but St. Clair assured him that they would join him eventually. Wayne went so far as to promise a thousand men.[24]

In Philadelphia Lafayette also met his friends Duportail, Charlus, and Dillon.[25] He hastened Duportail toward New Windsor, where Washington awaited him to act in Lafayette's place as liaison officer on the trip to Newport. The two younger men lost no time in begging Washington to let them accompany the marquis to the field of glory as volunteers.[26] Meanwhile, Lafayette sent Lieutenant-Colonel Gouvion ahead to inform Baron von Steuben, who commanded in Virginia, and Tilly, who commanded the small French squadron in the Chesapeake, of his orders and expectations. Steuben, who had already been informed that Lafayette was coming, was now reminded that no promise must be given Arnold that he would be treated as a prisoner of war.[27] This was in keeping with Washington's instruction that Lafayette was to "do no act whatever with Arnold that directly or by implication may skreen him from the punishment due to his treason and desertion, which if he should fall into your hands, you will execute in the most summary way."[28]

In three days at Philadelphia Lafayette had thus taken every precaution that lay in his power to assure the comfort of his men and the success of his mission. Yet even his optimistic spirit had been dampened by the news that recent dispatches from

[24] Lafayette to Washington, March 7, 1781, LC, Washington papers, no. 47, fol. 87.

[25] Lafayette to Washington, March 2, 1781, *loc. cit.; Calendar of Washington correspondence with officers*, III, 1741; Washington to Charlus and Dillon, March 23, 1781, Fitzpatrick, XXI, 359–60.

[26] *Calendar of Washington correspondence*, III, 1741.

[27] Lafayette to Steuben, February 26, 1781, Gates papers, box 16, no. 13; Lafayette to Washington, March 2, 1781, *loc. cit.*

[28] Washington to Lafayette, February 20, 1781, *loc. cit.*, p. 255.

Washington conveyed.[29] The waves had once more shown their favoritism to Britannia. The damage to Arbuthnot's ships was found to be of such a nature that it was possible, by taking parts from the most severely battered, to refit the less damaged ones. Within a short time he again was numerically superior to Destouches, who had only weakened himself by sending off Tilly's small squadron to the Chesapeake. It seemed unlikely now that further naval aid could be expected from the French generals in Newport, since up to that time they had shown themselves unwilling to fly in the face of British maritime supremacy. In fact, it was doubtful whether Tilly would dare stay in the Chesapeake with his few ships and incur the risk of being cut off from his base. And if he sailed away, no matter how skilfully Lafayette maneuvered the land forces, the sea would always offer Arnold an avenue of escape.

Nevertheless, Lafayette went on with his plans. At sunrise on March 1, Colonel Vose, in accordance with the marquis' instruction,[30] embarked his men at Trenton and sailed down the Delaware. They anchored for half an hour at Philadelphia and then sailed on.[31] Lafayette watched them proudly as they floated past the city in the early afternoon, their sails bellied out "by a wind which was extremely favorable."[32] They would be at Head of Elk by March 3, three days before Washington or anyone else had thought they could get there.

Yet the marquis had already begun to believe all his efforts had been in vain. Before leaving Philadelphia he wrote to Washington that if he learned that Tilly had left the Chesapeake, he would march his detachment back immediately and try to regain headquarters in time to accompany the commander-in-chief on the still delayed visit to Newport.[33] If he were not to be disappointed on both scores, however, he must

---

[29] Washington to Lafayette, February 25, 1781, Fitzpatrick, XXI, 289; Lafayette to Washington, March 2, 1781, *loc. cit.*

[30] Lafayette to Vose, February 28, 1781, *loc. cit.*

[31] "Wild's journal," p. 132.

[32] Lafayette to Washington, March 2, 1781, *loc. cit.*   [33] *Ibid.*

hurry. In the afternoon of March 2, he left Philadelphia, expecting to arrive at Head of Elk that evening. His men had landed early that morning at Wilmington, Delaware, and had marched through a cold rain to Christiana, where they had halted. The next afternoon they joined their commander at Head of Elk.[34]

There a dispatch from Washington awaited him with information that was somewhat discouraging. It announced that Tilly and his little squadron had returned to Newport. Destouches promised, however, to fit out a prize that Tilly had captured and to send it back to the Chesapeake, perhaps accompanied by other vessels. Lafayette and Steuben were therefore not to slacken their preparations. The marquis was to embark his men on transports and be ready to sail the moment he learned that the French once more controlled the Chesapeake.[35] Lafayette acknowledged this letter immediately, answering that he hoped "we may be embarked before we hear of the arrival of our friends."[36] He also hurried off dispatches to the military and civil officers in Virginia, urging them not to relax the siege of Portsmouth, because a new French fleet was on its way.[37] Again he warned that if Arnold were captured he was not to be treated as a prisoner of war.

Many hands had been busy preparing supplies and transportation for Lafayette's Continental force even before he arrived. Letters from Pickering to his deputy in Baltimore, Donaldson Yates, and to Governor Thomas Sim Lee, and from Lafayette to James McHenry, who once more called himself Lafayette's "volunteer aide-de-camp," had set in motion Maryland's ma-

---

[34] "Wild's journal," p. 32; Lafayette to Washington, March 3, 1781, LC, Washington papers, no. 47, fol. 72. Cf. E. W. Cooch, "Lafayette at Christiana, Delaware," *Daughters of the American Revolution magazine*, LXVI (1932), 556–59.

[35] Washington to Lafayette, February 27, 1871, Fitzpatrick, XXI, 309.

[36] Lafayette to Washington, March 3, 1781, *loc. cit.*

[37] Lafayette to Jefferson, March 3, 1781, "Letters of Lafayette," *Virginia magazine of history and biography*, VI (1899), 55–57; to Gist, March 3, 1781, LC, U.S. Revolution collection; to commanding officer before Portsmouth, March 3, 1781, Gates papers, box 16, no. 16. The commanding officer before Portsmouth proved to be Steuben, though Lafayette at the time he wrote was under the impression that Steuben had gone off to join Greene: see Lafayette to Washington, March 2, 1781, *loc. cit.*

chinery of government.[38] But the machinery creaked and moved much too slowly for the impatient commander of the expedition. On arriving at Head of Elk he found that not enough boats had been provided to ship all the men, horses, guns, and supplies that he had gathered together. That necessitated another volley of cajoling letters. Governor Lee was urged to send "the totality of the vessels at Annapolis and Baltimore."[39] Brigadier-General Mordecai Gist, who commanded the Maryland militia at Baltimore, received a similar request.[40] And Dr. McHenry again was called upon to use his influence with the Maryland authorities.[41] These letters were sent on their way to Baltimore and Annapolis by an express who was ordered to ride both "day and night with the greatest dispatch."[42] The effect was immediate. On the next day ships began coming up the Elk River, with the cheering news that more were to follow.[43]

The days that followed were given to increasing exertions to equip Lafayette's army. Renewed entreaties went forth to the governments of Maryland and Virginia. McHenry arrived at Elk to resume his duties as aide-de-camp, and Lafayette permitted him to do what he could not himself do with propriety— appeal personally to the merchants of Baltimore for their private support. They responded nobly. They held a meeting at which they vied with one another in a display of patriotism. They pledged themselves to pay for the supplies purchased, hoping that the Maryland government would reimburse them. A committee of three was appointed to make contracts and pur-

---

[38] McHenry to Lee, March 3 and 4 [incorrectly dated February 3 and 4], 1781, Shriver, pp. 49–50; see also "Archives of Maryland," XLV, 334–43.

[39] Lafayette to Lee, March 3, 1781, J. H. Pleasants (ed.), *Journal and correspondence of the State Council of Maryland* (*letters to the governor and council*), *1781* ("Archives of Maryland," Vol. XLVII [Baltimore, 1930]), pp. 101–2.

[40] Lafayette to Gist, March 3, 1781, *loc. cit.*

[41] Cited in McHenry to Lee, March 3, 1781, *loc. cit.*

[42] Endorsement in Lafayette's hand on back of letter to Gist, March 3, 1781, *loc.cit.*

[43] Lafayette to Wayne, March 4, 1781, Historical Society of Pennsylvania, Wayne papers; see also *The casket or flowers of literature, wit and sentiment,* IV (1829), 495–96.

chases in the common cause.[44] Boats, guns, ammunition, bread, meat, clothing, money, horses, oxen, wagons, fodder, stoves, medicines, and a hundred other more or less prosaic articles became the major interest of military, merchants, and statesmen as Lafayette and his subordinates relentlessly prodded them on. Despite contrary winds and heavy rains some of these much-needed supplies trickled toward Lafayette's encampment or were stored near the wharves along the bay. On March 7 he had thirty boats[45] and began to embark his detachment.

And still no word came of Tilly or the approach of any French vessel. On the contrary, disquieting intelligence arrived of English boats in the neighborhood of the James River.[46] Meanwhile, Lafayette's natural restlessness was increased by dispatches from Steuben to himself and Washington (which he took the liberty of opening), all conveying the idea that everything had been fully prepared for the capture of Arnold if he could be blockaded by sea.[47] Steuben with four thousand Virginia militia had bottled him up and was sure that he could be taken by storm. Lafayette was inclined to be less optimistic on that score than the baron, but was, nonetheless, anxious to see for himself. Greene, hitherto hard pressed by Cornwallis, was also now reported to have forced the British to retreat in North Carolina. The prospect of striking a telling blow against the "villainous traitor"[48] at Portsmouth was tantalizing.

Then came the marvelous news that not a mere detachment but the whole of Destouches' fleet was coming. It was contained in a message from Washington which had taken a whole week to reach Head of Elk.[49] Intelligence that had fallen into

[44] Shriver, pp. 48–61; Steiner, *McHenry*, pp. 35–37.

[45] Lafayette to La Luzerne, March 7, 1781, *AHR*, XX (1915), 594.

[46] Steuben to Lafayette, March 7, 1781, New York Historical Society, Steuben papers, Vol. XI, no. 119; Maryland Council to Lafayette, March 9, 1781, Shriver, p. 58.

[47] Steuben to Lafayette, March 7, 1781, *loc. cit.*; Lafayette to Washington, March 3, 1781, *loc. cit.*, and March 7, 1781, LC, Washington papers, no. 47, fol. 87; Sparks, *Correspondence of the American Revolution*, III, 254–57.

[48] Lafayette to Washington, March 7, 1781, *loc. cit.*

[49] Washington to Lafayette, March 1, 1781, Fitzpatrick, XXI, 322–23; Lafayette to Washington, March 8, 1781, *Mémoires* (Amer. ed.), pp. 387–90.

Rochambeau's hands with Tilly's prize vessel had persuaded the French commanders that the capture of Arnold was a vital matter, and they had at last determined that the necessity for action would justify the risk. A detachment of eleven hundred grenadiers and chasseurs was to sail with Destouches, and, since this body of troops was to be independent of Lafayette, no less a person than the Baron de Vioménil, Rochambeau's second in command, had consented to take charge of them. Washington now countermanded his earlier order that Lafayette was to stay in the Elk River and urged him to make every effort to be in a position to co-operate with Vioménil upon his arrival. Lafayette communicated the good news to General Greene.[50] He assured Greene that it was a compliment to have a soldier of Vioménil's rank named to co-operate with them. To be sure, he outranked them both, but that would not matter, since by the king's orders "the commanding generals of both nations in any expedition where they are not under His Excellency's orders must be independent of each other." Win or lose, the formidable combination of French and American forces would furnish a most welcome diversion for the hard-pressed Greene.

In expressing to La Luzerne[51] his thankfulness for the new turn in his fortunes, Lafayette playfully pretended to consider Rochambeau's newly found energy as a sign of confidence in himself. Yet playfulness disappeared at the thought that Vioménil might possibly feel strong enough to proceed without him and thus rob him of the glory he so jealously desired. He hoped (but was not altogether sure) that Destouches would see to it that the Americans would not remain blockaded above the James River by English vessels, while Vioménil fought it out with Arnold alone. He apprehended that if the French lost the combat without the co-operation of his division—or even if they won—there would be dissatisfaction among his men, who had marched so far and endured so much. Moreover, the "two barons" (Vioménil and Steuben), he feared, would probably dis-

[50] March 8, 1781, New York Historical Society, Benedict Arnold MSS, BU, Sec.A.
[51] March 8, 1781, *AHR*, XX (1915), 595.

agree and quarrel. Consequently, he determined, even without being sure that the English vessels in the bay might not prevent him, to send his force to Annapolis "under God's protection."[52] There they would await a French frigate to escort them farther down the bay, while he himself went out to seek Destouches and Vioménil in order to persuade them not to proceed without full co-operation with the Americans. He announced his intentions to Washington, assuring his chief that "whatever determination I take, great deal must be personally risked, but I hope to manage things so as to commit no imprudence with the excellent detachment whose glory is as dear and whose safety much dearer to me than my own."[53]

Lafayette's plan was immediately carried into action. On March 8 he moved his men down the river to Plum's Point and Cecil's Ferry and spent that day and the next in embarking them. He had expected to have to act as "admiral" to his little fleet, but fortunately Commodore James Nicholson of the Continental Navy had responded to Lafayette's requests and consented to take command. Nicholson promised to get them to Annapolis sooner than Lafayette had thought possible. Against an unfavorable wind the armada set sail on the ninth toward Turkey Point at the mouth of the river. There Lafayette left them to proceed on his self-appointed mission. The next day Nicholson's fleet anchored at Pool's Island, about fifteen miles out in the bay, and they arrived at Annapolis two days later, having been delayed by a storm which had scattered them.[54]

Lafayette had meanwhile dropped down the bay in the "Dolphin," a sloop armed with only swivels and carrying only thirty soldiers besides himself and Charlus. Charlus owed this distinction to the fact that he was his father's son. "I have clapped on board my boat," Lafayette candidly informed Washington,[55] "the only son of the minister of the French navy,

[52] *Ibid.*   [53] Lafayette to Washington, March 8, 1781, *loc. cit.*

[54] *Ibid.;* "Wild's journal," pp. 132–33; Lafayette to Lee, March 8, 1781, NYPL; McHenry to Lee, March 9, 1781, Shriver, p. 57; Lafayette to Washington, March 9, 1781 (two letters), *Mémoires* (Amer. ed.), pp. 390–91 and 496–97.

[55] March 9, 1781, *Mémoires* (Amer. ed.), p. 391.

whom I shall take out [to the French fleet] to speak if circumstances require it."

The marquis was in Annapolis on the tenth, pushing the Maryland council on to still greater efforts.[56] In order better to elude the enemy, he and his party left Annapolis in a small, open barge, intending to be picked up lower down the bay by the "Dolphin," which was to follow them at a distance. The precaution turned out to be wise. Lafayette had hoped to reach the mouth of the Chesapeake no later than the eleventh. But wind and weather once more proved hostile to youthful fervor, and he got no farther by that date than Herring Bay. There he found that the "Dolphin" for some reason had gone back to Annapolis. He could only conjecture that it was the possibility of attack by a superior English force that had led to her retreat.[57] The conjecture was right. As Lafayette and his men proceeded in their barge, they soon discovered British vessels sailing toward Annapolis to blockade his armada there. Sending warning to Commodore Nicholson, he nevertheless continued on his way.[58]

It was not until the afternoon of March 14 that Lafayette's open boat, carefully hugging the shore, reached Yorktown. He immediately sent an express to General von Steuben, who had been waiting for him for two days at Williamsburg and Yorktown, with an invitation to meet him.[59] Steuben found it a little hard to have bottled up Arnold at Portsmouth only to have a much younger general come to preside at Arnold's capture. But he played his part nobly. The two foreign generals, who had not met since 1778, now began to concert plans for the safety of Virginia. In going back and forth from his boat, Lafayette narrowly escaped drowning. Shallow water had obliged his heavy launch to anchor some distance off shore. On one occasion, Lafayette drove his horse into the water. The animal stepped into

[56] Shriver, pp. 58–59.

[57] Lafayette to Lee, March 11, 1781, Sparks MSS XXIX, fol. 523.

[58] McHenry to Lee, March 14, 1781, Shriver, pp. 62–63.

[59] Claiborne to Jefferson, March 13, 1781, W. P. Palmer et al. (eds.), Calendar of Virginia state papers and other manuscripts (11 vols.; Richmond, 1875-93), I, 569; Lafayette to Steuben, [March] 14, 1781, Tower, II, 243.

a hole and threw his rider, who could not swim, into deep water. The soldiers in the boat jumped in and pulled him aboard.[60] It looked as if the sea, in its stubborn preference for British rule, had reached out to get him.

Since the "Dolphin" had not come down to pick him up and since no one at Yorktown knew where to look for the French fleet, it seemed foolish even to the energetic Lafayette to go on. He determined to stay at Yorktown until he and Charlus might with more point start out to find Vioménil. Realizing the delicacy of Steuben's position, he refused to take command in Virginia and, in reporting to Washington what he had done, asked the commander-in-chief to compliment Steuben upon the excellent preparations around Portsmouth. Lafayette was certain that Arnold would be captured as soon as the French fleet came up the river; in fact, Steuben's militia and his own Continentals might be able to take Arnold without the aid of Vioménil's men.[61]

Having learned that his men were safe in Annapolis,[62] the marquis felt free to go upon a reconnoitering tour of the enemy's posts. On March 16 he went to Williamsburg. There he communicated with Governor Thomas Jefferson regarding the needs of the forces opposing Arnold.[63] Jefferson had frequently reminded him in earlier letters that it would be no simple task to equip his army in Virginia. That was due, Jefferson admitted, not only to the exhaustion of Virginia after the several invasions it had recently had to endure but also to "mild laws" and "a people not used to prompt obedience."[64] Lafayette, protesting his determination to "conquer or die" in "our noble contest" (as befitted one who had the honor to address the author of the Declaration of Independence), nevertheless with equal candor confessed: "Long since have I been used to these

[60] Sparks MSS XXXII, p. 131.

[61] March 15, 1781, LC, Washington papers, no. 47, fol. 156.

[62] Cf. Lafayette to McLane, March 16, 1781, New York Historical Society, McLane papers, Vol. II.

[63] Chinard, *Lafayette and Jefferson*, pp. 24–26; see also pp. 2–24.

[64] Jefferson to Lafayette, March 10, 1781, *ibid.*, p. 20.

inconveniences that are so far compensated by the numberless blessings of a popular government."[65] As if to indicate that he set greater store by the blessings than by the inconveniences, he made it clear that he would not hesitate to call upon Virginia's exertions. And, indeed, he soon began again the persistent demands for supplies which had met with such good results in Maryland, this time insisting upon a measure which he had been content to leave to the civil authorities in Maryland—the impressment of military necessities. "A people not used to prompt obedience" and unable to provide the horses he needed for his artillery found that two hundred of their oxen were impressed instead. The marquis apologized obligingly, however: "It is with the greatest reluctance that I sign any impressing warrants, but I hope my delicacy in this matter will be such as to render me worthy of the approbation of the state." Jefferson approved.[66]

A short jaunt across the James River brought Lafayette to Suffolk, south of Portsmouth, and thence he proceeded to the camp near Sleepy Hole, where General Peter Muhlenburg and some Virginia militia were situated. Here, out of deference to Muhlenburg, Lafayette again refused to assume command.[67] With a detachment of the few men he could find who had cartridges, he went out on reconnaissance. On the way his party met and cut up a small patrol of Hessian yagers. The Americans lost one man killed and two wounded and took four prisoners.[68] It was the first time in three years that Lafayette had been under fire. Lack of ammunition made it imprudent to push this advantage, and he complained to the governor and Brigadier-General George Weedon, of the Virginia militia, at the carelessness which had robbed him of a more striking victory.[69] But

[65] Chinard, *Lafayette and Jefferson*, pp. 24–25.

[66] Lafayette to Jefferson, March 17, 1781, *ibid.*, pp. 26–27.

[67] Lafayette to Weedon, March 20, 1781, collection of A. K. Ford, Minneapolis, Minn.; cf. H. A. Muhlenburg, *Life of Major-General Peter Muhlenburg of the Revolutionary army* (Philadelphia, 1849), p. 239.

[68] *Ibid.*; Simcoe, p. 185; Max von Eelking, *Die deutschen Hülfstruppen in nordamerikanischen Befreiungskriege, 1776 bis 1783* (Hanover, 1863), pp. 107–8.

[69] Lafayette to Jefferson, March 20, 1781, Chinard, *Lafayette and Jefferson*, pp. 30–31.

even a small victory was welcome. More welcome still was the news, received soon after, that the French fleet had actually sailed from Newport on March 8 and could not now be far away. Rejoicing, however, was somewhat tempered by the information that reinforcements from New York were coming to Arnold's relief.[70]

Then came the report that the French squadron had actually been sighted. Great bustle and high hopes spread through the several camps around Portsmouth. Lafayette took up his post at Williamsburg to be within easier communication of them all. Now the traitor would surely be caught, and American honor would be redeemed. Rumors of confusion in Arnold's ranks only increased the joy in the American camps. But hope was soon dashed. The vessels that had been sighted turned out to be the British under Admiral Arbuthnot.[71] He had met Destouches on March 16, and, though the French fleet had inflicted some serious damage on him and claimed the victory, he had succeeded in sailing to the Chesapeake while Destouches returned to Newport. Arbuthnot thus snatched victory from under Lafayette's nose. For Arnold's forces were short of provisions and could not have lasted much longer.[72]

Lafayette did not know of Destouches' retreat. He still hoped the French fleet might come and challenge Arbuthnot. For greater security, meanwhile, Muhlenburg's militia retreated to Suffolk, and Steuben took every precaution against surprise; and all continued to look for Destouches and Vioménil. Nevertheless, Lafayette sent word to his officers in Annapolis to be ready to move northward at a moment's notice to rejoin Washington.[73] It was only on March 25 that Lafayette learned of

[70] Smith to Steuben, March 21, 1781, K. M. Roof, *Colonel William Smith and lady* (Boston, 1929), facsimile between pp. 28 and 29.

[71] Lafayette to Jefferson, March 23, 1781, New York Historical Society, misc. MSS; Lafayette to Washington, March 23, 1781, *Mémoires* (Amer. ed.), pp. 391–95.

[72] Arbuthnot to Stephens, March 20, 1781, *Gazette de Leyde*, May 4, 1781.

[73] Cf. Lafayette to Washington, March 23, 1781, *loc. cit.*, pp. 393–94; to La Luzerne, March 23, 1781, *AHR*, XX (1915), 595–96; to Jefferson, March 23, 1781, *loc. cit.*; to Jefferson, March 24, 1781, Chinard, *Lafayette and Jefferson*, p. 33.

what had happened in the sea battle off the Capes of Virginia.[74] He did not know, however, that the French fleet had retreated and was only one day's sailing from Newport by that time; and, when the English fleet once more left its moorings and a three hours' cannonading was heard in the distance, he felt certain that the French had again challenged the British for supremacy in the bay. In the end the cannonading turned out to be only distant thunder, for no action took place that day. When the English fleet returned, the reason for their having sailed became clear: they had gone out to meet and escort to Portsmouth some transports sent from New York with reinforcements for Arnold.[75] That news definitely "destroys every prospect of an operation against Arnold," Lafayette reluctantly admitted, although "never has an operation be[en] more ready (on our side) nor conquest more certain."[76]

Lafayette's pride now made him cling to the hope that the French fleet had gone to Greene's aid instead of retreating. He determined, nevertheless, to return to Annapolis and to lead his disappointed division back to headquarters again. That seemed the wisest course to pursue, especially since, in reinforcing Arnold at Portsmouth, Clinton must have weakened the garrison at New York and Washington might thus be induced to begin action in that quarter. He was ready to admit that he had made a mistake in sending his men to Annapolis, as it had resulted only in their having to retrace their steps for a longer stretch. And he was also ready to apologize to Jefferson for having caused so much fruitless expense to the state of Virginia. "How much the disappointment is felt by me, Your Excellency will better judge than I can express."[77]

Before leaving Williamsburg, Lafayette approved of a scheme proposed by Steuben for catching Cornwallis between two

[74] Lafayette to Washington, March 25, 1781, LC, Washington papers, no. 47, fol. 231; Tower, II, 246-47.

[75] Lafayette to Washington, March 26, 1781 (two letters), LC, Washington papers, no. 47, fols. 233 and 235; to Jefferson, March 27, 1781, Jackson Collection.

[76] Lafayette to Washington, March 26, 1781, *loc. cit.*, fol. 235.

[77] March 27, 1781, *loc. cit.*

fires. The siege of Portsmouth would be abandoned (since there was small prospect of success against the increased British forces), and the Virginia militia would march quickly (before their brief terms of enlistment should expire) into North Carolina. The scheme would not only have aided the hard-pressed Greene, who had just lost an important battle at Guilford Courthouse, but might have relieved Virginia of her invaders, since they would have felt obliged to follow Steuben into North Carolina. But the civil authorities of Virginia felt that their men, and particularly their arms, ought to stay at home for the protection of their own state. And so nothing came of the proposal, though Greene sent an aide to beg Lafayette to move southward.[78]

It fell to Steuben to tell Greene's aide of the unfortunate decision of the Virginia council.[79] For by that time Lafayette was well on the road back to Maryland. Proceeding overland, he went several miles out of his way to Fredericksburg and Mount Vernon. This deliberate detour, he apologized to Washington, was due to "an ardent desire I had long ago of seeing your relations and above all your mother." "In order to conciliate my private happiness to duties of a public nature, I recovered by riding in the night those few hours which I had consecrated to my satisfaction." Unhappily, he confessed to his commander-in-chief, "my duty and my anxiety for the execution of your orders" prevented meeting more of Washington's family. No act on Lafayette's part could have been better proof of his youthful devotion to his chief.[80] There was no motive but loyalty for his taking a roundabout route, though on urgent military business, merely to make the acquaintance of his beloved general's family.

Lafayette rejoined his detachment at Annapolis on April 3.

[78] Memorandum of Steuben, endorsed by Lafayette and Gouvion, March 27, 1781, Historical Society of Pennsylvania; Lee to Jefferson, March 27, 1781. J. C. Ballagh, *Letters of Richard Henry Lee* (2 vols.; New York, 1914), II, 217; Greene to Washington, March 29, 1781, Sparks, *Correspondence of the American Revolution*, III, 278; Steuben to Lafayette, March 29, 1781, New York Historical Society, Steuben papers, Vol. IX, no. 145; J. M. Palmer, *General von Steuben* (New Haven, 1937), pp. 259-60.

[79] Steuben to Lafayette, March 29, 1781, *loc. cit.*

[80] Lafayette to Washington, April 8, 1781, *Mémoires* (Amer. ed.), p. 397.

Still blockaded by the English sloops "Hope" and "General Monk," his division, the crack troops of the Continental Army, had done nothing during his entire absence except to fortify a defensive position. On his arrival the marquis found urgent requests from Greene for men and artillery. His own orders and precarious situation made it difficult for him to part with either, but, placing a few cannon where they would be most effective against the British blockaders, he sent all the guns he could spare under the escort of some Maryland troops.[81]

Lafayette at first planned to move his men back to Head of Elk by an overland route. Several days' combing of the neighborhood of Annapolis for wagons to carry his supplies failed to produce enough of them. There was no choice left but to go by sea. Yet how get past the two English sloops? Colonel Stevens made a suggestion that seemed feasible. In accordance with that suggestion, on April 6, Commodore Nicholson, mounting two of his largest pieces (eighteen pounders) on a small merchant boat and accompanied by another vessel carrying two hundred men, went out to challenge the two English vessels. Having nothing so large as eighteen's, not realizing that their enemy had only two of them, being unable to maneuver as quickly as their improvised opponent, and perhaps fearing to be boarded by the two hundred men on the other craft, the Englishmen retreated.[82] Packing his men and stores onto all the available river craft, now numbering around ninety, Lafayette stole out under cover of night and sailed toward the Elk River. He reached Head of Elk in the morning of April 8.[83] Had he remained cautiously on the defensive at Annapolis, he might have regretted it. For the British had already begun to make plans to transfer their major attention from Greene's army to his, which they believed helplessly cooped up at Annapolis. And yet Nicholson's brilliant maneuver soon proved to be only another waste of effort.

[81] Shriver, pp. 71–74; Lafayette to Morris, April 4, 1781, collection of Drayton Burrill, Montclair, N.J.; Lafayette to Steuben, April 4, 1781, Gates papers, box 16, no. 25; *Calendar of Virginia state papers*, II, 23; Arbuthnot to Stephens, March 20, 1781, *loc. cit.*

[82] Lafayette to Washington, April, 8 1781, *loc. cit.*, p. 398; to Noailles, April 8, 1781, Patou, pp. 38–39; cf. Stevens, "Ebenezer Stevens," pp. 605-7.

[83] "Wild's journal," p. 135.

BIBLIOGRAPHICAL NOTES

In addition to his article on "Ebenezer Stevens," which has been cited above, John Austin Stevens has written *The expedition of Lafayette against Arnold* ("Publications of the Maryland Historical Society," No. 13 [Baltimore, 1878]). Both studies are now out of date, though still useful for certain details. The most helpful study for Maryland's part in the campaign of 1781 is Shriver's, *Lafayette in Harford County*, since it republishes the pertinent documents (not always in their proper order) from the Maryland archives; Mr. Shriver's introductory narrative contains several striking errors, however. Walter W. Preston, *History of Harford County, Maryland, from 1608 . . . . to . . . . 1812* (Baltimore, 1901) is outmoded, but useful as a source of Maryland tradition. The article by Cooch on "Lafayette at Christiana," based largely on Shriver, is misnamed; it deals with Lafayette's army, Lafayette himself not having visited Christiana at this time.

Chinard's *Letters of Lafayette and Jefferson* reprints several letters to be found also in his *Lafayette in Virginia: unpublished letters from the original manuscripts in the Virginia State Library and the Library of Congress* (Baltimore, 1928). Each of these works contains for the most part, however, documents not included in the other. Sometimes, too, the letters of Jefferson published in both works are taken from A. A. Lipscomb and A. E. Bergh (eds.), *Writings of Thomas Jefferson* (memorial ed.; 20 vols.; Washington, 1905). Whenever a letter of Jefferson was found in any two or all three of these sources, reference has been given above only to Chinard's *Lafayette and Jefferson*.

The "standard" life of Steuben is that by Brigadier-General John McAuley Palmer. The pioneer *Life of Frederick William von Steuben, major-general in the Revolutionary army* by Friedrich Kapp (New York, 1859), though still a good source for primary materials not otherwise easily available, suffers greatly from Kapp's effort to prove that the Germans (and therefore Steuben) contributed more to the cause of American freedom than the French (and therefore Lafayette).

CHAPTER X

Lafayette Checks Phillips and Escapes Cornwallis

AT ELK, Lafayette found several packets of letters waiting for him. Some of them were from abroad, containing heartening promises from Castries and Vergennes as well as a disturbing report about malicious gossip in Paris coupling his name with that of Aglaé de Hunolstein.[1] More pressing, however, were the dispatches from headquarters, the last of which ordered him to retrace his steps and move southward again with his detachment.[2]

Washington would have issued those upsetting orders earlier had he not been faced with a delicate point of military etiquette. It involved the jealousy of foreign officers that still persisted in the Continental Army. Some of the American officers at West Point had protested because several Frenchmen like Gimat and Galvan had been given commands under Lafayette while they were left behind in ignoble idleness.[3] Even General Heath confessed that he could not smother his own feelings, "which had been exceedingly wounded" because the expedition against Arnold had been entrusted to Lafayette, who was his junior. "I never will admit an idea to enter my breast that it is possible for any officer in the army, especially a foreigner, to have the interest or the honor of *my country* more at heart than I have, and if the conduct of my general in any instance should discover that he places less confidence in me, it cannot fail to make a painfull

---

[1] Cf. Lafayette to Noailles, April 8, 1781, Patou, pp. 38–39; Gottschalk, *Lady-in-waiting*, pp. 77–78.

[2] Washington to Lafayette, April 5, 1781, Fitzpatrick, XXI, 419–20; April 6, 1781, *ibid.*, pp. 421–23.

[3] Washington to Lafayette, April 6, 1781, *loc. cit.*, pp. 422–23.

impression."[4] Washington felt called upon to explain that the officers he had chosen had been designated because they had no other more important assignments and could be spared, that he did not consider Lafayette's assignment a more important one than Heath's at West Point, and that there were political motives behind Lafayette's appointment.[5]

Washington had, nevertheless, come to feel (once Lafayette's mission had failed) that the sooner the marquis and his fellow-officers returned, the better it would be for the promotion of good feeling in the service. So at first he ordered Lafayette to rejoin the main army with all speed,[6] planning to reorganize the detachment to everyone's satisfaction. Soon after, however, Greene demanded immediate support.[7] Even before Greene's pleas reached Washington, he had realized that a diversion or a reinforcement was essential if the southern army was not to be shattered between the recently augmented British forces in Virginia and Cornwallis' troops in North Carolina. And so he finally (and quite suddenly) set aside the finer points of military etiquette and instructed Lafayette to return southward and put himself under Greene's orders. Lafayette would have been better off to have stayed in Annapolis.

The marquis could not put Washington's new commands into effect immediately. Having made all his preparations for marching northward, he had to have a few days in which to reorient his commissary and transportation departments. A further delay of a few days was inevitable. But there no longer appeared to be a vital need for hurry. The latest reports from Greene indicated that Cornwallis' victory at Guilford Courthouse had been so costly that he was in full retreat, with Greene at his heels. The few days spent in resting and reconditioning his army Lafayette planned to use in rapid communication with headquarters. The re-establishment of the chain of expresses

[4] Heath to Washington, March 2, 1781, *Heath papers, part III*, pp. 178–79.

[5] Washington to Heath, March 21, 1781, Fitzpatrick, XXI, 342–44.

[6] April 6, 1781, *loc. cit.*

[7] Greene to Washington, March 29, 1781, Sparks, *Correspondence of the American Revolution*, III, 278.

had made it possible to send a message and receive a reply in five or six days. He hoped to be able to communicate to Washington his doubts regarding the wisdom of the new orders and to receive either a confirmation of them or different ones by the time his men were again ready to march.[8]

Lafayette felt it was altogether necessary thus to question Washington. A new problem now faced the harassed marquis. His men had left New York and New Jersey expecting to be gone only a few days. They had already been away for nearly two months. Having started back, they would be disappointed to find themselves ordered still farther away from their own states.[9] That disappointment would be due not only to their feeling that their need of shoes and clothing would better be cared for at home but also to a fear prevalent among the northern troops that the air of the South was unhealthy. They were afraid of the ague and fever, "which would certainly kill as the smallpox."[10] Some of Lafayette's officers told him that since his hair was sparse and he wore no wig, the sun might cause his death.[11] The marquis did not try to hide the hardships which Washington's sudden change of plans would cause his men. "They will certainly obey," Lafayette assured Washington,[12] "but they will be unhappy, and some will desert."

Washington did not need this warning to make him realize that Lafayette's position was precarious. He had already taken steps to get Congress to reinforce Lafayette and to pay his men.[13] He counted, too, on Wayne to join Lafayette with his Pennsylvanians, though "how either can march without money or credit is more than I can tell."[14] This was the time when Washington admitted to John Laurens: "Day does not follow night more certainly than it brings with it some additional proof of the impracticality of carrying on the war without the aid you

[8] Lafayette to Washington, April, 8, 1781, *Mémoires* (Amer. ed.), pp. 399–401.

[9] Lafayette to Greene, April 17, 1781, Clements Library.

[10] Unsigned interview with Lafayette in 1824–25, Virginia State Library.

[11] *Ibid.*   [12] April 8, 1781, *loc. cit.*, p. 400.

[13] Washington to Congress, April 8, 1781, Fitzpatrick, XXI, 429–31.

[14] Washington to Laurens, April 9, 1781, *ibid.*, p. 439.

were directed to solicit. . . . . We are at the end of our tether.
. . . . Now or never our deliverance must come."[15]

Without knowing how discouraged his idol had become, Lafayette, though usually most optimistic when others were disheartened, had begun to wonder whether a big mistake were not being made. His own preference was for a return northward. Recent dispatches from France had once more raised his hopes that ships and money would soon arrive. Their arrival ought to mean that there would be lively action around New York. The post he would most covet in that event was the command of a real advance guard. Instead it appeared that he would be leading "to exile"[16] a body only partly light infantry, destined to a minor role in the southern army.

To make matters worse, on April 9 Lafayette went to a nearby port on Delaware Bay and dined on board the frigate "Hermione," which Captain Latouche had recently brought down. Latouche confirmed his belief that the second French division would soon be at hand with the intention of acting against New York. Moreover, Latouche assured him that on Washington's orders ships would be sent speedily from Newport to carry reinforcements to Greene. That confirmed what Lafayette was thoroughly prepared to believe—that while he returned with his New England troops to re-establish the Light Division, some other corps could be sent southward by water and arrive in better condition and at an earlier date than his detachment possibly could by going on foot.[17]

Returning to Elk, Lafayette politely but clearly indicated his preference to Washington. Nevertheless, he promised, despite "the great want of monney, baggage, cloathing under which both officers and men are suffering,"[18] to start toward Virginia in the morning. Lafayette was no less in need than his men, for most of his baggage had been lost, some of it appearing later on

[15] *Ibid.*, pp. 438–39.

[16] Lafayette to Hamilton, April 15, 1781, LC, Hamilton papers; *Works of Hamilton*, I, 219.

[17] Lafayette to Washington, April 10, 1781, *Mémoires* (Amer. ed.), pp. 500–501.

[18] *Ibid.*, p. 499.

the backs of prisoners taken in Maryland.[19] Clothed or naked, they were required to make haste, because Governor Lee begged for the protection of Maryland's seaports from a deliberate policy of arson upon which the enemy had embarked.[20] Besides Lafayette soon began to feel "the desire of having as many rivers as possible behind us to prevent desertion."[21] Several of his best officers, including Charlus and Colonel Vose, were, in fact, asking for leaves, and he could not well refuse.[22]

Both heart and mind told Lafayette he ought to go north. Appealing to Hamilton, who, he hoped, might still be at headquarters, he complained more freely than he dared complain to any other. "After a march of forty days," he grieved, "we will arrive at a time when the heat of the season will put an end to operations. . . . . Before we arrive we shall perhaps be reduced to five or six hundred men. There will be no light infantry formed, no attack against New York, none of those things which have flattered my mind." It all made sense only if Washington, having at last had an interview with Rochambeau at Newport, had decided to transfer the principal seat of the war to the South.[23]

Yet, as a soldier, Lafayette did not think "any consideration must delay the execution of superior orders."[24] And so, though "our officers and men are none too happy about it," though "we have neither money, nor clothes, nor shoes, nor shirts and in a few days shall be reduced to green peaches," though "our feet are torn for want of shoes and our hands itchy for want of linen . . . . all that will not prevent us from marching . . . . and

[19] Shriver, p. 85.

[20] Council to Lafayette, April 8, 1781, *Archives of Maryland*, XLV, 383; cf. Lafayette to Lee, April 10, 1781, J. T. Scharf, *Chronicles of Baltimore* (Baltimore, 1874), pp. 193–94. The original of this letter is in Sparks MSS XLIX, fols. 220–21.

[21] Lafayette to Lee, April 17, 1781, Shriver, pp. 83–84.

[22] Lafayette to Washington, April 10 (second letter), and April 12, 1781, LC, Washington papers, no. 48, fols. 53 and 70; to La Luzerne, April 10, 1781, *AHR*, XX (1915), 597.

[23] Lafayette to Hamilton, April 10, 1781, LC, Hamilton papers; *Works of Hamilton*, I, 217–19.

[24] Lafayette to Washington, April 10, 1781, *Mémoires* (Amer. ed.), p. 500.

tomorrow we shall set out to execute the orders of the general who believes that course necessary."[25] He likewise pressed his dire need upon the Board of War in such words as to raise in their minds the suspicion that he wished them to override Washington's orders and to send him back. When they, however, seemed to suggest a qualified obedience to his general's commands,[26] he wrote them a letter which he himself thought might perhaps appear "disrespectful and impolite."[27] "Nothing could stop me," he explained to Washington by way of apology for that burst of indignation, "when it might be suspected I objected to your plans or even differed in opinion."

Lafayette's moving description of his men's sufferings was perhaps somewhat too vivid for the facts. Some of them could not have looked very much more ragged and hungry than the enemy at this time, because Lafayette was able to detect and capture several spies and traders-with-the-enemy by their mistaking him and some of his officers for Britishers.[28] Nevertheless, the prospect of having to return south after having headed toward home was not attractive to his men. When orders to face about and march to Baltimore were issued, wholesale defection began. On April 10 eight men deserted from the Massachusetts battalion alone, eleven more on the next day,[29] and nine from the Rhode Island battalion a few days later ("the best men they had").[30]

New and unexpected difficulties caused a postponement of Lafayette's march. A sudden rainstorm made the roads impassable, and to secure enough wagons and teams he had to resort to impressment. Starting out a day later than he had promised, his forces reached the Susquehanna on April 12.[31] There letters

---

[25] Lafayette to La Luzerne, April 10, 1781, *loc. cit.*, p. 598; cf. Lafayette to Greene, April 17, 1781, *loc. cit.*

[26] Cf. Lafayette to Greene, April 17, 1781, *loc. cit.*

[27] Lafayette to Washington, April 13, 1781, *Mémoires* (Amer. ed.), p. 503.

[28] Dispatch dated Baltimore, April 24, 1781, *Newport Mercury*, May 19, 1781; cf. Lafayette to Lee, April 10, 1781, *loc. cit.*; Shriver, p. 78.

[29] "Wild's journal," p. 135.

[30] Lafayette to Washington, April 14, 1781, *Mémoires* (Amer. ed.), p. 505.

[31] Lafayette to Washington, April 12, 1781, *loc. cit.*; April 13, 1781, *loc. cit.*

were received from Greene and Washington. They coincided in making Lafayette more satisfied with his new duties. Washington gave him permission to remain in Virginia practically independent of Greene, if Greene approved.[32] Greene asked him to proceed against Arnold, intending himself to move farther into South Carolina. In that way Greene hoped to prevent a junction of Arnold, who would be obliged to devote his energies to Lafayette, and Cornwallis, who would be obliged to follow him into South Carolina.[33] Lafayette considered that plan "a great piece of generalship,"[34] and he hastened to comply. Though he still retained confidence in his troops, he expected that further desertions would continue to diminish their numbers.[35] And the deserters were "our best, finest and most experienced soldiers."[36]

Three days were taken in hanging one of the captured spies and in putting the soldiers and the baggage across the Susquehanna River. Because of a high wind the marquis had not dared to place his wagons on board the ferry boats and impressed others on the other side of the river. "The Susquehanna," Lafayette said,[37] "was my Rubicon." Once past it he expected to give up all hope of being recalled to headquarters and to devote his entire energy to the British in Maryland and Virginia. While waiting at Susquehanna Ferry, he received a letter from Washington,[38] explaining that the project of attacking New York had once more been postponed. That cleared the atmosphere, though not altogether.

Lafayette spent the day on which he crossed the "Rubicon" in a sort of confessional, retailing to Washington his remaining grievances. A letter of Washington's, intercepted and published

[32] Washington to Lafayette, April 11, 1781, Fitzpatrick, XXI, 445; Lafayette to Washington, April 13, 1781, *loc. cit.*, p. 504.

[33] Greene to Lafayette, April 2, 1781, Johnson, II, 39.

[34] Lafayette to Greene, April 17, 1781, *loc. cit.*

[35] Lafayette to Washington, April 14, 1781, *loc. cit.*, p. 504.

[36] Lafayette to Washington, April 15, 1781, LC, Washington papers, no. 48, fol. 144a.

[37] Lafayette to La Luzerne, *AHR*, XX (1915), 598.   [38] April 11, 1781, *loc. cit.*

by the Tory press, indicated that, whatever Washington's public attitude toward Rochambeau might be, privately he regarded the French lack of enterprise as responsible for the failure to capture Arnold. Lafayette frankly declared that that letter gave him "pain on many political accounts." He also mentioned for the first time that he had long known of Washington's
quarrel with Hamilton and he now wanted Washington to know
that from the first he had exerted every means in his power "to
prevent a separation which I know was not agreeable to your
Excellency." He unmistakably indicated, too, his doubts regarding the wisdom of Washington's decision to send him south.
The commander-in-chief thus had deprived himself of "confidential communications . . . . which my peculiar situation with
both sides of the alliance would enable me to make." In addition, he had offended the French minister, who had sent Lafayette a letter which it would be improper to show Washington
because it was "too expressive of his grief for my departure
owing to a particular friendship for me." That "confessional"
the marquis sent to Washington by Gouvion, another of his best
officers, who was returning to headquarters.[39] With Gouvion
went also a new protest to Hamilton that "while the French are
coming I am going." But, the perplexed young general concluded, "if I go to exile, come and partake it with me."[40]

Once the high winds permitted the "Rubicon" to be crossed,
Lafayette proceeded to act with greater vigor than he had
shown of late. He requested the Maryland militia to arrest deserters. He also endeavored to shame his men into a contempt
for disloyalty. "The detachment," he announced in general orders, "was intended to fight an enemy far superior in number.
The general was, for his part, determined to encounter them,
but such of the soldiers as had an inclination to abandon him,
might dispense with the danger and crime of desertion, as every
one of them who should apply to headquarters for a pass to join

[39] Lafayette to Washington, April 15, 1781, *loc. cit.;* cf. Washington to Lund Washington, March 28, 1781, Fitzpatrick, XXI, 385–86; and Washington to Lafayette,
April 22, 1781, *ibid.,* pp. 490–91.

[40] April 15, 1781, *loc. cit.*

their corps in the North might be sure to obtain it immediately."[41] It was a risky thing to do, as Lafayette might well have been left to face the enemy nearly alone. But it worked. The prospect of glorious action, the efforts of their young leader to clothe and feed them, his attitude that only those who wished might stay had telling results. Soldiers who had already received permission to return now begged leave to remain. A sick sergeant tearfully pled to be allowed to trail after the army in a cart, and Lafayette yielded. Eight deserters returned and confessed their remorse.[42] Lafayette followed the policy of mixing kindness with severity. He hanged one deserter, discharged another in dishonor, and refused to permit those who had been ordered north to stay. Those who remained began to think of being sent home as a disgrace.[43]

Preceding his men by a day, Lafayette reached Baltimore on April 16. He stayed there, while his troops marched south of the town and crossed the ferry, where nine men were drowned.[44] Despite accidents and desertions, they had reached Baltimore with "about thousand men rank and file and a company of artillery."[45] In Baltimore Lafayette witnessed preparations for the defense of Maryland that gave him new courage. McHenry was now president of the Baltimore Board of War. Availing himself of McHenry's influence with the merchants of that town, Lafayette decided to raise money on his own bond. It was an expedient, McHenry thought, which "no one but himself would have thought of."[46] Lafayette was thus able to obtain about £2,000. With that sum he bought "a few hats, some shoes, some blankets, and a pair of linen over alls and a shirt to each man."[47]

[41] As quoted in Lafayette to Washington, April 18, 1781, *Mémoires* (Amer. ed.), pp. 405–6.

[42] Lafayette to La Luzerne, April 22, 1781, *AHR*, XX (1915), 599.

[43] *Ibid.*; and Lafayette to Greene, April 17, 1781, *loc. cit.* Lafayette's story in *Mémoires*, I, 267–68, does not mention the deserter who was hanged.

[44] "Wild's journal," pp. 135–36; Lafayette to Lee, April 17, 1781, *loc. cit.*

[45] Lafayette to Greene, April 17, 1781, *loc. cit.*

[46] McHenry to Greene, April 16 [18?], 1781, [Paris M. Davis], *Complete history of the Marquis de Lafayette . . . . by an officer in the late army* (Columbus, 1858), p. 100.

[47] Lafayette to Greene, April 17, 1781, *loc. cit.*

The foremost ladies of Baltimore were easily induced by the charming marquis, at a ball given in his honor,[48] to make the shirts, once the linen was paid for; and the overalls were left to the army tailors. Lafayette hoped that the £2,000 could be redeemed eventually from the money which France was expected to lend to the United States, but meanwhile pledged himself to reimburse it (with interest) in two years (when he should be twenty-five, the age at which the French law gave him complete control of his own property), if no one else did.[49]

By the time all these steps had been taken, Lafayette saw some prospect of clothing his men and stopping desertion, and began to be more cheerful. Although his pen had not been idle of late (he had written to Washington alone at least one letter nearly every day of the preceding week), his dispatches had been brief. But now he became effusive again and poured forth the entire history of his expedition since he had left New Windsor in February on eight foolscap pages addressed to General Greene.[50] Once more glory seemed to beckon. "You have so little ambition, my dear general," he wrote, "that you could not conceive my vishes on those accounts, was it not for the knowledge you have been able to get from our intimacy. But those motives are to be out of the question when public good is interested, and whenever it can be done with propriety, I know you will be glad to gratify me." And now in addition to the love of glory he was impelled by the desire for revenge. He had learned that General William Phillips was in command of the reinforcements that had joined Arnold at Portsmouth and, as Arnold's senior officer, was now in charge of the troops which opposed him in Virginia. Out of his childhood came the memory of the story of how his father had died, shot to pieces by English cannon at the Battle of Minden. The artillery officer who had commanded those cannon was Phillips! He told Greene of that

[48] Lafayette to La Luzerne, April 22, 1781, *loc. cit.*, p. 601; *Mémoires*, I, 267.

[49] Shriver, facsimile of bond, opp. p. 28; J. C. Fitzpatrick, *Spirit of the Revolution* (Boston, 1924), facsimile of subscription list, opp. p. 214 and pp. 215-16).

[50] April 17, 1781, *loc. cit.*

strange coincidence and added laconically, "I would have no objection to contract the latitude of his plans."

The marquis' intention now was to reach Richmond as quickly as possible. "The common way of marching troops" appeared to him "so dilatory that I would be upon the roads or at the ferry for an eternity." He determined to discard it. Instead he proposed to leave his artillery, tents, sick, and other incumbrances behind, impress as many horses and wagons as he could find, and advance by forced marches. He immediately sent letters to Governors Lee and Jefferson, apologizing for the "inconveniences" he had inflicted and would have to inflict. "Nothing makes me more unhappy than a necessity to impress private property, thereby distressing our best citizens,"[51] but "uncommon dangers require uncommon remedies."[52] Lafayette's next report to Washington[53] was much more cheerful than his earlier ones had been because of the "pleasanter prospect" he saw before him.

On April 19 Lafayette rejoined his division, but bad weather kept him in camp until the twentieth.[54] When they began their march again, half of the men rode in the impressed wagons, the other half proceeded on foot. They changed at regular intervals. In that way the ones tired from marching rested in the wagons though the whole contingent kept moving. It imparted to the painful experience of forced marches, McHenry thought,[55] an air of novelty and frolic. They covered twenty-eight miles the first day and, crossing the Potomac into Virginia on the twenty-first, arrived at Alexandria.

Lafayette had sent ahead one of his aides-de-camp to ask the civil authorities of Alexandria to prepare for his route to

---

[51] Lafayette to Lee, April 17, 1781, *loc. cit.*

[52] Lafayette to Jefferson, April 17, 1781, Chinard, *Lafayette and Jefferson* p. 37.

[53] April 18, 1781, *Mémoires* (Amer. ed.), pp. 403–6.

[54] "Wild's journal," p. 136. See also Lafayette to Jefferson, April 21, 1781, Jackson Collection, and Lafayette to La Luzerne, April 22, 1781, *AHR*, XX (1915), 600. On the basis of these letters, the itinerary given here differs somewhat from Nolan's (p. 168) and Charavay's (pp. 72–73).

[55] McHenry to Greene, April 16, 1781, *loc. cit.*

Fredericksburg.[56] Nevertheless, he found that Alexandria had not been co-operative. He had to buy some more shoes on his own credit;[57] not a single wagon was available for transportation, and he had again to resort to military impress. He was careful to avoid unnecessary roughness, putting the unpleasant task in the hands of an aide who was a Virginian[58] and sending only noncommissioned officers with him ("to be more certain of their delicacy toward the inhabitants"). But, he insisted, "my respect for the rights and convenience of the citizens cannot be equalled but by my zeal to forward every means of securing their freedom." He flattered himself, he said, that Virginia's inhabitants "could not deny us the means of advancing to their defense." For "there is not one soldier but who sacrifices more in this expedition than would be the very loss of the articles which we borrow for two or three days." Again he appealed to Governor Jefferson,[59] apologizing for what had been done to private property and urging that the civil authorities exert themselves more vigorously in the future if property were to be respected on his march between Fredericksburg and Richmond. Having already sent Colonel Barber to Philadelphia to plead with the Board of War, he also addressed Congress once more for provisions and money.[60]

The need for haste and strenuous measures was instant, since Phillips was reported to be on the offensive, with Richmond, the capital of Virginia, as his objective. Several of the enemy's ships

[56] Lafayette to Jefferson, April 21, 1781, loc. cit.

[57] Lafayette to La Luzerne, April 22, 1781, loc. cit.

[58] Lafayette to Jefferson, April 21, 1781, loc. cit. On Lafayette's staff at this time were several Virginians. Among them were Richard Clough Anderson ("Ye Andersons of Virginia," Old Northwest genealogical quarterly, XI [1908], 241), William Langborn (Virginia state papers, II, 92), Cadwallader Jones (Lafayette to Greene, May 18, 1781, Clements Library), and William Constable (Virginia state papers, II, 122–23). It seems very likely that George Augustine Washington, the general's nephew, was also one of them at this time, as he certainly was later (see Lafayette to "my dear George," April 21, 1781, Gardner-Ball Collection, and G. A. Washington to Weedon, June 2, 1781, APS, Weedon papers, no. 100), though Fitzpatrick (XXI, 488 n. and XXII, 66 n.) implies that he remained at New Windsor until May.

[59] Lafayette to Jefferson, April 21, 1781, loc. cit.

[60] Lafayette to Congress, April 22, 1781, PCC, no. 156, fols. 127–29; Tower, II, 261–62.

had actually come up the Potomac and had plundered and burned some plantations. Lafayette learned that, by going on board the enemy's vessels and consenting to give them provisions, Lund Washington, the general's nephew and agent at Mount Vernon, had saved all Washington's property but some slaves that deserted. Ashamed that anyone representing his friend should have acted in that fashion, he related the episode in his next dispatch to New Windsor.[61] Lund Washington's action, as Lafayette had foreseen, was repudiated by the general —in fact, even before he received the marquis' report of it.[62]

When Lafayette moved forward again from Alexandria, he could do so without fear of putting a greater distance between himself and a more glorious field of action around New York. For to Alexandria had come a note from headquarters assuring him that the interview with Rochambeau had at last taken place and had confirmed Washington in his decision to remain on the defensive.[63] "What the devil could he have told them?" Lafayette wondered,[64] still convinced that his superiors were making a mistake in not pushing the New York enterprise. If honor was to be won during that campaign, however, it was now obvious that it would have to be sought in the South.

As Lafayette's army advanced toward Fredericksburg, it became clear that his impressments were having the effects he feared. On their approach horses and wagons were hidden or put out of reach. Lafayette contented himself with the reflection that "when we are not able to do what we wish, we must do what we can"[65] and made his men go on foot as fast as dust and heat would allow without ruining them as a military unit. Crossing the Rappahannock, he reached Fredericksburg only on April 25. There a letter from Governor Jefferson[66] informed him

[61] April 23, 1781, *Mémoires* (Amer. ed.), pp. 406–7.

[62] Washington to Lund Washington, April 30, 1781, Fitzpatrick, XXII, 14; to Lafayette, May 4, 1781, *ibid.*, pp. 31–32.

[63] Washington to Lafayette, April 14, 1781, *ibid.*, XXI, 455–57.

[64] Lafayette to La Luzerne, April 22, 1781, *loc. cit.*, p. 600.

[65] Lafayette to Jefferson, April 25, 1781, Historical Society of Pennsylvania.

[66] April 23, 1781, *Jefferson's writings* (mem. ed.), XIX, 344–45 (which must be read together with the letter of Jefferson to Washington, April 23, 1781, *ibid.*,

that the enemy had moved up the James River and was advancing upon Petersburg. Steuben with his Virginia militia did what he could to oppose Phillips but was unable to save that town. Stopping barely long enough to give his men a chance to wash and rest, Lafayette forced them on toward Bowling Green, over roads now made muddy by rain.[67]

At Bowling Green Tavern, Captain William North, Steuben's aide, was waiting.[68] Lafayette learned from North that the English under General Phillips and Arnold were probably 2,500 strong and that Steuben and Muhlenburg, with only about 1,000 militia behind them, had been gallantly but ineffectually attempting to impede their progress. By that time Phillips and Arnold had captured Petersburg and had marched to Osborne's, thirteen miles from Richmond, leaving a trail of burning ships, barracks, and warehouses behind them. Sending North back to Steuben with the request that he center his operations as long as possible south of the river, Lafayette hurried on to Richmond, several hours ahead of his detachment, now numbering about eight or nine hundred infantry eager for a fight.[69] They arrived there on the evening of April 29—not a moment too soon.

The rapidity of Lafayette's march surprised the enemy.[70] Only on the next day did Phillips and Arnold occupy Manchester, just across the river from Richmond. Had Lafayette come a day later, Richmond, defended only by a feeble corps of militia hastily gathered by General Thomas Nelson, must have fallen. It was afterward reported to Lafayette that when Phillips found

---

IV, 175–76, or the letter of Jefferson to the president of Congress, April 23, 1781, P. L. Ford [ed.], *Writings of Thomas Jefferson* [10 vols.; New York, 1892–99], III, 21–22, for a complete text); the text in Chinard, *Lafayette and Jefferson*, p. 38, is incomplete. Cf. Lafayette to Steuben, April 25, 1781, Tower, II, 287–88.

[67] "Wild's journal," p. 136.

[68] Lafayette to Jefferson, April 27, 1781, Chinard, *Lafayette and Jefferson*, p. 39; Lafayette to Steuben, April 27, 1781, Gates papers, box 16, no. 30.

[69] Lafayette to Greene, April 28, 1781, *Mémoires* (Amer. ed.), p. 506; May 3, 1781, Gardner-Ball Collection, Indiana University Library; May 3, 1781 (another letter), LC, Washington papers, no. 96, fol. 253.

[70] Lafayette to Greene, May 3, 1781, Ball collection; Lafayette to Washington, May 4, 1781, *Mémoires* (Amer. ed.), pp. 508–9.

Lafayette's corps already in possession of a good position outside the city, he "fell into a violent passion and swore vengeance
against me and the corps I had brought with me."[71] Several
hundred of Phillips' men ventured to cross the river but,
charged by a few militia dragoons, retreated to their boats and
back to Manchester. Finding that they might be caught between Lafayette and Steuben if they attempted to attack the
city, Phillips and Arnold vented their chagrin by destroying
some buildings and burning twelve hundred hogsheads of tobacco at Manchester. The Americans were too weak to go to
the defense of the noble weed.[72] Still fearing attack, Lafayette
directed Steuben to bring his detachment to Richmond. The
attack did not come. That evening the British returned to Osborne's and soon fell down the river again. The marquis had
saved Richmond—for the moment at least.[73]

The only serious passage that Lafayette had had with Phillips while the fate of Richmond was thus being determined was
not one of the sword but of the pen. Phillips accused a party of
American soldiers of having fired upon his troops from a flag-of-
truce vessel during one of the skirmishes preceding Lafayette's
arrival at Richmond. He wrote an angry letter, whose holier-
than-thou tone might easily have offended even a less Anglo-
phobe soul than the marquis, threatening reprisal unless the
guilty persons were surrendered and their conduct publicly dis-
avowed. That letter was followed by another accusing the
American commander of imprisoning and mistreating various
Virginians merely because they had accepted "protection for
their persons and properties" from the English. Again Phillips
threatened violent redress if Lafayette did not show himself to
be "a gentleman of liberal principles" who would not "countenance, still less permit to be carried into execution, the bar-

[71] Lafayette to Washington, May 4, 1781, *loc. cit.*, p. 509.

[72] *Ibid.*; Arnold to Clinton, May 12, 1781, Lieutenant-Colonel Banastre Tarleton,
History of the campaigns of 1780 and 1781 in the southern provinces of North America
(Dublin, 1787), pp. 247-48.

[73] Lafayette to Washington, May 4, 1781, *loc. cit.*, pp. 509-10; Lafayette to Greene,
May 3, 1781, LC, Washington papers, no. 96, fol. 253.

barous spirit which seems to prevail in the council of the present civil power of this colony."[74]

Phillips' letters were delivered to Lafayette upon his arrival at Richmond. It was only after Phillips' powers of reprisal were greatly diminished by his retreat that Lafayette found time to answer them. He promised to investigate the alleged violation of a flag of truce and to give every redress in his power "in case the report made to you is better grounded than the contrary one I have received." That subject, he said, he considered the only part of Phillips' letter that required an answer. "The style of your letters, sir, obliges me to tell you that, should your future favours be wanting in that regard due to the civil and military authority in the United States, which cannot but be construed into a want of respect to the American nation, I shall not think it consistent with the dignity of an American officer to continue the correspondence." Later, upon investigation, Lafayette concluded that there had been no violation of flags of truce by his troops and sent Phillips a brief note "to set you right in this matter."[75] The British general, Lafayette learned afterwards, received both communications "with a degree of politeness that seemed to apologize for his unbecoming stile."[76]

When it was definitely ascertained that the enemy had gone away, Lafayette celebrated his victory by a grand review of his entire command.[77] On a large plain outside the city the French marquis and the German baron examined an army of New England regulars and Virginia militia, as they paraded and presented arms. But there was little time for celebration. Lafayette feared that Phillips might try to land at Williamsburg or elude him and advance upon Fredericksburg. By building a redoubt commanding a bend in the James River at Hood's and stationing General Nelson with some militia at Williamsburg, he hoped to put Richmond beyond further attack; and he gave

[74] Phillips to Lafayette, April 28 and 29, 1781, *Mémoires* (Amer. ed.), pp. 412–14.

[75] Lafayette to Phillips, April 30, and May 3, 1781, *ibid.*, pp. 414–15.

[76] Lafayette to Washington, May 17, 1781, *ibid.*, p. 410.

[77] "Wild's journal," p. 137.

Brigadier-General Weedon orders[78] to raise a corps of militia for the defense of Fredericksburg. Then he moved toward Bottom's Bridge across the Chickahominy River to a position in a thick pine woods closer to Williamsburg and Fredericksburg, though only sixteen miles from Richmond.

The weather having again turned warm and sunny, Lafayette had ordered his men to cut off the lower parts of their coats so that they might move faster. Now complaints about rain and mud gave place to outbursts against heat and ticks.[79] But his troops were at last allowed to rest for a few days, and the new clothing from Baltimore, their tents, and baggage had a chance to catch up with them. Lafayette, too, found the leisure to reply to recent letters he had received from headquarters. Washington had met all his complaints by simply acknowledging that his hardships were inevitable, would have been inevitable for any other corps that had been sent upon the same errand, and were necessary for the public service; but, he added, Lafayette might return to headquarters if he preferred, leaving Steuben in command in Virginia. Washington reaffirmed his personal preference to have Lafayette at New Windsor because of their friendship but made it perfectly clear that he must not expect to be more honorably employed in the North than in the South, because the weight of the war would probably shift to the South that year.[80] Lafayette decided to stay where he was, though his position, he confessed, was far from enviable. He could fight only on the defensive. "No boats, no waggons, no intelligence, not one spy could be obtained. . . . . A defeat would have scattered the militia, lost the few arms we have, and knocked down this handfull of Continental troops." The general's kindliness once more dispelled the several doubts that had momentarily arisen. "Any mark of friendship I receive from you adds to my happiness, as I love you with all the sincerity

[78] May 3, 1781, collection of A. K. Ford, Minneapolis, Minn.

[79] "Wild's journal," p. 137.

[80] Washington to Lafayette, April 21, 1781, Fitzpatrick, XXI, 488–89; April 22, 1781 (two letters), ibid., pp. 489–91 and 493–96.

and warmth of my heart and the sentiment I feel for you goes to the very extent of my affections."[81]

A few days passed in wondering where the British would strike next. Suddenly Phillips appeared to change his plans. At the mouth of the James River, instead of stopping at Williamsburg or rounding the Capes and sailing toward Fredericksburg, he faced about and sailed up the river again. The reason for this unexpected maneuver, it later developed, was that Cornwallis was now expected in Virginia. Leaving his lieutenant, Lord Rawdon, to attend to Greene in South Carolina, he had decided to turn his own attention to Virginia. In order to unite with the British forces there, he instructed Phillips to wait for him at Petersburg. Lafayette's intelligence service was again in good working condition, for he knew of Phillips' orders almost as soon as Phillips himself did.[82]

Lafayette hastily returned to Richmond. He was in great danger. In a country cut up by bays and rivers, he would now be obliged to move rapidly on foot against two forces, either of which was in itself more than a match for him and could move at will and without fatigue in its boats. He could think of only one source of quick support. That was Wayne. Delayed at first by the slowness of recruiting and then by "want of cash,"[83] Wayne had been expected daily for about a month. He was now reported to have started out from York, Pennsylvania, and actually to be on the way. Lafayette sent him a hasty note.[84] Outside he wrote, "Public service. This letter being of grim importance must be forwarded day and night." Inside, after telling of the new danger he was in, he entreated, "Hasten to our relief, my dear Sir, and let me hear of you that I may regulate my movements accordingly." In the hope that the North Caro-

[81] Lafayette to Washington, May 4, 1781, *loc. cit.*, pp. 508–9.

[82] Lafayette to Wayne, May 7, 1781, Historical Society of Pennsylvania; *Casket*, IV (1829), 496–97; Lafayette to Sumner, May 7, 1781, Walter Clark (ed.), *State records of North Carolina* (16 vols.; Goldsboro, 1895–1907), XV, 454–55; Simcoe, pp. 202–3; Tarleton, p. 349.

[83] Henry P. Johnston, *The Yorktown campaign and the surrender of Cornwallis, 1781* (New York, 1881), p. 44 n.

[84] May 7, 1781, *loc. cit.*

lina militia might present an obstacle to Cornwallis' advance, he began communication with their general, Jethro Sumner.[85] He also reported his new predicament to Congress[86] and the commander-in-chief.[87] Steuben, meanwhile, was ordered to raise as many new recruits as he could and proceed to the relief of Greene.[88]

On May 8 the marquis crossed to the south bank of the James River and marched his men toward Petersburg, determined to do what he could to impede Phillips without risking a battle. The British got there first. Lafayette had to halt at Osborne's outside the town and wait. Taking possession of a camp which the English had established only a few days before, Lafayette slept in General Phillips' bed that night but would be, he confessed, "too polite not to return it to him as soon as he needs it."[89] To make matters worse it was now reported that Clinton was coming south to join with Cornwallis and Phillips in the "party." "So here I am proscribed by that triumvirate," Lafayette joked bitterly, "though, not being as eloquent as Cicero, it is not my tongue that those gentlemen will cut off."[90] Faced by the excellent mounted units of Lieutenant-Colonels Simcoe and Tarleton, Lafayette implored La Luzerne to send him Lauzun's Legion: "Although my situation is not marvelous, I can not help smiling at the ridiculous figure . . . . which our militia dragoons cut without pistols, swords, saddles, bridles, and boots. . . . . What annoys me most is the shortage of everything, the total want of resources, the slowness in filling orders that we are forced to put up with in this region."[91]

Fortunately, Phillips was content to wait at Petersburg for Cornwallis. Lafayette's men were given a chance to catch their breath and reconnoiter the enemy's position.[92] He decided that

[85] Lafayette to Sumner, May 7, 1781, *loc. cit.*; May 11, 1781, *ibid.*, pp. 458–59.

[86] May 8, 1781, LC, Washington papers, no. 96, fol. 253.

[87] May 8, 1781, *Mémoires* (Amer. ed.), pp. 511–12.

[88] Lafayette to Steuben, Sparks MSS LXXXIV, p. 18.

[89] Lafayette to La Luzerne, May 9, 1781, *AHR*, XX (1915), 596.

[90] *Ibid.*

[91] *Ibid.*, p. 597.   [92] Tarleton, p. 349.

he could better protect Richmond by crossing to the north side of the river and yet not lose contact with the British if he left Muhlenburg with the militia on the south side. Accordingly, he took a new post around Kingsland Ferry and Wilton, part of his men crossing and recrossing the river at frequent intervals and making camp wherever they chanced to be, sometimes without tents.[93] Meanwhile, appeals to the governor of Virginia went forth by letter and by aide-de-camp. Jefferson made clear that he had done all he could to meet Lafayette's demands. If sufficient reinforcements did not now arrive, "I shall candidly acknowledge that it is not in my power to do anything more than to represent to the General Assembly that unless they can provide more effectually for the execution of the laws it will be vain to call on militia."[94]

The sincerity of Jefferson's own efforts could not be doubted. If they produced men and boats only very slowly, they nevertheless were important to the young marquis because they brought him into close though harried association with another leading American democrat. The readiness of Jefferson to admit that as the executive in a democratic government he could assume very little responsibility may have been exasperating to the French aristocrat-soldier, but it helped him to understand (none too sympathetically) the democratic process. He found that even the doctors were unable to take obvious measures for the care of sick and wounded such as establishing hospitals in safe places "unless authorized by a higher power."[95] Lafayette was impatient with such democratic dilatoriness. "With the handful of men I have there is no chance of resisting the combined armies unless I am speedily and powerfully reinforced," he notified Weedon from Wilton.[96] ". . . . There is more militia going off than there is militia coming in. What we have is, how-

---

[93] "Wild's journal," p. 138.

[94] Langborn to Jefferson, May 12, 1781, *Virginia state papers*, II, 92; Jefferson to Lafayette, May 14, 1781, Chinard, *Lafayette and Jefferson*, pp. 40-42.

[95] Cf. Surgeon Mathew Pope to Jefferson, May 17, 1781, *Virginia state papers*, II, 104.

[96] May 15, 1781, Tower, II, 308-9.

ever, called the Army, and that is expected from us which an Army could perform." He also turned for advice to Steuben, whose experience in Virginia was greater than his: "You perfectly know, my dear Baron, what ought to be done by the assembly to give energy to governement. Unless spirited measures are entered into we are certainly ruined. Raising, mounting, arming, transporting, subsisting a body of troops are things that cannot be done under the present regulations."[97]

And where was Wayne? The "grim" dispatch that Lafayette had sent to him to be "forwarded day and night" had already been on the road for over a week and was not to be delivered until a few more days had gone by.[98] Even after its late delivery Wayne was not ready to march for yet a few days. Because the men had been paid in depreciated currency which would buy little since few would receive it as money, another mutiny in the Pennsylvania line had broken out. It was scotched only by the severest measures. Twelve of the leaders were sentenced to death. At the first volley by the executing platoon seven fell, six dead. The seventh was bayoneted, Wayne forcing the execution at the point of a pistol. The remaining five leaders were hanged. Then at length the Pennsylvanians, a few days after Wayne had promised, began their southward march, "mute as fish."[99]

In daily expectation of Wayne's arrival Lafayette once more sent him a plea for "the greatest celerity,"[100] urging him to march without his baggage. Meanwhile, he issued orders to the local militia to impede Cornwallis' approach as much as possible, to send reinforcements, and to impress horses, saddles, bridles, and wagons, though "with the greatest delicacy."[101] Somehow he must create a cavalry unit. "Unless we have a re-

[97] Lafayette to Steuben, May 17, 1781, Gates papers, box 16, no. 34.

[98] Endorsements on Lafayette's letter to Wayne, May 7, 1781, *loc. cit.;* Wayne to Lafayette, May 19, 1781, Historical Society of Pennsylvania.

[99] Fitzpatrick, XXII, 191 n.

[100] May 15, 1781, Historical Society of Pennsylvania.

[101] Lafayette to Lawson, May 16, 1781, Jackson Collection.

spectable body of horse," he insisted, "Simcoe and Tarleton will over run the country."[102]

Lafayette's good fortune, nevertheless, did not altogether fail. Relief from unexpected quarters came to make his situation more hopeful. General Greene had succeeded in inflicting a rather costly victory upon Lord Rawdon before Camden, South Carolina. When Lafayette learned of that glorious defeat he congratulated Greene upon it: "The late engagement of Camden is like every action you risk. No ill consequences in a defeat—the enemy's ruin if victorious. I wish I had abilities, and I wish I had circumstances that could admit of such opportunities." Greene's position being less exposed than it had been, he gave permission to Lafayette to devote attention exclusively to the defense of Virginia.[103]

Lafayette thus found himself in independent command of Virginia. Though he instructed Steuben to continue southward with his new levies, he felt at greater liberty to take action free of any consideration but his own military position. Furthermore, from the Board of War, on Washington's repeated insistence, had come eleven hundred stands of arms. Lafayette, feeling that "the South Carolina troops are entitled to every preference and from their successes depends our delivery," requested Steuben to take as many of these new arms as he needed. The new supplies, he believed, would enable Steuben's levies to leave behind their old arms.[104] Not yet having learned that the state had provided only two men to repair arms (though on Steuben's insistence six more would be added in May),[105] he hoped he might use re-worked pieces to relieve his own want.

For several reasons the British did not move to crush Lafa-

[102] Lafayette to Weedon, May 16, 1781, Historical Society of Pennsylvania, Gratz collection.

[103] Lafayette to Greene, May 18, 1781, Clements Library; cf. Lafayette to Steuben, May 17, 1781, *loc. cit.*

[104] Lafayette to Steuben, May 17, 1781, *loc. cit.*

[105] Steuben to Lafayette, May 22, 1781, New York Historical Society, Steuben papers, Vol. XII, no. 66.

yette. Their hesitation was caused in part by their unfounded suspicion that Wayne's forces had already joined him and that he was stronger than he actually was.[106] In part, too, it was explained by the enemy's unwillingness to raise any new complications while waiting for Cornwallis. But the chief reason, Lafayette eventually learned, was that General Phillips had lain mortally ill for several days with some kind of fever. There was a certain ironic justice in an event immediately preceding his death. Gimat's battalion, to divert the enemy's attention from a shipment of cartridges to North Carolina, went to the Appomattox River across from Petersburg and bombarded the British for a while. A cannonball passed through Mrs. Boland's house, where Phillips lay dying, and killed a negro woman, slave of Mrs. Boland. Shortly afterwards Phillips died (May 13). It had not been Lafayette's intention to add to a sick man's suffering. He had not, in fact, known that Phillips was sick, but tradition quickly embroidered the facts into a romantic story of revenge for the death of Lafayette's father at Minden.[107]

Now Arnold commanded the British in Virginia once more. Just before Phillips' death, Arnold, wishing to arrange an exchange of prisoners, sent an officer under a flag with a letter signed by him. Lafayette asked the officer whether Phillips was dead yet. On receiving a negative reply, he availed himself of Phillips' seniority as an excuse for refusing to receive a renegade's letter, though he admitted that he would have been willing to communicate with any other British officer. The next day the same officer returned. Phillips was dead now, he said, and Arnold was once more commander of the British forces.

---

[106] Arnold to Clinton, May 12, 1781, Tarleton, p. 349; Cornwallis to Tarleton, May 15, 1781, *ibid.*, pp. 298 and 343-44; Arnold to Clinton, May 16, 1781, I. N. Arnold, *Life of Benedict Arnold* (Chicago, 1880), pp. 334-47, and *Mercure de France*, July 7, 1781, pp. 16-17.

[107] Lafayette to Washington, May 18, 1781, *Mémoires* (Amer. ed.), pp. 512-15; Lafayette to Noailles, May 22, 1781, Patou, pp. 41-47. Cf. J. J. Graham (ed.), *Memoir of General [Samuel] Graham* (Edinburgh, 1862), p. 37; Tarleton, p. 349; Alexander Garden, *Anecdotes of the American Revolution* (3 vols.; Brooklyn, 1865), III, 169-71. For the legend see Sparks MSS XXXII, pp. 131-32. The date of Phillips' death is usually given as May 13, but May 15 is correct: see Clinton to Eden, May 31, 1781, Stevens, *Facsimiles*, VII, no. 748. See p. 245 below.

Lafayette still refused to deal with the "English general who is at this moment commander-in-chief." But he added, "In case any other English officer should honour him with a letter, he would always be happy to give the officer every testimony of his esteem." Arnold avenged himself by refusing in his turn to communicate with officers subordinate to Lafayette and by threatening to send all his prisoners in the future to the West Indies. Lafayette reported his conduct to Washington[108] and Greene.[109] "A correspondence with Arnold is so very repugnant to my feelings that I can never conquer them so far as to answer his letters," he wrote Greene. "I am the more averse to it as Arnold is a very proud correspondent, and I can not submit to such a stile from the rascal." Washington approved wholeheartedly of the jealousy for American honor which Lafayette had thus exhibited.[110]

Having taken independent command in Virginia, Lafayette now felt a greater sense of responsibility than he had ever felt as commander of a dependent unit. In close collaboration with Steuben, who stopped at Camp Wilton on his way to join Greene's army, he reorganized the quartermasters' corps, the commissary, and the hospitals.[111] He also continued his valiant efforts to create a cavalry unit. Major Nelson's state troop "fatigued to death" and with broken-down horses, ten or twelve[112] men from Colonel Armand's partisan corps who had been left behind in Virginia and who "excite compassion," a few volunteers who were "very clever but volunteers," and thirty-two Continental cavalry under Colonel Anthony Walton White were the best he could gather. He had had a few militia cavalry, but "their time was out and they went home this morning," he reported to Greene in the midst of his efforts.[113] With the handful

[108] Lafayette to Washington, May 17, 1781, *loc. cit.*, pp. 410–11, in which was enclosed (p. 415) the correspondence with Arnold's aides.

[109] Lafayette to Greene, May 18, 1781, *loc. cit.*

[110] Washington to Lafayette, May 31, 1781, Fitzpatrick, XXII, 139.

[111] Lafayette to Greene, May 18, 1781, *loc. cit.*

[112] The figure *ten* comes from *ibid.*, but in his letter to Greene, May 24, 1781, Morgan Library, Yorktown, Vol. I, Lafayette says *twelve*.

[113] May 18, 1781, *loc. cit.*

that remained he would have to cope with crack troopers numbering about ten times his total cavalry force and led by reputed veterans like Colonel Tarleton.

In reorganizing his corps, Lafayette acted always on the principle that his army was to be looked upon "but in an inferior and secondary light" to Greene's.[114] When his reorganization was complete, he found he had around nine hundred Continentals, two brigades of militia under Muhlenburg and Nelson numbering between twelve and fifteen hundred (he could never be sure how many because they were constantly coming and going), about forty cavalrymen, and six pieces of artillery.[115] Arnold lay before him with one superior force, and Cornwallis was on his way with another. It was a situation calling for caution, a quality which Lafayette had not so far exhibited conspicuously. But he recognized all too easily that he must now move only with extreme circumspection. "To speak truth," he told Greene, "I become timid in the same proportion as I become independent. Had a superior officer been here, I could have proposed half a dozen of schemes."[116]

Cornwallis joined Arnold at Petersburg on May 20. Fewer than a hundred and fifty militia had turned out south of the Appomattox to stop him.[117] Lafayette did not blame the Virginia farmers for not leaving their spring plowing to leap to the sword. "There are no arms in this country, any more than in the provinces of France," he explained.[118] The combined British force was, Cornwallis reported, "superior to La Fayette even after Wayne joins him."[119] The marquis sought refuge in retreat to Richmond. There he began a polite correspondence with

[114] *Ibid.*

[115] On the number of cavalry see Lafayette to Morgan, May 21, 1781, James Graham, *Life of General Daniel Morgan of the Virginia line of the army of the United States* (New York, 1856), pp. 375–76; on the other figures, see Lafayette to Greene, May 18, 1781, *loc. cit.*

[116] Lafayette to Greene, May 18, 1781, *loc. cit.*

[117] Lafayette to Noailles, May 22, 1781, *loc. cit.*, pp. 42–43.

[118] *Ibid.*, p. 44.

[119] Cornwallis to Rawdon, May 20, 1781, Charles Ross (ed.), *Correspondence of Charles first Marquis Cornwallis* (2d ed.; 3 vols.; London, 1859), I, 99.

Cornwallis regarding the relief and exchange of prisoners, which he had refused to carry on with Arnold. This correspondence continued in gentlemanly tones throughout the whole of the bitter campaign that followed.[120]

At Richmond, Lafayette also renewed his efforts to increase his army. He sent requests to the governor of Maryland for militia from that state.[121] Learning that General Daniel Morgan of the Virginia riflemen, who had gone home on account of ill-health and had recently been ordered to join the Carolina army, was still in the state, Lafayette turned to him too, and "with the freedom of an old and affectionate friend" begged him to bring his riflemen to the rescue as well as to aid him with his own military ability.[122] Similar personal appeals went out to other officers of influence;[123] and to La Luzerne another plea for Lauzun's Legion.[124] Despite all these efforts, the promised contingents from Virginia fell far short of expectations.

In fact, Lafayette's demands were beginning to cause some grumbling among the people of the state. Why had he stayed north of the river while the enemy had massed on the south bank? "The people in this county don't like people that they can't understand, so well as they used to do," wrote a Virginia militia officer.[125] "I fear the Marquis may lose his credit. Deserters, British, cringing Dutchmen, and busy little Frenchmen swarm about Hd. Quarters. The people do not love Frenchmen; every person they cant [sic] understand they take for a Frenchman." Lafayette knew that the "Dutchman" Steuben was un-

[120] Copies of Lafayette's several letters to Cornwallis were sent both to Congress and to Washington and are now to be found in PCC, no. 156, and Washington papers.

[121] Lafayette to Lee, May 21, 1781, Sparks MSS XXIX, pp. 528-30.

[122] May 21, 1781, loc. cit.

[123] Lafayette to Parker, May 17, 1781, J. F. Crocker, "The Parkers of Macclesfield, Isle of Wight County, Virginia," Virginia magazine of history, VI (1899), 423; to Moseley, May 22, 1781, Morristown (N.J.) National Historical Park; to Lawson, May 23, 1781, Jackson Collection. Cf. Nelson to Jefferson, May 25, 1781, Virginia state papers, II. 118.

[124] Lafayette to La Luzerne, May 22, 1781, AHR, XX (1915), 601-2.

[125] Captain H. Young to Colonel William Davies, May 21, 1781, Virginia state papers, II, 111-12.

popular[126] and admitted that he did not regret losing him, "as the hatred of Virginians toward him was truly hurtful to the cause."[127] But he would have been pained and surprised to find anyone doubting his own popularity. He still counted on Wayne's Pennsylvanians to save him. "On their arrival we shall be in a position to be beaten more decently, but at present we can only run away."[128]

Still the Pennsylvanians did not come, and no one seemed to know where they were. Lafayette began to fear that his reputation would be lost in Virginia. He turned once more to Hamilton for consolation. Laughing at himself for having objected to going southward because there would be nothing to do, he lamented that he had "so many arrangements to make, so many difficulties to combat, so many enemies to deal with, that I am just that much of a general as will make me an historian of misfortunes and nail my name upon the ruins of what good folks are pleased to call the Army in Virginia." He was particularly fearful that people would accuse him of lacking boldness. "To speak truth, I am affraid of myself as much as of the enemy. Independance [*sic*] has rendered me the more cautious as I know my warmth. But if the Pennsylvanians come, Lord Cornwallis shall pay some thing for his victory."[129] He also appealed to his brother-in-law to defend him among the French at Newport. Enumerating the tremendous odds he had had to cope with since his return to Virginia, he complained, "Excepting General Washington, none of my friends in the North has sent me any news. If they know no more than that about our affairs, I am afraid I shall be severely, even unjustly, judged. If I am wrong, I ask no better than to be blamed and shall plead guilty of lack of talent, lack of experience, or even of both; but as my numerical inferiority is immense, and our difficulties indescribable, I

[126] Lafayette to La Luzerne, May 22, 1781, *loc. cit.*, p. 601.

[127] Lafayette to Hamilton, May 23, 1781, LC, Hamilton papers; *Works of Hamilt,* I, 262–64.

[128] Lafayette to Noailles, May 22, 1781, *loc. cit.*, p. 45; cf. Lafayette to La Luzerne, May 22, 1781, *loc. cit.*, p. 601; and to Hamilton, May 23, 1781, *loc. cit.*

[129] Lafayette to Hamilton, May 23, 1781, *loc. cit.*

hope that you will tell our friends what you know about them, so that, if condemned, I shall at least be condemned only in so far as I deserve."[130]

In this letter Lafayette showed that he was not so busy that he could forget personal affairs. He expressed his concern about "the mean trick" that had been played in Paris on "a person whom I love." He was indignant that gossip should "come two thousand leagues looking for me in order to make me the hero of the current scandal, and for a woman who is two thousand leagues from the flirtations and intrigues of Paris in order to make her the victim of some wicked fiction." Someone had apparently written a song about his relations with Mme de Hunolstein which Lafayette did not think funny. And the author was one so high in society that Lafayette felt, if he challenged him, he could "in all conscience" defend himself "only half way." That would seem to point to the Duc de Chartres as the culprit —or perhaps even the king's brother, the Comte de Provence.[131]

Being for the moment challenged in a more ardent duel than Mme de Hunolstein's honor called for, Lafayette soon forgot his personal chagrin. His reputation as a soldier in America was of greater immediate concern than his honor in Parisian society. He sensed that people in Virginia had begun to think he might "lose his credit." He frankly expressed his concern to his commanding generals.[132] "I ardently wish my conduct may meet with your approbation," he wrote to both Washington and Greene. "Had I followed the first impulse of my temper," he said to Washington, "I would have risked some thing more. But I have been guarding against my own warmth; and this consideration that a general defeat which with such a proportion of militia must be expected would involve this state and our affairs into ruin, has rendered me extremely cautious in my move-

---

[130] Lafayette to Noailles, May 22, 1781, *loc. cit.*, pp. 46–47.

[131] *Ibid.*; cf. Gottschalk, *Lady-in-waiting*, pp. 77–78. The suggestion that the object of Lafayette's wrath was the Comte de Provence has been made by M. Bernard Faÿ, who informs me that he has discovered a satirical song about Lafayette and Mme de Hunolstein which was written by Provence.

[132] Lafayette to Washington, May 24, 1781, *Mémoires* (Amer. ed.), pp. 416–18; to Greene, May 24, 1781, *loc. cit.*

ments." Yet he did not dare to avoid fighting entirely because "the country would think herself given up." So he had determined to skirmish, "but not to engage too far, and particularly to take care against their immense and excellent body of horse, whom the militia fears as they would so many wild beasts." He begged again and again for a cavalry reinforcement. "I am not strong enough even to get beaten. Government in this state has no energy, and laws have no force." His letter to Greene showed the same uneasiness about his reputation as a soldier. "As I expect people who don't judge upon any rational scale will find it very strange that I have not yet beaten the ennemy to pieces, my comfort will be in the approbation of the general, yours, and that of a few friends, who, I hope, will think with me I could not do better."

At long last the marquis heard from Wayne.[133] The Pennsylvanian's message was none too encouraging. Even if Wayne had been able to leave York on the day his letter mentioned, he would not reach Richmond for a while. Lafayette decided to retreat if Cornwallis crossed the river and threatened the city. He moved all public stores and private property to Point of Fork, farther up the river, determined not "to expose the troops for the sake of a few houses, most of which are empty."[134] The government of Virginia had already fled to Charlottesville. Meanwhile, the enemy roamed the neighboring country with very little molestation. They surprised and captured some militia in Chesterfield County, destroyed a bridge at City Point, and crossed the river in force some miles below Richmond at Westover. There they were joined by a reinforcement of two thousand men sent from New York.[135] The British now numbered about seven thousand men; against them Lafayette could lead no more than three thousand.[136]

[133] Wayne to Lafayette, May 19, 1781, Historical Society of Pennsylvania, which Lafayette refers to in the letters to Washington and Greene, May 24, 1781, *loc. cit.*

[134] Lafayette to Washington, May 24, 1781, *loc. cit.*, p. 417.

[135] Lafayette to Washington, May 24, 1781 (a second letter), *Mémoires* (Amer. ed.), pp. 517-18.

[136] Jefferson to Washington, May 28, 1781, *Writings of Jefferson* (mem. ed.), IV, 182-83.

Counting upon his tremendous superiority in both the quantity and the equipment of his troops, Lord Cornwallis expected to meet with very little opposition from Lafayette. His purpose was not, however, as the marquis feared,[137] to capture the American army. It was rather to destroy the manufactories and warehouses of Virginia. Ever since Cornwallis had taken charge of the British army in the south, he had intended to cut off the southern states from the northern ones completely. He had found, however, that that was not easy to do, in large part because they were kept supplied by the arsenals and stores of Virginia. His purpose in joining forces with the British troops already in Virginia was therefore to bag Lafayette if he could, but principally to destroy the resources of the Old Dominion.

General Clinton did not approve entirely of Cornwallis' strategy. His own pet scheme was to attack Philadelphia, the American capital, again; and Cornwallis knew that he was expected to hold his army in readiness to co-operate in such an enterprise if the proper opportunity arose. He nevertheless felt that he could carry out his own purpose by a quick raid of the principal Virginia towns and return to the Chesapeake in time to carry out any new orders that Clinton might send him. As soon as he began his march of destruction, he notified his commandant of his intentions: "I shall now proceed to dislodge La Fayette from Richmond, and with my light troops to destroy any magazines or stores in the neighbourhood, which may have been collected either for his use or for General Greene's army. From thence I purpose to move to the neck at Williamsburg, which is represented as healthy, & where some subsistence may be procured, and keep myself unengaged from operations, which might interfere with your plan for the Campaign, untill I have the satisfaction of hearing from you."[138]

As soon as Lafayette learned that the British had crossed the

[137] For the origin of the belief that Cornwallis had announced on entering Virginia, "The boy cannot escape me," see Appen. II.

[138] Cornwallis to Clinton, May 26, 1781, B. F. Stevens (ed.), *The campaign in Virginia: an exact reprint of six rare pamphlets on the Clinton-Cornwallis controversy*, etc. (2 vols.; London, 1888), I, 488. See also *ibid.*, p. 489, and R. G. Adams, "A view of Cornwallis's surrender at Yorktown," *AHR*, XXXVII (1931), 28–29.

Campagne en Virginie du Major Général M. de La Fayette, où se trouvent les Camps et Marches, ainsy que ceux du Lieutenant Général L. Cornwallis. en 1781.

ve re-inked Lafayette's route. Thus it appears here as a darker line than Cornwallis'. The reverse is true on

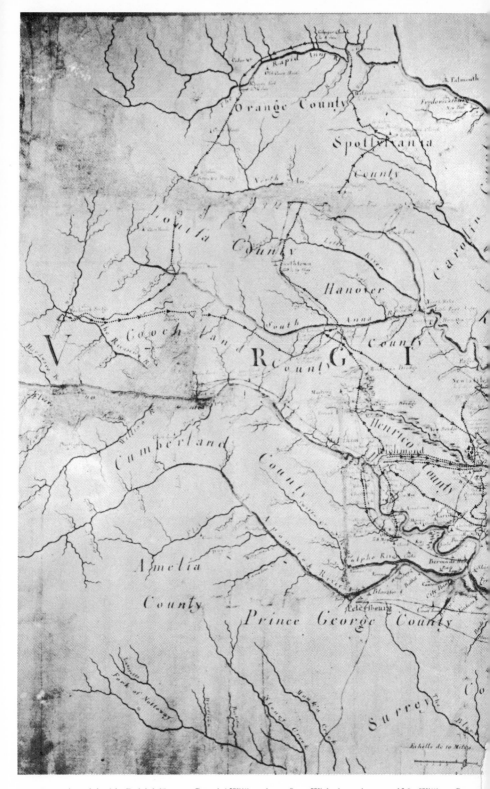

From the original in Raleigh Tavern, Colonial Williamsburg, Inc. With the assistance of Mr. William Cates, reproductions of the original.

James, he suspected an effort to turn his flank. Outnumbered by more than two to one, he immediately abandoned Richmond. He first moved seven miles north of the deserted capital, crossing the Chickahominy River. His chief desire was to avoid battle, if he could, for fear that his militia would turn and run, abandoning the few arms which he had succeeded in getting for them only by dint of great effort and earnest prayer. Yet he must also stop Cornwallis from getting to the north or to the west of him, for in the one direction lay Wayne's division, carrying with them, if they ever came, his one chance to achieve glory and in the other, his most valuable stores. He must, therefore, always keep a safe distance between him and the enemy and retreat in the direction of Fredericksburg, toward which Wayne was marching.

As Cornwallis advanced, unopposed except by felled trees and ruined bridges, Lafayette fell back. His purpose was, by moving in a line parallel to the enemy, always to keep to the upper country, north and west of Cornwallis. In that way he could cover either Point of Fork or Fredericksburg as emergency might require. By the time the British, avoiding Richmond, crossed the Chickahominy at Bottom's Bridge, which they repaired after Lafayette destroyed it, he had moved northwest and established camp between Allen's Creek and Gold Mine Creek, branches of the South Anna River.[139] On the way he learned that Greene had forced Lord Rawdon out of Camden. It was welcome news but offered him no immediate relief, as Greene not only did not turn northward to his help but, not knowing that Cornwallis was in Virginia, called upon Generals Steuben and Lawson to join him with the troops under their command.[140]

The peculiar nature of the terrain in tidewater Virginia proved to be a great boon to an army in retreat. True, it made it easy for the enemy, who had boats, to ferry across wherever

[139] "Wild's journal," p. 139; "Précis de la campagne de 1781," *Mémoires*, I, 477–78; Lafayette to Wayne, May 27, 1781, Historical Society of Pennsylvania; Tarleton, pp. 301–2; *Archives of Maryland*, XLVII, 261.

[140] Johnson, II, 127; Lafayette to Jefferson, May 28, 1781, Huntington Library, HM 22685; Lafayette to Steuben, May 29, 1781, Gates papers, box 16, no. 39.

they chose or to use the rivers for the transport of troops. But it also made it possible for Lafayette's army to cross the rivers by fords, bridges, or ferries and, destroying the bridges, hiding their boats, and guarding the fords, to take strong positions covered by bodies of water which could not easily be passed against resistance. The farmers, who refused to conceal their horses but grumbled if Lafayette impressed them, soon found that Tarleton did not observe that delicacy and respect for Virginia's civil authorities upon which Lafayette had insisted. Tarleton's dragoons were right behind him at Hanover Courthouse. At the same time a British force under General Alexander Leslie was sent down the James by water. Lafayette began to fear for the safety of Fredericksburg and particularly that the armament factory known as Hunter's Works, at Falmouth across the Rappahannock from Fredericksburg, might fall into the enemy's hands. He sent new exhortations to Wayne to hurry by forced marches.[141]

The marquis' fear of being caught on the flank by Tarleton and in the rear by Leslie while Cornwallis still lay before him with his main army was reason enough for insistence. There was the further risk that, in maneuvering to avoid being outflanked, Lafayette would uncover his stores at Point of Fork. He begged Steuben, if he could persuade himself that it would not be contrary to his orders to join Greene, to go with his new levies and with Lawson's militia and superintend the removal of the stores from Point of Fork.[142] He himself marched to the protection of Fredericksburg, ordering Weedon to move his livestock and stores, particularly those of Hunter's Works, to destroy all bridges and boats that the enemy might use, to gather together all the militia and volunteers he could find, and to inform Washington's family, so that they might get out of the enemy's reach.[143] Upon the receipt of urgent demands from Congress, he also ordered that the large number of Hessian prison-

[141] May 27, 28, 29, and 31, and June 4, 1781, Historical Society of Pennsylvania.

[142] Lafayette to Steuben, May 26, 1781, cited in Steuben to Lafayette, May 28, 1781, New York Historical Society, Steuben papers, Vol. XII, no. 73.

[143] Lafayette to Weedon, May 28 and 29, 1781, APS, Weedon papers.

ers, taken with Burgoyne's army and kept at Winchester, be started on their way to Massachusetts.[144] On his own responsibility he issued orders to Colonel White to impress two hundred horses and to create a cavalry worthy of the name, informing the governor that "nothing else will put it in my power to prevent the enemy from ravaging the country in small parties."[145] Meanwhile, the British burned warehouses and took prisoners at will.[146]

As Lafayette hastened to make a juncture with Weedon, the full significance of Greene's strategy was revealed to him in a letter which had been two weeks on the road. Greene had not only forced Rawdon out of Camden but had taken several of the posts in its neighborhood and was pushing his opponent hard. By the time Greene imparted this glorious news, he had learned of Lafayette's dire position. He therefore instructed him to keep Steuben's and Lawson's men in Virginia—as well as Wayne's, if they ever arrived. Lafayette congratulated Governor Jefferson and General von Steuben on this fortunate turn in Virginia's affairs. The pleasure of overrunning Virginia would now cost the British something, he exulted. "Time will come, I hope, when Lord Cornwallis will see his expedition in this state will amount to nothing."[147] The mere overrunning of a state did not mean its conquest, he stated[148] with something of his old self-confidence. The certainty that Wayne was not far off increased his cheerfulness.

Nevertheless, Lafayette continued to retreat from river to river. He had expected Weedon to join him at Mattapony Church, about twenty miles south of Fredericksburg, but Weedon had stayed at Fredericksburg to superintend the removal of his stores to a point of greater safety and to assemble militia

---

[144] Lafayette to Wood, June 3, 1781, *Virginia state papers*, II, 145–46.

[145] Lafayette to Jefferson, May 29, 1781, Chinard, *Lafayette and Jefferson*, p. 44.

[146] *Virginia state papers*, II, 129.

[147] Lafayette to Steuben, May 31, 1781, Public Record Office (London), C.O. 5/102, America and West Indies series 140/529–31.

[148] Lafayette to Jefferson, May 31, 1781, *ibid.*, 140/521–22.

around Hunter's Works.[149] Lafayette continued northward, moving not directly to Fredericksburg but somewhat to the west of it, crossing a branch of the Mattapony River at Corbin's Bridge and the Rapidan River at Ely's Ford. His purpose was to avoid being outflanked by the rapidly moving cavalry of the enemy which would thus prevent his union with Wayne. In that way Lafayette ran the risk of losing Hunter's Works without any greater resistance than Weedon could put up, but he had to take that risk, since for him the all-important objective was to effect a union with Wayne.[150]

Cornwallis marched to the vicinity of Cook's Ford on the North Anna River, and there he stopped. He had decided that Lafayette's maneuvers had made it impossible to prevent the junction with Wayne and that there was not enough property left at Hunter's Works to make an attack on Fredericksburg and Falmouth worth the cost. Moreover, Lafayette's position was such as to enable him to make a flank attack upon the British as they moved upon the town. So, as soon as it became clear that the marquis would cross the Rapidan, Cornwallis sent Simcoe and Tarleton to raid in the south, which Lafayette had left particularly undefended. Charlottesville was an especially tempting prize.[151] The governor and the Virginia legislature (being, as Lafayette said, "less dilatory in their motions than they had formerly been in their resolutions")[152] had fled from Richmond and assembled there; and there too the state had removed its stores. Steuben was nearly surprised by Simcoe's corps at Point of Fork and retreated hastily to the south side of the James, losing some of the stores that Lafayette had counted on him to defend.[153] Charlottesville was less fortunate. Tarleton, riding

[149] Weedon to Lafayette, June 1 and 4, 1781, "Letters of General Weedon," *William and Mary quarterly*, XXVII (1918–19), 167–68; *Calendar of the correspondence . . . . of Brig. Gen. George Weedon*, etc. (Philadelphia, 1900), nos. 102 and 104.

[150] "Wild's journal," pp. 137–40; *Mémoires*, I, 478.

[151] Tarleton, p. 302; Cornwallis to Clinton, June 30, 1781, Stevens, *Clinton-Cornwallis controversy*, II, 31–32.

[152] Lafayette to Greene, June 20, 1781, Clements Library.

[153] Steuben to Lafayette, June 5, 1781, New York Historical Society, Steuben papers, Vol. XII, no. 84; J. L. Whitehead (ed.), "Autobiography of Peter Stephen DuPonceau," *Pennsylvania magazine of history and biography*, LXIII (1939), 310–21.

his horses seventy miles in twenty-four hours, fell suddenly upon the small detachment that defended the temporary capital
and captured seven members of the legislature and some officers. The governor and the assembly barely had time to run
for safety to Staunton, where they set up a new capital.

Meanwhile, around Fredericksburg, there was panic. The inhabitants fled to the hills or across the river. Almost no one was
left in the town. General Weedon had himself taken his post on
the heights above Hunter's Works at Falmouth. The militia
from near-by counties came rushing in but always in pitiable
numbers and insufficiently armed.[154] Lafayette was now at Cul-
peper Church, about twenty miles farther upland, on the Rapidan River, ready to surrender Fredericksburg rather than risk
his junction with Wayne. But the expected blow never came.
Cornwallis began what looked like a retreat and certainly was a
retrograde movement, though its intention was only, after re-
uniting his infantry with Tarleton's dragoons and Simcoe's
yagers, to return to the neighborhood of Williamsburg, as he
had originally planned.

Lafayette decided to follow. Despite bad weather Wayne's
brigade was not very far off now. He was known to be marching
through Maryland.[155] Lafayette moved to Raccoon Ford,
farther up the river and somewhat south, closer to both Wayne's
and Cornwallis' lines of march. Lafayette's aide, Major Richard C. Anderson, had for several days been riding back and
forth between the two American generals with suggestions and
exchanges of notes.[156] At the very last minute "a deluge of rain"
made "impassable" the last river (the Rappahannock) that
Wayne would have to cross to join Lafayette.[157] Wayne, therefore, let his worn and bedraggled men rest a day at Norman's
Ford and dry out. For some time false rumors had spread in
official quarters and the hiding places of scared inhabitants that

---

[154] Weedon to Lafayette, June 4, 1781, *loc. cit.*; *Archives of Maryland*, XLVII, 271.

[155] Wayne to Lafayette, May 30, 1781, Johnston, p. 45; June 1 and 4, NYPL,
Bancroft transcripts.

[156] Lafayette to Wayne, June 4 and 5, 1781, Historical Society of Pennsylvania;
Wayne to Lafayette, June 6, 1781, *ibid.*

[157] Wayne to Lafayette, June 7, 1781, *ibid.*

the American armies had at last joined forces.[158] These rumors were perhaps due in part to the apparent transformation of the marquis' retreat into a pursuit. The change in the British line of march and the certainty that Wayne would soon catch up had induced Lafayette to move rapidly to the southward again. On June 10 he crossed the North Anna River at Brock's Bridge and moved forward to the banks of the South Anna. There the Pennsylvanians marched into the camp and placed themselves under the marquis' command.[159]

Lafayette now had nearly two thousand regular troops. Recent drafts by the state had increased his militia to about three thousand, not counting those under Steuben and Weedon. Morgan's riflemen were on their way, too; and the finest horsemen of Virginia and Maryland, mounted on their own thoroughbreds and paying their own expenses, daily augmented his cavalry.[160] His army, if not as seasoned as Cornwallis', was now nearly its equal in numbers. The young Frenchman had shown himself as resourceful in retrograde tactics as he had been daring in offensive strategy. At last he would not have to run so fast or so far and might even take up the chase himself.

[158] Iredell to Mrs. Iredell, May 30, 1781, G. J. McRee, *Life and correspondence of James Iredell* (2 vols.; New York, 1858), I, 517–18; Mason to Pearson Chapman, May 31, 1781, K. M. Rowland, *Life of George Mason (1725–1792)* (2 vols.; New York, 1892), II, 10–11; R. H. Lee to Weedon, June 1, 1781, Ballagh, II, 228; Hooe to Lee, June 9, 1781, Shriver, p. 93.

[159] "Wild's journal," p. 140, says Wayne joined them on June 11, 1781, but see *Mémoires*, I, 478; Colonel Richard Butler to Irvine, July 8, 1871, *Pennsylvania archives*, X (1896), 543; "The Yorktown campaign. Journal of Captain John Davis of the Pennsylvania line," *Pennsylvania magazine of history and biography*, V (1881), 292; J. A. Waddell (ed.), "Diary of Capt. John Davis of the Pennsylvania line," *Virginia magazine of history*, I (1893–94), 12; "Journal of Lieut. Wm. McDowell of the First Pennsylvania Regiment, in the southern campaign, 1781–2," *Pennsylvania archives*, 2d ser., XV (1890), 298; and "Diary of the Pennsylvania line" [compiled from the journals of Captain Joseph McClellan and Lieut. William Feltman], *ibid.*, 2d ser., XI (1896), 710. The place of the juncture of Wayne's force with Lafayette's is subject to even greater discrepancy among the sources than is the date, but it was probably at an unnamed station on the South Anna River almost due south of Brock's Bridge, from which Lafayette wrote to Washington earlier on June 10, 1781 (LC, Washington papers, no. 49, fol. 343); see Major Capitaine's map of the campaign in Virginia, Raleigh Tavern, Williamsburg, Va., reproduced between pp. 238 and 239 above.

[160] Lafayette to Washington, June 18, 1781, LC, Washington papers, no. 50, fol. 59; Lafayette to Greene, June 20, 1781, Clements Library; *Mémoires*, I, 271 and 273.

BIBLIOGRAPHICAL NOTES

The best sources for the English side of the Virginia campaign are the journals of Tarleton and Simcoe and the correspondence of Clinton and Cornwallis, which has been published in several versions but is most critically edited with variant readings in Stevens' *Clinton-Cornwallis controversy*.

Capitaine, who had been Lafayette's aide since his first campaign in America and was an excellent cartographer, made a huge map of the campaign of which at least two copies are now extant. One is described in André Girodie, *Exposition du centenaire de La Fayette 1757–1834, Catalogue* (Paris, 1934), pp. 67–68, no. 101; the one at Raleigh Tavern in Williamsburg, Va., is better known. The "Précis de la campagne de 1781 pour servir à l'intelligence de la carte" in *Mémoires*, I, 477–80, was obviously intended to accompany this map. There is no map in Vol. I of the *Mémoires*, but a map of the Virginia campaign is to be found in Vol. IV, frontispiece. It is not Capitaine's map, however, and is, in fact, untrustworthy in several points, such as the date of junction with Wayne's army. Mr. Jackson owned the manuscript that is probably the original of the "Précis." A copy of it is also to be found in the Sparks MSS LXXXVI, part 2. It is by Capitaine and not by Lafayette.

Several studies of the Virginia campaign have been published. Among those may be mentioned H. B. Carrington's, "Lafayette's Virginia campaign 1781" (*Magazine of American history*, VI [1881], 340–52), which is largely the same as the pages on the Virginia campaign in his *Battles of the American Revolution 1775–1781* (New York, 1876); M. J. Wright, "Lafayette's campaign in Virginia," *Publications of the Southern History Association*, IX (1905), 234–38; E. M. Allen, *Lafayette's second expedition to Virginia in 1781* ("Maryland Historical Society publications," no. 32 [Baltimore, 1891]); and Tower, II, 286–457. There are, however, inaccuracies and omissions in all these accounts. Moreover, they fail to understand, because they relied exclusively on the testimony of Lafayette, who was himself deceived, that Cornwallis was not retreating from Lafayette but acting according to a preconceived purpose.

Wayne's correspondence is now largely to be found in the Historical Society of Pennsylvania. Mr. Julian Boyd first made me acquainted with this correspondence. Much of it was published in the periodical called *The casket or flowers of literature, wit and sentiment*, IV (1829) and V (1830). Copies are also available in the Bancroft transcripts at the New York Public Library.

Carl Van Doren, *Mutiny in January* (New York, 1943), pp. 234–36 and 250–57 gives different figures from those on p. 229 above for the number executed.

Since the first printing of this book I have edited *The letters of Lafayette to Washington, 1777–1799* (Privately printed, 1944). The date of General Phillips' death is correctly given there (p. 194) and revised accordingly above (p. 231).

CHAPTER XI

Cornwallis' "Retreat"

THE general who runs away lives to fight another day. When Lafayette decided that the day had at last come when he need no longer run away, the enemy had, on their side, decided no longer to run after him. Since both the marquis' army and the Virginia legislature had vanished as Cornwallis' contingents approached, the British commander considered part of his purpose fulfilled. There remained only his mission of destruction. The moderate success of Simcoe in destroying Steuben's supplies at Point of Fork induced him to look for other supplies to destroy before returning to Williamsburg to await Clinton's further orders.

In the anxiety to move fast before the enemy, Lafayette had concentrated most of the Continental stores and much of the state's at Albermarle Old Court House. Their loss would have spelled disaster. For the Americans, even when they could count upon their meager supplies, were inadequately furnished with the things that distinguished an army from a band of marching men. Cornwallis, moving toward Elk Island near Point of Fork to rejoin Simcoe, intended to advance upon Albermarle Old Court House and cut off Lafayette from his food and equipment.[1]

Cornwallis was several days' march on his way when Wayne joined the marquis. Though still inferior to the enemy, Lafayette decided to risk a battle, if necessary, in defense of his supplies. Cornwallis' forces had by that time united at Point of Fork. Albermarle Old Court House lay only about twenty miles

---

[1] Cornwallis to Clinton, June 30, 1781, Stevens, *Clinton-Cornwallis controversy*, II, 32.

246

west of them up the James River, while Lafayette was a much greater distance away to the northwest. The rescue of the American supplies would have been impossible had not Lafayette had the advantage of commanding a militia who were fighting in defense of their own soil. The men of Virginia knew every creek and path of their country. They found a disused road which was generally deemed impassable. Happily, it proved to be pervious, though inhospitable. Lafayette forced his men through it in quick time.[2] Long afterward it continued to be known as "The Marquis' Road."[3] On the way the light infantry in Lafayette's army were cheered by the arrival of their new shirts from Baltimore. Though they found the woods "disagreeable"[4] and lacked water, they marched to Mechunk Creek, a branch of the Rivanna River, in two days. There some Virginia riflemen joined them[5]—all crack shots and some well mounted. Light horsemen soon began "crowding in from all quarters."[6] Lafayette also sent new orders to Steuben to come up.[7] His army seemed likely to become a formidable force.

In the meantime, uncertain where Lafayette was, Lord Cornwallis had divided his forces. Keeping most of his men with him in the neighborhood of Elk Island and at Bird's Ordinary, he had ordered Tarleton to march toward Albermarle Old Court House, destroy the stores there, then cross the James, scatter Steuben's new levies, and comb the south bank of the river before rejoining the main army. Cornwallis would, meanwhile, by

---

[2] *Mémoires*, I, 477, 480; Sparks MSS LXXXVI, Part II, pp. 136–45; McHenry to Lee, June 19, 1781, Elizabeth Kite (ed.), *A sidelight on history, being the letters of James McHenry . . . . to Thomas Sim Lee . . . . written during the Yorktown campaign* (Southhampton, N.Y., 1931), p. 18; Lafayette to Greene, June 18, 1781, PCC, no. 156, fols. 151–52, and Morgan Library, Yorktown, Vol. I.

[3] John Burk *et al.*, *History of Virginia* (4 vols.; Petersburg, 1804–16), IV, 506–7.

[4] "Wild's journal," p. 141.

[5] McHenry to Lee, June 19, 1781, *loc. cit.*; Lafayette to Greene, June 18, 1781, *loc. cit.*

[6] Letter of "a gentleman at Dumfries, Virginia," [June 28, 1781], *Independent Chronicle and Universal Advertiser* (Boston), July 26 ,1781.

[7] June 13, 1781, Tower, II, 336–37.

easy stages move to Richmond.[8] When Lafayette reappeared out of the unknown path, His Lordship discovered that the Americans were in a strategic position. The marquis could readily throw his men upon the road which Tarleton's cavalry must take to reach Albermarle Old Court House. Tarleton reported to his commander that the American army had crossed the South Anna River only after they had, in fact, drawn much closer and were but seven miles distant from the British outposts at one point—in a position for their scouts to intercept the letter which Tarleton wrote informing Cornwallis of Lafayette's maneuver.[9] The British general, though still superior in numbers and the quality of his troops (since the greater part of Lafayette's men were short-term militia), nevertheless decided not to take the risk of battle in an unfavorable terrain and of delay in his return to Williamsburg. He recalled Tarleton, reunited his forces, and began to withdraw toward Richmond. Once again the energy of the younger commander had frustrated his more experienced opponent.

Lafayette followed the British down the James River. Cornwallis' movements were leisurely, and Lafayette did not dare to press his opponent too hard. He had neither wagons enough to carry his meager supplies nor sufficient cavalry to pursue the enemy. There was also "an amazing scarcity of musket cartridges in camp,"[10] and once more Lafayette had to beg "for god's sake" for a supply of shoes.[11] He found, too, that he needed vinegar and rum to disinfect "the water of this country" which was "very unhealthy to Northern soldiers."[12] Moreover, he had to slow down for Steuben. Lafayette had begun to feel that Steuben's recent abandonment of part of his stores at Point

[8] Cornwallis to Tarleton, June 9, 1781, Lee, *War in the southern department*, II, 211–12 n.; Tarleton to Cornwallis, June 13, 1781, PCC, no. 156, fol. 159; Lafayette to Weedon, June 13, 1781, Ford collection; Carrington, *Battles*, p. 603. See also the Capitaine map of the Virginia campaign, *loc. cit.*

[9] Tarleton to Cornwallis, June 13, 1781, *loc. cit.;* Lafayette to Steuben, June 13, 1781, *loc. cit.*

[10] Major J. Pryor to Colonel Davies, June 15, 1781, *Virginia state papers*, II, 162; cf. also pp. 157 and 165.

[11] Lafayette to Weedon, June 16, 1781, APS, Weedon papers, no. 123.   [12] *Ibid.*

of Fork and his present tardiness in coming up despite frequent requests were perhaps in great need of investigation.[13] But Steuben was not altogether to blame. Effective English patrol of the highways had made them unsafe for the American mails. The baron's letters from both Greene and Lafayette had frequently been intercepted. He had thus been uncertain whether Greene wanted him to go to North Carolina or whether Lafayette wished him to stay in Virginia.[14] Having at last become convinced that he was expected by General Greene to remain with the marquis, he was now forcing his men to stretch their legs in long and tedious marches.[15] Lafayette did not dare to get too close to the English without him.

Thus the progress of Cornwallis toward Richmond was not, in fact, a retreat, and Lafayette knew that it was not. But he tried to make it look as if Cornwallis were running away from him. "It appears to me," he declared,[16] "that the enemy want to create the impression that the states of the south belong to them. Lord Cornwallis in one of his letters puts that idea forward as a matter quite well settled. My conduct in relation to him has been based upon the same political motives. When he changes his position, I try to give to his movements the appearance of a retreat. God grant that there be an opportunity to give to them the appearance of a defeat."

Political shrewdness seemed more than ever necessary. It was rumored in Virginia that neutral powers had met in Vienna to mediate between England and France. In Portsmouth the odds were five to one that there would be peace before Christmas.[17] Lafayette was himself inclined to credit those rumors. He hoped that an air of military success would so affect the peace negotiations that they would result in the independence of all thirteen states. "My heart beats, Monsieur le Chevalier," he wrote to

[13] Lafayette to La Luzerne, June 16, 1781, *AHR*, XX (1915), 602; cf. Lafayette to Steuben, June 15, 1781, Gates papers, box 16, no. 47; Kapp, p. 452.

[14] Steuben to Lafayette, June 13, 1781, New York Historical Society, Steuben papers, Vol. XII, no. 98.

[15] Lafayette to Steuben, June 15, 1781, Gates papers, box 16, no. 47.

[16] Lafayette to La Luzerne, June 16, 1781, *loc. cit.*, p. 603.

[17] Parker to Jones, June 27, 1781, *State records of North Carolina*, XXII, 1029.

La Luzerne,[18] "when I think of that treaty of peace. On the one hand, I see America independent. I see the ambassador of England paying his respects to the ambassador of the United States; I see all the English biting their lips whenever by chance the name of America and the American war is pronounced; I see Frenchmen and Americans marching arm in arm in foreign countries, passing by the English in attendance. In short there are a thousand little pleasures that I promise myself exclusive of the great end of the revolution. But on the other hand, I feel that I would consent to an eternal silence rather than say 'the English colony of Georgia or of Carolina.' Even in writing it I experience the uneasiness of a man who blasphemes for the first time."

The "appearance of a retreat" continued, and every day grew more realistic. And with it grew what Lafayette might have been tempted to call "the appearance of a pursuit." Nelson, who commanded the second line of Lafayette's army, composed of the Virginia militia, had recently been chosen governor of Virginia in Jefferson's place.[19] To be sure, Lafayette continued to complain of the state's niggardliness and particularly of mismanagement in the commissary department; and the scarcity of horses, which the slaves hid from the Americans and sold freely to the English, continued to aggravate him.[20] Nevertheless, increased exertions had recently been made,[21] and volunteers continued to come in. Credit for this burst of energy was due to the new governor of Virginia, but not entirely, for the initial steps had been taken even while Jefferson was still governor.[22] The Continental Board of War had also discovered a

[18] June 16, 1781, *loc. cit.*, pp. 603–4.   [19] *Ibid.*, p. 604.

[20] Lafayette to Washington, July 20, 1781 (public letter), LC, Washington papers, no. 51, fol. 49; the version of this letter in *Mémoires* (Amer. ed.), pp. 422–23, has been sadly truncated.

[21] Cf. *Calendar of Weedon correspondence*, nos. 123, 125, 126, 127, and 128; Shriver, p. 97; *William and Mary quarterly*, XXVII (1918–19), 173–74.

[22] Cf. Jefferson to Lafayette, May 29 and 31, 1781, Chinard, *Lafayette and Jefferson*, pp. 42–43 and 45–47; Burk, IV, 500–501 n.; *Journal of the House of Delegates of the Commonwealth of Virginia* (sess. of June 12, 1781), pp. 14–15; *Virginia state papers*, II, 155.

sudden vigor and had begun to send from Philadelphia the clothing and munitions that Lafayette had been entreating since April.[23] By September the Board of War was to spend over four million pounds in Continental money on the marquis' warrants—a sum it could not well afford even in its grossly inflated currency.[24]

The sight of British and German guards, dragoons, and light infantry retreating before a smaller force of Continentals, militia, and raw recruits raised depressed spirits in Maryland, Virginia, and North Carolina. Rumors of great battles and glorious victories spread rapidly through the country.[25] But Lafayette still marched at a safe distance from an opponent he preferred not to fight. When Cornwallis reached Richmond (June 18), Lafayette had already halted (June 17) at Colonel Dandridge's house near Allen's Creek,[26] about twenty-two miles northwest of Richmond. There Lafayette stopped for Steuben to join him.

As the impatient commander waited for his older subordinate, his impatience grew. He complained to Washington of Steuben's increasing unpopularity in Virginia. He all but accused the baron of either cowardliness or treason in having abandoned part of his stores at Point of Fork in the face of an inferior opponent. Even the militia, Lafayette reported, were refusing to serve under Steuben, and many of the new levies had deserted because they lacked confidence in him. Still the marquis, preferring not to register a formal charge against his older colleague, resorted to the subterfuge of sending these complaints "not to the Commander-in-Chief" but to his friend General Washington.[27] In a public letter to General Greene, a copy of

[23] Board of War to Lafayette, [ca. June, 1781], New York Historical Society, Steuben papers, Vol. XII, no. 100; *Virginia state papers*, II, 209.

[24] Benj. Harrison, Jr., to Washington, September 23, 1781, LC, Washington papers, no. 52, fol. 175.

[25] Cf. Gates to Morgan, June 15, 1781, Gaillard Hunt (ed.), *Fragments of Revolutionary history* (Brooklyn, 1892), p. 14; Bignall to Sumner, June 16, 1781, *State records of North Carolina*, XV, 486–87.

[26] Capitaine's map of the Virginia campaign, *loc. cit.*

[27] Lafayette to Washington, June 18, 1781 (private letter), LC, Washington papers, no. 50, fol. 59; Tower (II, 333–34) gives only part of this letter.

which he sent to Congress,[28] he made no recriminations, though one could read between the lines of his matter-of-fact account of events since the beginning of June that he did not approve of Steuben's behavior. Thus it was left to Washington and Congress to decide what to do. Lafayette would not commit himself openly. Half a century later he was still anxious that his letter to Washington should not be made public,[29] though he continued to believe Steuben's behavior "hardly judicious although well-intentioned."[30] If the English had intercepted and published it, as they frequently did other letters of Lafayette and Washington, Steuben would scarcely have been satisfied with the explanation that the uncomplimentary opinion had been expressed only privately.

Fortunately, Steuben never learned of this letter. When he finally joined Lafayette (June 19) there was little to disturb the ostensible friendliness between them. Even after listening to Steuben's account of what had happened at Point of Fork, Lafayette was not appeased, however. In a report to Greene,[31] which he likewise urged should be considered private, he insisted: "Had the Baron held 24 hours every one of the articles might have been carried up as high as Albermarle Old Court House where they [the British] did not venture. Instead of it he went to Staunton River 15 miles from the Point of Fork and crossed it. General Lawson with the militia left him. His new levies deserted. All Virginia was in an uproar against him. The enemy laughed at him, and I cannot describe to you what my surprise has been." Though the actual loss was not considerable, Lafayette was concerned about its effect upon public morale. It "will show great deal in newspapers," he lamented.

When Steuben finally joined Lafayette, the young commander began once more to think in terms of battle. "Wayne

---

[28] June 18, 1781, *Mémoires* (Amer. ed.), pp. 522–23. Copies signed by Lafayette are in the Morgan Library, Yorktown, Vol. I, and PCC, no. 156, fols. 151–52.

[29] Endorsement by Lafayette on copies sent to Sparks, 1829, Sparks MSS LXXXIV; see Justin Winsor, *Calendar of the Sparks manuscripts in Harvard College Library, etc.* (Cambridge, Mass., 1889), pp. 76–77.

[30] "Observations du Gal Lafayette," *loc. cit.*, p. 54.

[31] June 20, 1781, Clements Library.

was impetuous, and the Marquis loved glory," explained James McHenry,[32] who had once more joined Lafayette as aide-de-camp. They believed (mistakenly, it eventually proved) that they now had numerical superiority. Steuben's new Continentals together with 800 light infantry and 700 Pennsylvanians made 1,900 regulars, and they could count upon 3,000 militia and riflemen until the harvest set in. But the harvest was not far off. If they did not strike now, they might never have another good chance.

McHenry was himself opposed to an attack. A partial victory, he argued, would bring small advantage; a partial defeat would be disastrous, while a general defeat would undo everything so far gained. For the moment McHenry's advice prevailed. He privately appealed to Greene "to confirm it with as much expedition as possible . . . . lest military ardor should be too powerful for reason," at the same time warning Greene to "contrive your advice in such a way as to drown any suspicion of my interference."[33] Greene shared McHenry's feelings. Although McHenry had indicated a desire to join his staff, he urged his correspondent to stay with the marquis. "I am persuaded," he wrote,[34] "you are useful to him in moderating his military ardor, which no doubt is heated by the fire of the Modern Hero [Wayne], who by the by is an excellent officer." So McHenry stayed in Virginia and in the end was not sorry.

The marquis and "the Modern Hero" were not the only ones itching for a fight. Tarleton's respect for Virginia militia was none too wholesome, though he never underestimated the ability of the youthful commander opposite him. With about 700 men he had moved (on June 18) to within twelve miles of Dandridge's, intending to fall upon the militia. Spies brought word of this maneuver to Lafayette's quarters. He sent Muhlenberg with some light infantry to cut them off, moving the rest of the Continental line to their support, but "some rascals" (the en-

[32] McHenry to Greene, June 20, 1781, catalogue of the American Autograph Shop, Merion Station, Pa., November, 1938, no. 17.

[33] *Ibid.*

[34] Greene to McHenry, July 24, 1781, Steiner, p. 38.

emy's spies were always "rascals") informed Tarleton in time for him to retreat to Richmond in safety.[35] Lieutenant-Colonel John F. Mercer with a troop of volunteer horse meanwhile captured one of Tarleton's patrols in the rear of the enemy.[36] They were the first prisoners to be taken since Cornwallis had arrived in Virginia. With leaders of both sides sparring for a fight, a decisive action might soon have taken place had not chance decreed that the very advantages of the British should cause their undoing.

The superiority of the British in money, cavalry, and scouts had resulted once more in the collapse of the Continental express service. Couriers were frequently intercepted and their dispatches became the property of the enemy. Since the end of May, Lafayette had had frequent reason to complain that letters exchanged with Washington, Jefferson, and Steuben had gone astray. Sometimes he read them in the Tory press, which was careful to quote those parts that might show a smoldering hostility below the placid surface of the Franco-American alliance. Sometimes duplicates reached him if the sender had taken the precaution to forward more than one copy by different routes. Sometimes they never reached him in any form, and he learned only long afterward that they had been captured on the way.

While on the march to Dandridge's, Lafayette had learned that such interception was the reason for the apparent silence of Washington.[37] Somewhere between New Windsor and Morristown a courier had been taken by the British and with him two letters of Washington to Lafayette. One of those letters was intended for public consumption[38] (as Lafayette found from duplicates which Washington sent him as soon as he heard of the capture of the originals).[39] It contained no message more

[35] Lafayette to Greene, July 20, 1781, *loc. cit.*

[36] Mercer to Simms, [date unknown but between 1809 and 1817], Hunt, p. 44; Tarleton, pp. 308–9; "Military journal, kept by Major Ebenezer Denny 1781–1795," *Memoirs of the Historical Society of Pennsylvania*, VII (1860), 239–42.

[37] Lafayette to La Luzerne, June 16, 1781, *loc. cit.*, p. 603.

[38] Washington to Lafayette, May 31, 1781, Fitzpatrick, XXII, 139–40.

[39] June 4, 1781, *ibid.*, p. 161.

significant than praise for Lafayette's conduct of the campaign in Virginia, approving especially of his unwillingness to deal with Arnold and his avoiding battle with Cornwallis.

But the other was a private letter.[40] It revealed to Lafayette that Washington, toward the end of May, had had a third conference with Rochambeau at Wethersfield, Connecticut. Rochambeau's son had just returned from Paris with assurances that a fleet sufficient to control the American coast would arrive in July or August. At Wethersfield, Washington, Rochambeau, and the Comte de Barras, the new commander of the French fleet at Newport, had discussed plans for the bright campaign that lay ahead. The French officers, still unwilling to risk an attack on New York, felt that the wisest course would be to go to the assistance of Greene and Lafayette in the South. Washington, on the other hand, fearful that his army might melt away on a long march under the hot southern sun, maintained that an attack on New York would oblige the enemy to recall their troops from the South, thus diminishing the pressure on the overmatched forces in Virginia and the Carolinas. Washington's view prevailed despite Rochambeau's uneasiness, and plans were immediately set afoot for an attack upon New York. In the private letter in which Washington revealed this decision he gave Lafayette permission to return to New York if he wished, provided he left his Virginia command in capable hands.

Though it seemed at first a calamitious trick of fate that that letter should fall into the enemy's hands, it proved to be the enemy's undoing. Clinton was now convinced that he was in greater danger in New York than Cornwallis could possibly be in Virginia. By his calculations there were 7,724 British effectives in Virginia, and Lafayette's force was much smaller, with the Pennsylvania line "so discontented that their officers were afraid to trust them with ammunition."[41] On the other hand, he himself, with a garrison that he had stripped of some of its best units in order to reinforce Cornwallis, would soon be faced

---

[40] Washington to Lafayette, May 31, 1781, *ibid.*, pp. 143–44.

[41] Clinton to Cornwallis, June 11, 1781, Stevens, *Clinton-Cornwallis controversy*, II, 19.

by the combined forces of Washington and Rochambeau. There seemed to him to be only one thing to do, since Washington had put his finger on the weak spot in the British plans. That was to strengthen that spot. Hence in several letters which he dispatched in quick succession, he recommended that Cornwallis take a defensive position and send back such of his forces as he could spare to reinforce the garrison of New York.[42]

Cornwallis' rapid movements through Virginia prevented these letters of Clinton from reaching him for some time. Nevertheless, he continued to act in a way which suggested to the puzzled Lafayette that he was retreating, possibly for the purpose of re-embarking some of his troops but also perhaps because he feared Lafayette's growing strength. The sober fact was, however, that Cornwallis was of his own volition returning to Williamsburg, in the belief that his raid of Virginia had been quite successful. His estimate of the damage done differed widely from Lafayette's. It was to his interest to exaggerate the harm he had inflicted just as it was to Lafayette's interest to minimize it. Probably the truth lay somewhere between the low figures that Lafayette reported to Washington and the high ones that Cornwallis reported to Clinton. Moreover, Cornwallis made no allowance for the cannon and arms which Lafayette's friends fished out of the rivers again after the enemy had thrown them in. But Cornwallis was himself convinced that he had destroyed about 5,000 stands of arms, about 600 barrels of powder, and 2,000 hogsheads of tobacco, as well as a great number of guns, some clothing, harness, salt, and other supplies.[43] The results of his Virginia campaign seemed therefore sufficiently great no longer to require heavy exertion in the insalubrious swamps of Virginia. He could now afford to evacuate Richmond and retire to the healthier atmosphere of Williamsburg, there to await Clinton's further orders. So far was he from regarding his movements as a retreat that he did not even take the trouble to find out whether Lafayette was following him, satisfied that

[42] June 8, 1781, *ibid.*, pp. 14–17; June 11, 1781, *ibid.*, pp. 18–23; June 15, 1781, *ibid.*, pp. 24–25; June 19, 1781, *ibid.*, pp. 26–29.

[43] Cornwallis to Clinton, June 30, 1781, *ibid.*, p. 32.

his superiority in horsemen would cover his flanks and rear
from any surprise that his antagonist might attempt.[44]

Cornwallis evacuated Richmond on the morning of June 21.
At first he headed toward Bottom's Bridge over the Chicahomi-
ny. The marquis, undecided whether the enemy intended to
move toward the Potomac again or to withdraw to Williamsburg, sent orders to Weedon to be on the *qui vive*[45] and to Wayne
to stay close behind the British, ready to attack during the night
if an opportunity presented.[46] For the moment the cautious advice of McHenry seemed to carry great weight. Lafayette assured Greene that "as the fate of the southern states depends
on the preservation of this army, if mylord chooses to retreat
I had rather loose some share of glory than to risk a defeat by
which Virginia would be lost."[47]

That letter to Greene was one of the most cheerful the marquis had sent since he first came to Virginia. Not only did good
fortune seem to have given him the upper hand ("this retreat
will not read well in newspaper"), but recent reports from La
Luzerne indicated that the mission of young Rochambeau and
Laurens had not been futile. Ships and clothing had been promised, and "hard money has been given and permission to draw
for more." To Lafayette's great satisfaction "the disposal of
the money will be settled by General Washington." The prospect that peace negotiations would result in complete American
independence once more seemed certain, since Louis XVI had
assured Congress that all the resources of France would be employed to secure it.

Smiling fortune rapidly seduced Lafayette from all the principles of caution that had so far guided him. As soon as he
ascertained that the enemy's object was Williamsburg, he divided his forces in an effort to bring on an action. The American
army advanced in two columns. Wayne headed one that kept
close to the James River, while Lafayette himself accompanied

---

[44] Simcoe, p. 235.

[45] June 21, 1781, Ford collection.

[46] June 21, 1781, Historical Society of Pennsylvania.

[47] June 21, 1781, LC, Lafayette misc. MSS, acq. 3434.

the main body, which moved on the north bank of the Chicka-hominy, with Muhlenberg in the van and Steuben in the rear.[48] Wayne and Muhlenberg were ordered to press the British hard and to try to bring on a battle in the hope that the enemy might be caught between the two American columns. But Wayne, having marched his men through Richmond for a dis-tance of twenty-two miles in one day, dared not force them. farther.[49] And so the first engagement between Lafayette and Cornwallis had to be postponed.

On June 23 the American forces joined again near Mr. Sav-age's house, east of Richmond.[50] The enemy lay at New Kent Court House less than two miles below them. Lafayette waited for the British to move again, meanwhile appealing to Maryland for reinforcements, particularly cavalry.[51] He and Wayne now agreed to maneuver chiefly at night in an effort to draw Tarle-ton's cavalry into ambuscade or intercept Simcoe's rearguard.[52] When the enemy marched down toward Williamsburg again (June 24), Colonel Richard Butler was given command of an advance corps with orders to follow. Major William McPherson conceived of the idea of mounting some light infantry behind the fifty dragoons in his party.[53] This doubly laden body of horse, with some unmounted light infantry, formed Butler's van. Ingenuity thus made up in part for poverty.

That day the British stopped at Bird's Tavern, about ten miles from Williamsburg. On the next they reached Williams-burg.[54] Lafayette did not dare to push them too hard. Only on June 25 did he proceed, reaching Bird's Tavern two days

[48] See Capitaine's map, *loc. cit.*; Lafayette to Wayne, June 22, 1781, Historical Society of Pennsylvania; Lafayette to Steuben, June 22, 1781, Gates papers, box 16, no. 51; Tower, II, 343–44.

[49] Wayne to Lafayette, June 22, 1781, NYPL, Bancroft transcripts.

[50] McHenry to Weedon, June 25, 1781, *Calendar of Weedon correspondence*, no. 138.

[51] Lafayette to Lee, June 25, 1781, Shriver, p. 102.

[52] Cf. Wayne to Lafayette, June 25, 1781, NYPL, Bancroft transcripts.

[53] Lafayette to Greene, June 27, 1781, *Mémoires* (Amer. ed.), pp. 524–25. Signed copies are to be found in the Morgan Library, Yorktown, Vol. I, and PCC, no. 156, fols. 165–67.

[54] Graham, *Memoir of General Graham*, p. 52.

after Cornwallis had left it.[55] General Wayne had meanwhile kept close behind the enemy. Once Simcoe barely escaped by a bridge that his men hastily repaired and burned again. "I have the best grounds to believe," Wayne reported to Lafayette,[56] "that the lads do not like our night maneuvers." Lafayette stopped at Bird's Tavern. Butler's van took post at Spencer's Ordinary, about halfway between the American main army at Bird's and the British at Williamsburg.[57]

Having obeyed Clinton's orders by establishing himself at Williamsburg, Cornwallis intended to await the transports that were to take some of his men to New York. Since leaving Richmond, he had not in fact realized that he had been followed all the time and that Lafayette had succeeded in giving to his movement from Richmond to Williamsburg the appearance of a retreat. The safe distance which the American van had kept had made detection difficult.[58] But now Simcoe sent out a spy to find out what the Americans were up to. Informed that a small force of river boats lay close by and some distance from the main body under Lafayette, Simcoe by a night march fell upon them with about four hundred men, burned them, and foraged the countryside for cattle. On his return he ran into Butler's van at Spencer's Ordinary. Major McPherson's men, two to each horse, charged Simcoe's corps and then fell back upon the battalions of riflemen who came to their support, leaving nine men dead, fourteen wounded, and fifteen missing or prisoners. Simcoe, faced by a force much greater than his own, did not follow up his advantage but retreated toward Williamsburg again. Both armies had by that time begun to move to the support of their vans, but as the British returned to Williamsburg, there was no general action.[59]

---

[55] Lafayette to Wayne, June 25 and 26, 1781, Historical Society of Pennsylvania.

[56] June 25, 1781, *loc. cit.*

[57] Chastellux, II, pp. 7–8.   [58] Simcoe, p. 229.

[59] Lafayette to Wayne, June 26, 1781, *loc. cit.;* Lafayette to Greene, June 27, 1781, *loc. cit.;* Lafayette to Nelson, June 26, 1781, Chinard, *Lafayette and Jefferson,* pp. 47–48; Butler to Lafayette, June 26, 1781, PCC, no. 156, fol. 169; Tarleton, p. 360; Chastellux, II, 7–8; Simcoe, pp. 229–35; Simcoe to Chastellux, January 20, 1787, *Gentleman's magazine and historical chronicle,* LVII (1787), 36–39.

Lafayette reviewed his men the next day and made them sleep through a rainy night on the field.[60] But Cornwallis did not come out. The marquis did not hesitate to report the skirmish between Butler and Simcoe as an American victory, announcing that Butler's riflemen had killed sixty of the enemy and wounded one hundred.[61] Simcoe maintained that Lafayette made his own casualties appear smaller than they were and exaggerated the British.[62] Cornwallis, in fact, reported only thirty-three British losses. He claimed the victory, too;[63] but, as the Americans remained in possession of the field, the strategic advantage lay with them. Richmond once more seemed safe, and Nelson soon moved the government of Virginia back to the capital.

From the prisoners whom Simcoe took back to Williamsburg with him Cornwallis at last learned that Lafayette had not remained in Richmond. It seemed to Cornwallis that Lafayette had acted hazardously "as on the least previous intimation he must have been cut off."[64] But that could have been only meager satisfaction to His Lordship now that, by the failure of the British intelligence, the American army had managed to creep up to within six miles of his position before encountering opposition. Having finally discovered where Lafayette's forces lay, Cornwallis resolved, "if I can get a favorable opportunity of striking a blow at him without loss of time," to do so.[65] But he was now distinctly under orders to lose no time, for some of the letters of Clinton urging him to spare as many troops as possible for the defense of New York had at last reached him in Williamsburg.[66]

[60] "Wild's journal," p. 142.

[61] Lafayette to Greene, June 27, 1781, loc. cit.; Lafayette to Nelson, June 28, 1781, Sparks MSS LXXI, p. 141; Tower, II, 348-49.

[62] Simcoe, pp. 236-37.

[63] Cornwallis to Clinton, June 30, 1781, Stevens, Clinton-Cornwallis controversy, II, 33; cf. Tarleton, p. 360, and the New York Gazette and Weekly Mercury, July 16 and 23, 1781.

[64] Simcoe, p. 235; cf. also p. 229.

[65] Cornwallis to Clinton, June 30, 1781, loc. cit., p. 38.   [66] Ibid., p. 33.

Lafayette still flattered himself that the reason for the enemy's retreat was that Cornwallis exaggerated the size of the American army and feared it. Yet, knowing his own weakness only too well, he had no intention of taking unnecessary risks.[67] The day after Simcoe's skirmish with Butler, the Americans made camp at Tyree's Plantation, about twenty miles northwest of Williamsburg.[68] There Lafayette waited for the British to act.

While the men rested from the fatigue of their marches, their young chief knew no rest. For the British were only one of his great enemies. Two others that worried him almost as much were smallpox and the harvest. "By the utmost care to avoid infected ground we have hitherto got clear of the small pox," he informed Governor Nelson. "I wish the harvest time might be as easily got over. But there is no keeping the militia into the field." The original three brigades had now been reduced to two. "You might as well stop the flood tide as to stop militia when times are out." Even the riflemen (whose commander, General Morgan, had succeeded in raising only about one-fifth of his full contingent of two thousand and had not yet come to camp) "are determined to go and take care of their harvest so that I shall be left with the Continentals." Lafayette also begged everywhere for cavalry, particularly well-mounted gentlemen volunteers, Negro wagoners and pioneers, provisions, shoes, and horses. Only now did he complete the signing of notes for the loan from the Baltimore merchants which had enabled him to buy shirts and other articles for the light infantry.[69] The money, however, had long since dwindled away. His commissary, he admitted, now showed a little more vigor than it once had shown, but he wished Nelson to threaten "the severest punishments in case the army is left in the least want," which

[67] Cf. Lafayette to Nelson, June 26, 1781, *loc. cit.*, and June 28, 1781 (another letter of that date), New York Historical Society, misc. MSS "L"; *Virginia state papers*, II, 184 and 186.

[68] Lafayette to Greene, June 27, 1781, *loc. cit.*

[69] Lafayette to the Committee of Observation in Baltimore, July 3, 1781, Scharf, p. 194 (incorrectly said to be from "Mr. Lyon's Plantation").

should be inflicted "the first hour the army wants any kind of provisions."[70]

Meanwhile, other embarrassments arose. A resolution of the Virginia delegates had recently requested a formal investigation into the loss of the stores at Point of Fork. Taking advantage of Baron von Steuben's plea of illness, Lafayette permitted him to go to a friend's house near Charlottesville to rest and recuperate. He expected his sick subordinate to use his leisure in pressing in that neighborhood the need for men and supplies. Lafayette thus used Steuben's illness as a pretext for postponing the inquiry demanded by the people of Virginia while continuing to employ him in a military fashion. In reporting to Greene,[71] Lafayette indicated he intended to avoid the assembly's charge. "What has been lost at the Point of Fork is in great measure recovered. Little will be lost, including the Baron's popularity in Virginia. . . . . I have enough to do to inquire into Lord Cornwallis's intention and will have the honor of refering [sic] the assembly to your superior authority."

That report to Greene indicated that Lafayette did not regard his own situation as enviable. To be sure, he was forcing the enemy to keep their distance, he stated, by sending out a detachment against every detachment that they sent out and by feinting night attacks. But, he added, "children sing when they are affraid [sic]." He was not really equal to Cornwallis in numbers or morale. "I wish we may induce him to run from us least [sic] I should be obliged to run from him. . . . . Since I am first in command I become a great coward. . . . . I do what I can, but cannot do what I wish. In a word, my dear general, I manage matters for the best, try to correct abuses, get angry five or six times a day, and I hope you will be satisfied at least with my good intentions."

While waiting for Cornwallis to unfold his plans, the Americans rested in a carefully chosen position. There they celebrated

[70] Lafayette to Nelson, July 1, 1781, Chinard, *Lafayette in Virginia*, pp. 18–22.

[71] Lafayette to Greene, July 4, 1781, Smith collection. See also Steuben to Meade, June 30, 1781, Hunt, p. 157 and n., and Steuben to Morgan, July 16, 1781, *ibid.*, p. 15; *Journal of the House of Delegates* (sess. of June 22, 1781), p. 29; Palmer, pp. 285 and 296; Kapp, p. 453.

the fifth anniversary of the Declaration of Independence with a *feu de joie*, a review, and a dinner given by the marquis to his officers.[72] Despite his lamentations, Lafayette's army was, in fact, at a high point in numbers and quality. He had three brigades of militia under Generals William Campbell, Edward Stevens, and Robert Lawson, numbering 2,180 men; and three contingents of Continentals under Muhlenberg (who commanded the 800 New England and New Jersey soldiers whom Lafayette had brought), Wayne (who commanded 750 Pennsylvanians), and Colonel Christian Febiger (who commanded 450 new levies in Steuben's place). The three battalions of light infantry Lafayette described as "the best troops that ever took the field . . . . far superior to any British troops," who would not "venture to meet them at equal numbers."[73] In addition he could count on fifty Continental dragoons and sixty ("very bad") militia cavalry, as well as 300 artillerymen. Yet Lafayette's officers were uneasy, knowing that they had "to oppose an enemy at least equal in numbers, and certainly superior with respect to discipline."[74]

Festivities and leisure came quickly to a close. That day the English evacuated Williamsburg and marched toward James Island. Reconnaissance in the neighborhood of Williamsburg and Yorktown had convinced Cornwallis that he could not take a good defensive position there from which to embark the contingent which Clinton persistently demanded.[75] He must con-

[72] "The Marquis de La Fayette's movements and operations in Virginia in 1781: an extract from a small pamphlet entitled *A narrative of my life for my family*, by the late Judge Brooke," *Virginia historical register*, VI (1853), 201; McClellan and Feltman, "Diary of the Pennsylvania line," p. 713; "Journal of Lieut. McDowell," p. 300; St. George Tucker to his wife, July 5, 1781, C. W. Coleman, Jr., "The southern campaign from Guilford County Court House to the siege of York: the Peninsula campaign," *Magazine of American history*, VII (1881), 207.

[73] Lafayette to Washington, July 20, 1781, *loc. cit.*

[74] Febiger to Bland, July 3, 1781, Charles Campbell (ed.), *The Bland papers: being a selection from the manuscripts of Colonel Theodorick Bland, Jr.* (2 vols.; Petersburg, Va., 1840-43), II, 71; Tower, II, 354-55.

[75] Cornwallis to Clinton, June 30, 1781, *loc. cit.*, pp. 35-36. See also n. 42 above. Cornwallis did not receive Clinton's letter of June 28 (Stevens, *Clinton-Cornwallis controversy*, II, 29-30), which peremptorily repeated the request for troops, until July 8, 1781, after he had moved from Williamsburg.

tinue his retrograde movement (and now it might more accurately be called a "retreat") until he joined General Leslie's force at Portsmouth on the other side of the James. Lafayette had been paying ten guineas and more to anyone who would bring him "material information" from the British encampment.[76] He learned of the new British plans quickly[77] and immediately went in pursuit. The whole of his army moved to Chickahominy Church on the fifth. The next morning he sent Wayne ahead with about five hundred troops. After a forced march ("having had nothing to eat for more than 24 hours"[78]) Wayne's corps reached Green Spring Farm, a mile or two from the enemy north of James Island.

Here conflicting intelligence manufactured by hirelings of Tarleton[79] led to disaster. That morning Colonel Mercer, who had been reconnoitering near James Island, reported that the main body of Cornwallis' army had not yet crossed the river. Other gentlemen of the volunteer cavalry (including a Washington and a Lee) maintained that it had. At this point Lafayette himself came up and, fearing that a strong English force still lay on the near side of the river, sent for the rest of his troops. Yet, not wishing to lose contact with the enemy if only a rearguard remained, he also sent Wayne ahead with his corps and one cannon. Wayne made contact with the enemy near James Island early in the afternoon. For two hours his riflemen and cavalry kept up a steady fire upon the British outposts.[80]

The stubbornness with which these small parties held their position made Lafayette suspect that they were not a mere rear-

[76] Colonel James Innes to Governor Harrison, February 11, 1782, *Virginia state papers*, III, 58.

[77] Lafayette to Sumner, July 5, 1781, *State records of North Carolina*, XV, 508. Tarleton (p. 362) says that on their march on July 4 he drove in Lafayette's pickets and "communicated a general alarm" to Lafayette's corps; I have found no confirmation of this statement.

[78] "Wild's journal," p. 143; cf. "Denny's journal," p. 241.

[79] Tarleton, p. 363.

[80] Wayne to Washington, July 8, 1781, Sparks, *Correspondence of the American Revolution*, III, 347-48; Mercer to Simms, [1809-17], Hunt, pp. 45-46; Galvan to Peters, July 8, 1781, Historical Society of Pennsylvania.

ruins appears, but the handwriting and the style are the same as those on other

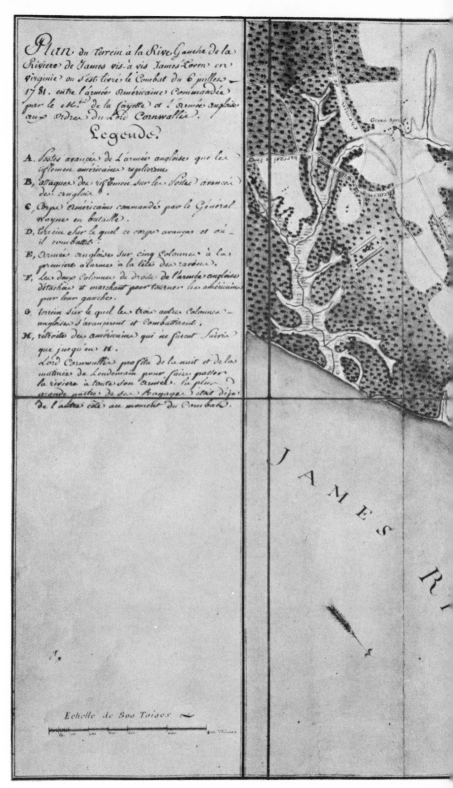

From the original in the Rochambeau papers, Library of Congress. Below the map the name *Desandr*
maps attributed to Capitaine.

guard as they appeared to be. Sending orders to the main body of his Continentals and militia to come up, he himself rode out to a near-by promontory to examine the enemy's position. He soon convinced himself that the enemy's baggage had already been safely delivered to the other side of the river and that the enemy lay in force before him. Spurring his horse full speed to warn Wayne, he found he was too late.

Wayne had already fallen into a trap skilfully prepared by Cornwallis. As the Continentals had begun to arrive bringing two other field pieces with them, Wayne had felt himself distinctly superior to the small enemy contingents he had uncovered. When Major de Galvan asked permission to take a British piece that had opened fire on them, he therefore consented. As Galvan's party advanced, they suddenly came upon the main force of the British, and for fifteen minutes the major's small command faced the fire of the whole enemy line alone. Then the British began an outflanking movement on their right, which, if successful, would have cut off Wayne from the reinforcements on the way.

Quickly realizing what had happened, Wayne had to make a decision on the spot. He could either retreat, leaving Galvan's men to the mercy of the enemy, or charge, giving them a chance to extricate themselves. For "Mad Anthony" Wayne the choice was clear. He took the bolder course. Now reinforced by the rest of his Pennsylvanians, he formed a line of about eight hundred men and three pieces of artillery, hoping to give the appearance of leading a larger body than he actually had. They charged toward the only causeway over the marsh beyond which the enemy lay concealed. Then Cornwallis uncovered his plot. Against Wayne's charge the British advanced in full force, outnumbering their adversaries three or four to one.[81]

Upon nearing Wayne's detachment Lafayette found that a general action had already begun and was proceeding disas-

[81] "Observations du Général Lafayette," p. 58; *Mémoires*, I, 273 and 274 n.; map by [Capitaine or] Desandrouins of the battle, LC, Rochambeau papers, reproduced between pp. 264 and 265 above; Galvan to Peters, July 8, 1781, *loc. cit.*; Wayne to Washington, July 8, 1781, *loc. cit.*, pp. 348–49; Tarleton, pp. 363–65.

trously.[82] Wayne's men charged boldly at first and kept up a good fight for a while, but the "close, warm and well directed fire"[83] of the enemy wilted the American line. They slowed down. First the right and then the left gave way, "the enemy making a devil of a noise of firing and huzzaing."[84] Soon "all on our side became a scene of confusion,"[85] and flight became too rapid to check. Lafayette ordered Galvan to try to rally the men on the other side of the marsh. He himself galloped from group to group, risking himself in a manner which his officers afterwards said was foolhardy. "Not a man in the whole detachment was more exposed."[86] He lost two horses in the mêlée. One was the beautiful animal which Holker had given him, shot from under his groom as it moved by its master's side. The other had its jaw fractured. Many other field officers lost their animals in similar fashion. Two of the fieldpieces had to be abandoned because their horses had all been killed.[87] Their loss was an especially disgraceful calamity in days when fieldpieces were few, expensive, and much more important than militia, whom Lafayette seldom counted among his casualties. The American general was particularly apologetic and the English general particularly pleased over these two cannon because one of them was marked "Captured at Bennington."[88]

Lafayette's men halted their flight at a brick house near Green Spring, half a mile away. There the marquis succeeded in restoring order, as Colonels Vose and Barber brought up the main body of the Continentals, Lawson with the Virginia militia being not far behind. After a few hours' rest Lafayette's troops

[82] *Mémoires*, I, 273–74; Lafayette to Greene, July 8, 1781, *Mémoires* (Amer. ed.), pp. 525–26.

[83] Lafayette to Greene, July 8, 1781, *loc. cit.*, p. 536; cf. Graham, *Memoir of Gen. Graham*, pp. 53–54.

[84] Galvan to Peters, July 8, 1781, *loc. cit.*   [85] *Ibid.*

[86] *Ibid.*; cf. Wayne to Washington, July 8, 1781, *loc. cit.*, p. 350.

[87] Lafayette to Greene, July 8, 1781, *loc. cit.*, p. 526; Lafayette to Noailles, July 9, 1781, Patou, p. 50; Wayne to Washington, July 8, 1781, *loc. cit.*, pp. 350; *Mémoires*, I, 274.

[88] Cornwallis to Leslie, July 8, 1781, Ross, *Correspondence of Cornwallis*, I, 106; cf. Lafayette to Greene, July 8, 1781, *loc. cit.*, p. 526.

retraced their march, arriving about midnight at Chickahominy Church, from which they had departed in better spirits early that morning. At dawn the next day Tarleton mopped up the woods and roads near Green Spring, encountering only a small body of mounted riflemen whom he easily routed. He wished to pursue and follow up the advantage the British had won, certain that Lafayette's army could now be annihilated. But Cornwallis, feeling his main purpose must be to send reinforcements to Clinton, preferred to continue on toward Portsmouth.[89]

And so Lafayette and Wayne were able to extricate themselves from a dangerous position with only the losses sustained in the fighting near James Island. Those losses were the greatest that had ever befallen any army that the marquis had so far led into battle. Lafayette, who usually understated his casualties, admitted 139 killed, wounded, and missing (not counting the riflemen wounded).[90] That was more than the total number of casualties inflicted on Lafayette's forces in all the other engagements in which he had been commanding officer. He had witnessed greater bloodshed only in the battles of Brandywine and Monmouth, where he had been subordinate to others.

In private Lafayette granted that "there were serious blunders on both sides," but, since the enemy chose to retreat, in the end "it will look well in a gazette."[91] In reporting the action to Congress, General Greene, and Governor Nelson, however, he was somewhat less candid. Calling it only a "short skirmish,"[92] he praised the gallantry of Wayne's Pennsylvanians, Galvan's light infantry, and the Virginia riflemen. He described

[89] Tarleton, pp. 362–67; Lafayette to Greene, July 8, 1781, *loc. cit.* Cornwallis to Clinton, July 8, 1781, Stevens, *Cornwallis-Clinton controversy*, II, 59; Galvan to Peters, July 8, 1781, *loc. cit.;* "Wild's journal," p. 144.

[90] Return of killed and wounded, signed by Major William Barber, PCC, no. 156, fols. 173–74.

[91] Lafayette to Gimat, [*ca.* July 9, 1781], typescript in the Gardner-Ball Collection.

[92] Lafayette to Greene, July 8, 1781, *loc. cit.*, copy of which is to be found in PCC, no. 156, fols. 171–72. Exactly the same letter was sent to Nelson, July 8, 1781, Sparks MSS LXXI, pp. 144–45.

the enemy's losses as far greater than his own, though the reverse was true. He made it appear (indeed, he honestly believed) that the English had continued their retreat because they feared a renewed attack. He flattered himself that he had induced them to believe his force much greater than it actually was.[93]

And, indeed, the effect upon Lafayette's reputation could have been no more favorable if he had won a great victory. On the day after the "skirmish," Cornwallis completed the crossing of the river, leaving some stores at Williamsburg and some wounded American prisoners and some horses at Jamestown. On the next morning Lafayette's soldiers occupied the island which they had failed to capture two days before. The marquis issued his general orders that day from Ambler's House near James Island, and they were the general orders of a victor, liberal in citations of merit and valor.[94]

The next day Lafayette proceeded to occupy Williamsburg. He chose not to follow the enemy until their plans became clearer. Meanwhile, he took advantage of the lull in retreat and pursuit to look after his men in the hospital. He visited wounded officers and men, asked after their needs, and gave instructions to the attendants to take good care of them. The sight of the marquis from this "most amiable point of view" drew grateful and warm praise from both officers and men.[95]

Lafayette had hardly started to rest from his strenuous labors of the preceding five months, when he began again to fear inaction. His first duty now seemed to be to reinforce the army in South Carolina, and he contemplated sending the new levies and the Pennsylvanians to Greene,[96] who once more reported

[93] Lafayette to Washington, July 8, 1781, *Mémoires* (Amer. ed.), pp. 420–21 (more complete text in Sparks MSS LXXXIV); to Noailles, July 9, 1781, *loc. cit.*; to Huntington, July 9, 1781, PCC, no. 156, fols. 174–75; to La Luzerne, July 9, 1781, *AHR*, XX (1915), 604; to General Allen Jones, July 10, 1781, *State records of North Carolina*, XV, 521–22; to Sumner, July 10, 1781, *ibid.*, pp. 522–23. Cf. Tarleton, p. 365.

[94] *Remembrancer*, XII (1781), 264–65; Tower, II, 369–70.

[95] Letter of an unknown soldier, July 11, 1781, Moore, *Diary of the American Revolution*, p. 453 n.; Lafayette to Nelson, July 10, 1781, Chinard, *Lafayette in Virginia*, p. 25.

[96] Lafayette to Huntington, July 9, 1781, *loc. cit.*; to Steuben, July 10, 1781, Gates papers, box 16, no. 53; to Nelson, July 12, 1781, Chinard, *Lafayette in Virginia*, p. 26.

that he was in difficulty.[97] He also urged the North Carolina militia to go to Greene's support and instructed the Virginia militia south of the James (now under Colonel Josiah Parker) to do what they could to intercept Cornwallis' forces if they moved to reinforce Rawdon.[98] Nevertheless, he knew that there was little glory to be won in such precautionary measures and began to think once more of returning north. He planned with warm pleasure to visit La Luzerne and to take part in the attack upon New York with Washington and Noailles.[99] It was good to have leisure, for he could write to them once more. He had neglected them of late, he explained to La Luzerne, because "when one is twenty-three, has an army to command and Lord Cornwallis to oppose, the time that is left is none too long for sleep."

Few persons even among those who were over twenty-three could have done better than Lafayette had done in Virginia. Though there had been some grumbling at first, he had won the affection of the people and the co-operation of the government. Steuben, whose ill-health increased the difficulties he had so far met in raising recruits, confessed in calling on Lafayette for help that "a word from you may have more effect than all the representations I have made;"[100] and Barbé-Marbois reported to Vergennes that "no man . . . . but Washington . . . . could have won such universal popularity."[101]

Some, in fact, had questioned Washington's choice of his young friend for so difficult a post. But from the first the commander-in-chief had persisted in believing that the marquis

[97] Greene to Lafayette, June 23, 1781, Gardner-Ball Collection; Lafayette to Greene, July 12, 1781, Morgan Library, Yorktown, Vol. II.

[98] Lafayette to General Allen Jones, July 10, 1781, *loc. cit.*; to Sumner, July 10, 1781, *loc. cit.*; to Parker, July 13, 1781, *Virginia historical register*, IV (1851), 206–7; to Governor Thomas Burke of North Carolina, July 16, 1781, LC, U.S. Revolution.

[99] Lafayette to La Luzerne, July 9, 1781, *loc. cit.*, pp. 604–5; to Washington, July 8, 1781, *loc. cit.*; to Noailles, July 9, 1781, *loc. cit.*, pp. 49–50.

[100] Steuben to Lafayette, July 13, 1781, New York Historical Society, Steuben papers, Vol. XII, no. 102.

[101] [1781], John Durand (ed.), *New materials for the history of the American Revolution* (New York, 1889), p. 242.

would be successful if anyone could. At the time of Virginia's gravest danger, when certain leading citizens were urging Washington to come to his own state's rescue or at least to send Nathanael Greene, when complaints were loudest against Steuben and did not spare Lafayette, Washington replied: "The command of the troops in that state cannot be in better hands than the Marquis's. He possesses uncommon military talents, is of quick and sound judgment, persevering, and enterprizing without rashness, and besides these, he is of a very conciliating temper and perfectly sober, which are qualities that rarely combine in the same person; and were I to add that some men will gain as much experience in the course of three or four years as some others will in ten or a dozen, you cannot deny the fact, and attack me upon that ground."[102]

General Greene, too, had defended the young Frenchman from unfriendly criticism. When Jefferson had complained that Virginia was overrun and begged for Greene's protection, Greene replied[103] that if Virginia had provided Lafayette with enough cavalry, it would not have been in such dire straits. "I have the highest opinion of the Marquis's abilities and zeal," he added, "and flatter myself that nothing will be left unattempted to give all the protection to the state that his force will admit." Such defense of the young soldier had been necessary before he took Jamestown and Williamsburg. Now those who had been the first to lose faith proclaimed him the loudest,[104] little realizing that their hero's success was more apparent than real. All they could see was that Cornwallis had run and that Lafayette had followed right behind him. To be sure, the one time (at Green Spring) Cornwallis had refused to be chased, Lafayette in his turn had had to flee. But since Cornwallis immediately resumed running again, Lafayette immediately resumed pursuit. Therefore, every patriotic American, including Lafayette, came to believe that Cornwallis ran because Lafayette chased

---

[102] Washington to Joseph Jones, July 10, 1781, Fitzpatrick, XXII, 353.

[103] June 27, 1781, G. W. Greene, *Life of Nathanael Greene, major-general in the army of the Revolution* (3 vols.; New York, 1871), III, 557.

[104] Cf. Nelson to Washington, July 27, 1781, *Virginia state papers*, II, 259.

him,[105] though in actuality Lafayette chased him because he ran.

The effect was the same in either case. Virginia north of the James was once more free of marauders, and Lafayette received applause on all sides for having freed her. McHenry thought that it was a kind of "sorcery and magic." "Legerdemain is a very necessary science for an American general at this moment."[106] And there was rejoicing, too, among the Frenchmen in the North. Rochambeau's chaplain, the sentimental Abbé Claude Robin, wrote admiringly of the young man "who left the arms of a tender and loving wife, the scene of pleasure and prestige where his name and his illustrious connections would without difficulty have opened to him the road of honor, to come to defend liberty under the American Fabius and to learn how to serve his country." The word *marquis*, the abbé continued, "which so often has served among us to indicate levity and frivolity, has become for Americans a beloved symbol which rouses their admiration and their gratitude."[107]

BIBLIOGRAPHICAL NOTES

The general impression given by all but a few writers on the Virginia campaign is that Cornwallis retreated because of the superior strategy of his young adversary. This is largely due to the fact that Lafayette, in his desire to make Cornwallis' retrograde movements seem like a retreat, deceived the early historians of the Revolution (see Appen. II). The testimony of the English commanders, contained in the Clinton-Cornwallis correspondence and Tarleton's and Simcoe's journals, is alone enough to correct that impression. The letter of Simcoe to Chastellux, January 20, 1787 (see n. 59 above) was intended to correct Chastellux's story of the battle at Spencer's Ordinary.

Several American sources, likewise, are far from being as enthusiastic about American successes as was Lafayette. The letter of Mercer to Simms (see n. 36 above) is very hostile to Lafayette's generalship; Mercer wrote long after the event, however, and seems besides to have been personally displeased with Lafayette. Galvan's letter to Peters (see n. 80 above) is not open to the same criticism, though Galvan probably overemphasized his own

[105] Cf. Jonathan Trumbull, Jr., to Jonathan Trumbull, July 9, 1781, *The Trumbull papers*, IV, 237; dispatch from Philadelphia, [*ca*. July 4, 1781], *Newport Mercury*, July 21, 1781.

[106] McHenry to T. S. Lee, July 11, 1781, Kite, p. 24.

[107] *Nouveau voyage dans l'Amérique septentrionale en l'année 1781, etc.* (Philadelphia and Paris, 1782), pp. 71–72.

part in the battle at Green Spring in his anxiety to secure a promotion. "Wild's journal" is, however, both thoroughly matter of fact and immediately contemporary; it too makes clear that Green Spring was the scene of a distinct American defeat.

Lafayette's story lost none of its glamour even after the political reason for painting his situation in rosy hues had passed. When he came to write his memoirs he had become convinced (if, indeed, he had not been earlier) that he had outwitted the British commanders at every turn. Hence the stories in *Mémoires*, I, 272–74, and in the "Observations du Général Lafayette," as well as in Capitaine's "Précis de la campagne de 1781" (*Mémoires*, I, 478–79), give the impression of a confused Cornwallis running away from a smaller force. Henry Lee's *War in the southern department*, published in 1812, appeared before Lafayette's *Mémoires* could lead him too far astray; moreover, Lee seems to have used the testimony of Mercer as well as that of Tarleton and Cornwallis. In some ways his account of the June, 1781, campaign is therefore the best available. Several more recent historians of the Virginia campaign (Carrington, Conrad, Johnston, Tower, and M. J. Wright, among others) have, however, followed Lafayette's testimony too confidently. Doniol (IV, 659 n.) goes as far as to refute La Luzerne, who, on August 4 and October 2, 1781, had written Vergennes that Cornwallis' retreat might be due to orders sent him by Clinton rather than to Lafayette's skill. Two recent scholars, at least, held a less biased point of view. E. E. Hale in his "Report of the Council" (*Proceedings of the American Antiquarian Society*, new ser., I [1880–81], 328, 336, and 337 n.) indicated all too casually that Lafayette was not the best source for knowledge of the Virginia campaign; and R. G. Adams in his very able "View of Cornwallis's surrender" (though he deals only briefly with the events of June, 1781) makes clear that the British general maneuvered as he did because of pressure from Clinton and not from Lafayette.

Some biographers of Wayne (cf. J. W. de Peyster, "Anthony Wayne," *Magazine of American history*, XV [1886], 134–45) have placed the blame for falling into Cornwallis' trap on Lafayette alone, giving "Mad Anthony" the honor of extricating his superior from a bad error. Wayne was no less responsible than Lafayette, however. In fact, since he gave Galvan the order to charge the British fieldpiece and thus made general action necessary, he was more to blame. Wayne's account of the battle (see n. 80 above) like Lafayette's (and for the same reasons) underestimated the damage done to the American army and made it appear almost a victory.

Since the first printing of this volume William B. Willcox has published *Portrait of a general: Sir Henry Clinton in the War of Independence* (New York, 1964), which portrays Cornwallis' and Clinton's reactions to Lafayette's maneuvers (see esp. pp. 403–6).

CHAPTER XII

Lafayette Coops Up Cornwallis

THE temporary rest from marching and countermarching was welcome to the weary American army. While Lafayette himself went to Richmond, his men, taking time to wash and to rest as they moved, proceeded by slow stages to a camp site which he had selected at Malvern Hill. He considered it "the most airy and healthy place this side of the mountains."[1] It was a strategic spot on a height about halfway between Richmond and Williamsburg and within covering distance of the stores at Albermarle Old Court House and Amelia.

Lafayette had been especially cautious in choosing this site because his army was once more but a skeleton. He had allowed many of the Virginia gentlemen volunteers to go home, and those who remained ("most of them men of fortune who made great sacrifices to this country") he did not wish to ask to do "common camp duties which can be as well performed by the continental horse."[2] The militia had dwindled to around fifteen hundred; and he had sent Wayne with all the Pennsylvanians and the new levies to the other side of the James to watch Cornwallis, who had stopped for a few days at Cobham, directly opposite Jamestown. Wayne might protect the stores on the south side of the James at Amelia if Cornwallis made an attempt in

---

[1] Lafayette to Washington, July 20, 1781 (public letter), LC, Washington papers, no. 51, fol. 49. *Calendar of Washington papers* (pp. 1899–1900) erroneously says this letter is marked "private"; it is, however, another letter of Lafayette to Washington, July 20, 1781 (LC, Washington papers, no. 51, fol. 53) which is so marked. *Mémoires* ([Amer. ed.], pp. 421–23) publishes only brief extracts from both letters. See also "Wild's journal," pp. 944–45.

[2] Lafayette to Morgan, July 16, 1781, NYPL, Myers, 913, 2.

that direction, or march to join Greene if Cornwallis moved to reinforce Rawdon.[3] Lafayette's remaining troop was not much more than twenty-two hundred now. If Cornwallis were to move again across the James, the marquis would have to retreat just as he had done before. So he begged Governor Nelson to place the army's stores in a less exposed place than Albermarle Old Court House had turned out to be.[4]

Those precautions proved to have been wise, for Cornwallis, before proceeding to Portsmouth, dispatched Tarleton with his dread cavalry and some mounted infantry to destroy the stores he could find in the Appomattox valley. For several days Tarleton wandered unmolested in the neighborhood of Petersburg and Prince Edward Court House, destroying what little he could find.[5] To intercept him Lafayette ordered some Virginia cavalry and riflemen under General Daniel Morgan (who had taken his post under the marquis only after the battle of Green Spring)[6] to a point above Petersburg. Wayne was instructed to reinforce Morgan.[7] But Tarleton succeeded in avoiding them.

After a few days at Richmond, Lafayette rejoined his men at Malvern Hill and established his headquarters at the house of William Randolph.[8] Spies soon reported to him that Cornwallis constantly kept asking when he was to leave for the North. That made it apparent that the British expected the main sphere of action to be transferred there. It now was believed that Cornwallis intended to send a good part of his men to New York. That suspicion was confirmed when Lafayette's aides cross-examined a talkative young officer of Tarleton's legion

[3] Lafayette to Wayne, July 13, 1781, Historical Society of Pennsylvania; to Burke, July 16, 1781, LC, U.S. Revolution papers.

[4] Lafayette to Nelson, July 13, 1781, Chinard, *Lafayette in Virginia*, pp. 27–28.

[5] Tarleton, pp. 368–73.

[6] Morgan to Greene, July 24, 1781, Graham, *Morgan*, pp. 394–95; cf. also *ibid.*, pp. 388–89.

[7] Lafayette to Wayne, July 15, 1789, Historical Society of Pennsylvania, and *Casket*, IV (1829), 533; to Morgan, July 16, 1781, *loc. cit.*, and July 17, 1781, NYPL, Myers, 914, 2; Lafayette to Wayne, July 21 and 23, 1781, Historical Society of Pennsylvania; to Morgan, July 21, 1781, NYPL, Myers, 916, 2.

[8] *American historical record*, I (1872), 31 n.

who had been taken prisoner. The picture of an attack upon New York by the combined forces of French and Americans with Lafayette nowhere in the picture seemed to Lafayette, who had planned and dreamed of it for two years, to be a sort of Hamletless *Hamlet*. He appealed to Washington again, resorting once more to the expedient of sending two letters, one of a public nature to the commander-in-chief and the other described as "not by any means directed to the commander-in-chief, but to my most intimate and confidential friend."[9]

Both letters conveyed the same impression. Since operations in Virginia were "for the present in a state of languor" and Lafayette was homesick (or, as he wrote it, "home sick") he hoped that Washington would find some place for him in the Grand Army even if nothing more than that of volunteer aide-de-camp. Forgetting for the moment how bitterly he had complained of Steuben's unpopularity and mismanagement, he suggested that the baron should be put in command in Virginia in his stead. Since no great maneuvers were likely to take place again in Virginia, "a prudent officer will do our business here, and the Baron is prudent to the utmost." While going into detailed suggestions on how Washington might manage to find a good post for him in the combined armies, the ambitious young soldier betrayed the emotional conflict that had characterized his behavior since he first became an American officer. Loyalty to Washington and a desire for glory struggled for supremacy in his soul. He tried to make them appear now to coincide. "I know the command of a separate army ought not to be quitted. But besides the service I may render to the cooperation, some arrangements which I leave to your goodness for me to think of may put me in very brilliant station. . . . . But do not, I pray, believe I have the least notion of calculating upon commands (tho' in my personal circumstances they become peculiarly important to me)."

Meanwhile, languor continued to reign in Virginia. Tarleton

---

[9] See n. 1 above. A version of the "private" letter, with only minor corrections, is to be found in Sparks, *Correspondence of the American Revolution*, III, 360–63. The *Mémoires* ([Amer. ed.], pp. 421–23) give only extracts from both letters.

had returned to Portsmouth, having encountered some militia
on the way and suffered some losses but with little addition to
his reputation as a destroyer.[10] Otherwise no military encounter took place. Lafayette himself disturbed the sultry air of
Malvern Hill by the constant scratching of his pen, addressing
Nelson, Steuben, and other civil and military authorities upon
the needs of his army, particularly on the shortage of horses
and the necessity for impressments.[11] "Upon my word," he declared in exasperation to the Virginia commissioner of war,[12]
"unless we have a cavalry the defense of this state wholly depends upon the mistakes of the ennemy." All reports from
Portsmouth indicated that an embarkation was taking place in
force. Though still fearing that the British might have in view
some further depredations in Virginia,[13] Lafayette began to feel
more and more certain that New York was their destination.
He sent word to Washington and Congress[14] to warn them
against that possibility, which, if realized, might frustrate the
contemplated attack upon New York. He also communicated
his conviction to the Comte de Grasse,[15] the new commander
of the French fleet in the West Indies. De Grasse had won a

[10] Lafayette to Greene, July 21, and August 12, 1781 Morgan Library, Yorktown,
Vol. II; Wayne to Parker, July 24, 1781, courtesy of Mrs. Helen Pierce Parker Chalmers, Smithfield, Va.; Lafayette to Wayne, July 25, 1781, Historical Society of Pennsylvania; Lafayette to Washington, July 26, 1781, LC, Washington papers, no. 50,
fol. 348 (extract in *Mémoires* [Amer. ed.], p. 423).

[11] Lafayette to Governor Lee, July 17, 1781 (from Richmond), Shriver, p. 102; to
Nelson, July 21, 1781, Chinard, *Lafayette in Virginia*, pp. 29–30; to Jefferson [?], July
22, 1781, Historical Society of Pennsylvania, Dreer collection; to Morgan, July 24,
1781, Gardner-Ball Collection; to Steuben, July 23, 25, and 28, 1781, Sparks MSS
LXXXIV, pp. 28–30, and Gates papers, box 16, nos. 55 and 56; to Nelson, July 26,
1781, New Jersey Historical Society.

[12] Lafayette to Colonel William Davies, July 27, 1781, Gardner-Ball Collection.

[13] Lafayette to Weedon, July 27, 1781, Ford collection; to Parker, July 27 and 28,
1781, "Revolutionary correspondence of Col. Josiah Parker, of Isle of Wight County,
Va.," *Virginia magazine of history and biography*, XXII (1914), 263–66 (also in "Letters from Baron Steuben, and others, to Colonel Josiah Parker, of Isle of Wight,"
Virginia historical register, IV [1851], 209–11).

[14] Lafayette to Washington, July 26, 1781, *loc. cit.*; to Congress, July 26, 1781, PCC,
no. 156, fol. 204.

[15] The original of this letter has not been found; it is mentioned in Lafayette to
Washington, July 26, 1781, *loc. cit.*

victory recently in West Indian waters, and Lafayette felt that there was room to hope that the admiral might see fit to strike a blow at Cornwallis' transports while they were at sea. Meanwhile, the marquis maneuvered so as to take advantage of Cornwallis' station in the town where he had nearly bagged Arnold. Should some lucky chance bring a French naval force to the Chesapeake, he wished to be in position to begin a siege of Portsmouth immediately. Assuming that Greene could dispense with Wayne's troops as long as Rawdon was not reinforced, he ordered the Pennsylvanians and the other forces south of the James to prepare to take a post closer to Portsmouth.[16]

But in a few days Cornwallis' plans changed again. It had previously been his intention to send the troops that Clinton had asked for and, abandoning Virginia entirely, to lead most of the others to Charleston.[17] But, on learning of that intention, Clinton disapproved. He wished to retain a foothold on the Chesapeake, since he planned to make that area a center of future operations against Philadelphia. For that reason he proposed to hold a naval base that would be deep, large, and safe enough for big line-of-battle ships.[18] He, therefore, suggested that Cornwallis either reoccupy the neck of land between the James and the York on which Williamsburg and Yorktown stood or, if that were not practicable, garrison Old Point Comfort, which Clinton hoped might secure control of Hampton Roads and thus answer the same purpose.[19] When Rear Admiral Sir Thomas Graves, the new naval commander of His Majesty's fleet at New York, agreed with Clinton that it was necessary to retain on the Chesapeake a winter naval station for big ships,

[16] Lafayette to Parker, July 18, 1781, "Revolutionary correspondence of Josiah Parker," pp. 262–63; to Greene, July 23, 1781, Morgan Library, Yorktown, Vol. I; to Wayne, July 25, 1781, "Extracts from the papers of General William Irvine," *Pennsylvania magazine of history and biography*, V (1881), 262–63.

[17] Cornwallis to Clinton, June 30, 1781, Stevens, *Clinton-Cornwallis controversy*, II, 37.

[18] Clinton to Cornwallis, July 8, 1781, *ibid.*, pp. 51–52; cf. *idem* to *idem*, August 2, 1781, *ibid.*, p. 114.

[19] *Ibid.*, pp. 53–54.

Cornwallis was given more peremptory orders. To a disconcerting degree they seemed to reverse previous plans and instructions. Not only was he to reoccupy the Williamsburg neck in order to support a garrison at Old Point Comfort, which he was "at all events to hold," but he was also for that purpose to retain all his troops if necessary.[20]

Cornwallis immediately sent his engineers to inspect Old Point Comfort. They reported that it was so situated that a land garrison there could not give sufficient protection to a naval force in its harbor because the river at that point was too wide to come fully within the range of shore batteries. His Lordship, therefore, determined to move his men back to Yorktown. If he also occupied Gloucester, immediately opposite on the York River, he reasoned, that would answer Clinton's purpose of providing a station on the Chesapeake which would be safe for big as well as little ships.[21]

Cornwallis' movements baffled Lafayette. Latest rumors had it that he was going to attack Baltimore. But if that were so, the marquis could not understand why Cornwallis' men had been prepared to embark for several days and yet had not sailed anywhere, though the winds were favorable. Still, knowing that he could do nothing to stop them from moving on the water wherever they wished, he continued to do all he could to check them on the land.[22] In addition to the forces of Wayne and Muhlenberg, the Virginia militia of Colonel Parker and the North Carolina militia of Brigadier-General Isaac Gregory were required to guard the southern areas and the roads toward the south. They might at least hinder, if too weak to arrest, any British effort to retreat toward Charleston.[23] And cavalry were

[20] Clinton to Cornwallis, July 11, 1781 (two letters), *ibid.*, pp. 61 and 62–63; Graves to Cornwallis, July 12, 1781, *ibid.*, p. 68. See also p. 306 below.

[21] Cornwallis to Clinton, July 27, 1781, *ibid.*, pp. 107–8.

[22] Lafayette to Parker, July 21, 1781, courtesy of Mrs. Chalmers; to Nelson, July 27 and 29, 1781, Chinard, *Lafayette in Virginia*, pp. 33–34 and 36–38; to Weedon, July 27, 1781, Ford collection; to Wayne, July 29, 1781, Historical Society of Pennsylvania; to Governor Lee, July 30, 1781, Shriver, p. 103; to Greene, July 31, 1781, Morgan Library, Yorktown, Vol. I.

[23] Lafayette to Washington, July 30, 1781, Sparks, *Correspondence of the American Revolution*, III, 365.

begged from every quarter in order to keep the British under constant surveillance and to harass them should they move out of Portsmouth. All that Lafayette needed to undertake a siege was an assurance of naval superiority, if only for a brief period.[24]

In the midst of these activities came a cryptic but encouraging word from Washington.[25] The commander-in-chief, while informing Lafayette that Rochambeau's forces had joined his for the proposed attack upon New York, added, "I shall shortly have occasion to communicate matters of very great importance to you." Meanwhile, Lafayette was to gather together as great a Continental force as he could and take every measure to augment his cavalry. He was also to keep Washington informed as quickly and as accurately as he could of Cornwallis' movements. Lafayette was able to read between the lines what Washington had not dared to say explicitly. The message seemed to hint quite clearly that there was some reason to hope that a siege of Cornwallis might be possible. The young Frenchman knew that that could happen only if the Americans had naval superiority, and naval superiority might come only in two ways. Either Barras would risk a dash from Newport to the Chesapeake or Admiral de Grasse would come to the continent from the West Indies.

That prospect made Lafayette's new role clear. He was to make every effort to retain Cornwallis where a superior naval and military force could capture him. At the same time he must keep informed and keep headquarters informed of any possible changes in Cornwallis' position. He took every measure to get accurate intelligence from Portsmouth. Not only did he urge the officers in charge of the troops close to the enemy to report to him frequently; he also stationed Commodore James Barron of the Continental Navy at Hampton to inform him as soon as the British vessels moved.[26] He sent spies into Portsmouth

[24] *Ibid.*, pp. 364–66; *Virginia state papers*, II, 274 and 689. See also n. 22 above.

[25] Washington to Lafayette, July 13, 1781, Fitzpatrick, XXII, 367–69.

[26] Cf. Barron to Lafayette, July 30, and 31, 1781, *Archives of Maryland*, XLVII, 386–87 and 383.

and even succeeded in suborning one of Cornwallis' servants.[27] A slave named James eventually won his freedom by act of the Virginia legislature for his services in this connection.[28] All Lafayette could gather led him to conclude: "Should a French fleet now come in Hampton Road, the British army would, I think, be ours."[29]

But the French fleet did not come. Nor did Cornwallis stay where he was. On the last day of July, two short, hasty notes from Commodore Barron informed Lafayette that the British had sailed and were heading upstream—not down the bay. Their destination, Barron announced, must be Baltimore.[30] Lafayette sent Major McPherson northward to report this unexpected move to Congress and the commander-in-chief.[31] He immediately took steps also to halt the Maryland troops that were supposed to be on their way to aid Virginia and to send them back for the protection of their own state.[32] Ordering Wayne to join him for a northerly march[33] and Parker to hasten intelligence of the enemy's movements,[34] he broke camp at Malvern Hill and set out to follow the British by land. He had pushed his men as far as Richmond when he learned that, instead of sailing up the bay, the enemy had begun to land unopposed at Yorktown and Gloucester.[35]

Once more Cornwallis had outwitted Lafayette. The Ameri-

[27] Lafayette to Washington, July 31, 1781, LC, Washington papers, no. 51, fol. 137, extracts of which are quoted in *Mémoires* (Amer. ed.), p. 425, and Tower, II, 411.

[28] *Journal of Virginia House of Delegates* (sess. of November 30, 1786; December 21, 23, and 25, 1786; January 1 and 9, 1787).

[29] Lafayette to Washington, July 31, 1781, *loc. cit.*

[30] Barron to Lafayette, July 31, 1781, *loc. cit.*

[31] Lafayette to Washington, August 1, 1781, LC, Washington papers, no. 51, fol. 141; to McKean, August 1, 1781, PCC, no. 156, fol. 215.

[32] Lafayette to Lee, August 1, 1781, "Extracts from the papers of General William Irvine," p. 265 (the original of which is now in the possession of the Essex County Club, West Orange, N.J.); McHenry to Lee, August 1, 1781, Kite, *Sidelight on history*, pp. 42–43.

[33] July 31, 1781, Historical Society of Pennsylvania; Tower, II, 411–12.

[34] Lafayette to Parker, August 1, 1781, courtesy of Mrs. Chalmers.

[35] Lafayette to Wayne, August 3, 1781, Historical Society of Pennsylvania; to Steuben, August 3, 1781, Gates papers, box 16, no. 59.

can army had gone in just the wrong direction—away from Yorktown, where they might, even with a small force, have hindered the enemy's landing and inflicted serious losses upon him. Believing that Cornwallis had learned of the late successes of the French fleet under Admiral de Grasse in the West Indies and therefore feared to be intercepted by De Grasse if he sailed for New York, Lafayette concluded that the British probably intended to remain at Yorktown and Gloucester.[36] If that were in truth their intention, the citizens of other cities in the Chesapeake valley might once more breathe freely. Yet Lafayette had to be on his guard against further subterfuges to throw him off the scent.[37]

Complaining that he was obliged to "walk in the dark" because he had to "guess at every possible whim of an enemy that flies with the wind and is not within the reach of spies or reconnoitrers,"[38] Lafayette decided to establish a new camp on the Pamunkey River. Meanwhile, he solicited funds for the sick and wounded in the hospital at Williamsburg, sent his aide Major Capitaine to move the hospitals out of Cornwallis' reach, redesigned the boats that were to carry his men and horses across the Virginia rivers, requested Maryland to forward once more the troops that had originally been intended to operate in Virginia,[39] and acted as peacemaker (without much success) between Nelson, who was furious because the Pennsylvanians had helped themselves too freely from Virginia's stores, and Wayne, who was equally furious at the reflection on the honesty of the officers and soldiers under his command.[40] Having made camp

[36] *Ibid.*

[37] Cf. Wayne to Lafayette, August 2, 1781, Historical Society of Pennsylvania.

[38] Lafayette to Wayne, August 4, 1781, *ibid.*

[39] Lafayette to Nelson, August 5, 1781, Chinard, *Lafayette in Virginia*, p. 41 (where it is erroneously dated August 6); Tucker to Nelson, August 5, 1781, *Virginia state papers*, II, 295; Lafayette to Smallwood, August 6, 1781, LC, Washington papers, no. 51, fol. 223; McHenry to T. S. Lee, August 6, 1781, Kite, *Sidelight on history*, pp. 47–49; Lafayette to Lee and Gist, August 6, 1781; Shriver, pp. 107–8; Wayne to Lafayette, August 5, 1781, Historical Society of Pennsylvania; and various correspondents to Davies, August 5–9, 1781, *Virginia state papers*, II, 295, 298, 307, and 308.

[40] Nelson to Lafayette, August 3, 1781, *Letters of Thomas Nelson, Jr., governor of Virginia* ("Publications of the Virginia Historical Society," new ser., no. 1 [Richmond,

at Newcastle on the Pamunkey, the marquis satisfied himself that, whatever the enemy's intention might once have been, they now meant to establish themselves in control of the York River between Yorktown and Gloucester. Moving cautiously (for "His Lordship plays so well that no blunder can be hoped from him to recover a bad step of ours"),[41] Lafayette, nevertheless, was convinced that the British had not much improved their position by exchanging Portsmouth for Yorktown. There, too, only naval superiority saved them. "Should a fleet come in at this moment, our affairs would take a very happy turn."[42]

At the new camp Lafayette's pen and aides immediately went to work. Washington's injunction to gather as big an army as possible was a word to one already wise to the peculiar needs of the army in Virginia. Relying on the effective assistance of McHenry, Lafayette sent his aide to concert plans with Governor Nelson. "I am sensible, Sir, of your difficulties," he assured Nelson.[43] "I am no less sensible that the Executive are as deeply interested as myself in the public welfare. On the first account it is useless to complain. On the second it is folly. I wish to surmount obstacles, and in this I solicit the honor to cooperate with the Executive of this State. Whatever means are put into my hands I shall endeavour to use, and with pleasure I see that the State is capable of exertions that will, if properly made, insue in safety." Again, as so often in the past, he clamored for magazines, arms, ammunition, means of transportation, more men, and better training for the men he had.[44] Despite "long conversations"[45] with the governor and council, McHenry could

---

1874]), pp. 63–64; Lafayette to Wayne, August 6, 1781, Historical Society of Pennsylvania; Wayne to Lafayette, August 9, 1781, *ibid.*; Lafayette to Wayne, August 11, 1781, Sparks MSS LXXI, p. 174; Lafayette to Washington, August 11, 1781, LC, Washington papers, no. 51, fol. 237.

[41] Lafayette to Washington, August 6, 1781, LC, Washington papers, no. 51, fol. 183.

[42] *Ibid.*, fol. 184.

[43] August 7, 1781, Chinard, *Lafayette in Virginia*, p. 44.

[44] *Ibid.*; and cf. *idem* to *idem*, August 6, 1781, *ibid.*, pp. 42–43.

[45] Lafayette to Washington, August 21, 1781, LC, Washington papers, no. 51, fol. 276. Sparks, *Correspondence of the American Revolution* (III, 389–92) amends the orthography and occasionally reinterprets the text of this letter.

not perform miracles and produce supplies without money. The old refrain about cavalry also rose from Lafayette's camp desk, and Steuben, still trying to mix the business of recruiting with his convalescence, was kept in a constant fret, remonstrating that he could not find accouterment enough even for the men he could raise, much less meet the demands that both Greene and Lafayette were making upon him.[46]

When Lafayette discovered that Cornwallis was indeed fortifying his position at Yorktown, he resolved to move closer to the enemy. After a few days on the Pamunkey River, he marched his men to New Kent Court House in a neighborhood where they had bivouacked just about a month earlier. But this time they crossed the Pamunkey River and made their way by slow marches to Montock Hill, close to the fork of the Pamunkey and the Mattapony. Here there was little fear of infection and "forage in plenty."[47] Lafayette posted the light infantry four miles from West Point and the militia four miles beyond them, stationing a reconnoitering party at West Point itself.[48] On the road near New Kent he became the hero of an anecdote that was remembered long afterward. As he stopped to talk to an old companion-in-arms and his wife, a cock under the arm of a child that stood near-by insisted upon crowing. To relieve the embarrassment of his friends, Lafayette said gallantly that the crowing was a good sign because the cock was the symbol of France.[49]

Chanticleer might well have crowed and the spirits of a young Frenchman might well have been high, for there were unmistakable signs from the northward of great things to come. Letters from Washington had recently come to him filled with grateful

[46] Steuben to Lafayette, August 6 and 9, 1781, New York Historical Society, Steuben papers, Vol. XII, nos. 107 and 108; Lafayette to Steuben, August 9, 1781, Gates papers, box 16, no. 64. Cf. Lafayette to T. S. Lee, August 10, 1781, Shriver, pp. 111–12.

[47] Wayne to Lafayette, August 10, 1781, NYPL, Bancroft transcripts; Lafayette to Greene, August 12, 1781, *loc. cit.*

[48] "Wild's journal," p. 147; Capitaine's map, *loc. cit.*; Lafayette to Greene, August 12, 1781, *loc. cit.*

[49] William Maxwell, "My mother," *Lower Norfolk Virginia antiquary*, III (1901), 49.

approval of Lafayette's generalship and with a broad hint that he stay in Virginia, since New York might not after all be the scene of the most glorious action that summer. All Washington waited for, it appeared, was that the means of transporting the Grand Army southward by water be made available, since he dared not risk tiring his men or encouraging them to desert in long land marches. And he added that there seemed to be "prospects of transporting ourselves in a manner safe, easy and expeditious." Unwilling to state plainly what he meant for fear that his dispatches might again be intercepted, he left his young friend to guess: "Your penetration will point out my meaning."[50]

To Lafayette that could signify only one thing—naval superiority at last. The commander-in-chief's letter made clear that Barras had considered, but had finally decided against, making the dash to the Chesapeake because "such a maneuvre might interfere with greater plans." It was obvious then that De Grasse was expected in the near future, and the imaginative Lafayette had no difficulty in picturing what that would mean. "For the present," he replied, "[I] am with you of opinion I had better remain in Virginia. . . . . I have pretty well understood you, my dear general. . . . ,"[51]

Assured of provisions along both the rivers that flowed past his camp, Lafayette was in a splendid position. He could bleed the country around Yorktown and Gloucester of food and forage, and "look down the river"[52] at both points occupied by the British. By crossing the Mattapony he could reach the area around Gloucester, which some militia commanded by Colonel James Innes kept under guard, and by crossing the Pamunkey he

---

[50] Washington to Lafayette, July 30, 1781 (public letter), Fitzpatrick, XXII, 431–32; *idem* to *idem*, July 30, 1781 (private letter), *ibid.*, pp. 432–34.

[51] Lafayette to Washington, August 11, 1781, *loc. cit.*; cf. Lafayette to Greene, August 25, 1781, Parke-Bernet catalogue no. 251 (sale of January 22–24, 1941), item no. 373. This exchange of letters makes clear the error of Lafayette's claim (letter to Sparks, November 26, 1830, Sparks MSS) that his requests "determined General Washington to adopt the measures which were terminated at Yorktown." Though Lafayette's reports undoubtedly were a factor in Washington's calculations, the ultimate decision turned on De Grasse's movements.

[52] Lafayette to Greene, August 12, 1781, *loc. cit.*

could get to Yorktown, which Colonel Thomas Mathew's militia held under surveillance. Moreover, he was not far from Wayne's camp, now at Bottom's Bridge over the Chickahominy. His chief concern still was his need of cavalry. Colonel Stephen Moylan with forty Continental dragoons arrived, and two hundred horses were found to be ready for Colonel White's troopers, but they were largely without equipment.[53] Couriers and aides, carrying more pleas to Nelson, Steuben, Morgan (who had once more gone home because of illness), and Colonel Davies, rode from his camp, threatening, cajoling, and begging cavalry and arms.[54] He even turned again to La Luzerne pleading for Lauzun's Legion.[55]

And now, too, Lafayette began to bicker with Governor Nelson upon several points. With Nelson's permission he had drawn money from the state treasury to defray the expense of recently exchanged American officers. Nelson found that the total expenditure for that purpose was extravagant. Lafayette retorted: "I readily confess the sums of monney that have been drawn are extravagant, as they are proportionate to the price extorted for every article and the lamentable depreciation of monney." Still far from the humanitarian he was one day to become, he suggested raising funds by reselling to their former owners at half-price in hard cash such slaves and other chattels as were recaptured from the English.[56] The old quarrel between Nelson and Wayne over some shoes that had been taken from Virginia stores continued; and Lafayette tried to mediate between the two angry men, fearful that Wayne might, as he threatened, return the shoes and then send his soldiers to a safe place because they would not be fit to continue the campaign.[57]

[53] *Ibid.*

[54] Lafayette to Nelson, August 12, 1781, Chinard, *Lafayette in Virginia*, p. 452 (the original of which is in the New York Historical Society, misc. MSS, "L," in McHenry's handwriting); to *idem*, August 12, 1781 (another letter), Historical Society of Pennsylvania; to Davies, August 13, 1781, Chinard, *Lafayette in Virginia*, pp. 46–47; to *idem*, August 14, 1781, Gardner-Ball Collection; to Steuben, August 13, 1781, Gates papers, box 16, no. 66; to Morgan, August 15, 1781, Graham, *Morgan*, pp. 396–98.

[55] August 14, 1781, *AHR*, XX (1915), 605.

[56] Lafayette to Nelson, August 12, 1781, Historical Society of Pennsylvania.

[57] Wayne to Lafayette, August 9, 1781, *loc. cit.*

Nor did it clear the atmosphere when Nelson complained that he in his turn had been insulted by Lafayette's subordinates.[58]

To make matters worse, a scandal had recently developed in the Virginia commissary department. The incompetence of Commissary-General John Brown led to a demand that he resign in order to avoid the embarrassment of a formal investigation,[59] but in the end Brown neither resigned nor faced an inquiry.[60] Though publicly Lafayette continued to declare that "no one is more fully impressed with the endeavours of the State,"[61] he attributed his financial difficulties not only to the inefficiency of certain officers but to the niggardliness of the state authorities.[62] Neither explanation increased his respect for the democratic way of life.

At this juncture a slight episode occurred which must have caused Lafayette to wonder still more about the blessings of a republic. As the possibility of a peace conference continued to grow, Congress had decided to name a commission of five to attend the negotiations if they materialized. Jefferson had been selected as one of the five. That had been in June, when Tarleton's horsemen had caused the Virginia legislature to run to the woods while they ensconced themselves in Charlottesville and Monticello. Not knowing where to address Jefferson, Congress had sent his appointment to Lafayette to deliver.[63] By the time Lafayette could do so, Jefferson had ceased to be governor of Virginia, and some of his political opponents had introduced a resolution to investigate his conduct in that office.

Jefferson was anxious to accept the post of peace commis-

[58] Nelson to Lafayette, August 15, 1781, *Letters of Nelson*, pp. 69–71.

[59] *Virginia state papers*, II, 218, 227, and 328; Lafayette to Nelson, July 23, 1781, Chinard, *Lafayette in Virginia*, p. 31; North to Wayne, July 24, 1781, *ibid.*, p. 32.

[60] *Virginia state papers*, II, 379.

[61] Lafayette to Davies, August 17, 1781, C. F. Libbie & Co. (Boston) catalogue, sale of May 20 and 21, 1892, p. 46, no. 490.

[62] Lafayette to Nelson, August 16, 1781, Chinard, *Lafayette in Virginia*, pp. 48–49; to Wayne, August 18, 1781, Historical Society of Pennsylvania; to Washington, August 21, 1781, *loc. cit.*; to Rudolph, August 22, 1781, Gardner-Ball Collection.

[63] Burnett, VI, 190, n. 2; Lafayette to Jefferson, June 26 and July 1, 1781, Chinard, *Lafayette and Jefferson*, pp. 47–48.

sioner, but he was also unwilling to leave for Europe until he had cleared his reputation. After much hesitation and a period of illness resulting from a fall from his horse, he declined the nomination. He asked Lafayette to deliver to Congress the letter in which he did so. In a private message to the marquis he explained: "I lose an opportunity, the only one I ever had and perhaps ever shall have, of combining public service with private gratification, of seeing countries whose improvements in science, in art, and in civilization it has been my fortune to admire at a distance but never to see, and at the same time of lending some aid to a cause which has been handed on from its first organization to its present stage by every effort of which my poor faculties were capable. These, however, have not been such as to give satisfaction to some of my countrymen, and it has become necessary for me to remain in the State till a later period in the present year than is consistent with an acceptance of what has been offered me. Declining higher objects, therefore, my only one must be to show that suggestion and fact are different things, and that public misfortunes may be produced as well by public poverty and private disobedience to the laws as by the misconduct of public servants. The independence of private life under the protection of republican laws will, I hope, yield me the happiness from which no slave is so remote as the minister of a commonwealth."[64] Lafayette had known something about Virginia's "public poverty" and "private disobedience to the laws." He might with reason, too, have made some mental reservations regarding the lack of vigor which the government of Virginia had shown while Jefferson was chief executive. To be sure, Jefferson easily cleared himself of all accusations when he at last was permitted to do so. Yet for a champion of the self-evident rights of man, "a man of intelligence" and "an eminent lawyer,"[65] to lament because he was the victim of the ingratitude of republics could not have helped the slow development of liberal ideas that was even then going on in the young aristocrat's mind.

[64] Jefferson to Lafayette, August 4, 1781, *Writings of Jefferson* (mem. ed.), IV, 184.
[65] Lafayette to La Luzerne, August 14, 1781, *loc. cit.*

But Lafayette had little time now for lessons on the ingratitude of republics. He contented himself with forwarding Jefferson's letter to Congress, indicating his belief that Jefferson
might accept the same offer at some future time.[66] For the moment the shortage of necessities disturbed him more than the
ingratitude of republics. "I cannot conceive what our commissaries are about," he protested.[67] "It is almost an age since
flour has been seen in camp, not even for the officers. . . . . Soap
and candles are entirely out of the question. Meat is hardly
eatable." Some shoes and clothing did come in from the Board
of War, but Lafayette, leaving many of his own men "bare-
footed,"[68] sent most of them to Wayne, who might have to make
a long march to South Carolina. Meanwhile, he continued to
wonder about the enemy's intentions. Why did Cornwallis fortify Gloucester? Why didn't he fortify Yorktown? Why did he
leave part of his forces in Portsmouth? "Lord Cornwallis's abilities are to me more alarming than his superiority of forces," he
conceded. "I ever had a great opinion of him. Our papers call
him a mad man, but was ever any advantage taken of him where
he commanded in person? To speak plain English, I am devilish
affraid of him."[69]

That fear vanished when next Lafayette received a dispatch
from headquarters. Washington had by that time learned definitely that De Grasse would come to the American mainland
with a force large enough to wrest command of the seas from
the British. Though the French fleet could stay only for the
summer, being obliged to return to West Indian waters in October, there would be time enough in the few weeks it remained
to deliver one decisive blow at least. De Grasse, on Rochambeau's persuasion, preferred to sail directly to the Chesapeake.
Washington, therefore, when he at last definitely confirmed the
glad tidings of which he had so long made a half-secret, ordered

[66] Lafayette to Congress, August 14, 1781, PCC, no. 156, fol. 222.

[67] Lafayette to Nelson, August 16, 1781, *loc. cit.*, p. 49.

[68] Lafayette to Wayne, August 18, 1781, *loc. cit.*

[69] Lafayette to Knox, August 18, 1781, *Historical magazine and notes and queries*,
VIII (1864), 73.

Lafayette once more to take steps to see that Cornwallis did not escape the net that was now sure to close in upon him, and promised "aid from this quarter."[70]

The young general's grateful heart leaped at the news. "I heartily thank you," he wrote Washington,[71] "for having ordered me to remain in Virginia and to your goodness to me I am owing the most beautifull prospect that I may ever behold." He reported in detail what he had done to surround Gloucester and Yorktown and the steps he had taken to raise men and provisions. He felt he could count on a goodly number of men. With the six hundred expected from Maryland and about four hundred exchanged prisoners who had been rearmed, he put the total of Continentals "at the lowest estimate" at twenty-five hundred rank and file, exclusive of artillery, "and three, or if more wanted, four thousand militia." As soon as accouterments were obtained he would have two hundred horsemen in addition to one hundred Continental dragoons. Of provisions, however, he was less confident. "There is such a confusion in affairs in this part of the world that immense difficulties are found for a proper formation of magazines." Though Virginia was well supplied in some kinds of provision like beef and corn, it would be desirable to call upon Maryland early. "Had we any thing like monney, matters would go on very well. . . . . We have no cloathing of any sort, no heavy artillery in order, some arms will be wanting, some horse accouterments, and great deal of ammunition. Nothing but your own entreaties may have a sufficient quantity of those articles transported to the head of the bay. In the present state of affairs, my dear general, I hope you will come yourself to Virginia, and that if the French army moves this way, I will have at last the satisfaction of beholding you myself at the head of the combined armies." In that case he hoped Washington would bring with him the heads of his several departments. "The men we have now here could not be equal to the task of a campaign upon so large a scale."

In the ensuing days Lafayette exhibited to an extraordinary

[70] August 15, 1781, Fitzpatrick, XXII, 501–2.

[71] August 21, 1781, loc. cit.

degree that meticulous attention to detail which made him a trustworthy commander. He sent Gimat and M. de Camus to Cape Henry to communicate with De Grasse as soon as his sails were sighted.[72] Lest the enemy reach North Carolina and escape across the Roanoke, he instructed Brigadier-General Allen Jones,[73] of the North Carolina militia, to destroy all the shipping on that river. Marching his own army to the ferries on the Pamunkey River, he ordered Wayne to move toward Westover and be ready to join him at a moment's notice.[74] The several militia colonels were likewise instructed to move in closer.[75] Though some of Wayne's men were still barefoot, they pushed onward cheerfully. Learning that Cornwallis had completely evacuated Portsmouth and its outposts, Lafayette sent engineers there to raze the fortifications.[76]

The romantic general busied himself also with improving his military intelligence in a fashion that others would have believed too histrionic. Still relying on the servants of Cornwallis whom he had in his pay, he also sent a New Jersey soldier named Charley Morgan to enlist in the British army, carrying false and misleading information. Not knowing about Clinton's orders to Cornwallis, Lafayette continued long afterward to believe that the British general did not endeavor to retreat south of the James because Morgan persuaded him to think it would be too hazardous. When Morgan deserted back to the Americans again, he refused to accept any reward or promotion and asked only that his old rifle be returned to him.[77]

[72] Lafayette to Washington, August 24, 1781, Sparks MSS LXXXIV, pp. 145–47 (erroneously dated as of June 24, 1781, inter alia in Sparks, Correspondence of American Revolution, III, 342–45).

[73] August 27, 1781, State records of North Carolina, XV, 626.

[74] August 22 and 25, 1781, Historical Society of Pennsylvania.

[75] Lafayette to Colonel Thomas Mathews, August 23, 1781, Virginia state papers, II, 353.

[76] Lafayette to Nelson, August 26, 1781 (one of three letters to idem of this date), New York Historical Society, misc. MSS, "L"; cf. Lafayette to McKean, August 23, 1781, PCC, no. 156, fols. 234–35.

[77] "Observations du Gén. Lafayette," p. 61; Mémoires, I, 453 n.; Sparks, Writings of Washington, VIII, 141 n. and 152–54 n; Lafayette to Washington, August 20, 1781, Gottschalk (ed.), Letters of Lafayette to Washington, pp. 223–24.

In the midst of these harried activities came one occasion for great rejoicing. Greene's aide, Colonel Lewis Morris, visited Lafayette again, carrying the heartening account of renewed success in North Carolina. Lafayette bade him speed to Washington with the tidings, sending with him a fresh report of his own activity. In this report congratulations were mixed with recriminations. There was neglect in Maryland now as well as in Virginia. "The conduct of some people in that state appears to me to be injurious to public interest," because the new Continental levies, long ago promised, had not yet arrived. And again he warned against the scarcity of hard cash. "From the moment I took the command of this army there has not been a farthing sent from the treasury and this state money is good for nothing."[78]

The discovery of a new object of reproach in the Maryland government did not, however, diminish complaints against Virginia. Once more the marquis threatened Nelson with disaster if the civil authorities continued to be "indifferent to the suffering of the army." "Unless vigorous measures are adopted," he warned, "we will be involved deeper and deeper in ruin. Few men in the field; not a sixth part of what is called for—a greater number without arms, the greatest part of whom live from day to day upon food that is injurious to their health, without six cartridges per man, and the poor Continentals that will soon be our only dependence falling off for want of spirits and flour. . . . . Should it be known to Lord Cornwallis, he may ruin us at one stroke, and defeat every project that may have been made for the protection of this state."[79]

The querulousness that frequently gave Lafayette's communications with American officials an unpleasant cast completely disappeared, however, when he wrote to his friends in France. He had not written often of late. But now he found time to send to Vergennes another packet of letters that the minister was requested to distribute to Adrienne, Poix, Maurepas, and

[78] Lafayette to Washington, August 24, 1781, *loc. cit.*

[79] Lafayette to Nelson, August 26, 1781 (another of three letters to *idem* of this date), Chinard, *Lafayette in Virginia*, p. 54.

others.[80] They all explained, with that kind of modesty which betrayed an inward pride, that he was stranded in the sands of Virginia four or five hundred miles away from any superior officer and facing the best general in the English army. He had been so harried in recent months that he had had neither the time to write nor the assurance that his letters would ever arrive. Now, however, he had a breathing-spell. "The heat of this country is so fierce," he informed Poix, "that you can hardly move in the month of August. It results in an additional difficulty, that of illness. Almost all my people at present have fever. I on the other hand have never felt better. . . . . Until now Fortune has treated me as a friend, but you know there is no chorus girl [demoiselle à l'Opéra] that is more fickle than she can be. Will she remain faithful to the end and pity my youth? I assure you that if she leaves me I shall be in a difficult position. A few months more, and I shall ask of her only a safe conduct back to France."

To his wife (in keeping with the eighteenth-century French aristocratic family tradition) Lafayette usually wrote tenderly but formally (much less intimately, for example, than to Poix). Again he used the same half-modest, half-boasting tone, quietly recalling the time when he had been considered gauche by many of her friends. "The pride with which you honor me has perhaps been flattered by the role that I have been called upon to play. You will have entertained the hope that a man could not be equally awkward in all spheres. But I should accuse you of a terrible case of conceit (since, everything between us being held in common, it would be conceited of you to think too highly of me) if you had not trembled at the dangers which I ran. . . . . It was not reasonable to trust me with such a command. If I had been unlucky, the public would have called such partiality blindness." To Adrienne he let slip a hint that "perhaps [the campaign] will end very agreeably," but with Maurepas he did not allow himself to be too optimistic: "Who knows if his

[80] Lafayette to Vergennes, August 24, 1781, Stevens, Facsimiles, XVIII, no. 43; to Mme de Lafayette, August 24, 1781, Mémoires, I, 454–57; to Poix, August 24, 1781, private collection; to Maurepas, August 24, 1781, Stevens, Facsimiles, XVII, no. 1636. The letters to others have not been found but are mentioned in these.

[Cornwallis'] maneuvres will not end in making us prisoners of war?"

A note of nostalgia also crept into the wanderer's letters—particularly that to Poix. He told of the good news he had received from the neighborhood of New York, where their friends Damas, Vauban, and Noailles were distinguishing themselves in skirmishes with the British. He missed them, to be sure, but "in the centuries" since he had reached America he missed "the Society" most. And those Americans who thought of Lafayette as a "republican" might have been surprised to read this injunction to Poix: "Place my most affectionate respects at the feet of the queen. Tell her how proud I am if I have had the necessary opportunities and talents to deserve her kindness by services to the common cause. She deigned to tell me when I left that she believed I would be helpful to it. But if to deserve it would be necessary only to love, then, my dear prince, never has sovereign had a more deserving subject." This was a courtly sentiment not only in its professions of loyalty to the queen but also in the note of assumed modesty that was allowed to enter it. A bourgeois would have fawned, a mere soldier would have boasted, but an officer and gentleman succeeded in doing both without quite doing either.

The "sands of Virginia," meanwhile, felt the tread of many feet. Lafayette's principal object now became the desire to prevent Cornwallis' escape to North Carolina. A sudden burst of energy in the fortification of Yorktown led him to believe that the British had learned of De Grasse's approach. Persuaded that they might try to cross the James again, Lafayette threw his men across the Yorktown peninsula, ready to resist if the enemy abandoned his new position.[81] In reality, however, Cornwallis did not guess the trap that was being prepared for him, though by this time the "secret" was known to several governors and generals on the American side.[82] He was, in fact, ex-

[81] Lafayette to Wayne, August 25, 1781, *loc. cit.*; to Allen Jones, August 27, 1781, *loc. cit.*; cf. Muhlenburg, pp. 266–67.

[82] *Ibid.*; Lafayette to Greene, August 25, 1781, *loc. cit.*; McHenry to T. S. Lee, August 28 and 30, 1781, Kite, *Sidelight on history*, pp. 55–57; Lafayette to Nelson, August 30, 1781, Gardner-Ball Collection.

pecting the arrival of the British fleet from the West Indies.[83] He had no intention of fleeing to North Carolina; the fortification of Yorktown was due to his effort to carry out Clinton's orders. Except for some foraging raids and a single attack by Tarleton upon some militia near Williamsburg,[84] the British remained on the defensive on both sides of the river. Nevertheless, Lafayette was justified in taking every precaution to keep them from escaping. Orders to the militia, entreaties to the governors of the neighboring states, continued in a steady stream.[85] They had as their supreme objective the welding of a land ring around Cornwallis which should keep him where De Grasse's fleet might, on its arrival, close up the only avenue of escape.

The arrival of Brigadier-General Duportail, America's ranking officer of engineers, from Washington's headquarters increased Lafayette's anxiety. Duportail brought the details that Washington had not dared to commit to writing. Not only was De Grasse coming with the West Indies fleet, but Barras might join him; and not only was a reinforcement to be expected from the north, but Washington and Rochambeau would themselves be there with the flower of their armies.[86] In fact Duportail thought they must already be in Philadelphia. A force of thirty-six ships and twenty thousand Frenchmen and Americans might soon be in Virginia to bag a quarry that Lafayette had been hoping to corner all summer, yet he feared he did not have it in his power to keep the quarry from escaping. And, if Cornwallis escaped, there seemed to be no chance of catching up with him again, because Duportail carried also the sobering in-

[83] Tarleton, p. 374.

[84] Ibid., p. 373; and McHenry to T. S. Lee, August 25, 1781, Kite, Sidelight on history, p. 54.

[85] See nn. 80 and 81 above; Lafayette to Greene, August 27, 1781, Morgan Library, Yorktown, Vol. I; to Nelson, August 27 and 29, 1781, New York Historical Society, misc. MSS, "L," and Sparks MSS LXXI, pp. 147–48; to Davies, August 30, 1781, Libbie catalogue, sale of May 20, 1892, p. 47, no. 495; to White, August 31,1781, University of Chicago Libraries, E 207, L2; to Taylor, August 31, 1781, Gardner-Ball Collection; Virginia state papers, II, 370–80.

[86] Washington to Lafayette, August 21, 1781, Fitzpatrick, XXIII, 33–34; cf. idem to De Grasse, August 17, 1781, ibid., p. 10.

formation that the French fleet could stay only about three weeks in American waters.[87]

The importunate young commander made a final appeal to the governors of Virginia and Maryland. McHenry wrote both letters, Lafayette dictating the one to Nelson and permitting McHenry to write and sign that to his own friend and governor, Lee of Maryland. "At the time that victory seems to be in our hands," McHenry wrote Nelson over Lafayette's signature,[88] "I am sorry to say that the disappointments I have met with renders it extremely precarious. . . . . We have not 2000 militia fit to bring into the field. We are destitute of ammunition, and the army living from hand to mouth and unable to follow the enemy. So that on the arrival of the Spanish, French and American forces, I may be reduced to the cruel necessity to announce that I have not, that it was not in my power to stop the enemy." Whatever might happen, he was resolved to resist all efforts by Cornwallis to escape to North Carolina. "But under the present circumstances of provisions, ammunition, men, and arms it is certain our attempt will be as fruitless as desperate. . . . . I expect every minute that our prey is escaping, and cannot express my feelings on the occasion. . . . . But I must attend to the most important point, and get as much clear of the impending disgrace as possible." On his own authority, Lafayette confessed, he had issued orders to several county lieutenants of Virginia to collect men. "But those who refuse obeying the laws of the Assembly and the calls of the executive will still less mind my request." Yet, for having acted independently of the civil authorities in ordering out militia, he felt he owed Nelson a personal explanation and in his own hand added to his lengthy letter a postscript of apology. McHenry's letter to Lee[89] was briefer but also directly to the point. "Should his Lordship succeed in this [effort to escape] it will be out of my power to prevent the Marquiss [*sic*] in his official letter from laying the blame on your Excellency and Council's not forwarding the troops agreeable to his repeated requests."

[87] Lafayette to Nelson, August 30, 1781, *loc. cit.*

[88] *Ibid.*   [89] August 30, 1781, *loc. cit.*

To prevent a sally from Yorktown, Lafayette once more moved to the camps in the neighborhood of Williamsburg, which his army had held in July. Colonel White's cavalry was instructed to come up with whatever accouterments they could find.[90] Wayne's men, marching day and night, proceeded to Cabin Point, on the south side of the James, ready to dissuade Cornwallis "by the most forceable arguments" from passing the river.[91] There, too, Lafayette sent some militia and dragoons. He also hurried off a special courier to inform General Greene of the latest developments.[92]

Sooner than expected, De Grasse appeared in Chesapeake Bay. He was sighted by one of Cornwallis' dispatch boats just in time to enable her to retreat to Yorktown.[93] Thus the British knew of the arrival of the French fleet on August 30. Lafayette learned of the appearance of a large number of sails only the next day, though he did not at first know whether they were French or British.[94] He soon learned to his great relief that they were, indeed, De Grasse's vessels. Twenty-eight line-of-battle ships and six frigates, carrying thirty-one hundred marines in addition to their crews, were now at hand. Not only would they prevent Cornwallis from crossing the James River, they would also be able to sail to Head of Elk and pick up Washington's and Rochambeau's men there, saving them the long trip by land which Washington had so much feared. There could have been no victory without them, that was clear; but it was not equally clear that victory was certain now that they had come.

Duportail, Gimat, and Camus had gone out to meet the fleet as soon as it passed Cape Henry. They informed De Grasse of their commander's position and of his suggestions for future action. De Grasse proved to be anxious to co-operate, and the

[90] Lafayette to Wayne, August 30–31, 1781, Historical Society of Pennsylvania; Lafayette to White, August 31, 1781, loc. cit.

[91] Wayne to Lafayette, August 31, 1781, Historical Society of Pennsylvania.

[92] Lafayette to unknown, August 31, 1781, Libbie catalogue, sale of May 20–21, 1892, p. 46, no. 487.

[93] Tarleton, p. 374.

[94] Lafayette to Wayne, August 31, 1781, loc. cit.; to Taylor, August 31, 1781, loc. cit.

Marquis de St. Simon, who commanded his marines, was extraordinarily gracious. He was willing, he said, to act as Lafayette's subordinate and to put his thirty-one hundred marines and eight cannons[95] under the younger man's orders, though in the French army he held a rank which might be senior to Lafayette's even in the American service. To St. Simon's three regiments of marines, De Grasse would be willing to add eighteen hundred sailors if Lafayette consented to storm Yorktown immediately. De Grasse felt that this force of nearly five thousand Frenchmen together with the five thousand or so that the marquis already had would be sufficient to justify risking a *coup de main*. In any event, St. Simon would be ready to begin landing his men at Jamestown soon.[96]

Duportail, for one, did not approve of an immediate assault and doubted whether the marquis would. The three deputies, nevertheless, sent a faithful account of their conversation to Holt's Forge, where Lafayette anxiously awaited their report. He made no effort to hide his joy at De Grasse's tempting offer, and sent couriers galloping off to carry the news to Washington, La Luzerne, Greene, Wayne, Steuben, and others.[97] Governor Nelson visited his camp personally and wrote the admiral a letter promising "to contribute every thing in my power towards the speedy and successful accomplishment of the object we have in view."[98]

Yet the marquis felt he could not take advantage of De Grasse's generosity. An assault upon Cornwallis' fortifications in Yorktown and Gloucester would perhaps be successful, but it would be risky. It would cost many lives, even if successful,

[95] St. Simon to Washington, September 8, 1781, [E. S. Kite (ed.)], *Correspondence of General Washington and Comte de Grasse, 1781* (Washington, 1931), pp. 26–27.

[96] Lafayette to La Luzerne, September 1, 1781, *AHR*, XX (1915), 606; Duportail to Washington, September 2, 1781, E. S. Kite, *Brigadier-General Louis Lebègue Duportail, commandant of engineers in the Continental Army 1777–1783* (Baltimore, 1933), p. 207.

[97] Lafayette to Washington, September 1, 1781, *Mémoires* (Amer. ed.), pp. 528–29; to La Luzerne, September 1, 1781, *loc. cit.*; to Greene, September 2, 1781, Morgan Library, Yorktown, Vol. I; to Wayne, September 1, 1781, Historical Society of Pennsylvania; to Steuben, [ca. September 1], Kapp, p. 671; to Weedon, September 1, 1781, Ford collection.

[98] September 2, 1781, *Letters of Nelson*, p. 9; cf. *Virginia state papers*, II, 380.

and would deprive Washington and Rochambeau, at that moment awaiting to be transported to the scene, of any share in the glory. Why chance with ten or eleven thousand men an action which within a few days might be undertaken by eighteen thousand? The only danger, if they waited, would be the enemy's escape. But Cornwallis could now hardly elude his doom, since the rivers would be blockaded by the French fleet.

Shortly after midnight on September 2, somewhat ahead of expectations, St. Simon's transports under escort of several frigates reached Jamestown and began to unload their men and supplies. "I do not think that any maritime operation was ever completed more rapidly than that of the French," said Lafayette proudly.[99] Colonels Butler and Stewart, of the Pennsylvania line, visited with the French commander before dawn.[100] "Never did I behold a more beautiful and agreeable sight," wrote one of Wayne's officers of the rejoicing that spread among the Pennsylvanians and Virginians.[101] Wayne, informing Lafayette of his own movements and the blockading of both the James and the York by contingents of the French fleet, exulted that "every door is shut by the hard-hearted fellows against poor Cornwallis."[102] As if to complete the day's list of wonders, it was also learned that Lord Rawdon, on his way to England for reasons of health, had been captured and was now a prisoner on board the "Ville de Paris," De Grasse's flagship.[103]

Nevertheless, a few things marred Lafayette's happiness that day. Virginia's commissary department proved no more competent to provide for the French than it had for the Americans, and Lafayette was embarrassed. He could hide the nakedness of his Virginia regiment ("I shall endeavor to keep it a little out of sight," he wrote to Colonel Davies);[104] but he knew he

[99] Lafayette to La Luzerne, September 8, 1781, *AHR*, XX (1915), 607.

[100] Wayne to Lafayette, September 2, 1781, NYPL, Bancroft transcripts.

[101] "Journals of McClellan and Feltman," p. 719.

[102] Wayne to Lafayette, September 2, 1781, *loc. cit.*

[103] Lafayette to Greene, September 2, 1781, *loc. cit.*

[104] September 2, 1781, Libbie catalogue, sale of May 20–21, 1892, p. 47, no. 496; cf. Lafayette to Nelson, September 5, 1781, Gardner-Ball Collection.

would have to borrow from the French in great quantities, and he felt somewhat humiliated. More serious was the accident that befell Wayne. In hastening to keep an appointment with Lafayette, Wayne had failed to halt when challenged by a sentinel and had received a discharge of buckshot in his leg. Wayne took no relish in the prospect of being absent from the ultimate victory which he had done so much to prepare. He angrily insisted on a court-martial for the offending soldier, which Lafayette reluctantly granted. The soldier was acquitted on the ground that he had done no more than was his duty. Wayne was able to hobble back to duty only after some days, meanwhile leaving his command to Colonel Butler.[105]

The several contingents under Lafayette now joined forces. The French transports brought Wayne's troops across the river close to James Island on September 3, and shortly afterward Lafayette marched his light infantry to a near-by station at Green Spring.[106] The Americans frankly admired "the very fine soldiery appearance" of the Frenchmen.[107] They were all "very tall men," splendidly uniformed in white coats turned up with blue,[108] "so well made, so robust."[109] Wayne described them as the finest body of troops he had ever seen.[110] The American soldiers quickly went out of their way to show their appreciation of their allies. Despite the poverty of his stores, Lafayette gave them all the flour he could spare, leaving his own soldiers to get along on corn meal. Some of his men yielded their horses for the French artillery and hussars. And there were no complaints because the French slept under tents while they biv-

[105] "Journal of McClellan and Feltman," p. 719; "Wild's journal," p. 149; Sparks MSS XXXII, pp. 200–201.

[106] De Grasse to Washington, September 4, 1781, *Correspondence of Washington and De Grasse*, pp. 19–20; *Virginia state papers*, II, 384–85.

[107] "Journal of Feltman and McClellan," p. 719.

[108] *Ibid.*, pp. 719–20.

[109] Letter from Williamsburg, September 1 [10 ?], 1781, *Magazine of American history*, VI (1881), 35.

[110] Wayne to Robert Morris, September 14, 1781, J. W. Wright, "Notes on the siege of Yorktown," *William and Mary College quarterly historical magazine*, 2d ser., XII (1932), 235, n. 11.

ouacked in the open. Long afterward Lafayette remembered with gratitude that his troops had played a generous role without grumbling, though "all the preferences were for the French."[111]

If Cornwallis had attacked the Continentals before they effected their junction with the French, they might have been too weak to hold their ground. Cornwallis might also have tried to prevent St. Simon's landing, as St. Simon himself thought he ought to have done.[112] Having decided not to risk a battle in order to prevent the uniting of Lafayette's forces,[113] Cornwallis was now outnumbered and distinctly at a disadvantage. His young adversary had combined an army of over fifty-five hundred regular troops, both Frenchmen and Continentals, under his direct command. In addition, scattered at various points throughout the state but chiefly in the neighborhood of Yorktown and Gloucester, were over three thousand militia, with three thousand more expected.[114] And French vessels patrolled the York and the James rivers, cutting off British retreat north or south.

The advance upon Yorktown began immediately. Wayne's division and the light infantry, making up the van, preceded the French army, which had no means of transportation. On September 4 they marched unopposed into Williamsburg and billeted in the buildings of William and Mary College. Though St. Simon's detachment, delayed by problems of food, water, horses and wagons, remained at Jamestown,[115] the American

[111] "Observations du Gén. Lafayette," p. 68; cf. *Mémoires*, I, 282, and Lafayette to Nelson, September 5, 1781, *loc. cit.*

[112] "Journal des campagnes de l'Amérique de 1781 à 1782" in Ludovic de Contenson, "Capitulation d'Yorktown et le Comte de Grasse," *Revue d'histoire diplomatique*, XLII (1928), 391. Cf. Clinton's "Observations on Earl Cornwallis's answer," Stevens, *Clinton-Cornwallis controversy*, I, 1222–24; also *ibid.*, p. 75.

[113] Tarleton, pp. 376–77.

[114] Lafayette to Greene, September 2, 1781, *loc. cit.*; cf. Lafayette·to Washington, August 21, 1781, *loc. cit.*

[115] Lafayette to Nelson, September 4, 1781, Chinard, *Lafayette in Virginia*, p. 56; September 5, 1781, *loc. cit.*; September 6, 1781, Smith collection. See also "General Richard Butler's journal of the siege of Yorktown," *Historical magazine*, VIII (1864), p. 103.

vanguard threw out skirmishers toward Yorktown. The Brit
ish, expecting to be relieved at any moment by their own fleet,
retired into the town and busied themselves with improving
their fortifications. Lafayette's repeated appeals to Governor
Nelson finally produced enough food and supplies to permit
St. Simon's army to march.[116] Using the private horses and
carriages of American officers and the wagons of the American
army, the French troops entered Williamsburg on September 8.

St. Simon had been persuaded that an attack would be too
hazardous and had agreed to wait for Washington and Rochambeau.[117] The armies encamped in and around Williamsburg.
There Lafayette re-formed his army. The light infantry that he
had brought with him from the North formed the right wing;
the Pennsylvania and Virginia Continentals made up the center; the French marines comprised the left wing.[118] The allies
"made a very elegant appearance" as they paraded between
the two rows of well-constructed and "handsome" houses which
made up the town.[119]

At Williamsburg, Lafayette soon learned of Washington's
movements. The whole of the French army under Rochambeau
and about two thousand Continentals under Major-General
Benjamin Lincoln were on September 2, the date of a dispatch
from Washington, still at Philadelphia. The commander-in-
chief approved wholeheartedly of everything that Lafayette had
done to keep Cornwallis bottled up on the York peninsula. But
he was still "all impatience and anxiety" and begged his "dear
marquis" if he learned "any thing new from any quarter" to
"send it . . . . on the spur of speed."[120] He had not yet learned
of De Grasse's arrival and hence was much distressed that an

[116] "Journal of McClellan and Feltman," p. 720; "Wild's journal," p. 149; Virginia
state papers, II, 401–6.

[117] De Grasse to Washington, September 2, 1781, Kite, Duportail, p. 206; Lafayette
to La Luzerne, September 8, 1781, loc. cit.

[118] "Butler's journal," p. 105; J. B. T. Phelps, "Extracts from the journal of Lieutenant John Ball Tilden, Second Pennsylvania Line, 1781–1782," Pennsylvania magazine of history and biography, XIX (1895), 56.

[119] "Butler's journal," p. 105; Journal de Blanchard, p. 96.

[120] Fitzpatrick, XXIII, 75–78.

English fleet, which was known to have sailed for the Chesapeake, might frustrate all allied efforts.

Lafayette himself had learned of that British fleet only the day before entering Williamsburg.[121] For a time it looked as if Cornwallis might yet be saved by his countrymen's hardihood upon the seas. But the British force proved to be inferior in numbers to the French, and its admiral, Thomas Graves, no match for De Grasse. Without Lafayette's knowledge, De Grasse had sailed out of Lynnhaven Roads with most of his vessels, leaving enough craft behind to keep the rivers blockaded, and in an all-day engagement on September 6 had inflicted serious damage on the smaller English fleet. The wind then separated the two antagonists. For two more days they watched each other without joining battle and then lost sight of each other. De Grasse returned to Chesapeake Bay. When Graves finally got to Cape Henry, he found the French in possession of the bay once more and decided to return to New York. The control of the waters around Yorktown thus remained in the hands of the allies. Cornwallis could no longer expect either to receive aid or to escape by sea. Shortly after reaching Williamsburg, Lafayette received a report of the naval engagement of the sixth. Without waiting for De Grasse's return, he hastened to send the report to Philadelphia.[122]

Washington's letter from Philadelphia had made victory seem doubly sure, since it promised a reinforcement of around seven thousand. Nevertheless it contained one element of disappointment. General Lincoln was senior to Lafayette in the American service. Hence he would command the American wing of the allied army, and Lafayette would have to serve under him. The junior major-general felt, however, that he might easily be compensated. "Your approbation of my conduct," he declared, "emboldens me to request that . . . . the division I will have under him may be composed of the troops which have gone through the fatigues and dangers of the Virginia cam-

[121] Lafayette to Washington, September 7, 1781, cited in *idem* to *idem* September 8, 1781, *Mémoires* (Amer. ed.), p. 529.

[122] *Ibid.*, pp. 529-30.

paign. This will be the greatest reward of the services I may have rendered, as I confess the strongest attachement to those troops."[123]

Lafayette's unremitting exertions throughout the summer around the malaria-ridden estuaries of Virginia at length belied his boasts about his health. While Wayne's command had been near Yorktown, the light infantry at Green Spring, and the French at Jamestown, he had galloped back and forth several times between the three camps. After he had finally conveyed his main army safely to Williamsburg and learned of the defeat of Graves's fleet, he came down with a violent fever: Reluctantly he took to his bed in the quarters that had just been set aside for him in Dr. St. George Tucker's house. Even in bed, however, he remained active. "I beg your pardon, Monsieur le Chevalier," he dictated to La Luzerne, "for not writing to you personally, but by dint of acting as quartermaster and commissary, stealing salt provisions, impressing beef, and clamoring for flour I have finished awkwardly enough by giving myself a fever and headache. . . . . Perhaps I am dying of old age since two days ago I rang out my twenty-fourth birthday."[124]

Lafayette hoped his illness would pass with a few hours' rest, but he proved too optimistic. Steuben, himself miraculously cured of an attack of gout by the news of the arrival of the French fleet, decided at last to join Lafayette again rather than go to Greene's quarters and arrived at Williamsburg a little later on the same day as Lafayette. He was not permitted to see Lafayette.[125] The marquis was, however, sufficiently strong to straddle a horse the next day and to review the army with St. Simon.[126] But he was not fully recovered.

On the following day, Gouvion returned, sent on ahead by Washington to aid Duportail in laying out plans for the siege of Yorktown. He brought the news that Washington had probably left Philadelphia by that time. In fact, about that moment the commander-in-chief, for the first time in six years, was visit-

[123] *Ibid.*, p. 530.   [124] September 8, 1781, *loc. cit.*

[125] Steuben to Ben Walker, September 9, 1781, Palmer, p. 288.

[126] "Journal of McClellan and Feltman," p. 721; "Wild's journal," p. 150.

ing his home at Mount Vernon. He had let his army proceed to Baltimore without him. Gouvion thought that he would soon be at Williamsburg. Lafayette wrote what was for him a brief note,[127] assuring Washington that, despite De Grasse's continued absence, there were enough vessels available in Chesapeake Bay to guarantee the safety of the allied forces.

The nearness of the combined armies was not an unmitigated pleasure. For how were they all to be fed? The harassed marquis' fever still consumed him when he wrote to Governor Nelson: "I could wish to sleep tonight but I fear it will be impossible with the prospect which is before us for tomorrow. There is not one grain of flour in camp either for the American or French army. What we are to do I know not. . . . . Has your Excellency any hopes for tomorrow? I am distressed in the extreme, in a thousand ways, and without the power of offering either myself or the soldiers the smallest relief."[128] He suggested that private supplies of flour be seized. He wrote to Weedon to send whatever he could find in the neighborhood of Fredericksburg.[129] Wayne, still at Jamestown with his wounded leg, sympathized with Lafayette. "I have not been pleased with Madame Fortune for some time. . . . . She has added to that displeasure in attacking you at this crisis with a caitiff fever. Try, my dear Marquis, to shake it off & I will endeavour to get clear of my complaint the soonest possible. We will then go hand in hand, & force her youngest daughters from the enemies [sic] arms. But as to Misfortune she may coquet it with the British as long as she pleases. For she is so d——d agile that I never wish to see her face again!"[130]

Fickle Dame Fortune, despite fever, wound, and famine, nevertheless did well by Wayne and his friend. For she at last brought "Mad Anthony" hobbling to camp,[131] and on the next

---

[127] September 10, 1781, *Mémoires* (Amer. ed.), pp. 530–31.

[128] September 11, 1781, Chinard, *Lafayette in Virginia*, p. 59.

[129] September 11, 1781, Ford collection.

[130] Wayne to Lafayette, September 11, 1781, Historical Society of Pennsylvania.

[131] "Journal of McClellan and Feltman," p. 721; Wayne to Robert Morris, September 14, 1781, *New York Historical Society collections for 1878*, pp. 468–69; "Butler's journal," p. 105.

day Washington, Rochambeau, and Chastellux rode into Williamsburg with a small escort—several days ahead of their men, who were to follow under Vioménil and Lincoln. Royal salutes of twenty-one guns boomed out as they approached the camp.[132] Lafayette, despite his ague, jumped on a horse and rode full speed to greet his chief. On reaching his beloved friend he dismounted, rushed to him with outstretched arms, and to the amazement of several American officers standing about to be introduced, embraced him "with an ardour not easily described."[133] Perhaps Washington noticed, as Dr. Tucker had several weeks previously, that his young friend's hair had become remarkably thin for so young a man.[134]

The two armies soon turned out in dress parade for their commanding generals. Washington, Rochambeau, Chastellux, Lafayette, St. Simon, and their suites visited the French and then the American encampments. More salutes. At St. Simon's tent the French officers were introduced to Washington, after which the officers sat down to "an elegant supper." In honor of Washington the French army band played an overture from a French opera "signifying the happiness of the family when blessed with the presence of their father and their great dependence upon him." Only at ten o'clock did supper end. The guests separated "after mutual congratulations and the greatest expression of joy."[135]

Before midnight there was a new occasion for rejoicing. Letters arrived from De Grasse.[136] He had at last returned to the bay and there had met Barras's squadron, which had taken two British frigates on its way from Newport and had entered the harbor without encountering Graves's bigger force. The French fleet now included over forty large vessels; and they knew from

---

[132] "Butler's journal," p. 105; "Wild's journal," p. 150.

[133] Tucker to Mrs. Tucker, September 15, 1781, Coleman, "The southern campaign," p. 212; cf. W. C. Bruce, *John Randolph of Roanoke 1733–1833* (2 vols.; New York, 1922), I, 45.

[134] Tucker to Mrs. Tucker, June 24, 1781, Coleman, "The southern campaign," p. 205.

[135] "Butler's journal," pp. 103 and 106.

[136] "Journal of McClellan and Feltman," pp. 721–22.

experience that Graves was no match for them. No more did the allies need to yearn for that maritime supremacy which they had awaited since the distant spring of 1780, when Lafayette had first announced the great French armada. At last their dream had been realized.

But Lafayette did not learn of this good fortune until the next day.[137] He was now no longer the independent commander of the forces in Virginia. He was again only a major-general leading a division of Washington's army. So when the supper in honor of the ranking generals was over, he had returned with his ague to his sickbed. The good news was conveyed to him only in the morning.

BIBLIOGRAPHICAL NOTES

That Cornwallis moved to Portsmouth and then to Yorktown because of his interpretation of Clinton's orders is now well known and has been fully explained in R. G. Adams' "View of Cornwallis's surrender." Cornwallis' inaction does not diminish the credit due to Lafayette for the able precautions he took to prevent the expected retreat, though it explains his success more clearly than does his own explanation of it. Greater credit than he has often received, on the other hand, is due to Lafayette for his extraordinary efforts to move impoverished, incompetent, and lethargic commissary agents of Virginia and Maryland to effective measures. The prodigious energy that he showed in that connection can be understood only by an examination of the numerous pertinent documents in the *Virginia state papers* (supplemented by Chinard's *Lafayette in Virginia*) the *Archives of Maryland* (supplemented by Shriver's *Lafayette in Harford County* and Kite's *Sidelight on history*), and the *State records of North Carolina*. It is rather interesting that, while Sparks knew several of the documents in which Lafayette complained of the states' lack of co-operation (at least they are to be found in the Sparks MSS), he never published them, and the editors of Lafayette's *Mémoires* omitted them likewise. In that way Lafayette's real merits in the Virginia campaign have been doubly misunderstood. He has been lauded as a great strategist, though he had no real opportunity to show whether he was one or not; and he has never received due appreciation for his genius (I use the word advisedly) as what a later generation has come to call "a public relations man."

P. 278 above has been revised since the first printing to conform to the findings of William B. Willcox in "The British Road to Yorktown," *American Historical Review*, LII (1946), 19 n., and in *Portrait of a general*, pp. 403–6, esp. p. 405 n.

[137] Cf. "Butler's journal," p. 106; "Wild's journal," p. 150.

CHAPTER XIII

The Siege of Yorktown

NO ONE had earned a rest more honorably than the ague-stricken major-general. Though his own good luck and the bad judgment of Generals Clinton and Cornwallis had won for him much of his success, less perseverance or more rashness might easily have led to the annihilation of the force which he had commanded. If Cornwallis now faced the prospect of surrender, it was in large part because Lafayette had persisted where others might have given up or had been cautious where others, yielding to an alluring temptation, might have proved too bold. The commander-in-chief, immediately after reaching Williamsburg, publicly testified to his satisfaction "on joining the army under the command of Major-General the Marquis de La Fayette with prospects which (under the smiles of Heaven) he doubts not will drown their toils with the most brilliant success."[1]

Now that others could assume the responsibility for bagging the game that he had cornered, Lafayette might well have relaxed and let his fever run a normal course. But it was not in the young Frenchman's nature to rest if he could stand and move about. Besides, his fever was getting distinctly better. On shaky knees and with quivering hands he attended the dinners that the general officers of the two allied nations exchanged and was himself host at one of the most resplendent of them. Despite their host's discomfort, his guests "passed the afternoon in the greatest happiness and harmony," for on that day the news of Barras's arrival and De Grasse's return to Chesapeake

[1] General orders, September 15, 1781, Fitzpatrick, XXIII, 114–15.

Bay became general property.[2] Barras's nine vessels had transported from Newport the siege artillery of the French army. "The storm seems to thicken fast around Lord Cornwallis," Colonel Butler wrote in his journal with pardonable relish.[3]

Nevertheless, the marquis was too ill to move far from his quarters. That was why, when Washington and Rochambeau sailed down the York River to board the "Ville de Paris" off Cape Henry for a conference with Admiral de Grasse, Lafayette was not one of the officers to accompany them. He stayed at Williamsburg, once more in chief command of the army for a few days.[4] Claude Blanchard, commissary of war with the French forces in America, happened to come to camp during that interval, and, putting their heads together, they arranged the details of food, water, clothing, and other supplies for Rochambeau's troops. Lafayette's intendant in Paris, who had had several occasions to lament Lafayette's carelessness about money, would have been justly amazed at the change that recent experiences had wrought in his youthful client. "It is difficult," Blanchard declared,[5] "to put more order, patience, and integrity in the discussion of business matters. He reminded me of Scipio Africanus in Spain [though some others spoke of him as America's second Fabius[6]]. Young and modest though he was, he already had the reputation of a skilful warrior."

During the absence of Washington and Rochambeau, Lafayette received the visit of two of Rochambeau's aides, who had gone on ahead of the combined army. These compatriots were gladly made welcome,[7] but still more joyously received was John Laurens, who arrived from France the next day with a promise of "every thing which will be necessary to finish the

---

[2] "Butler's journal," p. 106.   [3] *Ibid.*

[4] Cf. Lafayette to Weedon, September 19, 1781, Smith collection.

[5] *Journal de Blanchard*, p. 96.

[6] Cf. letter of correspondent with Lafayette's army, September 6, 1781, *Magazine of American history*, VI (1881), 35; Wayne to Reed, October 3, 1781, Johnston, p. 127.

[7] "Journal de Closen," I, 328–30; "Diary of a French officer, 1781 (presumed to be that of Baron Cromot du Bourg, aide to Rochambeau)," *Magazine of American history*, IV (1880), 443–44.

war."[8] Even Steuben, generally not given to an easy optimism, found that "every thing is preparing for our grand enterprise, and, as far as we have gone, fortune seems to have seconded all our endeavors."[9]

Contrary winds kept Washington and his companions away from Williamsburg longer than had been intended. It was not until September 22 that they returned. Their interview with De Grasse had been most successful. The admiral had promised to keep his fleet in the bay until the end of October, half a month longer than he had originally agreed. He also undertook to examine the advisability of forcing his way up the York River beyond the batteries of the enemy at Yorktown and Gloucester, thus securing communication on both sides of the river. St. Simon's corps, he agreed, was to remain under Washington's command until the fleet sailed, and he was still ready to land eighteen hundred more men for a *coup de main*. Convinced that a decisive action could be forced before the date fixed for the fleet's departure, Washington was well pleased with his allies.[10]

As if to prove that good fortune must not long be consistent, De Grasse suddenly announced a change in his intentions. The new plans were due to intelligence which Washington had sent him immediately upon his return to Williamsburg. Dispatches from Congress and La Luzerne which had arrived during the commander-in-chief's absence announced that Admiral Robert Digby had reached New York with a large force and that a new effort to relieve Cornwallis was to be feared. Washington rushed the Baron von Closen, one of Rochambeau's aides, to De Grasse with this information,[11] meaning only to put the French admiral on his guard against surprise by an English force that by the most liberal count must yet be inferior. De Grasse, however, supposed that he ought to abandon his present post at

---

[8] Steuben to Greene, September 19, 1781, Kapp, p. 456.   [9] *Ibid.*, p. 455.

[10] Washington to Howe, September 24, 1781, Fitzpatrick, XXIII, 132. Cf. Washington to De Grasse, September 22, and to Congress, September 23, 1781, *ibid.*, pp. 127–28; also *Correspondence of Washington and De Grasse*, pp. 35–41.

[11] "Journal de Closen," p. 335; *Correspondence of Washington and De Grasse*, pp. 44 and 48.

Lynnhaven near Cape Henry, leaving a few vessels behind to guard the York and the James, and sail into open water, where there would be less chance of being outmaneuvered by a skilful opponent. He might even sail toward New York in search of the British, he implied.[12]

When Closen returned to tell of this new proposal, consternation immediately spread among the generals in Williamsburg. If De Grasse left his present moorings to go into open water rather than up the York River, as Washington hoped, unfavorable winds might take his fleet far enough from the bay to permit Admiral Digby to sail unopposed toward Yorktown and to steal off with Cornwallis' men before he could be intercepted. With or without Digby's aid, if once the allies lost control of the rivers by even a momentary absence of the French fleet, Cornwallis might retreat, saving most of his army by sacrificing his artillery, baggage, and rear guard. Furthermore, without the aid of fast sailing boats, the transportation and supply of the huge army that Washington was mobilizing on the Yorktown peninsula would take so long that the British could not possibly be taken before De Grasse would have to leave for the West Indies.

All these arguments against De Grasse's suggestion must be brought forcibly to his attention once more. Lafayette (now fully recovered from the fever) volunteered to carry out this mission.[13] Instructions for the marquis were carefully written out with Washington's approval under Laurens' supervision.[14] He was to present in detail the several disadvantages that were to be expected from De Grasse's desertion of the Chesapeake. Before Lafayette left Williamsburg, however, Washington decided that it would be more effective to address De Grasse personally in a letter which his emissary would deliver. The marquis would be free to add his own influence and persuasion as occasion might permit.

[12] De Grasse to Washington, September 23, 1781, *Correspondence of Washington and De Grasse*, pp. 45–47.

[13] "Observations du Général Lafayette," p. 66.

[14] Fitzpatrick, XXIII, 139, n. 23.

And so the marquis' instructions became a long letter to De Grasse.[15] It closed with the remark: "The Marquis de la Fayette who does me the honor to bear this to yr Excellency will explain many peculiarities of our situation which could not well be comprised in a letter; his candour and abilities are well known to yr Excellency and entitle him to the fullest confidence in treating the most important interests." Rochambeau also sent along a message setting forth his apprehensions.[16] Knowing Lafayette's impetuosity, Washington earnestly requested him not to go beyond the Capes if De Grasse had already put to sea when he arrived. In that event he was to write to the admiral a personal entreaty to return, and Baron von Closen, who was to accompany him, would be entrusted with delivering all the letters to their destination.[17] The need for haste was obvious. Before the two young noblemen left camp, all the French troops had arrived and the Americans were expected at any moment. If only De Grasse could be counted upon, the siege might begin immediately.

Near sundown on September 25, Lafayette and the Baron von Closen, still tired from his earlier mission, set out for the frigate "Richmond," recently captured from the enemy. At College Landing on the James River, they left their horses and boarded the boat. After supper they dropped down the James to Hampton, which they reached in the morning. There they went on board the frigate "Iris" and sailed in search of Admiral de Grasse, who had unexpectedly changed his moorings to the York River. It was only after sailing until another sundown that the "Iris" brought them to the "Ville de Paris."[18]

By that time, however, Lafayette's arduous journey had largely been deprived of its purpose. Even before Lafayette and Closen had set out from Williamsburg, a council of De Grasse's general officers had disapproved of his plan to sail out of the bay and recommended instead that the major part of the

[15] September 25, 1781, Fitzpatrick, XXIII, 136–39.   [16] Doniol, V, 546.

[17] Washington to De Grasse, September 25, 1781, *loc. cit.*, p. 139; "Journal de Closen," p. 335.

[18] "Journal de Closen," pp. 336–37.

fleet should anchor in the York River, while a contingent of four or five vessels cruised in the James. That was why Lafayette had found the "Ville de Paris" where she was. The new disposition of the fleet, it was hoped, would prevent both the retreat and the relief of Cornwallis. De Grasse had sent off a messenger to notify Washington of this decision a day before Lafayette arrived. Though the marquis did not know it, the most important point in his instructions had already been taken care of.[19]

Yet De Grasse's new position was not altogether satisfactory either, as the marquis was quick to perceive. On boarding the "Ville de Paris," Lafayette, having delivered Washington's and Rochambeau's letters, recommended a return to the moorings at the mouth of the bay. The admiral had already of his own accord come to the conclusion that the post he had taken in the York River was "bad and unsuited" for any service to the allied army. It left the James River and the lower part of the bay inadequately guarded against an enemy effort to relieve Cornwallis at the same time that it made it more difficult for the fleet to reprovision. He was therefore quite ready to agree that he ought to return to his original anchorage near Cape Henry.[20] In return for the promise to move down the bay again, Lafayette undertook to place before Washington some of De Grasse's needs, such as a hospital for his sick, American sailors to take their places, the transfer of his numerous English prisoners to the land, and a more regular correspondence between the land and naval forces.[21]

The glory-thirsty major-general also broached the subject of a naval operation against Wilmington or Charleston after Yorktown should have fallen. Washington had already tried to get the admiral to commit himself to an attack upon those Carolina points in order to relieve the pressure upon General

---

[19] De Grasse to Washington, September 25, 1781, *Correspondence of De Grasse and Washington*, pp. 51–52.

[20] De Grasse to Washington, September 26, 1781, *ibid.*, pp. 52–54; to Rochambeau, September [26], 1781, Doniol, IV, 546–47; "Observations de M. le Cte de Grasse dans sa conférence avec M. le Mis. de Lafayette," LC, Rochambeau papers.

[21] "Observations de M. le Cte de Grasse," *loc.cit.*

Greene's army, but to no avail.[22] Lafayette was only slightly more successful. De Grasse would not promise to stay in continental waters beyond the end of October, but he did not oppose the suggestion that on the way to the West Indies, if there were time enough, an attempt might be made upon Charleston.[23]

The meeting between the two Frenchmen brought great satisfaction to both. De Grasse gallantly implied in the letter which he sent to Washington by Lafayette that he was glad he had created some anxiety in the American camp, for "I should not have had the pleasure of greeting [the Marquis de Lafayette] except for my letter which caused him to come here."[24] Lafayette reported that he had been "enchanted by our admiral's candor and good will."[25]

Early the next morning Lafayette and Closen started their journey back to headquarters in a sloop. That evening they reached the "Diligente" and went on board for supper. They found Lord Rawdon and some other prisoners there.[26] Lafayette had met Lord Rawdon during the brief visit he had made in England before he first stole off to America, and so they were, in a sense, old friends. Rawdon freely lamented the fate that had befallen him and seemed to be in store for Cornwallis. He also was disturbed by Lafayette's belief that he might be turned over to the Americans, fearing less gentle treatment at their hands.[27]

After a leisurely supper Lafayette and Closen re-entered their sloop and proceeded up the James. Their conductors did not know the river well and ran their boat onto some oyster beds five or six times, but they made a landing close to Williamsburg at eight on the morning of September 28. Shortly after their departure, they learned, Lincoln's army had joined forces with

[22] *Correspondence of Washington and De Grassse*, pp. 40–41.

[23] Lafayette to Washington, September 30, 1781, *Mémoires* (Amer. ed.), pp. 531–32; to La Luzerne, September 30, 1781, *AHR*, XX (1915), 608.

[24] De Grasse to Washington, September 26, 1781, *loc. cit.*, p. 53.

[25] Lafayette to La Luzerne, September 30, 1781, *loc. cit.*

[26] *Ibid.;* "Journal de Closen," pp. 339–40.

[27] *Ibid.;* Sparks MSS XXXII, pp. 141–42.

the troops already on the peninsula, and that very morning the allied troops had left Williamsburg to begin the siege of Yorktown. Tired as they were from long voyages on comfortless boats, they mounted their horses and galloped to Williamsburg.[28] At his quarters there, Lafayette found a letter announcing that Greene had recently inflicted on the English at Eutaw Springs a telling defeat and had driven the enemy back almost to the gates of Charleston.[29] With this harbinger of success to speed them on, the two eager soldiers once more jumped into the saddle, and six miles on the road to Yorktown caught up with the army, which was still on the march.[30]

Washington and Rochambeau were pleased with the results of the two officers' mission. Yet in a sense it had been nothing more than a kind of carrying of coals to Newcastle. Even before their return De Grasse's messenger had reported to Washington the decision of the council on board the "Ville de Paris," and Washington had already thanked De Grasse for his decision to stay. "The resolution that your Excellency has taken in our circumstances," the commander-in-chief wrote, "proves that a great mind knows how to make personal sacrifices to secure an important general good."[31] Lafayette, nevertheless, continued to believe as long as he lived and induced others to believe that he had played a decisive role in persuading De Grasse to stay.[32]

Now that the admiral's latest decision was known, the possibility of Admiral Digby's appearance made no difference in the plans of attack upon Cornwallis' army. Nevertheless, it had a significant effect upon the outcome of the siege. Cornwallis had contemplated his position with an expert eye and had early concluded that there were only two possible ways of escape from the trap which Lafayette and Washington had prepared

[28] "Journal de Closen," pp. 340–41.

[29] Jones to Lafayette, September 8, 1781, referred to in a letter from Williamsburg quoted in *Newport Mercury*, October 20, 1781; cf. Lafayette to La Luzerne, September 30, 1781, *loc. cit.*

[30] "Journal de Closen," p. 341.

[31] September 27, 1781, Fitzpatrick, XXIII, 143.

[32] Cf. *Mémoires*, I, 278; "Journal de Closen," p. 339; G. W. P. Custis, *Recollections and private memoirs of Washington* (New York, 1860), pp. 236–37.

for him if he were not relieved. One of them would have been to risk a battle. Before the main army under Vioménil and Lincoln came up, he might have attacked the combined force of Lafayette and St. Simon and then attempted a retreat. It would have been a costly effort, but less costly in the end than the complete surrender that seemed certain when finally the main army joined forces with Lafayette and St. Simon. That way he had hesitated to try, however, because in the event of defeat (which was not at all improbable) there would be no possibility of retreat. He would thus have lost many lives without bettering his position. Unwilling to throw away his men's lives in what appeared to him to be a desperate gamble, Cornwallis might have considered stealing across the James River during the absence of the French fleet. In the end Cornwallis tried neither battle nor escape, chiefly because he had learned even before Washington and Rochambeau that Admiral Digby had arrived in New York and might come to his rescue. Depending upon being relieved in due time if he held out, he kept his men feverishly at work in making strong redoubts and fortifications.[33]

As Lafayette and Closen had learned, the junction of the troops under Lincoln and Vioménil with the army at Williamsburg took place on September 26.[34] The next day Washington created a new order of battle. The American army under Lincoln formed the right wing, and the French army under Rochambeau formed the left. The American army in turn was to be divided into two lines, the Continentals in front and the militia in the rear. The Continentals were again divided into left, center, and right divisions. Dayton's and Clinton's brigades made up the left; Wayne's Pennsylvania and Gist's Maryland lines made up the center under Steuben; and Muhlenburg's and Hazen's brigades made up the right.[35]

[33] Tarleton, pp. 376–77 and 379–80; Ross, I, 123; Moore, II, 517; Stevens, *Clinton-Cornwallis controversy*, I, 76–77, 84, and 163–67; Clinton to Eden, [end of 1781], Stevens, *Facsimiles*, VII, no. 753.

[34] See pp. 313–14 above; cf. "Dairy of Du Bourg," p. 449.

[35] General orders, September 27, 1781, Fitzpatrick, XXIII, 146–48; cf. J. W. Wright, "Some notes on the Continental Army," pp. 102–3.

Lafayette as next senior major-general to Lincoln commanded the two brigades on the right. Muhlenburg's command was made up of those regiments of light infantry under the command of Colonels Vose, Barber, and Gimat which Lafayette had brought from New York and New Jersey to Virginia; and Hazen's brigade contained, in addition to Hazen's regiment of Canadians, the regiments of Colonel Alexander Scammel and Lieutenant-Colonel Alexander Hamilton, which Washington had recently designated as "the Light Corps."[36] In that way the troops that officially or habitually were referred to as "light infantry" came under Lafayette's orders. Once more they took on the name and *esprit* of the Light Division. Thus at last there passed under Lafayette's command his good friend Alexander Hamilton. And after Colonel Scammel was captured and mortally wounded while reconnoitering the enemy's lines, John Laurens took his place as commander of the third battalion of Hazen's brigade.[37] The three young men who had probably been closest to Washington throughout the war were thus brought together in the right division of the right wing of the allied troops before Yorktown.

Immediately upon Lafayette's return to the army he took command of his division. Shortly afterward fifteen hundred men were put to work building a trench before Yorktown under cover of a guard of picked Americans commanded by Lafayette and the Bourbonnais and Soissonais regiments commanded by the Baron de Vioménil.[38] For a period of over two weeks siege operations were vigorously carried on by the allied army and doggedly resisted by the British. During those operations Lafayette's division bore a heavy share of the labor and the risks. Lafayette himself, often acting as major-general for the day,[39] kept the operations of the whole American force in mind without ever losing sight of his own immediate command. He made

[36] Fitzpatrick, XXII, 500; XXIII, 19, 59, and 134; cf. J. W. Wright, "The corps of light infantry," p. 461.

[37] General orders, October 8, 1781, Fitzpatrick, XXIII, 199.

[38] Robin, pp. 117–19.

[39] Fitzpatrick, XXIII, 148, 152, 176, 197, 216, etc.

several suggestions for the conduct of the siege to Washington;[40] and on at least one of them (a proposal to find some way to prevent Cornwallis from crossing the York River) Washington took immediate action.[41]

Meanwhile, the siege operations around Yorktown developed. On September 30 the enemy gave up their outer works, and the allies occupied them at small cost. They were soon converted by the besiegers to their own use, and a ring of bayonets encircled the beleagured city. Lafayette's division lay at the right extremity of the combined armies, holding a post southwest of the city with its right flank on Wormeley's Creek, a branch of the York River, and its left covered by Steuben's command. Until the French and American artillery were emplaced, action consisted chiefly of reconnaissance on the allied side and a feverish building of fortifications, especially under cover of night, by the British.

Operations began in earnest only on October 6. That night the first parallel of breastworks was opened up. There being only three major-generals in the American army, Lafayette had to mount the trenches every two or three days. The Light Division marched into the trenches for the first time on October 7, "with the tread of veterans, colors flying, drums beating, and planted their standards on the parapet."[42] Dr. James Thacher had orders to give his special attention to the marquis if he should be wounded.[43]

Three days later, while Lafayette and the Baron de Vioménil commanded in the trenches, the enemy's cannon were effectively silenced by a continuous bombardment of all the allied artillery, and the enemy's shipping in the York River was destroyed or forced to seek shelter on the Gloucester side. Gov-

[40] Lafayette to Washington, September 30, 1781, loc. cit.

[41] Cf. Washington to De Grasse, October 1, 1781, Fitzpatrick, XXIII, 160-63.

[42] Johnston, p. 135; "Diary of Captain James Duncan in the Yorktown campaign, 1781," Pennsylvania archives, 2d ser., XV (1890), 749 (also contained in the "Old Northwest" genealogical quarterly, VII [1904], 156); Fitzpatrick, XXIII, 197; Capitaine, "Journal du siège d'York en Virginie," Jackson Collection.

[43] Thacher, p. 273.

ernor Nelson was present with the army in his capacity of commander of the Virginia militia. By a simple act of patriotic self-
sacrifice Nelson that day did much to wipe out Lafayette's feeling of impatience with the Virginia government. Asked to designate a good target for the allied guns to aim at, Nelson pointed
out a large house which he said was probably Cornwallis' headquarters. It was his own house.[44] The allied bombardment did
great damage in the crowded town. The next day the second
parallel of trenches was begun but could not be carried completely around the defenders because of the fire from two redoubts on the enemy's left.

While these operations were in progress, Colonel Morris,
Greene's aide, came to Yorktown with dispatches for Washington and Lafayette. "I cannot help thinking it no less fortunate
for the public than happy for ourselves," wrote Greene to his
commander, "that so perfect a good understanding subsists between your Excellency, the Marquis and myself."[45] Washington
agreed that the "good effects" which had been achieved might
be attributed to "the perfect good understanding between you,
the Marquis and myself." He hoped that that understanding
would never be interrupted, "and I am sure it never can while
we are all influenced by the same pure motive, that of love to
our country and interest in the cause in which we are embarked." Not having forgotten that he had had to bear "much
for the sake of peace and the public good," he nevertheless was
grateful on the eve of apparent success that his conscience assured him that he had acted rightly, and he had happily had
"but few differences" with those who like Greene and Lafayette
had served under him.[46]

Greene's aide carried that affectionate admission of friendship and loyalty back to South Carolina together with a less
restrained declaration of devotion from Lafayette. Morris also

[44] Capitaine, "Journal," *loc. cit.*; Shaw to Knox, April 15, 1792, F. S. Drake, *Life and correspondence of Henry Knox* (Boston, 1873), pp. 106–7; Custis, pp. 336–37; Sparks MSS XXXII, pp. 147–48.

[45] September 17, 1781, LC, Washington papers, no. 52, fol. 155.

[46] October 6, 1781, Fitzpatrick, XXIII, 190–91.

had been initiated into the secret of the contemplated naval attempt upon Charleston. He took to his chief the assurance that Lafayette would do what he could to convince De Grasse that it ought to be undertaken. "I need not telling you," the marquis' letter ran, "that I will do what I can. I . . . . probably will join your army for the winter unless I return to France."[47] Indeed, the siege of Yorktown had progressed so far that it seemed likely that the British would surrender shortly, and Lafayette was not unduly optimistic in speaking of joining Greene before the winter.

The evening of October 14 was Steuben's tour in the trenches. That day, however, was chosen for an attack upon the two redoubts which had become the key defense of Yorktown, and the Light Division was selected for the hazardous work. In Washington's plans these redoubts were generally referred to as Number 9 and Number 10. Number 10 was on the enemy's extreme left on the river, hence immediately opposite Lafayette's division; Number 9 was farther to the British right and about two hundred yards from the end of the American second parallel. Reconnaissance by the French officers during the day led to a concerted plan for an attack at nightfall.

Lafayette designated Lieutenant-Colonel Gimat to lead the assault on Number 10. But Hamilton, insisting that it was his tour of duty, demanded that he be put in command. Lafayette explained that his officers would prefer the honor to go to one of those who had served throughout the whole of the Virginia campaign. He permitted Hamilton, however, to appeal to the commander-in-chief. Washington directed that Hamilton be placed in charge of the American assaulting party.[48] Vioménil chose the Comte de Deux Ponts for the attack upon Number 9, which had the larger garrison. Picked French grenadiers from regiments with long histories and magnificent traditions were placed under Deux Ponts. Vioménil could afford to feel proud and confident of their success. But when he implied some doubt that the Americans might be equally relied upon, Lafayette, somewhat

[47] October 6, 1781, Morgan Library, Yorktown, Vol. I.

[48] Lee, *Memoirs of the war*, II, 342 n.; Sparks MSS XXXIII, p. 204.

piqued, retorted (as nearly as he could afterward remember):
"We are young soldiers and have only one way in these cases.
That is to unload our rifles and march right in with our bayo-
nets."[49]

And that was exactly what Hamilton's party did. As agreed,
after darkness had begun to fall, Hamilton and Deux Ponts
formed their men for the attack. Washington examined and
approved the dispositions Lafayette had made and delivered a
short speech to the men on the importance of their objective.[50]
In the ranks the soldiers talked of the ruthlessness that the
British under Benedict Arnold had recently shown toward the
garrison of New London, Connecticut, after it had surrendered.
They threatened reprisals.[51]

Then six cannon shots boomed forth in rapid succession. It
was the signal to attack. The two forces advanced to the assault. Hamilton led the way for the Americans. About three
hundred men, with Gimat's battalion of New Englanders in
the van, followed by Hamilton's battalion of New Yorkers and
New Englanders (under Major Nicholas Fish) marched on their
leader's right in one column, while on his left proceeded another
column of about eighty men under Laurens with orders to get
behind the redoubt and prevent the escape of any of its defenders. Ahead of them went a score of sappers and miners,
who were to clear away abatis and palisades. But the men did
not wait for the obstructions to be removed. They advanced
steadfastly with bayonets fixed. "Not a gun had been loaded."[52]
In the face of an enemy fire which cut down forty of them, they
clambered swiftly into the redoubts, Gimat's battalion in front
and Fish's on the left, while Laurens covered the rear and the
river prevented retreat on the right. Behind them, meanwhile,
the rest of Muhlenburg's and Hazen's brigades had been drawn

[49] *Mémoires*, I, 278-79; Sparks MSS XXXII, pp. 204-5.

[50] Stephen Olney quoted in Catherine R. Williams, *Biography of Revolutionary heroes*,
etc. (New York, 1839), p. 276; E. M. Stone, *Our French allies*, etc. (Providence, 1884),
p. 441.

[51] Lafayette to La Luzerne, October 16, 1781, *AHR*, XX (1915), 611.

[52] Lafayette to Cooper, October 14, 1781, *AHR*, VIII (1902), 90.

up in supporting columns, led by Lieutenant-Colonel Francis
Barber's battalion of New Hampshire and New Jersey troops.
Wayne's brigade of Steuben's division had been placed so as to
support them in turn.

But victory was won so rapidly that of these supporting columns only Barber's battalion got into action. Within only a
few minutes from the time the guns had boomed out the signal
to march, Number 10 was in American hands.[53] "To see this
afair [sic] transacted under the eyes of foreign armies gave me
unspeakable satisfaction," Lafayette owned.[54] Only eight of the
defenders were killed or wounded, the attackers, despite their
resentment over New London, giving quarter as soon as resistance ceased. Hamilton himself intervened to save the commandant from an enraged soldier who sought revenge for the death
of Colonel Scammel.[55]

The French had not had equal success at Number 9. Halting
for their pioneers to clear away the abatis, they waited while the
enemy poured a murderous fire into their ranks. Deux Ponts
had ordered his men not to return the enemy's fire until they
had reached the crest of the parapet. Their losses in killed and
wounded soon were more than twice as many as the Americans
had suffered.[56] Lafayette sent his division inspector, Major William Barber, to inform Vioménil that he had captured his re-

[53] McHenry to Governor Lee, October 15, 1781, Kite, *Sidelight on history*, pp. 71–72;
"Butler's journal," p. 109; Hamilton to Lafayette, October 15, 1781, Lodge, *Works of
Hamilton*, IX, 247–50; Lafayette to Washington, October 16, 1781, *Mémoires* (Amer.
ed.), pp. 443–44.

[54] Lafayette to Cooper, October 14, 1781, *loc. cit.*

[55] Hamilton to Lafayette, October 15, 1781, *loc. cit.*, p. 249; Thacher, p. 341; *Mémoires*, I, 280 n. The story that Lafayette ordered his men to give no quarter is to be
found in William Gordon, *History of the rise, progress and establishment of the independence of the United States of America*, etc. ([3 vols.; New York, 1794], pp. 257–58), from
which it passed into current belief among English writers: cf. *Gentleman's magazine*,
LVIII (1788), 1165 (reviewing the London [1788] edition of Gordon) and William
Cobbett, *Porcupine's works*, etc. (12 vols.; London, 1801), XII, 151. Gordon claimed
to have derived this statement from a manuscript journal of Major Gibbs. The story is
not to be found in any other primary source, however, and was explicitly denied by
Hamilton in a letter to the *New York Evening Post*, August 2, 1802 (Lodge, *Works of
Hamilton*, X, 441–42).

[56] Count William de Deux Ponts, *My campaign in America*, ed. S. A. Green (Boston,
1868), pp. 58, 67, 127, 144–45, and 148.

doubt and stood ready to assist in the capture of the other. The gesture was the retort courteous to Vioménil's earlier doubts of American soldierliness.

By that time the batteries in Yorktown, roused by the noise of battle, had opened fire all along the American line. Barber was wounded in the side by a cannon shot as he moved from post to post but carried on his mission. Refusing to allow his wound to be dressed until he had completed his duty, he returned with Vioménil's message: the French were not yet masters of their redoubt but soon would be! And they soon were. But they did not win their victory by cold steel alone. Deux Ponts had not required his men to unload their pieces. When they reached the top of the parapet, he ordered them to fire. Then they charged with bayonets fixed, and the enemy fled or surrendered.[57]

Vioménil made noble amends for his previous lack of confidence. In reporting to his general the results of the assaults upon the redoubts, he praised the marquis (who, being his junior in rank, he regarded as under his command) for behaving "with as much intrepidity as intelligence" and the American infantry for conduct that made them appear "like grenadiers accustomed to difficult things."[58] Lafayette's report to his general did not mention the French but cited for bravery Colonels Hamilton, Gimat (who was shot in the foot), Laurens, and Barber (who was slightly wounded), and Major Barber.[59] The most grievously injured of the French officers was Colonel Charles de Lameth, who had served as a subaltern with Lafayette under the command of his uncle, the Comte de Broglie, in the remote years of peace. Shot through both knees, he was saved from a double amputation only by a wise doctor who decided to leave his cure to nature.[60]

[57] *Ibid.*, pp. 58 and 145; Thacher, p. 342 and n.; Sparks MSS XXXII, pp. 204–7; Lee, *Memoirs of the war*, II, 343; Lafayette to La Luzerne, October 16, 1781, *loc. cit.*, pp. 610–11; Aaron Ogden to unknown, May 6, 1835, Jackson Collection.

[58] Vioménil to Rochambeau, October 16, 1781, Deux Ponts, pp. 156–61; *Magazine of American history*, VI (1881), 47–49.

[59] Lafayette to Washington, October 16, 1781, *loc. cit.*

[60] Dumas, I, 51 n.; Eugène Welvert (ed.), *Mémoires de Théodore de Lameth* (Paris, 1913), p. 108 and n. 2.

The day after the capture of the two redoubts, Lafayette complimented the Light Division (and entirely unintentionally roused a deep resentment in one of his most seriously wounded officers, Captain Stephen Olney, by citing him only after mentioning a subordinate).[61] In general orders Washington thanked Vioménil and Lafayette "for the excellency of their dispositions and for their own gallant conduct upon the occasion." He begged them "to present his thanks to every individual officer and to the men of their respective commands for the spirit and rapidity with which they advanced to the attacks and for the admirable firmness with which they supported themselves under the fire of the enemy without returning a shot." Perhaps because he had heard of Vioménil's doubts regarding American prowess in assault, Washington added: "The General reflects with the highest degree of pleasure on the confidence which the troops of the two nations must hereafter have in each other."[62] The capture of the two redoubts had enabled the allies to complete their second parallel to the river. During the night the line of trenches had been continued to Number 9, and by morning both of the erstwhile enemy fortifications had become part of the besiegers' ring around Yorktown. That day Lafayette had his first occasion to rebuke Cornwallis for his conduct as a gentleman.[63] Hitherto all correspondence between them had been on a high level of gentlemanliness, and each had shown a becoming humanity in carrying out requests on behalf of wounded and prisoners. This time, however, Cornwallis sent out a flag without ceasing his fire, and Lafayette, retaining the flag officer, sent back one of his own to Cornwallis to inform him of the impropriety of his conduct. Cornwallis apologized, saying the offense was unintended. Firing accomodatingly ceased on both sides till the flag officers could be exchanged and then began again in earnest. The enemy made a sortie upon the French part of the line at midnight and succeeded in damag-

[61] Olney's testimony cited in Williams, pp. 784–85; Lafayette to Olney, October 18 [?], 1781, *ibid.* (original in the Illinois State Historical Society Library).

[62] Fitzpatrick, XXIII, 223. For a discussion of the meaning of the apparently inexact phrase, "without returning a shot," see p. 328 below.

[63] "Butler's journal," pp. 109–10.

ing a few guns before they were driven off, but within a few hours those guns were again pouring shell into Yorktown along with the others.

All day of the sixteenth a steady cannonading rained shot and shell on the besieged, making their position untenable. A storm frustrated a final desperate effort by Cornwallis' army to steal across to Gloucester during the night. On the next morning he determined to ask for a cessation of hostilities for twenty-four hours. The Light Division was in the trenches when the British drummer first appeared upon the parapet and beat the signal for parley. Lafayette received the enemy's offer to surrender and sent it to headquarters.[64] Washington after some parleying finally granted a two-hour truce for the discussion of capitulation terms. The negotiations were still in progress when noon arrived and the marquis was relieved as usual by Steuben's division.[65] When Steuben's turn to be relieved came the next noon, he refused to leave his post, claiming that the laws of war permitted his men to stay in the trenches until the negotiations were completed in order that they might plant their divisional standards over the conquered town. Washington agreed, and countermanding earlier orders to General Lincoln's division to mount the trenches that day, granted the baron the honor which he claimed.[66] If Lafayette had been as familiar with the customs of war as Steuben, he might with equal justice have refused to be relieved by Steuben and thus have reserved all honors for his own division.[67]

Outnumbered two to one (5,745 Continentals; 3,200 militia; and 7,800 Frenchmen—not counting about 15,000 sailors under

[64] "Wild's journal," p. 155; journal of an American officer quoted in Joseph Martin, *Comprehensive description of Virginia*, etc. (Richmond, [1835 ?]), p. 295. The story that Cornwallis asked as a favor that he be allowed to treat with Lafayette alone but that the marquis modestly refused that honor is a myth, based apparently on the statement of [L. P. de Bérenger], *Mémoires historiques et pièces authentiques sur M. de Lafayette* (Paris, [1790]), p. 9.

[65] Martin, p. 295; General orders, October 16, 1781, Fitzpatrick, XXIII, 233.

[66] "Butler's journal," p. 110; General orders, October 17, 1781, Fitzpatrick, XXIII, 234; and After orders, October 18, 1781, *ibid.*, p. 238.

[67] For the legend about a quarrel between Lafayette and Steuben over this question, see Appen. I, pp. 429–30 below.

De Grasse—to 8,800 English, provincials, and Hessians),[68] the British after a good fight, not free from errors and miscalculations, formally signed a capitulation at noon on October 19. The terms had been arranged by Lafayette's two companions, Laurens (for the Americans) and Noailles (for the French) assisted by M. de Grandchain (for the French fleet). At first the allied generals had been inclined to favor most liberal terms, but in the end, on Lafayette's suggestion, the British were not permitted to march out of their positions with full honors of war. Lafayette remembered that the garrison of Charleston, commanded by General Lincoln, had been required to sheath its standards and to march to a tune that was not a national anthem. The same terms were now imposed upon the garrison of Yorktown.[69]

The ceremony of surrender began at two o'clock on October 19.[70] With arms on shoulders, colors incased, and band appropriately playing a tune called "The World Turned Upside Down," the British marched between the lines of American and French soldiers drawn up facing each other in their best uniforms. Cornwallis was not with his army. Pleading illness, he had sent his men out to surrender with General Charles O'Hara at their head. O'Hara made it obvious that they wished to be regarded as surrendering to the French and not to the Americans. Turning to Lafayette's friend Mathieu Dumas, one of Rochambeau's aides assigned to escort him, O'Hara asked where

[68] The numbers of the military groups that participated in the siege of Yorktown are much in dispute. Several of the above figures are taken from *Special news releases relating to the life and times of George Washington* by the United States George Washington Bicentennial Commission (Washington, 1932), p. 382. The estimate of 15,000 sailors under De Grasse is derived, however, from Lafayette's statement (letter to La Luzerne September 1, 1781, *AHR*, XX [1915], 606) that there would be 18,000 men under De Grasse when Barras arrived (allowing for the 3,100 men under St. Simon who were landed from De Grasse's force and are therefore more properly included among the 7,800 Frenchmen). Hughes's figure (III, 659; cf. Keim, p. 441) of 24,000 men for De Grasse seems to count Barras's force twice. The figure of 8,800 British and Hessians is derived from British state papers as analyzed in Sparks, *Writings of Washington*, V, 545. The usual figure of 7,500 British and Hessians seems to omit the provincials.

[69] Knox to Jay, October 21, 1781, Drake, p. 71; Lafayette to Mme de Lafayette, October 22, 1781, *Mémoires*, I, 472; *ibid.*, p. 280; Sparks MSS XXXII, p. 208.

[70] Knox to Jay, October 21, 1781, *loc. cit.*, p. 72.

Rochambeau was. On receiving an answer, he started toward the French general. Both Dumas and Rochambeau reminded O'Hara that Washington was the commander-in-chief of the allied army.[71] O'Hara turned to Washington "with much embarrassment in his countenance."[72] Washington indicated that he was to take further orders from General Lincoln, who had had to surrender his own army at Charleston. Lincoln led the British and Hessians through the lines of their conquerors. They kept their eyes turned toward the French ranks, until Lafayette, resenting their studied disregard, ordered his drum-major to strike up "Yankee Doodle." The band's blare made them turn their eyes toward his side of the line.[73] At the end of the double formation the British turned to the right, marched a short distance, deposited their arms, surrendered their standards (the officers being permitted to keep their side arms), and then returned to Yorktown under guard of the militia.[74] The same day the British at Gloucester surrendered to M. de Choisy.

In general orders the next day Washington congratulated the army "on the glorious event of yesterday." He was careful first of all to thank Louis XVI and the allied fleet and army, singling out several of the most prominent officers for special mention. Then he turned to the American army. "The General's thanks to each individual of merit would comprehend the whole army. But he thinks himself bound, however, by affection, duty and gratitude to express his obligations to Major-Generals Lincoln, de La Fayette, and Steuben for their dispositions in the trenches." And he enumerated several others who had especially distinguished themselves.[75]

---

[71] Dumas, I, 52–53 and n.; Rochambeau, I, 295. The story that O'Hara offered his sword to Lafayette (or Washington or Lincoln) is ably refuted in "Le vase offert à la famille du Général Lafayette: lettre de M. le Major Lee," *Journal de l'Institut Historique*, III (1835), 59–62.

[72] Lee, *Memoirs of the war*, II, 361.

[73] Sparks MSS XXXII, p. 248; Custis, p. 248; cf. O. G. T. Sonneck (ed.), *Report on "The Star-Spangled Banner," "Hail Columbia," "America," "Yankee Doodle"* (Washington, 1909), p. 109.

[74] Noailles to Molly Robinson, October 26, 1781, A. W. Wood, "The Robinson family and their correspondence with the Vicomte and Vicomtesse de Noailles," *Bulletin of the Newport Historical Society*, no. 42 (October, 1922), pp. 24–25.

[75] General orders, October 20, 1781, Fitzpatrick, XXIII, 244–47.

The commander-in-chief could not mention the services of his young friend more conspicuously than that without violating military etiquette. But others did not feel under equal restraint. The next day was Sunday, and Rev. Israel Evans, chaplain of the New Hampshire troops, delivered a sermon which he dedicated "to the honorable Major-General the Marquis de la Fayette, whose disinterested services in the cause of America prove him to be the friend of mankind, and whose well known amiable virtues render all panegyric needless."[76] And in France when news of the capture of Yorktown was learned by a proud and jubilant people, the praises of Lafayette were unstinted. Several newspapers published the same comments: "The general who contributed most to the success of this great enterprise is without contradiction the Marquis de la Fayette. It is he who followed Cornwallis step by step, who harassed him unceasingly, who drove him back into Yorktown, and who prepared his downfall. Americans as well as Frenchmen, and even the enemy pronounce the warmest praise of this young nobleman. . . . . He is already compared to Turenne for the gentleness and simplicity of his manners, his calm and his excellent power of observation."[77] If there was a generous degree of journalistic license in that estimate, the sober truth remained that no other person (except perhaps De Grasse) had contributed so much or so directly to the capture of one of England's finest armies as had the young general fresh from the "Society" of Paris.

BIBLIOGRAPHICAL NOTES

Despite the embarrassing number of books and articles on the siege of Yorktown, several questions have not been carefully treated hitherto (see above, nn. 68 and 71, for examples). One of the most difficult of the moot points arises in connection with the attack upon the redoubts on October 14, 1781. There is an apparent conflict of testimony as to whether or not the French fired before entering Number 9. Deux Ponts says unmistakably that

[76] *A discourse delivered near York in Virginia on the memorable occasion of the surrender of the British army . . . . before the brigade of New York troops and the division of American light-infantry under the command of the Marquis de Lafayette* (Philadelphia, 1782). Cf. [Israel Evans], "Journal of the siege of York," *Collections of the Massachusetts Historical Society*, 1st ser., IX (1804), 107.

[77] *Gazette de Leyde*, November 30, 1781, supplément; *Mercure de France*, December 1, 1781.

they did (pp. 144–45), and Lafayette's *Mémoires* (I, 279) speaks of "the fire of the French." On the other hand, Rochambeau (in his *Mémoires*, I, 293–94, and his "Journal des operations du Comte de Rochambeau," *Gazette de Leyde*, November 30, 1781, and suppléments), Lafayette (to La Luzerne, October 17, 1781, *loc. cit.*), and others speak of the French as taking their redoubt "sword in hand," or "at the point of the bayonet." The only way of resolving this conflict among firsthand witnesses is to assume that, as Deux Points says, the French fired at the parapet, and then, as the testimony of the others would imply, took their redoubt at the point of the bayonet. Lafayette's story (see p. 320 above and n. 49) of his exchange of words with Vioménil would otherwise have no meaning. Moreover, Lafayette is always careful to point out that his men's guns had been unloaded, implying that those of the French were loaded (cf. letter to La Luzerne, October 16, 1781, *loc. cit.; Mémoires*, I, 279).

It is a little more difficult to explain Washington's statement in General orders for October 15, 1781 (Fitzpatrick, XXIII, 223), that both attacking parties "supported themselves under the fire of the enemy without returning a shot." Unless Deux Ponts and Lafayette are both wrong in stating that the French did return the enemy's fire, the explanation of Washington's words can be only that he meant that the French "supported themselves under the fire of the enemy without returning a shot" for a good part of the fight. It should be remembered that Washington and Rochambeau, as well as Lafayette when writing to La Luzerne, were in a position where they could make no comparisons, inevitably odious, between the conduct of the French and that of the Americans. In their memoirs, Deux Ponts and Lafayette were not under any such compulsion. (I am indebted to Mr. Thomas M. Pitkin, associate historical technician, Colonial National Historical Park, Yorktown, Virginia, for his aid in helping to resolve this conflict of testimony.)

In addition to the eyewitnesses cited in this chapter, there are other primary sources for the siege of Yorktown. Among them, Tarleton's *Campaigns*, the *Clinton-Cornwallis controversy*, the manuscript "Journal du siège d'York" by Capitaine in the Jackson Collection, and the *Diaries of George Washington 1748–1799*, ed. J. C. Fitzpatrick (4 vols.; Boston, 1925), have been used for this account. Of the secondary sources that have already been cited, Johnston's *Yorktown campaign* has been especially useful; and J. W. Wright's "Notes on the siege of Yorktown" should also be mentioned again. J. A. Stevens, "The Allies at Yorktown, 1781" (*Magazine of American history*, VI [1881], 1–53), quotes from many contemporary sources. J. F. Shafroth, "The strategy of the Yorktown campaign 1781" (*United States Naval Institute proceedings*, LVII [1931], 721–36 and 1368–69), is helpful for its maps. H. L. Landers, *The Virginia campaign and the blockade and siege of Yorktown 1781*, etc. (Washington, 1931) does not supersede Johnston's monograph as the "standard" work on the subject.

Special mention should be made of Miss Kite's edition of the *Correspondence of Washington and De Grasse*, without which the story of Lafayette's relations with De Grasse would have to be told in the traditional (and incorrect) fashion derived from Lafayette's romanticized version of it (*Mémoires*, I, 278).

CHAPTER XIV

Lafayette Returns Again to France

LORD CORNWALLIS, notwithstanding current allega-
tions to the contrary and his systematic destruction of
property, had consistently acted in a manner becoming
an officer and gentleman in his transactions with Americans.
Elation at his capture in the allied camp was, therefore, tempered with a certain sympathy for his misfortune.[1] That he had
pleaded illness in order to avoid having personally to surrender
his army indicated mental distress if not physical discomfort.
On the day after the capitulation, Washington, Rochambeau,
and Lafayette sent their aides to him to present their compliments. Lafayette's aide was Major George Augustine Washington. Cornwallis received those officers with a grace and dignity
becoming the mighty who had fallen. He was especially interested in Major Washington, who had the double honor of
being his uncle's nephew and his general's aide. He hoped that
Lafayette, with whom unseen he had conducted a duel all summer long, would come to call on him. He wanted Lafayette particularly to understand the reasons which had dictated his surrender and explained to young Washington some of his controversy with Clinton.[2]

When Major Washington returned to camp and delivered this
message, Lafayette felt that he could afford to be gracious to a
once-feared adversary who had now become an unwilling guest.
The next day he visited Cornwallis' quarters. With a map of
Virginia in hand, the British commander explained how he had

---

[1] Cf. Noailles to Molly Robinson, October 26, 1781, Wood, "The Robinson family,"
pp. 24–25.

[2] *Mémoires*, I, 280–81 and n.; Sparks MSS XXXII, pp. 249–50.

planned to escape to Gloucester if storms had not prevented, and Lafayette revealed to him the precautions that had been taken to cut him off even if he had succeeded.[3] Cornwallis returned the marquis' call before they left the vicinity of Yorktown. He found at Lafayette's quarters a Negro servant who, he had thought, had been in his employ to spy on the Americans, but, he now discovered, had been spying upon him instead.[4]

Other allied officers saw Cornwallis often and were charmed by his simplicity.[5] They readily adopted his explanation of his misfortune and placed the blame for it upon his superiors. "Sir Henry Clinton has deceived him," Lafayette announced to his friends, though only because Clinton was himself deceived by the "pretenses" of an attack upon New York.[6] Other British generals likewise received such civilities as the allied camp would permit. General von Steuben, whose pocket was not so well lined as Lafayette's, even borrowed money with which to dine them.[7] At one such dinner General O'Hara, making a mock effort, Lafayette thought, to keep from being overheard, stated confidentially to some French generals that he was glad not to have been taken by the Americans alone. "It's obvious," Lafayette retorted, "that General O'Hara does not like second performances (*répétitions*),"[8] thus reminding all present that once before (at Saratoga) O'Hara had been taken prisoner, and then by the Americans alone.

Cornwallis himself seemed to be apprehensive that his army might receive bad treatment at American hands. Lafayette pointedly remarked that Americans had always been "humane to armed prisoners."[9] On the other hand, he insisted that the British government had blundered in placing Henry Laurens, "being a public minister and not a military man," in close

[3] Sparks MSS XXXII, p. 249.

[4] *Ibid.*, p. 250.

[5] Noailles to Molly Robinson, October 26, 1781, *loc. cit.*

[6] Lafayette to Poix, October 20, 1781, private collection; cf. Lafayette to Cooper, October 26, 1781, *AHR*, VIII (1902), 89–91.

[7] Garden, p. 323; cf. Kapp, pp. 464–65, and Palmer, pp. 294–95.

[8] *Mémoires*, I, 281 n.   [9] *Ibid.*, p. 281.

confinement in the Tower of London. Thereupon Cornwallis expressed a strong desire to be exchanged for Laurens, and Lafayette undertook to broach the subject to his commander.[10] If in peace as in war Lafayette thus jealously guarded the honor of America, he was no less gracious than any of his colleagues. A Loyalist colonel who was ill was Lafayette's guest for several days and long remained grateful for the marquis' hospitality.[11]

Sympathy for a gallant adversary did not, however, spoil the joy of victory. When the last soldier of Cornwallis had laid down his arms, Rochambeau decided to send Lauzun back to France with an official report of the shining glory that the allies had won. Lafayette prepared an account of his own, to be carried by the same messenger. Reverting again to a favorite figure of the stage, he announced to Maurepas: "The play is over, Monsieur le Comte, and the fifth act has just ended. I was a little uneasy during the first ones, my heart rejoiced greatly at the last, and I have no less pleasure in congratulating you on the happy conclusion of our campaign."[12] He dared to hope now that the war would soon be over. After what had happened to the talented Cornwallis, "What English general," he asked rhetorically of Vergennes, whom he congratulated with equal enthusiasm, "will come to put himself in charge of conquering America?"[13] The great merit of his illustrious opponent also received honorable mention in his letter to Adrienne: "The capture of Cornwallis is a most agreeable reward for me. It has made me forget the disappointments, pains and anxieties with which the superior talents of my enemy only too well surrounded me throughout the campaign."[14]

[10] Moses Young to Henry Laurens, April 10, 1782, Frank Moore (ed.), *Materials for history . . . . correspondence of Henry Laurens of South Carolina* (New York, 1861), pp. 218–20.

[11] "A narrative of the transactions, imprisonment, and sufferings of John Connolly, an American Loyalist and lieut.-col. in His Majesty's service," *Pennsylvania magazine of history and biography*, XXIII (1889), 284.

[12] October 20, 1781, *Mémoires*, I, 470.

[13] October 20, 1781, Stevens, *Facsimiles*, XVII, no. 1639 (and, with omissions, *Mémoires*, I, 471).

[14] [October 20, 1781], *Mercure de France*, December 1, 1781, pp. 35–36.

As usual the marquis reserved his most intimate reflections for the Prince de Poix.[15] He explained the fortunate chain of events which had led to victory, expressing his gratitude to St. Simon for placing a French army under his command, distributing credit freely also among De Grasse, Barras, Rochambeau, Chastellux, and Vioménil, and citing for valor their mutual friends Lauzun, Noailles, Charlus, Damas, and Vauban. But he reserved the highest praise for the "Generalissimo": "His genius, his greatness, and the nobility of his conduct bring to him the hearts and the veneration of both armies." Of the friends at home to whom the jubilant general, fresh from a brilliant victory which might assure the firm foundation of a young republic, wished especially to be remembered, last (and therefore first) was his queen, to whom he sent his "most tender and most respectful regards." Republican generals, if French noblemen, must not forget that they are courtiers too.

Lafayette's declaration that the capture of Cornwallis was the fifth act of a tragedy was an example of his Gallic penchant for hyperbole. Actually, the war was not yet over; and no one knew what still remained to be done better than the exultant marquis. While the British still controlled New York and Charleston, the United States could hardly claim to be entirely free or expect unconditional recognition of its independence at a peace conference. Lafayette's plan to go to Greene's aid in the siege of Charleston had already won Washington's approval and had roused a tentative interest in De Grasse. As soon as the amenities required of a gallant conqueror toward a worthy foe were acquitted, Washington and Lafayette set out to visit De Grasse, thank him for his part in the victory, and discuss future operations. Washington stayed but a short time—only long enough to portray the significance of an attack upon Charleston and the brilliant chances of success if De Grasse's boats were to take some troops from Yorktown to reinforce Greene. If the attack upon Charleston seemed impracticable, Washington maintained, a subordinate though still significant

[15] October 20, 1781, *loc. cit.*

objective for a joint effort would be the enemy's post at Wilmington.[16]

Washington did not wait for a decision. Hastening back to his army, he left Lafayette behind on the "Ville de Paris," promising him command of the enterprise against Wilmington if he could win the admiral's support. The young general stayed on board with his aide McHenry for another day.[17] But no arguments could move De Grasse from his persuasion that it was his duty to the king and his obligation to the Spanish allies to return to the West Indies by November. He would be ready, however, to take Lafayette and two thousand American troops as far as Wilmington, if they could be got ready to leave by November 1.[18]

While Lafayette was on the "Ville de Paris," the frigate that was to carry Lauzun back to France left port. The young husband took advantage of its departure to add a last-minute note to the letter he had already written to Adrienne. He frankly confessed to her that among his "most beautiful moments" were the times when he had commanded St. Simon and other *maréchaux-de-camp* together with the troops under them. "I am sorry for Cornwallis," he wrote, "having the highest regard for him. He is kind enough to show some respect for me, and since at his surrender he gave me the pleasure of making amends for the improper acts of Charleston, I do not expect to insist upon further revenge."[19]

Back in camp, Lafayette busied himself with preparations for the voyage to Wilmington. As De Grasse had requested, he sent Gouvion and several expert pilots to the "Ville de Paris" to give the admiral details on the navigation of the Carolina coast. But when De Grasse examined these men carefully, he became persuaded that conditions were unfavorable for the pro-

[16] *Diaries of Washington*, II, 270; *Correspondence of Washington and De Grasse*, pp. 119-21; Fitzpatrick, XXIII, 250 and n.

[17] McHenry to Governor Lee, October 23, 1781, Kite, *Sidelight on history*, p. 75.

[18] Lafayette to Washington, October 23, 1781, *Correspondence of Washington and De Grasse*, pp. 121-23 (where this document is erroneously said to be by De Grasse; cf. LC, Washington papers, no. 54, fol. 53).

[19] October 22, 1781, *Mémoires*, I, 471-72.

posed expedition. He had too few boats to transport two thousand men without crowding his vessels, and the danger of storms made it wise to avoid heavy loads. Besides, his main objective, he insisted, must be to reach the West Indies in November. If he met the enemy, he might therefore have to run away, carrying Lafayette and his men with him to the Caribbean. Thus "instead of doing good for the Americans, I shall take away from them for a long time one of their best defenders and do harm to the cause." Yet, if the Americans could manage to provide their own vessels and to join him, he announced his willingness to escort them as far as Cape Fear. He hoped his young countryman would not feel too disappointed in him. "Do not deny me your friendship. On the contrary, pity me for not being able to finish my work by dealing a second deathblow to our enemies."[20]

Subsequent messages to Washington and Lafayette made it clear that for De Grasse (as, indeed, for the French government) the American continent was but a minor arena of war. The major field of action was the rich islands of the Caribbean. De Grasse again insisted that he was honor bound to get to the West Indies soon. Therefore, he could do no more than escort vessels which Lafayette would himself provide.[21] Washington had already composed a letter to Congress stating that Lafayette would with De Grasse's aid sail to the reduction of Wilmington, when the admiral's new conditions became known. They were obviously impossible to meet. Even if enough vessels were available to transport two thousand men, they could not be brought together in time. Reluctantly, Washington added a postscript to his letter, stating that he would now be obliged to send Greene's reinforcements by land.[22]

Washington's reason for having promised command of the

[20] De Grasse to Lafayette, October 24, 1781, *Correspondence of Washington and De Grasse*, pp. 129–32. (I have departed in some minor details from Miss Kite's translation.)

[21] De Grasse to Lafayette, October 26, 1781, *ibid.*, pp. 136–37; to Washington, October 26, 1781, *ibid.*, pp. 133–36; to Charlus, October 26, 1781, *ibid.*, p. 138.

[22] Washington to president of Congress, October 27–29, 1781, Fitzpatrick, XXIII, 294–99.

Wilmington expedition to Lafayette in preference to several senior major-generals was that a Frenchman could better co-operate with De Grasse, who could speak no English. Now that De Grasse was no longer counted on, the command could safely be entrusted to an American officer; and Major-General St. Clair was placed in charge.[23] Lafayette thus found himself faced with the prospect of being engaged in nothing more exciting than camping in the neighborhood of Yorktown, idly awaiting developments beyond his control. He began to think of home once more. He had, in fact, mentioned to some friends that he would soon return to France.[24] His mind began to teem again with grandiose schemes. He would go to the French government with demands for huge sums of money, a large reinforcement for Rochambeau, a big naval force. "Halifax, Newfoundland, Penobscot" still figured prominently in his plans.[25] Other French officers had already received permission to return to France, carrying certificates of high praise from the commander-in-chief and Congress.[26] Honor and promotion awaited them in France. Lafayette, too, asked for a furlough. Washington granted it readily—all the more so because Lafayette promised to use his influence to secure a larger navy and a reinforcement of Rochambeau's army for the next campaign.[27]

Before leaving Virginia the marquis felt that he must make his peace with the government of that state on two counts. In a letter to Governor Nelson he apologized both for any violation of "all those forms which I could have wished" in the confiscation of property and for having done nothing to push the investigation of Steuben's behavior at Point of Fork.[28] On the latter score, indeed, Greene had already expressed complete confidence in Steuben, and Lafayette had also announced

[23] Washington to St. Clair, October 29, 1781, *ibid.*, pp. 292–93.
[24] Lafayette to Poix, October 24, 1781, private collection; to Cooper, October 26, 1781, *loc. cit.*
[25] Lafayette to Cooper, October 26, 1781, *loc. cit.*
[26] Cf. Lafayette to Poix, October 24, 1781, *loc. cit.*
[27] Lafayette to Cooper, October 26, 1781, *loc. cit.*; cf. Washington to Lafayette, January 4–5, 1782, Fitzpatrick, XXIII, 429–31; and pp. 337–40 below.
[28] Lafayette to Nelson, October 31, 1781, Chinard, *Lafayette in Virginia*, p. 60.

full approval of the baron's conduct during the entire campaign.[29] The Virginia Assembly let the investigation go by de-
fault. For years to come, however, it was called upon to listen
to claims of indemnity for damage done by the marquis' soldiers.[30]

At the end of October, Lafayette bade farewell to the troops
that he had led to victory from the ice-covered Hudson to the
muggy swamps of the Chesapeake. "In the moment the Major
General leaves this place," his address ran,[31] "he wishes once
more to express his gratitude to the brave corps of light infantry
who for nine months past have been companions of his fortunes.
He will never forget that with them alone of regular troops, he
had the good fortune to manoeuvre before an army which after
its reduction is still six times superior to the regular forces he
had at that time." On November 5, accompanied by McHenry,
his beloved brother-in-law Noailles, and several other returning
Frenchmen, he reached Baltimore. There the citizens drew up
an address assuring him that he would "always hold a first
place" in their hearts. Lafayette replied graciously: "My campaign began with a personal obligation to the inhabitants of
Baltimore; at the end of it I find myself bound to them by a
new tie of everlasting gratitude."[32] Leaving Baltimore the next
morning he was in Philadelphia by November 8. James Madison, deputy to the Continental Congress, writing to a friend in
Virginia, expressed the wish that "some handsome compliments" might be paid the marquis for his "judicious and zealous
services."[33]

[29] Lafayette to Steuben, October 26, 1781, New York Historical Society, Steuben
papers, Vol. VIII, no. 79; Kapp, pp. 470 and 472; Palmer, pp. 295-96.

[30] Cf. Anne W. Ready (ed.), "Lafayette at Providence Forge," *William and Mary
quarterly*, 2d ser., XI (1931), 241; "Lafayette in New Kent County," *Virginia magazine of history and biography*, XLI (1933), 76.

[31] Anonymous, "General Lafayette," *Atlantic magazine*, I (1824), 400; Thacher,
p. 536.

[32] *Newport Mercury*, December 15, 1781; *New York Gazette and Weekly Mercury*,
November 19, 1781; Scharf, pp. 194-95; Hezekiah Niles (ed.), *Principles and acts of
the Revolution in America* (Baltimore, 1822), p. 399; Nolan, pp. 206-7.

[33] Madison to Edmund Pendleton, November 13, 1781, Gaillard Hunt (ed.), *Writings of James Madison* (8 vols.; New York, 1900-1908), I, 161-62.

In Philadelphia, as so often elsewhere, dramatic events seemed to wait for the marquis to arrive on the scene before they happened. On the day of his arrival, Lawrence Marr and John Moody, Tory spies, were arrested for attempting to steal the secret journal of Congress. Lafayette was appointed president of the court-martial that tried them. On November 10, they were sentenced to death.[34]

Before leaving Yorktown, Lafayette had arranged to meet Washington in Philadelphia. The death of John Parke Custis, Mrs. Washington's son, detained the general at Mount Vernon, however, and he was obliged to write to his young friend in explanation. His letter was filled with glowing words of appreciation for Lafayette's "military conduct and other important services in the course of the last campaign" and of "affectionate regard . . . . too well riveted to undergo diminution or change." But it was meant chiefly to confirm Washington's approval of the marquis' return to France, since he intended to press for an augmentation of Rochambeau's army and particularly for naval reinforcements. "It follows . . . . as certain as that night succeeds the day that without a decisive naval force we can do nothing definitive, and with it every thing honourable and glorious. A constant naval superiority would terminate the war speedily; without it, I do not know that it will ever be terminated honourably."[35]

When this letter reached Lafayette, he had already spent a fortnight in Philadelphia. He had conferred with Robert Morris on financial matters and with Robert R. Livingston on foreign policy in order to be well informed on America's needs and wishes when he again saw his king.[36] The departing general, now unable to count on his commander to present his petition, addressed Congress directly for permission to return to France. "There is no prospect of active operations before the time at

[34] *Gentleman's magazine*, LII (1782), 89; *Newport Mercury*, December 1, 1781; *Gazette de Leyde*, February 12, 1782, supplément; Nolan, pp. 207-8.

[35] November 15, 1781, Fitzpatrick, XXIII, 340-42.

[36] Lafayette to Greene, November 22, 1781, Morgan Library, Yorktown, Vol. II; Robert Morris, "Diary in office of finance, 1781," LC, Robert Morris papers, under dates of November 8, 9, and 22, 1781.

which I may be able to return," he explained. Meanwhile, his absence "might also become serviceable to our views for the next campaign." Despite his earlier announcement of the "fifth act of the play," he now felt the drama was far from ended. In writing Greene an affectionate farewell, he declared: "I am not of those who think we will have peace this winter. I think Great Britain will make a last effort. . . . . In a word, I depend upon an other campaign, and hope I will be once more a soldier in your army."[37]

Lafayette's letter to Congress was referred to a committee of three, of whom James Madison was one.[38] Madison did not overlook this opportunity to pay the "handsome compliments" that he had suggested. The committee the next day moved that Lafayette be granted a furlough and "that he return at such time as shall be most convenient to him." They warmly commended his "zealous attachment to the cause . . . . his judgment, vigilance, gallantry, and address . . . . his merits and military talents," and the bravery and enterprise of the men who had served under him. They proposed that "the Secretary of Foreign Affairs acquaint the ministers plenipotentiary of the United States [Franklin, Adams, and Jay] that it is the desire of Congress that they confer with the Marquis de la Fayette, and avail themselves of his informations relative to the situation of public affairs in the United States" and "that the Secretary of Foreign Affairs further acquaint the minister plenipotentiary at the Court of Versailles [Franklin] that he will conform to the intention of Congress by consulting with and employing the assistance of the Marquis de la Fayette, in accelerating the supplies which may be afforded by his Most Christian Majesty for the use of the United States." They also recommended that the superintendent of finances and the secretary of foreign affairs communicate with the marquis so as to enable him to be of greatest service in his new capacity of adviser to the American diplomats abroad. Finally, they suggested that the United States government assume Lafayette's debt to the merchants

[37] November 22, 1781, PCC, no. 156, fols. 248–50; Tower, II, 462.
[38] *Journals of Congress*, XXI, 1131 n., and 1134.

of Baltimore. Congress quickly accepted these resolutions. In addition they ordered that Morris send Lafayette to France in "a proper conveyance" and that Livingston draw up a letter to the young Frenchman's ruler for their approval.[39]

Congress' letter to Louis XVI was not completed for several days, but the resolutions were immediately sent to Lafayette.[40] He replied gracefully: "My attachement to America, the sense of my obligations and the new favors conferred upon me are so many everlasting ties that devote me to her. At every time, in every part of the world my heart will be panting for opportunities to be employed in her service."[41]

In keeping with the wishes of Congress, the superintendent of finance and the secretary of foreign affairs once more conferred with the young general. They met at Livingston's office. A representative of the Board of War was also present.[42] They agreed upon the nature of the dispatches that the marquis would carry back to France for Franklin and Vergennes. The next day Washington came to town. Morris invited the two soldiers to his quarters, and they reached the conclusion that Lafayette ought to ask for a subsidy or loan of ten millions. Morris thought that sum sufficient for the ensuing campaign.[43] Washington particularly emphasized the need for additional naval and land assistance from France.[44]

Livingston's draft of the letter to Louis XVI was not submitted until November 29. With some amendments it was quickly adopted. It expressed to America's "great, faithful and beloved friend and ally" the congratulations of Congress on the

[39] *Ibid.*, pp. 1134–36.

[40] Hanson to Lafayette, November 24, 1781, Burnett, VI, 268.

[41] Lafayette to Hanson, November 25, 1781, PCC, no. 156, fols. 252–54.

[42] Morris, "Diary," under date of November 25, 1781. From Morris' diary it would appear that this representative was Richard Peters, but Lafayette's letter to Greene, November 22, 1781 (*loc. cit.*), indicated that he expected to confer with General Lincoln, who, though recently appointed secretary of war, had not yet accepted that office.

[43] Morris, "Diary," under date of November 26, 1781; Lafayette to Vergennes, April 18, 1782 [?], Stevens, *Facsimiles*, XVII, no. 1641.

[44] Lafayette to Franklin, Adams, and Jay, November 21, 1782, NYPL, Bancroft transcripts.

recent victory and their deep appreciation of Lafayette as well as of Rochambeau and De Grasse. "Major General the Marquis de la Fayette [it ran] has in this campaign so greatly added to the reputation he had before acquired that we are desirous to obtain for him, on our behalf, every notice, in addition to that favourable reception which his merits cannot fail to meet with from a generous and enlightened sovereign; and in that view we have directed our minister plenipotentiary to present the Marquis to your Majesty."[45]

When resolutions and letters were completed, Lafayette not only had a new claim to special consideration from "the greatest and best of kings"[46] for his military services to a grateful ally but had added to his numerous military honors the right to take an official part in the peace and other diplomatic negotiations of that ally. The desire to represent the United States in the peace negotiations, long ago expressed by Lafayette, was now to be realized—and in the brilliant company of Franklin, Adams, and Jay. As the neophyte diplomat later imparted to Washington,[47] he was diffident about his diplomatic ability, though he would try to "justify the confidence of Congress by giving my opinion to the best of my power whenever it is asked." He felt more sanguine in pulling the purse strings. "The affair of finances will, I fear, be a difficult point for the American minister, in which, however, I will be happy to help him with my utmost exertions." Morris and Livingston, too, counted on Lafayette's "zeal and activity" to "go far in smoothing the way" toward the accomplishment of America's diplomatic objectives.[48]

New honors poured in upon the young soldier. La Luzerne lent his voice also to those who called Lafayette's "zeal" to the special attention of his king.[49] And within a few weeks the Gen-

[45] *Journals of Congress*, XXI, 1145-46.

[46] Hanson to Lafayette, November 24, 1781, *loc. cit.*

[47] December 21, 1781, *Mémoires* (Amer. ed.), p. 448.

[48] Morris to Franklin, November 27, 1782, Wharton, V, 12-13; Livingston to Jay, November 28, 1781, *ibid.*, p. 30.

[49] La Luzerne to Rayneval, November 25, 1781, AAE, corr. pol., É.-U., Vol. XIX, fols. 297-98.

eral Assembly of Virginia passed a resolution thanking Washington, Rochambeau, De Grasse, and Lafayette for their services. It likewise required that a bust of the marquis be made in Paris, inscribed with a suitable sentiment, and presented to him on their behalf.[50] Washington was asked to convey this resolution to his friend. The commander-in-chief gladly did so, frankly acknowledging his "peculiar pleasure in becoming the channel through which the just and grateful plaudits of my native state are communicated to the man I love."[51] To an American correspondent, however, Washington admitted that the Virginia resolution puzzled him a little. "I am not a judge of the etiquette on these occasions, but it really does seem odd to me to present a man with his own likeness."[52]

Morris had meanwhile secured for Lafayette the "Alliance," probably the best boat in the American navy, on which he had returned to France in 1779. The economical Morris, instructing Captain John Barry to take on board Lafayette, Noailles, Duportail, Gouvion, La Colombe, Poirey, and anyone else whom Lafayette might designate, urged the captain to lay in stores "with discretion." Barry was to "remember that we are not rich enough to be extravagant, nor so poor as to act meanly." The "Alliance" was to take Lafayette to France as quickly and safely as possible and to return in the spring.[53]

One other financial matter had to be adjusted before Lafayette could leave Philadelphia with a clear slate. He had long been living on borrowed funds. The French banker Leray de Chaumont had been lending him money through his Philadelphia agent John Holker. At various times since July, 1780, when the money that Lafayette had brought with him from France had been exhausted, Lafayette had borrowed large sums from Holker. By the time he left Philadelphia the total amount-

[50] *Journal of the House of Delegates* (session of December 17, 1781), p. 43.

[51] Washington to Lafayette, January 5, 1782, Fitzpatrick, XXIII, 431.

[52] Washington to Randolph, January 8, 1782, *ibid.*, p. 435, n. 65.

[53] "Sailing instructions to Commodore Barry to take General La Fayette to France 'on business of the utmost importance to America,' 1781," [November 27], *American Catholic historical researches*, X (1893), 33–35. Cf. Morris to John Brown, November 27, 1781, Historical Society of Pennsylvania, Dreer collection.

ed to £165,952 and some shillings in Continental paper. Holker had translated these sums into silver money at the rate prevailing at the time of borrowing. The rate had steadily mounted from 60 in July, 1780, to 262½ in May, 1781, but after Yorktown had dropped again to 225. Holker's accounts indicated that the total loan would be worth about £1,273 in silver. In part payment of the sum due, Holker accepted some of the household effects which Lafayette would leave behind. That brought the total debt to around £1,190 sterling. Lafayette agreed to reimburse this sum to M. de Chaumont in Passy at the low rate of 14 livres tournois to the pound sterling plus a 25 per cent charge to cover costs of exchange operations. Thus Lafayette promised to pay to M. de Chaumont nearly 21,000 livres tournois when he arrived in France.[54] The purchasing-power of the livre tournois was more than that of the dollar today;[55] and that sum represented only a fraction of the marquis' expenditures since his return to America a year and a half earlier.

Lafayette, Noailles, Duportail, and several other returning French officers left Philadelphia even before Congress' letter to Louis XVI was ready.[56] On December 6 they reached Hartford, Connecticut, and four days later were in Boston. The bells of the town rang forth in noisy welcome as soon as their arrival was known. The townsmen turned out to greet them and to show once more their affection for America's marquis, whose name alone "calls to our mind without a recapitulation a series of various and important services rendered by him to the cause of America besides his late brilliant ones in Virginia."[57] Lafayette visited old friends—General Hancock, Samuel Cooper, and the French consul Létombe. He was feted by the officers of the Massachusetts line, was visited by the town council, and addressed by Samuel Adams, making again the kind of gracious

[54] Receipt by Lafayette, November 23, 1781, Gardner-Ball Collection.

[55] The livre tournois was only a money of account in the eighteenth century. It did not exist in fact. It was worth approximately a shilling sterling.

[56] Morris, "Diary," under date of November 28, 1781; Lafayette to Reed, November 28, 1781, Reed, II, 377; *Gazette de Leyde*, February 26, 1781, supplément.

[57] *Boston Independent Chronicle and Universal Advertiser*, December 14, 1781. Cf. *Newport Mercury*, December 22, 1781; Nolan, pp. 211–12.

reply which the occasion demanded and at which he was rapidly becoming expert.[58] A subscription of twenty-five guineas to a fund to rebuild a meeting-house at Charleston, burned during the Battle of Bunker Hill, added greatly to his reputation for generosity.[59]

After several days, ovations began to pall. Noailles, anxious to sail now that the time had been set, wrote a young American friend in broken English: "I think indeed more easy to take a British army than to have a frigate out of Boston harbour. Since my arrival in this town I have been running, speaking, disputing, and I don't believe we shall be able to go to sea before these three days."[60] Twice "three days" passed, and still the "Alliance" lay in Boston harbor. Captain Barry could not get a crew to sail his vessel. He needed two hundred and forty men and had only one hundred and eighty-two. Morris' orders had permitted him to call on the French consul Létombe for French sailors or upon the Massachusetts government for impressed men. The very fact, however, that the "Alliance" was to carry distinguished passengers made it hard for Barry to fill his roster. Good seafaring men could not be induced to embark on a vessel which was forbidden to cruise after easy and profitable prizes but must make a French port as quickly as possible because of its precious passengers; and other naval officers refused to transfer their own men to Barry's frigate.[61] Meanwhile, Lafayette, politely declining an invitation from his old acquaintance, John Paul Jones, to visit Portsmouth, New Hampshire,[62] cooled his heels on board the "Alliance," busying himself in his well-inten-

[58] *Newport Mercury*, December 29, 1781; town records of Boston, December 14, 1781, quoted in Forbes and Cadman, I, 15–16; Nolan, pp. 212–13.

[59] *Newport Mercury*, December 22, 1781; Nolan, p. 213.

[60] Noailles to Molly Robinson, December 14, 1781, Wood, *The Robinson family*, p. 27.

[61] Barry to Samuel Nicholson, December 20, 1781, Barry letter book, Hepburn collection (from transcript in the possession of W. B. Clark, Evanston, Ill.); to Lafayette, December 21, 1781, *ibid.*; to Morris, December 22, 1781, *ibid.*; W. B. Clark, *Gallant John Barry, 1745–1803* (New York, 1938), p. 243.

[62] Lafayette to Jones, December 22, 1781, LC, John Paul Jones papers; De Koven, II, 219.

tioned, officious manner with sending to La Luzerne[63] advice on the affairs of Consul Létombe in Boston and to Washington[64] and Livingston[65] his opinion regarding the suspected patriotism of John Temple, Bowdoin's son-in-law.

At last the "Alliance" was ready to sail. Gradually the number of her crew had increased, and though her captain thought her "very indifferently manned"[66] she had more sailors than he had once believed he needed—two hundred and eighteen Americans and thirty-seven Frenchmen. Barry decided to delay no longer. Farewell notes went out hastily to Knox, Congress, and Washington from the marquis' desk.[67] The one to Washington betrayed his pathetic devotion: "We are going to sail and my last adieu I must dedicate to my beloved general. Adieu, my dear General. I know your heart so well that I am sure that no distance can alter your attachment to me. With the same candor I assure that my love, my respect, my gratitude for you are above expression, that on the moment of leaving you I more than ever felt the strength of those friendly ties that forever bind me to you, and that I anticipate the pleasure, the most wished for pleasure to be again with you and by my zeal and

[63] Lafayette to La Luzerne, December 22, 1781, *AHR*, XX (1915), 611–12.

[64] Lafayette to Washington, December 21–23, 1781, *Mémoires*, I, 474–75. Usually the American edition of the *Mémoires* gives a better text of letters in English than does the French edition. In this case, however, the American edition (pp. 448–49) has been led astray by the copy in Sparks MSS LXXXIV. The copyist here started to copy a long paragraph dealing harshly with Temple but thought better of it, crossed out what little he had copied, and skipped the rest. The French edition at least shows that something was skipped and that a postscript was added on December 23. The American edition and those that have borrowed from it (cf. Gilbert Chinard, *George Washington as the French knew him* [Princeton, 1940], pp. 9–10) omit even those two points. I fortunately discovered among the papers of Lafayette at the Château Lagrange-Blénau a mutilated copy of this letter which appeared to have been saved from a fire. Part of the section dealing with Temple and the whole of the postscript of December 23 were still legible. For the grounds of Lafayette's strictures on Temple see Wharton, IV, 638, and *Journals of Congress*, XXII, 101–2.

[65] Lafayette to Livingston, December 21, 1781, NYPL, Bancroft transcripts.

[66] Barry to Morris, December 22, 1781, *loc. cit.*; Clark, p. 243.

[67] Lafayette to Knox, December 23, [1781], Massachusetts Historical Society; to Congress, December 23, 1781, PCC, no. 156, fols. 256–57; to Washington, December 23, 1781 (postscript to letter of December 21, as cited in n. 64 above).

services to gratify the feelings of my respect and affection."
Any skeptic to whom this effusive language failed to carry conviction would have been convinced upon reading a letter Lafayette had sent the day before to George Augustine Washington.[68] "You will greatly oblige me, my dear friend," he had
written, "to get copies of my letters to the General, as you know
I never kept any, and when I grow old, I will find great satisfaction in reading over our correspondence during last campaign. There is an other thing that would give me great pleasure. The General has several orderly books from the begining
[sic] of the war, and there are orderly books of mine in the light
infantry of the two last campaigns which I would like to have
copied by some sergeant that writes a fair hand and bound up
in the same way as those of the General are." Imitation as well
as sentimentality—not only a sincere form of flattery but also
an undeniable token of the influence that the "General" exerted upon his protégé.

The "Alliance" weighed anchor and sailed down the harbor.
Early on Christmas morning the wind blew from the right direction, and the proud vessel majestically floated away from the
American shore.[69] Captain Barry was disappointed with his mission. He would much have preferred to be allowed to cruise the
Atlantic in search of unsuspecting British merchantmen. He
yielded, however reluctantly, to the orders of Financier Morris
to carry Lafayette and his companions to France as speedily
as wind and weather would permit. On one occasion he even
changed his course to avoid a British vessel that might have
given the "Alliance" some "sport." His crew did not hide their
disappointment, frequently expressing the wish "that the marquis was in France."[70] The captain's graciousness was some-

[68] December 22, 1781, Hunt, *Fragments of Revolutionary history*, pp. 63–64; also
Historical magazine, 2d ser., VIII, 353. The original is in NYPL, Myers, 1224, 2
(where it is incorrectly said to be to George Washington Lewis).

[69] "Rough sketch of the life of Commodore Barry" and "Life of John Kessler" (one
of the "Alliance' " crew), Minnesota Historical Society, Kessler MSS (transcripts in the
possession of W. B. Clark); Clark, p. 244.

[70] "Rough sketch of the life of Commodore Barry," *loc. cit.*; Clark, pp. 244–46.

what rewarded by Lafayette's and Noailles' promise to use their influence when they landed to get fifty or sixty French seamen to join him in a cruise of five or six weeks.[71] An uneventful voyage brought them after twenty-four days to Port Louis across the bay from Lorient. On January 17, Barry's passengers once more set foot on land. Barry soon fell to quarreling with the port authorities regarding the accounts of the Frenchmen in his crew and, getting little satisfaction, vented his anger with Frenchmen in telling Lafayette what he thought of them. The marquis saw to it that a well-filled purse found its way into Barry's hands.[72]

On the next day the French officers, hastening to Lorient, made preparations for a speedy voyage to Paris. Lafayette had barely a moment in which to announce his safe arrival to Washington and Congress.[73] His letters spoke of the happy effect that the capture of Yorktown seemed to have had all over Europe, of the death of Prime Minister Maurepas, and of the birth of a long-awaited dauphin to Marie Antoinette ("from attachment to the queen I have been made particularly happy by this event").[74] He assured both Congress and the general that he would soon return in order to gratify the "sentiments of affection, gratitude, and I may say patriotism" that bound him "so strongly" to America.[75] "However happy I am to be in France and to enjoy the sight of my friends, I anticipate the pleasure to find myself again in a few months on the American shore and to feel that unspeakable satisfaction I ever experi-

[71] Barry to Franklin, January 17, 1782, APS, Franklin papers, Vol. XXIV, Part I, no. 37.

[72] Barry to Lafayette, March 10, 1782, Barry letter book, Hepburn collection; Clark, pp. 245–46.

[73] Lafayette to Washington, January 18, 1782, Sparks MSS LXXXVIII, Part I; to Congress, January 18, 1782 (erroneously dated by Lafayette 1781), PCC, no. 156, fols. 260–61.

[74] Lafayette to Washington, January 18, 1782, *loc. cit.* This sentence has been omitted from the amended text given in *Mémoires*, II, 15–17 (the editors being careful to hide Lafayette's early loyalty to Marie Antoinette).

[75] Lafayette to Congress, January 18, 1782, *loc. cit.*

enced when after an absence I could once more arrive at head-quarters."[76] The letters dispatched, Lafayette and his friends set out on their journey. Three days of hard riding brought them at last to Paris.

BIBLIOGRAPHICAL NOTES

Tower and Doniol cease to be of value for the life of Lafayette after the capture of Yorktown. J. A. Stevens, "Visit of Lafayette to the United States 1784" (*Magazine of American history*, II [1878], 724–33) and Nolan's *Lafayette in America day by day* are helpful secondary sources for this chapter. I am especially indebted to Mr. William Bell Clark not only for his careful and charming biography of Barry but for his generosity in placing his notes on Lafayette at my disposal.

[76] Lafayette to Washington, January 18, 1782, *loc. cit.*

CHAPTER XV

Franklin's Aide

THE carriage that bore Lafayette rolled up before the
Noailles town house in the Faubourg St. Honoré early
in the afternoon. A joyous band of market women, having learned somehow that he was coming, had gathered at the
mansion gate. As he stepped out of his carriage, they crowded
around him, offering branches of laurel.[1] Inside the house he
found his two children—"grown up so much that I find myself
great deal older than I apprehended."[2] A rapid fire of questions
revealed that Mme de Lafayette was not at home. She had gone
to the Hôtel de Ville to attend a banquet given by the king and
queen to celebrate the birth of their long-awaited son three
months earlier. It would probably be hours before Their Majes-
ties could decently leave, and no one would presume to leave
before them. Then it would take hours for the procession of
coaches to move along the wintry streets in appointed order as
the ladies accompanied the queen to the château of La Muette
near the Bois de Boulogne.

The marquis prepared to wait for six or seven hours. Sooner
than he could have expected, however, a sudden commotion
filled the air. The clatter of hoofs and carriage wheels upon the
paving stones of the Rue St. Honoré revealed that the royal
procession would pass by his very door. He went to the gate to
pay his respects to Her Majesty and perhaps to catch a glimpse

[1] Métra, XII, 273–74; M. de Lescure (ed.), *Correspondance secrète inédite sur Louis XVI, Marie-Antoinette, la cour et la ville de 1777 à 1792* (2 vols.; Paris, 1866), I, 458–59.

[2] Lafayette to Washington, January 30, 1782, Sparks MSS LXXXVIII, Part I, pp. 3–4; *Mémoires*, II, 17–20.

of his wife. The queen's carriage stopped before the Noailles house, and sitting beside Marie Antoinette was his Adrienne![3]

The king and queen, when the news of the young husband's return reached the Hôtel de Ville, had tried to induce Adrienne to leave the banquet, knowing, as all Paris society knew, how hard the separation had been for the devoted wife. But Adrienne remembered her manners and begged only that the cortège should pass by the Noailles hôtel on the way to La Muette so that she might see her husband as he paid his respects to the queen. Her gracious Majesty immediately called her carriage, invited the astonished Adrienne to join her, and followed by a retinue of noblewomen who outranked the Lafayettes and should normally have preceded Adrienne they had come to where the marquis now stood to salute them. The queen spoke affably to him, congratulating him warmly on his victories and safe return and then, despite the gentle protests of Adrienne, ordered her to stay with her husband.[4] As Adrienne stepped from the royal carriage, a vast crowd that had gathered to see the queen and the victor of Yorktown broke into lively applause.[5] Trembling and faint with joy, Adrienne fell into her Gilbert's arms, and he carried her into the house. For a long time afterward, Adrienne later confessed, she would grow weak whenever her husband entered a room where she was and, afraid to become a nuisance to him, would try to restrain her feelings.[6]

The day after his return Lafayette went to La Muette to report to the king and to pay his respects. Louis XVI greeted him cordially and paid him many compliments. The king spoke of Washington in terms of "confidence, regard, admiration and affection,"[7] though he would make no promises of future aid to America. The noblemen of the court crowded around Lafayette

---

[3] Métra, XII, 273–74; Comte de Ségur, *Mémoires ou souvenirs et anecdotes* (3 vols.; Paris, 1825–27), I, 245–46; "Mes loisirs" (unpublished journal of the book dealer Hardy), BN, fonds français 6684, Vol. IV, fol. 97 (under date of January 22, 1782); *Gazette de Leyde*, February 1, 1782.

[4] Hardy, "Mes loisirs," *loc. cit.*

[5] *Gazette de Leyde*, February 1, 1782. [6] Lasteyrie, pp. 202–3 and 425.

[7] Lafayette to Washington, January 30, 1782, *loc. cit.*

and expressed their approval.[8] Many of them began to seek permission to go to America and emulate his example.

The approbation of several court nobles was short lived. It was already noised abroad that the king had awarded some signal honors to those who had distinguished themselves in the capture of Cornwallis. For Lafayette the king's award proved to be the rank of *maréchal-de-camp*. Lafayette's seniority rights were to date from the capture of Yorktown, though he was not to take his new rank until peace was declared. Meanwhile, he was to retain his rank of major-general (equivalent to that of *maréchal-de-camp*) in the American army. It was expressly stipulated that this honor was only for Lafayette and was not to be regarded as a precedent for any other French officer in the American service.[9] The marquis' command of the King's Dragoons, it was eventually decided, would go to the Vicomte de Noailles. He sold his commission to Noailles for 60,000 livres, though he had paid 80,000 for it himself. Poix provided the money for his younger brother.[10]

Many officers were wounded to the quick by the honors showered upon their colleague.[11] Some of them had been in the army before he was born and had now to watch him skip over the heads of all the older colonels and all the brigadiers to become *maréchal-de-camp* at the age of twenty-four. Every man to receive that rank in the next six years had been his senior in service.[12] Complaints came quickly to the ears of Lafayette and the Marquis de Ségur, the new minister of war. The young soldier offered to decline his promotion, but when the minister, father of Lafayette's friend and relative, the Comte de Ségur, maintained that his authority would then be jeopardized and

---

[8] *Gazette de Leyde*, February 1, 1782.

[9] Marquis de Ségur to Lafayette, December 5, 1781, *Mémoires*, I, 473–74.

[10] Poix to St. Paul, January 27, 1782, AMG, Lafayette dossier 1261; receipt of Lafayette, February 2, 1782, *ibid.*

[11] Comtesse de Boufflers to Gustavus III, February 18, 1782, A. Vivie, "Lettres de Gustave III à la Comtesse de Boufflers et de la comtesse au roi," *Actes de l'Académie Nationale des Sciences, Belles Lettres, et Arts de Bordeaux*, LX (1898), 239–40; Bachaumont, XX, 72.

[12] "Lafayette jugé par le Comte d'Espinchal," *Revue retrospective*, XX (1894), 293. Cf. Comte d'Allonville, *Mémoires secrets de 1770 à 1830* (2 vols.; Paris, 1838), I, 101.

he would feel called upon to resign, Lafayette decided to do nothing about it.[13] At that time began the hostility of some of the noblemen of France toward their youthful superior. "They say that he did nothing extraordinary," one of the *nouvellistes* of the day recorded, "and they might well have done as much if they had had the same opportunities."[14]

But for others the victor of Yorktown, the friend of Washington, remained a popular hero. Vergennes had written him (in a letter which Lafayette received only after his arrival in Paris), "History records few examples of as complete a success [as yours]. . . . . You may rest assured that your name is held here in veneration";[15] and Vergennes was not mistaken. Lafayette himself declared that his reception "surpassed my utmost ambition."[16] Despite his youth, he was feted by the old Maréchal de Richelieu. Together with all the marshals of France he drank to the health of George Washington "with great veneration" and was requested to present the homage of the marshals to Washington.[17] King Gustavus III invited him to visit Sweden.[18] Artists came to paint his portrait. His exploits received the attention of historians and dramatists. Verses and pamphlets were written in his honor, and well-known songs that referred to ancient heroes were now applied to him and sung with a new zest.[19] People followed him in crowds "to see a hero,"[20] among

---

[13] *Mémoires*, IV, 4–5.   [14] Bachaumont, XX, 72.

[15] December 1, 1781, AAE, corr. pol., É.-U., Vol. XIX, fols. 307–8; cf. Doniol, IV, 685–89, and Vergennes to Lafayette, January 23, 1782, Morgan Library, Lafayette, Vol. II.

[16] Lafayette to Washington, January 30, 1782, *loc. cit.*

[17] *Ibid.*; cf. Comtesse de Boufflers to Gustavus III, February 18, 1782, *loc. cit.*

[18] Vivie, "Lettres de Gustave III," pp. 216, 220, 221, and 251–52.

[19] Cf. I. M. Hays (ed.), *Calendar of the papers of Benjamin Franklin in the library of the American Philosophical Society* (5 vols.; Philadelphia, 1908), III, 430, and IV, 79; Bachaumont, XX, 127 and 313; M. R. Hillard d'Auberteuil, *Essais historiques et politiques sur la Révolution de l'Amérique septentrionale* (2 vols.; Brussels, 1781–82), II, 425–36; St. John de Crèvecœur, *Lettres d'un cultivateur américain*, etc. (3 vols.; Paris, 1787 [1st ed.; London, 1782]), I, i–v; APS, Franklin papers, Vol. LI, no. 86; *Journal de Paris*, March 1, 1782, p. 237; Métra, XII, 307.

[20] Basmarein to Lafayette, [*ca.* February, 1782], Robert Castex, "Armateur de La Fayette, Pierre de Basmarein," *Revue des questions historiques*, 3d ser., VI (1925), 123–24.

them Pierre de Basmarein, who had driven a hard bargain with Lafayette for the boat on which he had first gone to America but was now reduced by misfortunes to beg favors of his former customer. In her own hand the queen copied from Belloy's patriotic tragedy *Gaston et Bayard* some verses[21] that in the popular mind were frequently applied to the modern paladin. For he likewise "loved battles like a young soldier" but "like an old general knew how to avoid them." The lines ended on a note of unmistakable esteem:

> I admire his prudence and I love his courage;
> With those two virtues, a soldier has no age.

Street singers good humoredly protested the hubbub the young hero had caused:

> That a warrior flies to do battle
> To the far off American strand,
> That over the quarrels of England
> He gets himself all in a rattle—
> That's of no matter, I think.
> My humor's of peace-talk to tattle.
> That's of no matter, I think.
> As I carol and as I drink.[22]

One day when Paris' new darling went to the Opéra with some friends to see the famous Mme Darlay in *Iphigénie en Aulide*, the actress, at the point where she was supposed to crown Achilles with laurel, indicated that she ought to place the crown on Lafayette's head instead. Applause resounded through the house and continued until Lafayette satisfied the audience with a little speech of thanks.[23] But the reward that was perhaps most cherished by the new Achilles was the favor of Aglaé de Hunolstein. She now considered herself happy to be counted among his friends.[24] Soon gossip, not mistaken for once, reported that something more than friendliness existed between them.

[21] Mme Campan, *Mémoires sur la vie de Marie Antoinette*, etc. ("Bibliothèque de mémoires relatifs à l'histoire de France pendant le 18⁰ et le 19⁰ siècle," ed. F. Barrière, vol. X [Paris, 1886]), p. 178.

[22] Bachaumont, XX, 313; cf. Gottschalk, *Lady-in-waiting*, p. 90.

[23] Métra, XII, 307; Bachaumont, XX, 71–72; *Newport Mercury*, July 6, 1782; *Gazette de Leyde*, February 19, 1782.

[24] Cf. Gottschalk, *Lady-in-waiting*, pp. 54 and 90–95.

Amidst plaudits and admiration Lafayette did not forget that he was a soldier on leave for a special mission. In fact, "the reception I have met with," he wrote to Congress,[25] "is the more flattering to me as it evinces nothing weighs so much with the nation and her sovereign as an ardent zeal for the cause of America and honorable testimonies of her confidence." He had expected to call on Franklin on the day after his arrival in Paris,[26] but Franklin's gout had kept him away; and Vergennes in his turn pleaded (quite truthfully) the pressure of other duties as his excuse for not coming himself to call upon the marquis.[27] Franklin, nevertheless, greeted Lafayette's return with "great joy"[28] and proved only too willing to accept him as "a political aid de camp,"[29] while Vergennes begged his former protégé "to procure me as soon as possible the opportunity to speak with you."[30] Within the first week of his arrival in Paris, Lafayette had seen not only Franklin and Vergennes but also, on Franklin's request, every other one of the king's ministers and had argued for a new loan to America—"with greater weight than I could possibly do," Franklin admitted.[31] Vergennes on two recent occasions[32] had frankly confessed his distress over the lack of energy that he thought he saw in America and the too great willingness to depend upon France. "I am not marvellously pleased with the country that you have just left," he told Lafayette.[33] "I find it barely active and very demanding." Lafayette reported to Franklin that, though he still hoped to win over the ministers, the loan was bound to be small, and it would be best "to act as if none were to be expected."[34] To Washing-

[25] January 29, 1782, PCC, no. 156, fols. 264–66.

[26] Barry to Franklin, January 31, 1782, APS, Franklin papers, Vol. XXIV, Part I, no. 52; Lafayette to Franklin, January 22, 1782, *ibid.*, no. 39.

[27] Vergennes to Lafayette, January 23, 1782, *loc. cit.*

[28] Franklin to Carmichael, January 25, 1782, Smyth, VIII, 370.

[29] Lafayette to Congress, January 29, 1782, *loc. cit.*

[30] Vergennes to Lafayette, January 23, 1782, *loc. cit.*

[31] Franklin to Morris, January 28, 1782, Smyth, VIII, 374.

[32] December 1, 1781, *loc. cit.*; January 23, 1782, *loc. cit.*

[33] January 23, 1782, *loc. cit.*   [34] Franklin to Morris, January 28, 1782, *loc. cit.*

ton he wrote[35] that he found it "very difficult, next to impossible to get money." Nor would he promise much more on the score of major operations for the ensuing campaign. "For it is generally thought in this quarter that the exertions of America are not equal to her abilities."

In lesser undertakings Franklin's aide-de-camp encountered fewer obstacles. He was able to persuade the minister of the marine to ship American stores in stout bottoms. He secured for Captain Barry permission to apply for enough American sailors in French ports to enable him to make his cruise—too late, since Barry had started off without them.[36] He gave expert advice to agents of the American states on the proper choice of supplies and munitions.[37] He arranged at his own expense for a letter of credit of £500 for the use of Henry Laurens, now on parole in London,[38] and contributed generously to the support of the arts and the worthy poor.[39] He frequently exchanged calls with the friends of America and of Ireland.[40] Nor did he forget the French soldiers who had distinguished themselves under his orders in America, urging their promotion and reward, sometimes paying their expenses out of his own pocket.[41] Though he was richer now than he had ever been, having inherited while he was in America the lands in Brittany which had belonged to his great-grandfather, the Comte de La Rivière, his

[35] January 30, 1782, loc. cit.

[36] Lafayette to Franklin, February 12, 1782, Sparks MSS XVI, pp. 320–23; cf. Clark, p. 249.

[37] Lafayette to Searle, March 23, 1782, Historical Society of Pennsylvania.

[38] Lafayette to Laurens, April 14, 1782, [A. S. Sally, Jr. (ed.)], "Letters from the Marquis de Lafayette to Hon. Henry Laurens, 1777–1780," South Carolina historical and genealogical magazine, IX (1908), 173–75.

[39] Lafayette to Faget [or Inget], July 11, 1782, Historical Society of Pennsylvania; memoir of Gouvion, 1782, André Lasseray, Les Français sous les treize étoiles 1775–1782 (2 vols.; Macon, 1935), I, 237; ibid., p. 273 n.; letter of credit for Henry Laurens, April 12, 1782, "Letters from Lafayette to Laurens," p. 175; Girodie, p. 42, no. 56a.

[40] Cf. Edward Newenham to Miles, October 9, 1782, W. A. Miles, Correspondence on the French Revolution (2 vols.; London, 1890), I, 7–8; "Letters of Mrs. Ralph Izard to Mrs. William Lee," Virginia magazine of history and biography, VIII (1900), 21–22.

[41] Cf. receipt of Capitaine, May 8, 1782, Girodie, p. 68, no. 101; Marquis de Ségur to Lafayette, May 12, 1782, AN, C 358, dossier 1901; see also n. 39 above.

intendant Morizot soon began to complain that he would himself have to "resort to strange purses" in order to meet the demands that Lafayette was making on him.[42]

But Lafayette never lost sight of his major duties as Congress' diplomatic agent and gladly—persistently, in fact—took upon his own shoulders the responsibility of interviewing ministers. Franklin, much less mobile and somewhat less sanguine, willingly took advantage of "the general esteem and affection" of one who "promises to be a great man here."[43] And the marquis immensely enjoyed the new role of diplomatic agent. "Mr. Franklin cannot render his friend more happy," he admitted,[44] "than in employing him for the service of America, and he feels a particular pleasure in avoiding for the doctor the trouble of journeys to Versailles where his peculiar situation calls him two or three times a week." Finding that separate conferences with Vergennes, Castries, and Ségur created unnecessary duplication of effort, he induced them to form "a committee of the three ministers" that he might "debate with them all."[45] Finally, Vergennes asked him for a précis of the points he had made in their conversations; and Lafayette pointed out in a lengthy memoir[46] America's need for ten or twelve millions and the desirability of a powerful demonstration against New York or Charleston.

The young soldier's importunities at length were rewarded. After more than a month of interviews he was able to announce that Vergennes wished to communicate to the American minister personally the sum of money that would be forthcoming.[47]

[42] Quoted in Girodie, p. 25, no. 33.

[43] Franklin to Livingston, March 4, 1782, Smyth, VIII, 389.

[44] Lafayette to Franklin, February 25, 1782, APS, Franklin papers, Vol. XXIV, no. 100.

[45] Lafayette to Franklin, February 12, 1782, loc. cit.

[46] "Note de differents objets relatifs à l'Amérique sur lesquels M. le Comte de Vergennes demande un précis de nos conversations," Stevens, Facsimiles, XVII, no. 1641. This "Note" is filed in AAE, mémoires et documents, É.-U., Vol. II, fols. 97–99, just before another dated April 18, 1782. Stevens and others have therefore assumed it to be of about that date. The contents indicate, however, that it precedes Vergennes' endorsement (ca. February 25, 1782) of the first loan in 1782 to the United States.

[47] Lafayette to Franklin, February 25, 1782, loc. cit.

Though it would be small, Franklin could have it whenever he chose to ask for it. It proved to be a loan of six millions to be paid quarterly, beginning in March, 1782.[48] Shortly afterward the ministry also agreed to a reinforcement of Rochambeau's army.[49]

No sooner was success achieved in one diplomatic area than Lafayette's attention was called to difficulties in another. This time it was John Jay, accredited by the United States to the Spanish court, who needed his assistance. Though Spain had for nearly three years been an ally of France in the war against England, she had refused, on various pretexts but chiefly out of the fear of a strong Protestant republic in the Western Hemisphere, to recognize the independence of France's ally. Jay was constantly referred back and forth from one official to another until his patience was exhausted. When he received the resolution of Congress urging him to correspond with Lafayette, he was nothing loath to take advantage of the illustrious soldier's prestige.[50] The marquis immediately placed the details of Jay's frustration before Franklin, Vergennes, and other French ministers,[51] while he hastened to give the perplexed Jay an assurance he did not himself feel. Spanish "generosity and frankness," he wrote, would not leave to Holland, where Minister John Adams was daily expecting the recognition of American independence, "the credit of first entering into this measure."[52] But his carefully coded report to Washington indicated that he expected only delay—if not, indeed, interference—from Spain.[53] The unco-operative spirit of the Spanish government, as he had discovered in a long conversation with Louis XVI and his ministers, was one of the obstacles in the way of more vigorous French support to the United States. For the French ministers were

[48] Franklin to Morris, March 4, 1782, Smyth, VIII, 385–86.

[49] Lafayette to Vergennes, April 18, 1782, Stevens, *Facsimiles*, XVII, no. 1642.

[50] Jay to Franklin, March 1, 1782, H. P. Johnston (ed.), *Correspondence and public papers of John Jay* (3 vols.; New York, 1890), II, 263–64.

[51] Lafayette to Vergennes, March 20, 1781, *Mémoires*, II, 20–23.

[52] March 28, 1782, NYPL, Bancroft transcripts, America 1781, I, 281.

[53] March 30, 1782, Sparks MSS LXXXVIII, Part I, fols. 5–8 (of which a garbled version is given in *Mémoires*, II, 23–27, and hence elsewhere).

planning to fix their attention upon the Antilles, where Spanish support would be more readily available.

Yet other news from Spain and elsewhere was vastly encouraging. The Spanish captured Port Mahon in Minorca, and the siege of Gibraltar seemed to hold out a chance of success. New victories in the West Indies were also reported. The opposition to Lord North, the English minister who stubbornly refused to recognize defeat in America, had grown strong enough to force him out.[54] Having been invited with his wife for a few days' Easter visit at the Marquis de Castries' countryseat in Antony near Paris, Lafayette devoted part of his holiday to relaying these grounds for cheerfulness to friends and officials.[55] Again protesting his devotion to America, he explained that his only reason for not returning immediately was his feeling that he could be more useful as a diplomat in France than as a soldier in America. "I am perfectly satisfied with the dispositions of this Government. Both nations will forever be attached to each other; and I see both are so much the object of British envy and treachery that it will ciment [sic] among them an eternal amity and alliance."[56]

Faint signs of British willingness to sue for peace began to appear. An effort was made through an unofficial agent to seduce France to a separate negotiation, but Vergennes, seeing both sentimental and practical reasons for joint negotiations, replied that "France would never treat without her allies." Lafayette hastened to warn Livingston against similarly "insidious proposals" to win the United States away from France. "France is the only true friend on whom America should rely in Europe."[57] He learned shortly afterward that Adams, on being sounded out at The Hague on the prospects of a separate

[54] Lafayette to Washington, March 31, 1782, Sparks MSS LXXXVIII, Part I, fol. 9.

[55] Lafayette to Livingston, March 30, 1782, LC, Washington papers, no. 56, fol. 353; to Morris, March 30, 1782, Parke-Bernet Galleries catalogue, no. 251, January, 1941, John Griswold Collection, Part II, p. 88, item 375; to Congress, March 30, 1782, PCC, no. 156, fols. 270–71. (There is another letter of the same date, which, though it is said by Wharton [V, 283] to be to Livingston, is perhaps to the president of Congress [PCC, no. 156, fols. 274–75].)

[56] Lafayette to Washington, March 30, 1782, *loc. cit.*

[57] Lafayette to Livingston, March 30, 1782, LC, Washington papers, no. 56, fol. 353.

peace between England and the United States, had answered that "independence was the first step, and nothing could be done but in concert with France."[58]

Franklin, nevertheless, did not wish to close all doors to negotiations. Fortunately, one of his acquaintances proved to be a friend of some of the new British ministers. Franklin proposed to explain to him, if Vergennes consented, that France would make no unreasonable demands in return for peace, and Lafayette agreed to find out whether Vergennes would approve such a maneuver.[59] Franklin himself wrote to the new British secretary of state, Lord Shelburne, mentioning no particular demands but indicating a longing for general peace.[60]

Such maneuvers could not be expected to have immediate results; and Lafayette, too long delayed in France, began in April to prepare to return to America and his beloved Light Division.[61] Many ambitious young noblemen planned to precede him with a new expeditionary force into a campaign that all expected to be glorious and final. "Our young lords," one of the journalists of the day reported, "all want to become little Lafayettes."[62] Among them were several who had once thought of their now illustrious compeer in patronizing, if friendly, fashion—the Comte de Ségur (son of the minister of war), the Prince de Broglie (oldest son of the marshal), and the Chevalier de Lameth (nephew of the same marshal and brother of the man badly wounded before Yorktown). They carried warm letters of introduction from him to Washington, Morris, Knox, La Luzerne, George Augustine Washington, and Hamilton.[63] In

[58] Lafayette to Jay, April 28, 1782, NYPL, Bancroft transcripts, America 1782, II, 235–36.

[59] Lafayette to Vergennes, March 20, 1782, Doniol, V, 76.

[60] Franklin to Shelburne, March 22, 1782, Smyth, VIII, 460–61.

[61] Franklin to Morris, March 30, 1782, *ibid.*, p. 404; to Livingston, March 30 and April 8, 1782, *ibid.*, pp. 406 and 422; to Washington, April 2, 1782, *ibid.*, p. 412.

[62] Lescure, I, 462.

[63] Lafayette to Washington, April 12, 1782 (two letters), Sparks MSS LXXXVIII, Part I, fols. 10 and 12–13 (one of which is translated in *Mémoires*, II, 27–29); to Morris, April 12, 1782 (two letters), LC, Robert Morris collection, and Historical Society of Pennsylvania; to Knox, April 12, 1782, Massachusetts Historical Society; to La

those letters he lamented that his sense of duty retained him in France, where feelers for peace were being cautiously put out by both nations and where he therefore felt he would continue to be most useful. "The late change of ministry," he wrote to Henry Laurens[64] (still on parole in London), "is so far pleasing as Wighish [*sic*] appearances, tho' in an enemy, cannot fail to be agreeable. As a French man, as an American I very little care who governs Great Britain. Never shall I forgive (tho' it is pretty well paid for) British haughtiness and cruelty to *us poor Rebels*. But, on account of Humanity at large, I heartily wish, tho' I am far from believing, the sacred flame of Liberty may some what be kindled in that quarter." Meanwhile he promised to direct his energies toward obtaining a general, as opposed to a partial or separate, peace.

Time wore on without producing any definite bid for peace. The French government began again to think in earnest of a vigorous effort in the ensuing campaign. Vergennes once more asked the American major-general how best to aid the American cause. Lafayette replied in another of his lengthy memoirs[65] (perhaps previously submitted for approval to Franklin),[66] reminding the minister that he spoke not only as an emissary of America but also as "a Frenchman who submits everything to the good of his country." "The Americans," Lafayette confessed, "are tired of war, and the people long for the end of their suffering, but the most tempting proposals made by [British] ministers, once beloved and still respected, will obtain nothing contrary to the terms of the treaty [with France] or even to the obligations of gratitude." Under the circumstances, however, he felt that any retrenchment of the aid that France had led America to expect would have a bad effect. In addition to the

---

Luzerne, April 12, 1782, *AHR*, XX (1915), 612; to G. A. Washington, April 12, 1782, *Massachusetts Historical Society proceedings*, VI (1890–91), 169–71; to Hamilton, April 12, 1782, *Works of Hamilton*, I, 277–78.

[64] April 14, 1782, "Letters from Lafayette to Laurens," pp. 173–75.

[65] "Mémoire sur les affaires d'Amérique," April 18, 1781, Stevens, *Facsimiles*, XVII, no. 1642, enclosed in Lafayette to Vergennes, April 24, 1781, *ibid.*, no. 1643.

[66] Lafayette to Franklin, [*ca.* April 18, 1782], LC, Franklin papers, no. 2273.

promised reinforcement of Rochambeau, an earnest effort must be made to reduce either New York or Charleston; and he recurred once more to his old scheme of invasion of Newfoundland and Canada.

The new English ministry, prompted by Dutch readiness to recognize American independence, proved anxious not to fight another campaign. Emissaries soon came to Vergennes, Franklin, and Adams with proposals that met with a uniform reply: the allies would treat together, or they would not treat at all.[67] Lafayette began to fear that the Spaniards' desire to conquer Gibraltar would prove a stumbling block to an early peace and wished "the devilish rock was out of the way."[68] Just as he had come to the conclusion that there would be a new campaign, which "in Europe at least, is going to be a Spanish one,"[69] Franklin's old friend, Richard Oswald, sent by Lord Shelburne, came to see the American plenipotentiary, who introduced him to Vergennes. Lafayette learned about these visits from the French ministers.[70] It began to appear that England was willing to make a general peace based upon the acknowledgment of American independence. Without that acknowledgment, the young patriot declared, "I had rather fight for ten years longer."[71]

Lafayette now somewhat officiously urged Adams to come to Paris for the expected negotiations. And the invitation contained noteworthy evidence on the development of the marquis' political credo. Complimenting the Massachusetts republican on having won Dutch recognition of the United States, he employed terms that, more clearly than any language he had so far used, showed to what extent he had begun to question the divinity that doth hedge a king: "Though the court air has not so much altered my republican principles as to make me believe the opinion of a king is every thing, I was the other day pleased

[67] Lafayette to Jay, April 28, 1782, *loc. cit.*　　[68] *Ibid.*

[69] Lafayette to Adams, May 7, 1782, Adams, VII, 582.

[70] Benjamin Franklin, "Journal of the negotiations for peace with Great Britain," Smyth, VIII, 492.

[71] Lafayette to Adams, May 7, 1782, *loc. cit.*

to hear the King of France speak of you in terms of the highest regard."[72] Shortly afterward, in acknowledging the work of an author named Le Brigant on America's right to independence (apparently the first book of political philosophy he had read in a long time), Lafayette lauded the Declaration of Independence and for the first time wrote the fearsome words "natural right against tyranny."[73] The education of the young "republican" was fast nearing completion.

Adams replied didactically to Lafayette's letter.[74] The republican form of government, he announced, was "the best of which human nature is capable." For "two republican powers, Athens and Rome, have done more honor to the species than all the rest of it," and "America would at this moment have been a howling wilderness inhabited only by bears and savages without such forms of government" and "would again become a wilderness under any other." Yet he was not an enthusiast who wished to overturn empires and monarchies. "I am no king-killer, king-hater, or king-despiser." When kings were enlightened like Louis XVI of France, Frederick of Prussia, or the Emperor Joseph of Germany, he was ready to admire them. "You may well think, then, that the information you give me that the King of France was pleased the other day to speak to you of me in terms of the highest regard gave me great pleasure." If Adams might take such self-conscious delight in royal attention, Lafayette could be forgiven for not yet having become entirely republican.

Meanwhile, a little progress was made in the search for peace. Oswald was soon reinforced in Paris by Thomas Grenville. Lafayette then found that Franklin had paid several visits to Versailles in company with the British agents. Negotiations through two gentlemen who had no authority except to sound out the allied representatives and to report to London seemed patently awkward, and Lafayette immediately offered a suggestion that would have made communication between the two capitals more direct and effective. He had learned that the

[72] *Ibid.*, p. 581.

[73] May 16, 1782, Gardner-Ball Collection. [74] May 21, 1782, Adams, VII, 593–94.

French had sent a representative to London during the negotiations (likewise in Paris) that had brought the previous war between England and France to a close in 1763. Why not send him
on a similar mission now? He was "an American citizen,"
spoke both languages, and was well acquainted with American
interests.[75]

Franklin thought Lafayette's suggestion a good one and encouraged him to propose it to the French ministry. Lafayette
also asked to meet Oswald and Grenville, and Franklin agreed
to invite them all to breakfast together. The breakfast of the
American sage, the French-American soldier, and the two British agents proved a great success. "The gentlemen . . . . had a
good deal of conversation at and after breakfast, staid till after
one o'clock, and parted much pleased with each other."[76] For
two more weeks nothing happened to advance Lafayette's ambition. Then Grenville informed Franklin that he had at last
received full power to treat for peace with France and her allies,
but he would not enter upon his duties until France saw fit to
send a similar mission to London. That afternoon Lafayette
called on Franklin and learned of Grenville's conditions. It
seemed proper, they agreed, for the marquis now to propose to
Vergennes that he "be the person employ'd in that service."[77]

Lafayette's interview with Vergennes, however, proved to be
a great disappointment. The minister informed Lafayette that
Grenville had been empowered to treat only with France. Since
the French government had already on several occasions refused to enter upon negotiations unless the American commission were to enjoy an equal footing, there could be no question
of sending a similar mission to London. Lafayette imparted
this disturbing information to Franklin. Hastening to court,
the American diplomat was permitted to examine Grenville's
letter of power. It did, indeed, fail to mention France's allies.
Franklin, seeking for an explanation of this sudden change of
front on the part of a ministry that had seemed ready for any

[75] Franklin's "Journal," Smyth, VIII, 492–93.
[76] *Ibid.*, pp. 493 and 495–96 (under date of May 10–11, 1782).
[77] *Ibid.*, p. 512 (under date of May 26, 1782).

terms of peace, found it in the recent capture of De Grasse by Admiral George Rodney at the Saints in the Antilles. That victory led the British to believe that they could now avoid the humiliation of recognizing American independence. Vergennes assured the anxious American plenipotentiary that the king would never agree to any negotiations inconsistent with the dignity of his country.[78]

Once more Lafayette began to think of returning to the United States. English spies and Paris rumor, which he had not discouraged, already had him on his way; and in America he was daily expected—some said, with a numerous fleet and a large body of soldiers.[79] The Comte de Ségur, arrived in America, wrote to his wife: "Tell Lafayette that I am in a country filled with his name where everyone adores him."[80] None looked forward to his return with greater interest than George Washington. The affection of the two men had now become proverbial. French travelers in America considered it natural to speak to Washington of Lafayette as to a father of a son. One of Lafayette's friends, the Prince de Broglie, on arriving at Washington's headquarters, found that the stern soldier's face grew soft and wreathed in a kindly smile as they drank a toast to Lafayette.[81]

Yet, until it was certain that there would be no peace, Lafayette was unwilling to start off to rejoin his beloved general. Days passed without producing for Grenville the desired power to treat with France's allies as well as with France. Once when

[78] *Ibid.*, p. 513 (under date of May 28 and 29, 1782).

[79] Public Record Office, FO miscellany, 2 (1780–1805), intelligences, received from Lord North, March 13, 1782; *ibid.*, advices, received May 4, 1782, no. 32; *Heath papers, part III*, p. 361; Historical Manuscripts Commission, *Fifth report* (Shelburne MSS) (London, 1876), p. 253; *Maryland Gazette*, June 6 and September 26, 1782; *Newport Mercury*, June 22, 1782; *Boston Independent Chronicle and Universal Advertiser*, September 26, 1782; *Calendar of Washington correspondence*, III, 2129; Burnett, VI, 358; Muhlenberg, p. 415.

[80] [September, 1782 ?], B. Van Vorst, "L'Amérique au XVIIIᵉ siècle d'après un voyageur français," *Revue des deux mondes*, 5th ser., LX (1910), 209.

[81] E. W. Balch (tr.), "Narrative of the Prince de Broglie," *Magazine of American history*, I (1877), 309; Duc de Broglie, *Deux français aux États-Unis et dans la Nouvelle Espagne en 1782: Journal de voyage du Prince de Broglie et lettre du Comte de Ségur* (Paris, 1903), p. 58; cf. Clark, p. 268.

Grenville asked the marquis when he expected to go to America, the young man replied that he had already stayed longer than he had intended in order to learn whether there would be peace or war, but "I see that the expectation of peace is a joke and that you only amuse us without any real intention of treating." He therefore expected to set out in a few days.[82] Franklin, meanwhile, had nothing more vital to negotiate than the release from parole of Lord Cornwallis in exchange for that of Henry Laurens. As one of the generals to whom Cornwallis and his officers had surrendered, Lafayette was consulted at every stage in that negotiation.[83]

Cornwallis' release was somewhat delayed by the honors that were being showered upon the visiting Czarevitch Paul of Russia and his wife. Lafayette was called upon to attend many of these functions. Reviews, dinners, balls, and tours of the illustrious institutions of France consumed time that was needed for other things.[84] But such activity likewise had its compensations. Everywhere Lafayette received honors only second to those of the "Comte du Nord," as the heir to the Russian throne chose to be called; and on one occasion when the "Comte du Nord" visited the Grand Chamber of Parlement, the highest court in the land, and the advocate-general made a complimentary speech in his honor, modest Adrienne de Lafayette, who happened to be among the prince's escort, was singled out for similar compliments.[85] The festivities in honor of Paul wound up with a grand ball in the Hall of Mirrors at Versailles, lighted with five thousand candles for the occasion; and the Duc de Croÿ, who had already been charmed by Lafayette's manners, now felt that the most distinguished moment of the ball came

[82] Franklin's "Journal," Smyth, VIII, 535; cf. *ibid.*, p. 521.

[83] Grenville to Fox, May 23, 1782, John Russell (ed.), *Memorials and correspondence of Charles James Fox* (4 vols.; London, 1853), IV, 205; Franklin's "Journal," Smyth, VIII, 530–32 and 534.

[84] Cf. Franklin's "Journal," Smyth, VIII, 534; Gottschalk, *Lady-in-waiting*, pp. 91–94.

[85] M. F. Barrière (ed.), *Mémoires de Weber frère de lait de Marie-Antoinette, reine de France* ("Bibliothèque des mémoires relatifs à l'histoire de France pendant le 18ᵉ et le 19ᵉ siècle," Vol. VII [Paris, 1885]), p. 80.

when the queen, dressed as La Belle Gabrielle, danced with La-fayette.[86] The last time Lafayette had danced with Marie An-toinette, he had won only titters for his awkwardness; but that was long, long ago—before he had won glory and self-confidence in America.

When, finally, the Grand-Duke Paul left the capital, Lafa-yette found time to turn to diplomacy once more. He went to breakfast with Franklin at Passy, taking with him Major Alex-ander Ross, Cornwallis' aide-de-camp, who had come to push forward the release from parole of Cornwallis and his aides. Franklin felt he had only a shadow of authority to deal with Cornwallis' parole, since, having been empowered by Congress to exchange Laurens for General Burgoyne, he would have to take upon himself the responsibility of substituting Cornwallis for Burgoyne. As for the aides, he preferred to leave that en-tirely to Lafayette. He therefore drew up a release for Corn-wallis alone, subject to the approval of Congress. Major Ross proved unwilling to accept that condition and left dissatisfied. The next day Ross sought the advice of Oswald, who convinced him that Franklin had acted properly. The major returned to Franklin's house and declared his willingness to accept a con-ditional release for Cornwallis and his aides. Franklin, pleading that he had no authority whatsoever with regard to the aides, sent him again to the marquis.[87] Lafayette proved willing to assume that responsibility if Franklin concurred ("for you know in our American government one must be cautious").[88] "We must in this moment," he wrote, "do every thing we can to show our good disposition, so as to let the ennemy have the blame in every miscarriage of negotiations. And personally I wish to act politely by Lord Cornwallis."

The conditional release of Cornwallis and his aides was thus

[86] Croÿ, IV, 264.

[87] Franklin's "Journal," Smyth, VIII, 535–40 (under dates of June 10–12); Russell, IV, 218; Ross, I, 142 and 146.

[88] Lafayette to Franklin, June 12, 1782, LC, Franklin papers, no. 1054; Hale and Hale, II, 229–30.

arranged.[89] Lafayette on the first opportunity apologized to Washington for having assumed the prerogative of commander-in-chief and Congress, giving as his excuse the precedent of General Lincoln's release along with his aides.[90] Washington approved of what had been done as soon as he learned of it and urged Congress also to endorse it, not only as "a respect due to the character of the Marquis" but "best also in a political view."[91] Congress, somewhat less tactful, postponed action,[92] however, until peace made it no longer necessary.

In the course of these negotiations Lafayette had asked Ross why England was so backward in making peace proposals. "We are afraid," the major replied, "of offering you more than you expect or desire."[93] Grenville shortly received new and fuller powers to treat with both France and her allies and to recognize the independence of the United States unconditionally. Franklin found the language of Grenville's new powers somewhat ambiguous, however. They conferred authority to deal with France and "any other Prince or State";[94] but since the British government had hitherto denied the claim of the United States to being a "state" there remained a loophole by which England might yet escape from full recognition of American sovereignty. Lafayette discovered in another of his frequent visits to Versailles that Vergennes, nevertheless, was satisfied with Grenville's new commission. Franklin thereupon planned to go himself to place his doubts before the French minister, but an attack of influenza kept him at home. He asked the marquis to

---

[89] An earlier draft of the aides' release from parole [June 10, 1782] is contained in LC, Franklin papers, no. 1051; this is evidently the draft which Lafayette intended Franklin to sign (Smyth, VIII, 536). A copy of the final draft, as signed by Lafayette and endorsed by Franklin, is in Sparks MSS LXXXVIII, Part I, fol. 11 [June 12, 1782]. Lafayette apparently did not finally sign the aides' parole until about June 17, 1782 (Smyth, VIII, 545).

[90] Lafayette to Washington, June 25, 1782, Sparks MSS LXXXVIII, Part I, fols. 14–15.

[91] September 30, 1782, Fitzpatrick, XXV, 221–22.

[92] *Journals of Congress*, XXIII, 661 and 852–53.

[93] Franklin's "Journal," Smyth, VIII, 545.

[94] Franklin to Oswald, June 27, 1782, Wharton, V, 522; June 26, 1782, Smyth, VIII, 554.

go in his place. Lafayette saw Vergennes, who agreed to discuss the problem with Grenville and get a clear-cut statement of his intention.[95] On the next day Lafayette found that Grenville, having dined with Vergennes, had been induced to write again to London for clarification. "If this goes on," Lafayette reported to Franklin,[96] "at least it goes at a moderate gate [*sic*]." When he returned again to Passy that evening, he had no further details.

The interval before the next important development in Lafayette's diplomatic career witnessed his avowed affiliation with the philanthropic movement of his day. He had, up to this time, given little attention to questions of reform. The few comments he had made of a political nature had usually been salted to the taste of those for whom they were intended—republican for Americans, monarchical for Frenchmen. That did not indicate inconsistency or weakness so much as a desire to please and to be liked. Many other persons, more politically minded than the young American major-general, were in that day ready to advocate a federated republic for America and a tempered absolutism for France.

There was in France, however, a growing reform movement that centered around the numerous literary societies and Masonic lodges that were to be found in nearly every hamlet of France. Lafayette's literary interests were small. Though (and probably also because) he spent so much time at his desk in writing letters and reading official documents, only rarely is there to be found in his writings up to this time a literary or historical allusion to indicate that he had been reading the books that were helping to mold the ideas of his generation—the works of Voltaire, Rousseau, Montesquieu, Diderot, Raynal, and other so-called *philosophes*. Except for a passing reference to Raynal, not a single one of the *philosophes* is mentioned in the hundreds of letters he had written before June, 1782.[97]

[95] Franklin's "Journal," Smyth, VIII, 545–47.

[96] June 21, 1782, LC, Franklin papers, no. 1056.

[97] Cf. Louis Gottschalk, "Attitude of European officers in the Revolutionary armies toward General George Washington," *Journal of the Illinois State Historical Society*, XXXII (1939), 22–28; *Lafayette comes to America*, p. 51 n.

Even before Lafayette first went to make his reputation in America, he was a Mason.[98] There is, however, no thoroughly reliable record of his attendance at any lodge meetings in the six or seven years that followed. But now Lafayette made his first well-known gesture as a Mason. On February 6, 1782, he had allowed his name to be presented to the Lodge of St.-Jean d'Écosse du Contrat Social, which claimed to be the mother-lodge of the Scottish Rite Masons of France. The Grand Orient, the other association of French Masons, was, to be sure, less mystical than the Scottish Rite Masons and was headed by the Duc de Chartres, prince of the blood. But the Lodge of St.-Jean d'Écosse du Contrat Social had, as its name indicated, a philosophy of its own, though its activities were philanthropic and fraternal rather than political. It enjoyed the prestige of having among its members or visitors several prominent noblemen, clergy, ministers, philanthropists, and writers like Ségur, St. Germain, De Grasse, Chastellux, Pestalozzi, and Roland.[99]

Lafayette's candidature was accepted by unanimous acclamation instead of by the usual ballot, and it was agreed that all formalities were to be dispensed with in receiving him. He sent a letter of thanks, which was read at the next session. It was not, however, until the meeting of June 24 that he was able to appear in person.[100] In order to give their distinguished young brother "a clear indication of the value it places upon his military talents," the lodge received him "with honors which were ordinarily shown only to Masons of the highest degree."[101] When the marquis appeared at the door, the venerable sent several knights and officers to escort him. Having gone through the

[98] See Appen. III below.

[99] G. Clément-Simon, "La loge de 'Contrat Social' sous la règne de Louis XVI," *Revue des questions historiques*, CXXIX (1937), 4–8; letter of Lionel Hauser (Paris dealer who owned the register of the Loge de Contrat Social) to Theodore E. Norton, secretary of the American Friends of Lafayette, August 6, 1937.

[100] Clément-Simon (p. 8) says June 20, but this is a typographical error: see transcript of the meeting of June 24, 1782, in André Lebey, *La Fayette ou le militant Franc-Maçon* (2 vols.; Paris, 1937), I, 48–49.

[101] Lebey, I, 49.

regular ceremony, he was permitted to take the oath of full membership (*affilié*). Election by acclamation rather than by ballot was, as the lodge was careful to announce, a distinction which was "reserved for heroes" and "of which there have been no previous examples."[102] After a brief visit Lafayette begged to be excused because of his "civil occupations" and was escorted to the door "with the same honors."[103] Lafayette's connection with an organization that boldly proclaimed its belief in the social contract, in the notion that governments were bound to protect as well as the people to obey, was at the same time recognition of his past merits and a pledge of things to come.

Meantime, disappointments followed closely upon one another in diplomatic and military affairs. The defeat of De Grasse in the Battle of the Saints proved to be more serious than had at first been believed. Lafayette discovered that the ministry now felt that, with the French West Indies fleet so sadly depleted, no effort against Charleston or other Continental port could be made. He found some consolation in "the patriotic spirit" which was "diffused through every individual" at the report of De Grasse's surrender. Provinces, cities, Masonic clubs, and other groups offered to buy enough ships of the line to restore the French fleet to its former strength. "In the mean while," Lafayette reported proudly, "governement are using the greatest activity, and this has given a spur to the national exertions. But independant of the stroke in itself, I have been sighing upon the ruin of the plans I had proposed towards an useful cooperation upon the coasts of our America."[104]

The conversations with the English emissaries likewise proved disappointing. Part of the trouble, Lafayette soon discovered, lay in the fact that the new British government was divided. One faction, led by Lord Shelburne (to whom Oswald reported), was less ready to acknowledge American inde-

---

[102] Address of the Loge de Contrat Social, [1782], quoted by Charavay, p. 91, n. 2.

[103] Lebey, I, 49.

[104] Lafayette to Livingston, June 25, 1782, PCC, no. 156, fol. 290 (Wharton [V, 521] gives a slightly "Englished" version).

pendence than the other, led by Charles Fox (to whom Grenville reported).[105] The united efforts of Vergennes, Franklin, and Adams resulted in Grenville's finally agreeing that American independence might be recognized as a preliminary to negotiation. The British commissioner proved adamant, however, when Vergennes, asking him to sign a paper acknowledging American sovereignty, used the phrase: "The King of England is resolved to acknowledge. . . . ." Grenville wished "resolved" softened to "disposed."[106] He also proved less willing to treat with Franklin than with Vergennes and finally returned to London for new instructions. Meanwhile, the act enabling the government to acknowledge American independence was held up in the House of Lords. The marquis reported these dilatory tactics to Livingston in a detailed epistle that was greatly appreciated.[107]

Lafayette was ready to confess his diplomatic mission a failure and to return to America, where he was long overdue if he were to play his part in the year's campaign. Franklin and also Jay, recently welcomed to Paris by Lafayette, believed however, that he ought to remain. He was willing to admit that he would be more useful to the cause at King Louis' court than in a probably inactive campaign in America. For, as he was vain enough to see, "the footing I am upon at this court enables me some times to go greater lengths than could be done by a foreigner."[108] Franklin and Jay gladly acknowledged their indebtedness to their young adjutant,[109] and at his request[110] explained (though they did not belabor the point as did he) that it was their advice and approval which kept him from rushing

[105] Grenville to Fox, June 4, 1782, Russell, I, 362–63; Franklin's "Journal," Smyth, VIII, 545–46.

[106] Lafayette to Livingston, June 25, 1782, *loc. cit.*, fol. 286 (p. 519).

[107] Livingston to Lafayette, November 2, 1782, Wharton, V, 843.

[108] Lafayette to Livingston, June 25, 1782, *loc. cit.*, fol. 287 (p. 519).

[109] Franklin to Livingston, June 25, 1782, Smyth, VIII, 550; Jay to Livingston, June 28, 1782, *Correspondence of Jay*, II, 318.

[110] Lafayette to Franklin, June 25, 1782, LC, Franklin papers, no. 1068; Lafayette to Jay, June 25, 1782, NYPL, Bancroft transcripts, America 1782, III, 182; Jay to Lafayette, June 25, 1782, *ibid.*, p. 182½.

once more where "both duty and inclination"[111] led him. Unless unforeseen developments delayed him longer, however, he intended to be in America by September[112] and even asked that his horse be sent from Rhode Island to Philadelphia for him.[113]

Word finally reached Paris that the enabling act had passed both houses of Parliament. Lafayette, nevertheless, continued, as behooved a budding diplomat, to doubt British sincerity.[114] What he feared now was that the British would try to negotiate a separate peace in Philadelphia; and he added his warnings to those which Jay and Franklin had already sent against the insidious movements of the enemy.[115] He apologized for having to "be busy to distinguish between truth and falsehood in a line where cheating is considered as a very clever improvement." He felt all the "more tired of these political concerns" because he was "truly vexed not to join the army." He was ashamed that his friends were in the field while he was at such a distance from them. "They will think," he protested to Washington (perhaps too loudly), "I am much altered from what they have known me to be, unless you are pleased, my dear General, to let them know that your political people have kept me here for motives of public utility and that I never could make a greater sacrifice to my zeal for America than when I delay so much my return to the army where I heartly wish I could be immediately transported."[116]

During his venture into diplomacy, Lafayette declared, he had been guided chiefly by a single principle: he acted as he thought Washington wished him to act. "I hope you will ap-

---

[111] Lafayette to Washington, June 25, 1782, *loc. cit.*; cf. Duportail to Washington, June 27, 1782, Kite, *Duportail*, p. 254.

[112] Lafayette to Hamilton, June 29, 1782, *Works of Hamilton*, I, 283–84.

[113] Lafayette to G. A. Washington, June 29, 1782, Historical Society of Pennsylvania.

[114] Lafayette to Washington, June 29, 1782, Sparks MSS LXXXVIII, Part I, fols. 16–17.

[115] Jay to Livingston, June 28, 1782, *loc. cit.*, pp. 318–19; Franklin to Morris, June 25, 1782, Smyth, VIII, 553.

[116] Lafayette to Washington, June 29, 1782, *loc. cit.*; cf. also Lafayette to Congress, June 29, 1782, PCC, no. 156, fols. 294–96; and to Livingston, June 29, 1782, which is a postscript to the letter of June 25, 1782, *loc. cit.*, fols. 291–92 (p. 521).

prove my conduct," he wrote his "adopted father," "and in every thing I do I first consider what your opinion would be had I an opportunity to consult it." That rule of conduct had even become part of his family's code. Informing the revered leader that he hoped "in the course of some months your God son will have a brother," he added, "My little family . . . . are taught before all to revere and to love General Washington."[117] That reverence, that desire to do what Washington would approve, was indeed to become his standard of conduct in every new endeavor, as others were soon to discover.[118]

Lafayette's friends, continuing to rush to America, sympathized with him in his effort to "add the olive branch to the laurel."[119] The father of one of them held up the marquis' "good conduct and especially his modesty and simplicity" as a model.[120] Another, on leaving for America, said he was inconsolable over the prospect of "not finding you in a country which I shall find filled with your name and your deeds." He promised, however, to make the Americans appreciate fully the extent of Lafayette's sacrifice "in bartering your sword for a pen." The exchange, he thought, was not a fair one. "You are going to be more than ever revolted," he predicted, "by English pride, stupid Spanish vanity, French frivolity, and despotic ignorance. You will see that the cabinet creates as great impatience as a battlefield and that there are as many stupidities in a diplomatic transaction as in a campaign. You will see especially how often principle is sacrificed to form and you will say more than once, 'If chance had not made me one of the leading actors, I should certainly not remain on the stage.' But the more obstacles you find, the greater merit you will deserve. Why should you not achieve whatever you wish! You have genius and luck. That is half as much again as is necessary to

[117] *Ibid.*   [118] See below, pp. 391 and 421–22.

[119] Unknown [Ségur?] to Lafayette, July 7, 1782, private collection.

[120] Unknown [the handwriting seems to be Vioménil's, but there are reasons for doubting his authorship] to his son, [*ca.* September, 1782], collection of Judge W. B. Beals, Olympia, Wash. (I am indebted to Mr. J. F. Gough, Jersey City, N.J., for my understanding of this document.)

become a great man."[121] How different his friends' attitude was now from what it had been in the old days when they had thought him sluggish and unemotional![122]

Lafayette's friend was not mistaken about the impatience created by diplomatic delays. Grenville returned from London with the news that the resignation of Charles Fox had placed Lord Shelburne in unquestioned control of the British government.[123] Yet negotiations moved no faster. Grenville twice received new commissions which were regarded by Franklin as "imperfect"[124] and finally was recalled, leaving Oswald to carry on the negotiations. Soon Alleyne Fitzherbert arrived to replace Grenville, but with powers to treat only with France, Spain, and Holland. The whole month of July passed in relative inactivity, and yet the expectation that something would happen detained Lafayette in France. The frigate on which he had hoped to sail with his friends to America waited three weeks for him and finally put to sea without him.[125] The month of August, too, was spent in idleness. Lafayette railed at "that haughty, barbarous nation," the British, and particularly at Lord Shelburne, whose protestations were not "safe to be depended upon."[126] One day he found Oswald and Franklin peering at each other through their spectacles. Franklin's were of a rare kind, with double lenses. After the Englishman had left, Franklin said, "Oswald has but four eyes, and I have six; it will be a pity if I cannot see as far as he."[127]

Lafayette devoted part of his unwelcome leisure to a new philanthropic interest. He began to be interested in the peas-

[121] Unknown [Ségur?] to Lafayette, July 7, 1792, loc. cit.

[122] Gottschalk, Lafayette comes to America, pp. 52–53.

[123] Lafayette to Franklin and Franklin to Lafayette, July 9, 1782, Wharton, V, 603–4.

[124] Franklin to Livingston, August 12, 1782, Smyth, VIII, 579; cf. Franklin to Lafayette, July 24, 1782, ibid., p. 571.

[125] "Narrative of the Duke de Lauzun," American history magazine, II (1907), 294; M. F. Barrière (ed.), Mémoires du Duc de Lauzun ("Bibliothèque des mémoires relatifs à l'histoire de France pendant le 18e siècle," Vol. XXV [Paris, 1882]), p. 210.

[126] Lafayette to Henry Laurens, August 20, 1782, "Letters from Lafayette to Laurens," pp. 176–77.

[127] Sparks MSS XXXII, pp. 135–36.

ants on his estate and was no longer content, as he once had been, merely to make suggestions to Morizot. He personally brought to the attention of the new controller-general of finances, Joly de Fleury, a scheme which he believed would promote the welfare of his people in Auvergne. If the government would permit and help to support it, Lafayette was prepared to establish a school to teach the farmers to weave the yarn which they made from the wool of their own sheep. The new trade would not only increase the earning-power of the peasantry, he contended, but would keep them at home during the winter. Soon an inspector of manufactures was on his way to Haute Auvergne to look into the feasibility of Lafayette's scheme. Like everything else that required the approval of a bureaucracy not accustomed to impatient philanthropists, Lafayette's scheme encountered delays. Its realization was prolonged even beyond the peace negotiations.[128]

While waiting for bureaucrats and diplomats to act, Lafayette became twenty-five years of age. By French law he ceased to be a minor. Though he had led thousands of men in battle and had given weighty advice to men in two nations who had the power to wage war or make peace, only now did he become free from the restraints put upon him by guardians and older relatives in the control of his own affairs. His first important step was to reconfirm the powers of Jacque-Philippe Grattepain-Morizot as his intendant. He also proceeded to settle the problems recently inherited with the property of his great-grandfather. That property had fallen jointly to Lafayette and his cousin, the Comte de Luzignem. Morizot was authorized to look after his client's interests in the partition. He was likewise permitted to sell some lands in Brittany and Paris and to acquire other property instead, particularly a house in Paris where the Lafayettes might establish a home independent of the Noailles. In this way the marquis rounded out his estate and at the same time raised liquid funds for his huge expenditures

---

[128] AN, F¹² 1376, folder dated 1782; Germain Martin, *Buffon, maître de forges; Lafayette et l'école pratique de tissage de Chavaignac* (Le Puy, 1898), pp. 13–25, and "Buffon et La Fayette manufacturiers," *Réforme sociale*, XXXVIII (1899), 71–73.

in the American cause. Lafayette was described in these pompous documents as "Monseigneur Marie-Joseph-Paul-Yves-Roch-Gilbert du Motier, Marquis de la Fayette, major-general in the armies of the United States of North America, Baron of Reignac, Vissac, St. Romain, Seigneur de Kaufrait, St. Quihoet, Le Plessix, La Touche, and in part of the County of Ploeuc, L'Isle Aval, and Veau Couronné."[129] That title alone indicated that the twenty-five-year-old "republican" was one of the richest men in French society.

Eleven days after Lafayette attained his legal majority his wife gave birth to another girl, her third surviving child. It had been a hard confinement for Adrienne, and the baby had come sooner than expected.[130] The devout mother wished her to be named after a Catholic saint. The father wanted her to carry a name that had some meaning in his religion—America. Fortunately they hit upon the name Virginie, which satisfied them both. Lafayette hastened to inform Franklin of their decision. "Every child of mine that comes to light is a small addition to the number of American citizens. I have the pleasure to inform you that, tho' she was but seven months advanced, Madame de Lafayette has this morning become mother of a daughter, who, however delicate in its beginnings, enjoys a perfect health, and I hope will soon grow equal to the heartiest children. This reminds me of our noble revolution, into which we were forced sooner than it ought to have been begun. But our strength came on very fast, and upon the whole I think we did *at least* as well as any other people." He asked permission to name his daughter after Virginia. "I want to present her as an offering to my western country."[131] Franklin answered immediately: "I continue to suffer from this cruel gout; but in the midst of my pain this news of Mad^m de la Fayette's safe delivery and your acquisition of a daughter gives me pleasure. In naming our

---

[129] Power of attorney (*procuration*), September 9, 1782, Morgan Library, Lafayette, Vol. I; cf. "procuration generalle," February 20, 1782, University of Rochester Library; and documents dealing with the contemplated purchase of a house on the Rue de Bourbon dated November 12, 1782, AN, T 333.

[130] Lasteyrie, p. 203.   [131] September 17, 1782, Smyth, VIII, 595.

children I think it well to begin with the most ancient and as we cannot have too many of so good a race, I hope you and Mme. de la Fayette will go through the thirteen. But as that may be in the common way too severe a task for her delicate frame, and children of seven months may become as strong as those of nine, I consent to the abridgement of two months for each; and I wish her to spend the twenty-six months so gained, in perfect ease, health and pleasure. While you are proceeding, I hope our states will some of them new-name themselves. Miss Virginia, Miss Carolina and Miss Georgiana will sound prettily enough for the girls; but Massachusetts & Connecticut are too harsh even for the boys, unless they were to be savages."[132]

Lafayette still was torn between the desire to return to America and the fear that great events might take place in Europe. He had not given up hope that the English might see the light: "One day or other," he said, "the court of London may be in earnest, and then . . . . she will not intrude upon us with so strange an idea as that of treating upon an unequal footing."[133] On the other hand, writing again to his "best friend," Washington, he prayed: "God grant . . . . I may be with you before you get this letter!"[134] His prayer was not answered. The manner, if not the fact, of British recognition of the thirteen states remained in doubt. The British government proved willing to treat with the United States as an independent state, but in Oswald's commission to do so the thirteen states were enumerated separately and referred to as the "thirteen colonies."[135] The American commissioners demurred, asking Oswald to submit their objections to his government.[136]

Franklin's ill-health and his candid exploitation of Lafayette's popularity at court kept Lafayette scurrying between Paris,

[132] September 17, 1782, *ibid.*, pp. 595–96.

[133] Lafayette to Laurens, September 19, 1782, "Letters from Lafayette to Laurens," pp. 177–78.

[134] September 1, 1782, Sparks MSS LXXXVIII, Part I, fol. 19.

[135] Wharton, V, 712 n.

[136] Cf. Townshend to Oswald, September 20, 1782, *ibid.*, pp. 747–48.

Passy, and Versailles. Once Jay accompanied him.[137] Jay's doubt of France's loyalty had daily mounted. It was not allayed by his meeting with Vergennes. He learned, to his alarm, that the French minister seemed to think that the Americans ought to go ahead with the negotiations on the terms of Oswald's commission. Vergennes believed that he could induce Oswald to write a letter stating that "he will treat with the American plenipotentiaries in their capacity of plenipotentiaries of the United States and the first article of the preliminary treaty will contain the most explicit renunciation of all the rights and pretentions which the king and crown of England have held or might have held at any time in the lands composing the sovereignty of the United States."[138] Lafayette, on one of his numerous visits to Versailles, rapidly wrote this sentence down and without the usual amenities of salutation, sent it to Franklin. But Jay was not content with such "expedients."[139] His suspicion of French intentions was growing rapidly. He proposed to send to Vergennes a long protest, setting forth his objections to any conversations with Oswald unless the United States were recognized to be fully free and independent before negotiations began.

Before Jay could send his protest,[140] however, the atmosphere cleared. Oswald had sent to his government the Americans' request that they say "the thirteen United States" instead of "the thirteen colonies"; and they had acted on it favorably.[141] By the end of September, Oswald received a second commission. It authorized him to treat "with any commissioners or persons

---

[137] Lafayette to Vergennes, September 10, 1782, Doniol, V, 153, n. 1.

[138] Lafayette to Franklin, [*ante* September 18, 1782], LC, Franklin papers, no. 2594. This document is not dated, but Jay implies (letter to Livingston, November 17, 1782, *Correspondence of Jay*, II, 385-86) that it was written before the proposed letter to Vergennes, which was in the process of composition on September 18, 1782; see Jay to Livingston, September 18, 1780, *ibid.*, p. 346. There is a similar document in LC, Franklin papers, no. 2667.

[139] Jay to Livingston, November 17, 1782, *loc. cit.*, p. 385.

[140] Jay to Livingston, September 18, 1782, *loc. cit.*, p. 366; November 17, 1782, *loc. cit.*, p. 408.

[141] Townsend to Oswald, September 20, 1782, *loc. cit.*

vested with equal powers by and on the part of the Thirteen United States of America."[142]

It was now clear that full recognition of American sovereignty would precede the opening of peace negotiations. A great victory had been won. It had come as a result of the direct communication of Oswald with Franklin and Jay; yet, without the activity of Lafayette at Versailles, Vergennes' support might not have been so readily available, and the British government might therefore have been less willing to make the concession which the American commission thought so important for their dignity. Franklin's apprentice deserved part of the credit for the victory.

The problem of American dignity rose again over the question of the Spanish attitude toward a treaty of alliance with the United States. Jay took his problem to Vergennes. By chance he found Lafayette in Vergennes' antechamber; and the Spanish ambassador, the Conde de Aranda, entered shortly afterward. Jay and Lafayette pressed the embarrassed Aranda for a frank acknowledgment of American independence. When Vergennes arrived, he tried to effect a compromise among the heated debaters, suggesting that Jay might try to negotiate a treaty of alliance with the Spanish without raising the question of American independence. Jay felt that "the dignity of America" forbade his treating on "any other than an equal footing."[143] Thus nothing came of the episode. Moreover, startling reports reached suspicious American ears. Vergennes' secretary, Rayneval, had gone back and forth between London and Versailles on a secret mission. His errand not only deprived Lafayette of his hope of being sent as peace negotiator to London but also increased the uneasiness of the American agents regarding Vergennes' intentions.

By the beginning of October, Lafayette was convinced that peace would not be concluded before the next summer. The defeat of a Spanish attempt upon Gibraltar increased the un-

[142] September 21, 1782, Wharton, V, 749.

[143] Jay to Livingston, November 17, 1782, *loc. cit.*, pp. 443–45 (describing events of September 26).

willingness of the "haughty" British to make the concessions that were demanded of her; at the same time the Spanish government weakened the American position by its unwillingness to recognize the American nation or to accept the Mississippi River as its western boundary.[144] Lafayette, therefore, continued to believe himself too indispensable to leave for America.[145] Jay, becoming increasingly suspicious of Frenchmen, was less pleased with his helpfulness than Franklin and reported to Livingston that, "as we have a competent number of commissioners," it ought not to be necessary to trouble the marquis.[146]

The young general had himself concluded by this time that his voyage to France would not produce the distinguished results he had hoped.[147] He, therefore, accepted with great joy a chance to play a new role, again as a soldier. To make amends for De Grasse's defeat in the West Indies, the French government had proposed a joint Spanish and French expedition to the West Indies. Lafayette's old associate Admiral d'Estaing was to be placed in charge, and Estaing had asked that the marquis be given command of the land forces that were to go with him. Lafayette began to hint at this scheme to Washington as early as October 14. Ten days later he spoke more openly about it, though still "under the greatest secrecy."[148] Since he was not to have his rank of *maréchal-de-camp* until the peace, he was to keep his American rank, "and the outside as well as the inside of an American soldier." "In a month's time we must know if England is willing to make peace. . . . . I do not intend to set out before that time."

Days passed, and yet peace came no nearer to conclusion. Lafayette himself realized the truth: the Spanish were delaying

[144] Lafayette to Adams, October 6, 1782, Adams, VII, 645.

[145] Lafayette to Washington, October 14, 1782, Sparks MSS LXXXVIII, Part I, pp. 20–21 (tr. in *Mémoires*, II, 38–39).

[146] Jay to Livingston, October 13, 1782, *Correspondence of Jay*, II, 349.

[147] Lafayette to Washington, October 14, 1782, *loc. cit.*

[148] October 24, 1782, Sparks MSS LXXXVII, Part I, p. 22 (incomplete tr. in *Mémoires*, II, 40–41).

Vergennes' negotiations with Fitzherbert because they wanted Gibraltar, and Vergennes did not keep the Americans informed of the unsatisfactory progress out of fear of making them still more angry with Spain.[149] Delays continued. When Captain Barry returned to Lorient from a successful cruise and inquired whether peace was near, Lafayette answered: "I now am so far convinced that an other campaign is necessary that in a month's time I embark for America."[150]

The marquis' role as a diplomat became increasingly delicate. Adams, summoned by Jay upon the receipt of Oswald's new commission, quickly joined in doubting Vergennes' sincerity. He confided to his diary: "Mr. Jay likes Frenchmen as little as Mr. Lee and Mr. Izard did. He says they are not a moral people, they know not what it is; he don't like any Frenchmen; the Marquis de Lafayette is clever, but he is a Frenchman. Our allies don't play fair, he told me; they are endeavoring to deprive us of the fishery, the western lands, and the navigation of the Mississippi; they would even bargain with the English to deprive us of them; they want to play the western lands, Mississippi, and the whole Gulf of Mexico into the hands of Spain."[151] Adams did not even go through the formality of informing Vergennes of his arrival until the minister, having learned of it from police reports, mentioned the American's lapse of etiquette to both Franklin and Lafayette. It was only after the marquis "in a great air of confidence"[152] urged Adams to repair his error and Franklin gave him the same advice that Adams went. Nowhere, he himself admitted, had he been treated with half the respect now shown him at Versailles.[153] Lafayette also lionized him. He invited him to dinner at his house, where Poix, Noailles, Jay, Bancroft, and William Frank-

[149] "Diary," Adams, III, 314; Lafayette to Livingston, October 14, 1782, NYPL, R. R. Livingston papers, II, 337–38.

[150] Barry to Lafayette, October 28 and 31, 1782, LC, U.S. Navy collection; Lafayette to Barry, November 2, 1782, collection of Henry N. Haiken, Bronx, N.Y. Cf. Clark, pp. 278–79.

[151] "Diary," Adams, III, 303.

[152] Ibid., p. 304.   [153] Ibid., p. 306.

lin were among the guests, and initiated Adams into the secret of Estaing's proposed expedition against the West Indies.[154]

Since Franklin's gout and gravel kept him inactive in Passy and Jay was occupied by the Spanish business, the negotiations now fell largely to Adams. Adams, like Franklin and Jay, did not hesitate to exploit Lafayette's willingness to be helpful. On Adams' request the young Frenchman went often to see Vergennes upon American affairs. Congress' need of money was now the chief motive of his visits. Vergennes pointed out that the war had already been very costly to France; but would Mr. Adams try to get some of the needed money from Holland if the king stood guaranty of its return?[155] Lafayette then went to see Controller-General Fleury and dared to ask for 20,000,000 livres. Fleury, too, pointed out that the American war had cost a huge sum. Besides, the minister thought, there ought to be a good deal of money in America from the purchases of the French and British forces there. Lafayette replied that only Tories benefited from British spending. When he suggested that Adams might go to Holland for a loan, Fleury did not encourage it. The marquis even tried to enlist Queen Marie Antoinette's aid.[156]

But at last the time came when Lafayette felt he could no longer postpone joining the forces that were to sail for Cadiz. Dressed in the uniform of an American major-general, he went to Versailles to bid farewell to the royal family.[157] But, before he could actually leave Paris, new dispatches arrived from Congress pressing for immediate pecuniary aid. On the other hand, no intimation was received from La Luzerne of his opinion regarding the advisability of further stipends. Lafayette undertook to step into the breach. He made a lengthy appeal to Vergennes.[158] "In considering America, Monsieur le Comte," he wrote, "it is natural for me to take the point of view of a Frenchman. It is in that capacity alone that I examine the dangers of English influence. The people are tired of war, but at

---

[154] *Ibid.*, p. 303.
[155] *Ibid.*, p. 305.
[156] *Ibid.*, p. 314.
[157] *Ibid.*, pp. 317–18.
[158] Lafayette to Vergennes, November 22, 1782, *Mémoires*, II, 41–45.

present they love France and hate England. Help given now is an act all the more advantageous as it puts the seal upon all the others, raises courage, and closes the mouths of the English emissaries who increasingly accuse France of intending to build a fire without putting it out." He argued that there was less money in America than might be believed since much of it was in Tory hands. The great distances and the war had made tax collections difficult, though on that score, he agreed, the American government was to be blamed. The fact remained, nevertheless, that if their revolution was not to fail, they must have aid from France. He hinted that the prolongation of the war was not America's doing. "It should perhaps be remembered that that continent is the only quarter where we have had great success; and the reason for that is simple enough, since everything there is for us and against the enemy. In the happy event that we send forces there, we may expect to find an army capable of co-operation. There has never been a better one than that of the Americans. But if their patience is finally exhausted, if Congress wavers between the inconvenience of maintaining it and the inconvenience of disbanding it, if in the end it should be needed to prevent disturbances rather than to undertake an offensive operation, not only will it be impossible to attack the enemy's ports, but also it will be easy for them to reduce their garrisons . . . . and the men thus spared will be sent against our islands." Political as well as military factors therefore, he argued, dictated a new loan to America. "We have nothing to fear except her inability to carry on, and even then she would never consent to avoiding the obligations of alliance or of gratitude."

This was an effective appeal, setting forth the practical as well as the sentimental motives for French interest in supporting the United States to the last sou. Lafayette somewhat proudly showed it to the American commissioners when he went to Passy to bid them goodbye. Franklin was displeased (or at least so Adams thought) because "it seemed an attempt to take . . . . the merit of obtaining the loan if one should be procured." Lafayette's explanation was that he had written it because Vergennes in the absence of La Luzerne's long-overdue dispatches, "would do nothing in the affair of money without something French to go upon."[159]

Lafayette also presented a letter ostentatiously asking the commissioners' approval of his departure to Spain. It was a wooden document detailing his contributions to the American cause since 1777.[160] It was obviously a mere formality, since they had already approved his going and could have done little to stop him if they had not. Yet he felt uneasy lest Congress be displeased with him. "Without their approval, and without an acknowledged rank in the French army," he had explained to Vergennes, "I am going to undertake operations of which they do not know the origin."[161] Franklin and Jay both noted especially one passage in Lafayette's petition: "Had I not been detained by you, Gentlemen, upon political accounts which you have been pleas'd to communicate to Congress, I would long ago have returned to America."[162] It was true that they had found Lafayette's assistance useful, but this sentence seemed to imply that he had been "detained" by them against his own wishes, whereas they had merely consented to his own preference to stay.[163] Though it was true that Franklin had once written to Congress that he would try to "prevail" upon Lafayette to stay "a few weeks longer," he had written that on Lafayette's request, and Jay had written similarly for the same reason.[164] Moreover, several months rather than weeks had passed since then, and they had not insisted upon Lafayette's remaining that long. Both men, Adams noted, were "nettled" by their young friend's explanation of his conduct and denied it.[165]

After Lafayette left Passy, Adams privately wrote in his

[159] "Diary," Adams, III, 326–27.

[160] Lafayette to Franklin, Jay, and Adams, November 21, 1782, NYPL, Bancroft transcripts, America, 1782, IV, 278½.

[161] Lafayette to Vergennes, November 22, 1782, *loc. cit.*, p. 42.

[162] Lafayette to Franklin, Jay, and Adams, *loc. cit.*

[163] "Diary," Adams, III, 327.

[164] See above, p. 370, and nn. 109 and 110.   [165] "Diary," Adams, III, 327.

diary an unflattering opinion of him: "This unlimited ambition will obstruct his rise; he grasps at all, civil, political, and military, and would be the *unum necessarium* in every thing; he has had so much real merit, such family supports, and so much favor at Court, that he need not recur to artifice."[166] Adams' judgment was exceedingly keen; he had put his finger upon Lafayette's principal weakness—the desire to be wherever glory was to be won and to claim at least his full share of it, even if sometimes with assumed modesty. "You are condemned," Hamilton wrote to the marquis about this time,[167] "to run the race of ambition all your life." Yet if the young general had been ambitious, he had not acted without worthy motive and instigation. Adams would have been more charitable if he had acknowledged (as he did elsewhere in his diary)[168] that it had been with his approval that Lafayette had first approached Vergennes on the recent request for a loan; and Franklin, too, might have borne in mind his earlier admission that "our friend, the marquis, assisted me much" in obtaining a previous loan.[169]

Despite the displeasure of the three commissioners with their young friend, they sent a gallant answer to his request for their approval. "Our country has had early and repeated proofs both of your readiness and abilities to do her service. The prospect of an inactive campaign in America induced us to adopt the opinion that you might be more useful here than there, especially in case the negotiation for peace on the part of France in England should be committed to your management; for your knowledge of our affairs and attachment to our interest might have been very advantageous to us on such an occasion." Since the proposed expedition of the Comte d'Estaing might put "a glorious and speedy termination" to the war, however, they now thoroughly approved of his going.[170]

That letter had to be sent to Brest, for Lafayette had, in

[166] *Ibid.*   [167] November 3, 1782, *Works of Hamilton*, I, 320.

[168] Adams, III, 303 and 305.

[169] Franklin to Morris, March 4, 1782, *loc. cit.*, p. 385.

[170] Franklin, Adams, and Jay to Lafayette, November 28 [26 ?], 1782, Wharton, VI, 89.

fact, left Paris without their written permission, having learned from Dr. Bancroft that the ministers were agreed that he should go.[171] On his way he had to pass through Versailles. Without changing his traveling clothes,[172] he called on Vergennes. The minister promised that, whether or not he received La Luzerne's dispatches in the meantime, he would speak with Fleury the next day, though he seemed doubtful of any amount above 6,000,000 livres. Pleased with even that sum, Lafayette hastened on. From Rambouillet[173] the next morning he sent a hasty message to Franklin: "The six million, *between us*, I think we will have. . . . . You will oblige me to make these communications to Mssrs. Jay and Adams . . . . because I want them to see that nothing more on my part remains to be done."

It was only a year later that Lafayette learned that the American diplomats believed he had not been "so active as they in obtaining the last six millions."[174] Then he burst into indignation, in a letter to his former aide McHenry, regarding "the selfishness of others." "I cannot help remembering," he wrote, "that Jay and Adams never went to Versailles but twice, I think, when I pushed them to it, that Mr. Franklin did repose himself upon me, who went so far as to say that I had rather delay the departure of 8,000 men and nine ships waiting for me at Brest than to go without an assurance of the six millions." And, indeed, though the money might have been secured without Lafayette's constant darting back and forth to Versailles, he was right in maintaining that the three American commissioners had relied upon him as a ready and useful link with the French court.

Franklin, at least, was willing to let the marquis have part of the credit. He admitted that his "aide" had "likewise been im-

---

[171] Lafayette to Franklin, [November 26, 1782], LC, Franklin papers, no. 502. Cf. Mme de Lafayette to Jay and Jay to Mme de Lafayette, November 27, 1782, NYPL, Bancroft MSS, America 1782, IV, 279 and 280½; *Gazette de Leyde*, December 6, 1782.

[172] Lafayette to McHenry, December 26, 1783, Huntington Library, MH 157.

[173] In his letter to McHenry (*ibid.*), Lafayette says that he wrote to Franklin "upon his [Vergennes'] table" at Versailles, but the letter in question is dated "Rambouillet, Tuesday morning": Lafayette to Franklin, [November 26, 1782], *loc. cit.*

[174] Lafayette to McHenry, December 26, 1782, *loc. cit.*

portunate"[175] and had "employed himself diligently and warm-ly in the business."[176] But there was in Paris one American, who preferred to remain anonymous, whose praise of Lafayette was less chary. "His informations must have been such as no other person in France could have given to our ministers," he wrote to America, "and such perhaps as the whole body of Congress could not have communicated, because his knowledge was collected from observation and personal enquiries, and theirs, from the nature of their situation, cannot be so various, so critical and extensive." The young hero's spirit amazed this admirer. "This nobleman brings with him to France all our earliest and brightest enthusiasm with all our present firm-ness and virtue. Much may he be rewarded by his own country, for much he deserves from ours, which can give him nothing save gratitude." The unknown enthusiast was not so well in-formed as Franklin, Adams, and Jay regarding Lafayette's recent diplomatic role, but his unstinted encomium, printed in a Philadelphia paper,[177] reached a wider audience in America than the faint praise of the more restrained triumvirate.

As yet Lafayette knew nothing of this controversy over his share in the diplomatic glory. But he was not regretful at last to be leaving the strange atmosphere of diplomacy and to be once more on his way to breathe the smell of blood and gun-powder.

BIBLIOGRAPHICAL NOTES

The best studies of the negotiation of peace in 1782 are Doniol, Vol. V, and, less detailed but also less Francophile, S. F. Bemis, *Diplomacy of the American Revolution* ("Foundations of American diplomacy, 1775–1823"; New York, 1935). My article on "Franklin and Lafayette" covers the year 1782 very briefly. Van Doren's *Franklin*, Frank Monaghan's *John Jay* (New York, 1935), and Charavay's *Lafayette* (the "standard" biographies of their sub-jects) do not give their associations during that year very much space. P. E. Schazmann, *La Comtesse de Boufflers* (Lausanne, 1933) tells the story of Gus-tavus III's interest in Lafayette.

[175] Franklin to Morris, December 14, 1782, Smyth, VIII, 638.

[176] Franklin to Livingston, December 5, 1782, *ibid.*, p. 630.

[177] Extract from a letter from a gentleman in Paris, August 3, 1782, *Pennsylvania Gazette*, October 30, 1782.

CHAPTER XVI

Spain and the Peace

IN THE days when the best roads were paved with stone blocks and food could be transported over them no faster than by horse and wagon, an army of twenty thousand was enormous. Some of the bloodiest battles of the eighteenth century had been fought by less than that number on either side. Only in a few—like Blenheim, Fontenoy, Rossbach, Minden—did larger armies participate.

But the governments of Versailles and Madrid had now determined upon something spectacular. They were going to prepare an expedition whose success not only would be assured but would put an end to the war. The Spanish were chiefly concerned about Gibraltar. There was little advantage to be gained, however, by increasing the size of the army that for nearly four years had besieged that rock, since the failure of attacks upon it was not due to lack of numbers.

Next to Gibraltar the prizes which the Spanish sought the most were the British West Indies; and Vergennes, determined to follow where his Bourbon allies chose to lead lest the alliance prove ineffective, had agreed upon an imposing West Indian venture. A force of seven thousand men and nine warships were to sail from Brest to Cadiz, where about thirteen thousand men and forty warships were already to be gathered. Thus a force of about twenty thousand men and fifty ships of the line would be created. It was to sail to the West Indies and merge with the troops and vessels which were already operating there. Eventually the Franco-Spanish armada was expected to number at least sixty-six ships of the line and twenty-four thousand men.[1] The famous Spanish Armada which Good Queen Bess had defeated two centuries earlier had not had many more line vessels and men.

Of the whole body only Estaing and Lafayette knew the plans of the French ministry. Their enormous force was to capture Jamaica and then, as Lafayette had insisted, go on to besiege New York. If—and only if—the king of Spain consented, Lafayette might be sent with a French army of six thousand men into Canada in order to divide the English in the defense of New York. All that seemed to stand between Lafayette and his inveterate ambition to win "the fourteenth state" was the reluctance of Spain.

Estaing, who was to have command of the whole, had been in Spain for several weeks when Lafayette started out to join the French forces preparing at Brest. The Comte de Roux accompanied him in the expectation of being made his aide. Though wearing the uniform of an American major-general, the marquis was looked upon as Estaing's chief of staff and second in command of the land forces. His aides had been carefully selected with the approval of the French war office.[2] Among them were none of those who had distinguished themselves in America. They were all expected to go back to their posts in the Continental Army—except Capitaine, who was to join him later.[3]

From Rambouillet, Lafayette and Roux hastened to Brest. "Frightful roads and bad horses" brought them there late on December 1.[4] They had spent two sleepless nights on the road.

[1] *Mémoires*, II, 5; Roux to Poix, January 16, 1783, private collection; Lafayette to Hamilton, April 1, 1783, quoted in Historical Manuscripts Commission, *Report on American manuscripts in the Royal Institution of Great Britain* (4 vols.; London, 1904–9), IV, 142.

[2] Lafayette to Ségur, November 20, 1782, AMG, AH 3732, Lafayette, no. 114; memoranda regarding Barral and Roux, AN, Marine B4 210, fols. 107, 129, and 163.

[3] Lafayette to Poix, December 4, 1782, private collection.

[4] Roux to Poix, December 2, 1782, private collection. See also *Gazette de Leyde*, December 6 and 17, 1782, supplément. Lafayette gave the date of his arrival once as December 2 (letter to Poix, December 3, 1782, private collection) and once as December 3 (letter to Washington, December 4, 1782, Wharton, VI, 108–9). Roux seems to be less confused on this point.

Fearing that he had delayed his departure from Paris too long and that the fleet might already have sailed from Brest, Lafayette had insisted on going by way of Lorient to see Captain Barry. He wished to inquire whether, if he missed the boat that was to carry him to Cadiz, Barry would take him. They boarded the "Washington," a smaller vessel in the bay, and there Barry, whose ship was farther out in the roadstead, joined them. Barry promised to do what he could. As the "Washington" fired a salute of thirteen guns, Lafayette and his aide, without rest, started on the final lap of their journey.[5]

At Brest they encountered a refreshing atmosphere of activity. The fleet had not yet sailed. Troops arrived steadily and quickly embarked upon thirty-six transports, which were to make up the fleet under the escort of nine men-of-war. Lafayette and Roux boarded the flagship, the "Censeur," Admiral de Vialis commanding.[6] It soon became clear that they would not be able to sail immediately, and Lafayette found time to grow sentimental. "I am sad, very sad to leave," he wrote to the Prince de Poix,[7] "and the idea of leaving my friends has never before been so painful to me. You know how fond I am of you, my dear prince. It cost me more to go away from you than I can say." Twice before Lafayette had left Poix and France with less of a twinge. Could it be that his sadness this time was due to leaving Mme de Hunolstein behind?

Time began to weigh heavily on Lafayette's hands. Part of it he employed in his favorite pastime of letter-writing. Fearing that some member of Congress "might from public report, imagine that I enlarge so far their permission as to follow pursuits that would not particularly promote the views of America," Lafayette assured Congress[8] that his heart was "bound up to

---

[5] Roux to Poix, December 2, 1782, *loc. cit.;* interview with Barry reported in *New York Gazette and Weekly Mercury*, March 3, 1783, from the *Martinique Gazette,* January 15, 1783.

[6] Roux to Poix, December 2, 1782, *loc. cit.*

[7] Lafayette to Poix, December 3, 1782, *loc. cit.*

[8] December 3, 1782, PCC, no. 156, fols. 300–302 (and, with some omissions, Wharton, VI, 102–3).

America by every sentiment of a grateful, an everlasting, and I may add a patriotic love." His past actions, he repeated (though by this time he ought to have been less positive), were to be explained by his yielding to the opinion of the ministers of America in France, who had thought he might "serve her in the political field." Now that he was about to embark for Cadiz, he had done so "by their advice," too. "Upon the voyage, the mode, and time of it, I have taken their opinion and it has been that I was acting consistent with the interest of America and the instructions of Gal Washington."

The punctilious soldier, fearful that his absence might be misunderstood in the army, also wrote to Washington for approval.[9] He had accepted his new command, he claimed, because it seemed to be "the means, the only means in the world to bring about what you have directed me to obtain"—supremacy in American waters. He hoped his commander would be satisfied with his conduct and would tell Congress so. "Indeed, my dear General, it is necessary to my happiness, you will think so. When you are absent I endeavour to do the thing which you seem likely to have advised had you been present. I love you too much to be one minute easy unless I think you approve of my conduct."

The marquis showed a stickler's concern, too, lest Franklin, Adams, and Jay might not formally grant their sanction. He had left instructions with Adrienne to get it in writing from them and to forward it to Brest by special courier.[10] Since it had not yet arrived when the fleet seemed ready to sail, he wrote to Franklin[11] to send it to the minister of marine, who in turn would forward it to him. "Your opinion has been I should go, and I am pursuing an object that may I hope prove useful to America. Upon your opinion therefore, I determine my going." This formalism was something like the great vacillation that had beset him on his last voyage to Spain, where he had

[9] December 4, 1782, *loc. cit.*

[10] Mme de Lafayette to Jay, November 27, 1782, NYPL, Bancroft transcripts, America 1782, IV, 279.

[11] December 4, 1782, Hale and Hale, II, 231.

stopped in 1777 on his first trip to America. Then, too, he had tried to avoid complete responsibility for his own decision. At that time he had argued that, because the French ministers had not really objected (though ostensibly they had), they had therefore approved.[12] Now he reasoned that, because the American ministers had approved, they had insisted. He had been more correct then than he was now, though not altogether wrong now. But he had been an obscure boy then; now he was a famous man and should have been candid enough to act upon his own authority. Such unwillingness to assume full responsibility for his own major decisions when they were not explicitly in line with legality or instructions was of a piece with his tendency to act "as though he were following the advice of someone else" (the phrase is Talleyrand's)[13]—or (as he himself would have put it) to act as Washington might have acted in his place. Cropping up at crucial points in his later career, it was to serve as a brake on both his ambition and his achievements.

At last the "Censeur" lifted anchor and sailed. Just before she pulled away, Lafayette sent his last adieus to Poix.[14] "Never was I so unhappy at leaving my friends," he repeated. ". . . . Speak of me to the men and the women, the charming women, who are our friends." The fleet sailed from Brest on December 4 but was soon obliged by contrary winds to drop anchor again and then to return, as the winds developed into a gale. Lafayette apparently was developing a good pair of sea legs. Roux reported, "My general has not yet been seasick, but the aide-de-camp on the contrary has suffered very much."[15]

At Brest a letter from Poix awaited him. It informed him that malicious gossip had begun again to couple his name with that of Aglaé de Hunolstein. She had been distressed by such gossip even before there had been justifiable ground for it, and from the very start it had marred her happiness. Aglaé's hus-

---

[12] Gottschalk, *Lafayette comes to America*, p. 120.

[13] Duc de Broglie (ed.), *Memoirs of the Prince de Talleyrand*, tr. Raphael Ledos de Beaufort (5 vols.; New York, 1891), I, 52-53.

[14] December 4, 1782 (a second letter of that date), private collection.

[15] Roux to Poix, December 5, 1782, *ibid.*

band seemed more tolerant than her family; and Adrienne had all along observed (in her daughter's phrase) "an exalted delicacy which removed from her any suspicion of jealousy, or at least of the petty actions which ordinarily follow therefrom."[16] But Aglaé's mother was shocked, and those who had some reason to be jealous of Lafayette had shown no delicacy. His private affairs had become public property, and the public relished them. In indignation mixed with resignation, Lafayette protested to Poix: "The meannesses of the public of which you tell me make me almost sorry that we have not already sailed. I prefer to think that that public is a small number of little cliques. The more extensive public—the public in another sense—has honored me with its good will. In the society-public, on the contrary, some persons honor me with their jealousy. But why do they torment my angelic friend? Is that the penalty for her perfection? Or is she to blame if they make trouble for her in order to hurt me in the most painful way? That would show discernment in them, for I admit that nothing in the world could distress me more."[17]

Despite the growing danger that an English fleet might blockade Brest, Lafayette was obliged to contemplate the possibility of prolonged unfavorable winds. He took full advantage of his enforced idleness. He wrote to Franklin[18] again for the letter of approval, which had not yet arrived. "But," he consoled himself, "I know the opinion of the three gentlemen in the commission, and you have also thought that I ought not to detain the fleet on my account. And as I am still more anxious to do the best than to appear to have done so, my conscience is easy, and I would willingly loose [sic] the credit of past exertions rather than to neglect an opportunity of making new ones."

Lafayette had also learned that Rayneval had again returned from a speedy voyage to England. That made him hope that peace was not far distant.[19] As a matter of fact, though Lafayette did not yet know it, the American commissioners, dis-

[16] Lasteyrie, p. 194.

[17] December 6, 1782, private collection.

[18] December 6, 1782, Hale and Hale, II, 231–32.   [19] *Ibid.*, p. 232.

trustful of Rayneval's missions to London, had already agreed
with Oswald to the preliminaries of peace. Those preliminaries,
they pleaded, did not constitute a separate transaction since
they were not to become binding until the general peace was
signed. The separate American understanding with Oswald was
in part attributable to Lafayette. British anxiety for a speedy
peace was in some degree due to his political activity as well as
to the enormous armaments that were known to be ready to
start in the spring for the West Indies. Dispatches from Paris
to London pictured the marquis as a "vain and insolent young
man" who headed the war party in France. He had gone about
"fanning the waning flames of ill will" between France and England and trying to get himself sent on a mission to England—
for no other purpose, Fitzherbert said, than the satisfaction of
appearing before George III in an American uniform.[20]

Ignorant that the first important step toward a general peace
had already been taken, Lafayette knew only that the war
might end at any time. That would make it unnecessary for
his expedition to sail. And if the expedition should be called off,
he already had his eye on other employment. The final treaty
might well be signed in London, where he could be useful. Cautiously putting out his feelers, he wrote to Franklin: "In case
men of some rank are sent by France, I do not know who will
be the person. If it is not the one we spoke about together, it
will be the usual ambassador, my uncle the M^{quis} de Noailles.
This if you please (entre nous) unless you think useful to communicate it, under secrecy, to your colleagues. As to my part,
if matters were so ripe as to admit of my return, nothing would
more highly please me than the happiness, any how, to serve
America, and more particularly in the capacity of a man hon-
oured with her confidence."[21]

Peace continued to be the chief subject of conversation

[20] Fitzherbert to Shelburne, December 1, 1782, and January 15 and 19, 1783, cited
in Lord Edmond Fitzmaurice, *Life of William, Earl of Shelburne*, etc. (3 vols.; London,
1875–76), III, 320–21.

[21] Lafayette to Franklin, December 6, 1782, *loc. cit.*, pp. 231–32 (here quoted after
the original in APS, Franklin papers, Vol. XXVI, no. 89).

around Brest,[22] but wind and tide waited for no decision. Within two days of the "Censeur's" return, a sudden breeze once more sent her to sea at the head of the French fleet. Lafayette again sent hasty farewells to Franklin[23] and Poix.[24] Since "personal considerations ought to give way to motives of public utility," he wrote to Franklin, he had decided to sail with the fleet, "and untill peace is ascertained, will continue in promoting the views which you have decided to be the most advantageous to America." By this time, it appears, Lafayette had succeeded in persuading himself that Franklin was entirely responsible for his decision to go to Spain.

The voyage to Cadiz was uneventful. Lafayette proved not to have won complete immunity from seasickness, but poor Roux "looked less like a composer of letters than a man who is about to carry them into the next world."[25] They passed the region of bad winds and enemy fleets safely, though by that time Lafayette had begun to wish heartily for peace, if only for the sake of the "unfortunates shut up in these vile floating coffers."[26] When they had spent a little over a week on board and were only about twenty leagues from Cadiz, the wind again changed, and it looked as if they would take just as long to cover the remaining distance. Impatient to be on land and active once more, Lafayette now transferred to the frigate "Richmond" and sailed ahead of the fleet. Becalmed a few miles out of Cadiz, he succeeded in making the shore and reaching his destination by land on the evening of December 23. He found living quarters at the home of an American named Richard Harrison, who acted as a sort of American consul in Cadiz.[27] On his arrival

[22] Roux to Poix, December 8, 1782, private collection.

[23] December 8, 1782, Wharton, VI, 120 (here quoted after the original in LC, Franklin papers, no. 1098).

[24] December 8, 1782, private collection.

[25] Lafayette to Poix, December 18, 1782, *ibid.*   [26] *Ibid.*

[27] *Ibid.;* Lafayette to Jay, December 26, 1782, *Correspondence of Jay,* III, 12; Manuel Hermet to Rendon, December 24, 1782, *New York Gazette and Weekly Mercury,* March 3, 1783; Lafayette to Poix, December 24, 1782, private collection; Roux to Poix, December 31, 1782, *ibid.* The *Correspondence of Jay* calls Lafayette's host in Cadiz Mr. Hamilton; the correct name was more probably Mr. Harrison (see Wharton, V, 176 and 180; VI, 239 and 241).

Estaing appointed him *maréchal-général des logis* (quartermas-ter-general) of the combined armies. Roux was rewarded for his loyalty and seasickness by being made *aide-major-général* under Lafayette's direct orders.[28] The fleet did not enter the Cadiz harbor until December 30.

In Cadiz, Lafayette began to believe that his efforts had not been in vain. From the Spanish prospective, peace seemed far off. The Franco-Spanish forces still were besieging Gibraltar. "We shall have war," he decided. "I shall not return before next winter."[29] And again: "Peace seems to be moving further and further off, and we shall have one more campaign."[30] He found that Estaing was a worthy commander, and one could serve under him without qualms. Cadiz, however, was boring. "Its greatest merit is that it is less Spanish than the other cities."[31] Certain Spanish officials filled the marquis with repug-nance. Wherever he went, he found the fandango and the ro-sary, but rarely a beautiful woman. One lady with "big black eyes and hair that trails along the ground"[32] had once been a friend of the Vicomte de Noailles. Lafayette mentioned her several times in his letters to Poix. But, though he wrote amus-ingly enough about the amorous escapades of his friends in Cadiz, he remained, as he put it, "tranquilly in my savagery."[33] He claimed no credit for his good behavior, however. Except for the beauty with black eyes, a baronne still younger and prettier, and an English lady less beautiful than kind, "there isn't a woman here whose acquaintance is worth having."[34]

In Cadiz, Lafayette learned that, as far as the United States was concerned, the war was over. He was himself somewhat shocked that, despite commitments in the treaty of alliance

[28] Roux to Poix, December 31, 1782, *loc. cit.;* Lafayette to Poix, December 31, 1782, *ibid.*

[29] Lafayette to Poix, December 31, 1782, *loc. cit.*

[30] Lafayette to Vergennes, January 1, 1783, *Mémoires,* II, 47.

[31] Lafayette to [Mme de Tessé], January 1, 1783, *ibid.*, pp. 49–50.

[32] Lafayette to Poix, December 31, 1782, *loc. cit.*

[33] Lafayette to Poix, January 21, 1782, private collection.

[34] Lafayette to Poix, January 28, 1783, *ibid.*

and instructions from Congress, the American plenipotentiaries had signed separate preliminaries of peace but immediately undertook to apologize to Vergennes for his adopted country- men: "Having so little information, I hazard no opinion, but I am persuaded that you will be pleased with Congress. I can even repeat two things in addition—that the American minis- ters put great store by your communications, and that with fi- nancial help we shall have powerful co-operation in their coun- try."[35] A letter from Vergennes arrived even before Lafayette could send off his. It gave him few details that he did not al- ready know from current reports. He could only repeat in a postscript what he had already said: "You will, I hope, be pleased with Congress."[36]

The most crucial need of the United States, Lafayette real- ized, was money. In the hope of securing more effective finan- cial and military aid from Spain, he thought of writing a long letter on the subject to his old friend William Carmichael, who in Jay's absence was chargé d'affaires at Madrid. Knowing that letters sent by the post would probably be opened and re- ported to the Spanish government, he proposed to word it for Spanish eyes to read. Estaing approved of the idea, and Lafa- yette sounded out Vergennes upon it: "I am far from believing that that will bring us any Spanish money, but I did believe that I might make this little effort, inadequate though it is."[37]

While waiting for a reply from Versailles, the marquis kept busy with such things as wagons, hammocks, tents, guns, axes, and other humdrum objects of a quartermaster-general's care, quite content with the efforts of the Spanish and with "the very beautiful armament" being mobilized. Yet he feared that when all was ready and they were on the point of sailing, a courier would come with news of general peace. "But if I get back to

---

[35] Lafayette to Vergennes, January 1, 1783, *loc. cit.*, p. 48; cf. Lafayette to Jay, December 26, 1782, *loc. cit.*, p. 11.

[36] January 2, 1783, *Mémoires*, II, 48-49 (where the date is erroneously given as January 1: cf. AAE, corr. pol., É.-U., Vol. XXIII, fol. 28).

[37] Lafayette to Vergennes, January 1, 1783, *loc. cit.*, p. 48; cf. Lafayette to Jay, December 26, 1782, *loc. cit.*, p. 12; Lafayette to Livingston, February 5, 1783, Wharton, VI, 238-39.

Paris, I shall not regret the waste of our efforts," he wrote Poix, in a long and amusing letter. It was filled with superlatives on the merits of his friends in French society. There were no superlatives for Aglaé, but "when you learn of opportunities [to write me]," he begged, "don't forget to tell Madame de Hunolstein about them."[38]

The duty of his office soon took the quartermaster-general to the camps in the environs of Cadiz. Roux reported that his young commander "was quite satisfied" with the soldiers and that their officers "all want to serve under his orders."[39] Upon his return the marquis received an appeal for help from Carmichael. Like Jay before him, the American chargé was in the embarrassing position of not being recognized by the Spanish court as the representative of an independent state. He could not even get an audience with the Spanish minister of foreign affairs in order to present his credentials.[40] Lafayette, remembering his earlier scheme to befool the Spanish government, now sent off a letter much like the one he had previously proposed—ostensibly to Carmichael but actually for the Spanish authorities to read. He vigorously expressed the opinion that Spain ought to treat with the United States on a basis of equality. "Congress, I hope, & thro' them, the whole nation, do not intend their dignity to be trifled with & for my part, I have no inclination to betray the confidence of the American people. I expect we are going to have peace & I expect Spain is going to act by you with propriety; but should they hesitate to treat you as a public servant of the United States, then, however disagreeable is the taste, Mr. Carmichael had better go to Paris where France may stand a mediator & thro' that generous & common friend, we may come to the wished for connection with

---

[38] Lafayette to Poix, January 13, 1783, private collection. The documents on Lafayette's activity as quartermaster-general are to be found in AN, T 404³ and Marine B⁴ 210. Some of them have been published in Victor Advielle, "Quelques autographes inédits Lafayette relatifs à l'expédition de Cadix," *Révolution française*, XI (1886), 447–49.

[39] [Roux] to Poix, January 16, 1783, private collection; cf. Lafayette to Poix, January 16, 1783, *ibid*.

[40] Cf. Carmichael to Livingston, February 21, 1783, Wharton, VI, 259.

the Court of Spain "[41] To make doubly sure that his letter would be opened in the mails, a few days later he sent another copy of it; and he also advised Carmichael to show it to the French ambassador in Madrid.[42] Carmichael did so, and Lafayette soon learned that it had had "a pretty good effect."[43] Thus was Spanish espionage converted to the uses of democracy.

By the end of the month preparations at Cadiz were complete, and the armada was ready to sail. Estaing went to Madrid to arrange final details. The king of Spain, to Lafayette's surprise, had not only co-operated wholeheartedly but now even consented to his being sent to Canada with a French army to divert the English.[44] It began to look as if his favorite ambition—to conquer Canada—might at last become a reality, having won the approval of the government that had blocked it in the past. On returning from the court of Charles III, Estaing declared that the king of Spain was afraid of Lafayette. A single episode had sufficed to convince the admiral of that. When he had suggested that Lafayette be made provisional governor of Jamaica after its capture, the old king exclaimed, "No, never, not that! He'd create a republic there!"[45]

Despite Estaing's success at Madrid, his forces did not move. The expectation that peace had been, or soon would be, declared rendered them immobile. The Spanish wished Estaing, while waiting, to aid them in the Mediterranean, but Lafayette advised against it, fearing that the expedition might receive its orders to sail while it was away and precious time would thus be lost. On his insistence, Estaing remained idle in the Cadiz harbor.[46] Lafayette was in a quandary regarding his eventual

[41] Lafayette to Carmichael, January 20, 1783, PCC, no. 156, fols. 308–11 (and with some omissions, Wharton, VI, 222–23).

[42] Lafayette to [Carmichael], January 29, 1783, Jackson Collection.

[43] Lafayette to Livingston, February 5, 1783, *loc. cit.*, p. 240.

[44] *Ibid.*, p. 238.

[45] *Mémoires*, III, 198; Sparks MSS XXXII, pp. 112–13; Lapierre de Chateauneuf, *Le Général Lafayette: mémoires authentiques* (Paris, 1831), p. 52.

[46] Estaing to Ségur, January 29, 1783, AN, Marine B4 211, fol. 85.

destination. To Carmichael, he wrote, that if peace came—"and now I hardly question it"—he would "pay a visit to my friends on the other side of the Atlantic."[47] To Poix he wrote: "If I am permitted to consult my heart, it will not be long before I have the pleasure of greeting you."[48]

The preliminaries of a general peace were signed at Paris on January 20. An express, sent to Estaing to call off the expedition, arrived in Cadiz twelve days later.[49] Circumstances conspired to make Carmichael, who had been the American most concerned with Lafayette's first enlistment in the American war, also the first to whom he broke the news of general peace. "Remember the times, my good friend, when we have made our first acquaintance. Now our cause is gained, and the remembrance of past labours adds to the enjoyement." Since he could not "think of leaving this country before I pay my respects to the king" and since he also wished to know the Conde de Floridablanca, the king's chief minister, he planned to join Carmichael in a few days.[50]

Breaking up the armada that had been so painfully mobilized at Cadiz was not simple. There were accounts to balance, promotions and transfers to recommend, personal affairs to clear up, before he could properly leave.[51] Estaing had been ordered to send a fast vessel to cruise wherever French vessels might be found in order to inform them that the war was over. Lafayette persuaded him to let the vessel carry his personal servant to America with the news. Estaing fittingly chose a corvette named the "Triomphe"; and as the "Triomphe" prepared for its long journey Lafayette sat down at his desk to write another series of "gazettes" that his servant would carry to America. When his pen had ceased its scratching, he had composed long

[47] January 29, 1783, *loc. cit.*

[48] January 28, 1783, *loc. cit.*

[49] Floyd to Clinton, March 25, 1783, Burnett, VII, 102; Lafayette to Carmichael, February 2, 1783, LC, House of Representatives collection, no. 103.

[50] Lafayette to Carmichael, February 2, 1783, *loc. cit.*

[51] See n. 38 above.

dispatches to Washington,[52] Congress,[53] Livingston,[54] and Greene,[55] among others.[56] He congratulated them warmly on the successful conclusion of the war. "Our early times," he told Congress,[57] "I recollect with a most pleasing sense of pride. Our present ones make me easy and happy. To futurity I look forward in the most delightful prospects." His felicitations to Washington reached oratorical heights: "Were you but such a man as Julius Caesar or the King of Prussia, I should almost be sorry for you at the end of the great tragedy where you are acting such a part. But with my dear general I rejoice at the blessings of peace where our noble ends have been secured. Remember our Valley Forge times, and from a recollection of past dangers and labours, we still will be more pleased at our present comfortable situation. What a sense of pride and satisfaction I feel when I think of the times what have determined my engaging in the American cause. As for you, my dear General, who truly can say you have done all this, what must your virtuous and good heart feel on the happy instant which the revolution you have made is now firmly established. I cannot but envy the happiness of my grand children where they will be about celebrating and worshipping your name. To have one of their ancestors among your soldiers, to know he has the good fortune to be the friend of your heart will be the eternal honour in which they

[52] Lafayette to Washington, February 5, 1783, Sparks, *Correspondence of the American Revolution*, III, 545–59 (where it is slightly retouched). It is quoted below from the copy in Sparks MSS LXXXVIII, Part I, fols. 25–30. The passage quoted by Washington in his letter to Livingston (March 29, 1783, Fitzpatrick, XXVII, 266–67) is contained in neither version.

[53] Lafayette to Congress, February 5, 1783 (two letters), Wharton, VI, 237–38 (original in PCC, no. 156, fols. 312–14); and PCC, no. 156, fol. 336.

[54] Lafayette to Livingston, February 5, 1783, *loc. cit.*, pp. 238–40. Another letter of Lafayette to Livingston, February 5, 1783, marked "most private" is in LC, Hamilton papers. The presence of this letter in the Hamilton papers has led the editor of *Works of Hamilton* (I, 325–27), Wharton (VI, 240–41), and others to assume that it is to Hamilton. It is, however, clearly addressed by Lafayette to Livingston; its presence in the Hamilton papers is probably to be explained by several references to Hamilton which it contains and which presumably Livingston wished Hamilton to see.

[55] Lafayette to Greene, February 5, 1783, LC, Nathanael Greene collection.

[56] Lafayette to unknown, February 5, 1783, Sparks MSS XLIX, Part III, p. 273.

[57] Wharton, VI, 237.

shall glory, and to the oldest of them as long as my posterity will last, I shall delegate the favour you have been pleased to confer upon my son George."[58]

If he had had his own way, Lafayette declared, he would himself have brought the news of the peace to America. But Carmichael's needs called him to Madrid, and from there he would go to Paris, and so could not plan to be in America before the summer. He begged to be excused, pointing out again and again that his own wish was to go to America but that he remained because of his loyalty to Congress and the demands of American political agents in Europe. He suggested confidentially to Livingston that he would like Congress to approve of his conduct publicly. "The best way to manage it is to have a resolve of Congress published by way of answer to my letters."[59] And he promised Washington to embark for America in June. "Happy, ten times happy will I be in embracing my dear General, my father, my best friend, whom I love with an affection and a respect which I too well feel not to know it is impossible to me to express it."[60]

Lafayette's restlessness did not permit him to take advantage of the breathing-spell that peace now offered. He already had made many plans for the future. For one thing, he and Washington, he thought, ought to undertake a great humanitarian enterprise together. It was evidently a scheme which had developed from his observations in Virginia. "Now, my dear General, that you are going to enjoy some ease and quiet, permit me to propose a plan to you which might become greatly beneficial to the black part of mankind. Let us unite in purchasing a small estate where we may try the experiment to free the Negroes and use them only as tenants. Such an example as yours might render it a general practice, and if we succeed in America, I will cheerfully devote a part of my time to render the method fashionable in the West Indies. If it be a wild

[58] See n. 52 above, and Sparks, *Correspondence of the American Revolution*, III, 545–46.

[59] See n. 54 above and Wharton, VI, 241.

[60] See n. 52 above and Sparks, *Correspondence of the American Revolution*, III, 546.

scheme, I had rather be mad this way than to be thought wise in the other task."[61] This utterance was the first of a long series of humanitarian proposals that were to form a significant part of his future activity as a liberal. His earlier comments had given no hint that he thought of "the black part of mankind" as anything other than slaves and chattel.

The marquis still hoped also for a signal honor from his adopted country. Though the king of France could now be expected to send his regular ambassador, the Marquis de Noailles, to the Court of St. James, Lafayette continued to look forward to a diplomatic career. In a "most private" letter which accompanied his public dispatch to Livingston and which Livingston was requested to show to no one but Washington, he set forth his ambition. "Here is an other thing which would highly flatter me and lies within your departement. A ratification of the treaty will be sent by Congress to the court of England. It is but an honorary commission that requires only a few weeks, and even a few days attendance. The sedentary minister [and he suggested his friend Hamilton for that post] you may send or with me or after me, or what I would like better, at the time when Great Britain has sent hers to you. So many greater proofs of confidence have been bestowed upon me by Congress that I may freely tell you my wishes upon this very pleasing mark of their esteem." He explained that when he was last in England, just before going to America for the first time, he was looked upon as "an enthusiastic rebel and indeed a young madman." That was why he would now like to present himself there "in the capacity of an extraordinary envoy from the United States." At that time he had placed himself "on pretty bad terms" with Adrienne's uncle, the French ambassador, but "now our friendship has revived and I am in the situation to lead him into my measures and to know his secrets without telling him mine."[62]

Washington was the only American besides Livingston to whom Lafayette confessed his ambition. In an "entirely confidential" part of his letter to the general he frankly avowed: "I

[61] Sparks, *Correspondence of the American Revolution*, III, 547.
[62] See n. 54 above and Wharton, VI, 241.

would take it as a most flattering circumstance in my life to be
sent to England with the ratification of the American treaty; you
know it is but an honorary commission that would require the
attendance of a few weeks, and if any sedentary minister is sent,
I should have the pleasure of introducing him."[63] He imparted
his secret ambition to Estaing, too; and the admiral thought
that America "would do well by herself and us to ask you to
consent to be her ambassador to London."[64] Washington fell in
with his young friend's plan, believing that, if it proved "consistent with our national honor," Congress would "feel a pleasure in gratifying the wishes of a man who has been such a
zealous labourer in the cause of this country."[65] But in the end
Lafayette was not sent to London.

Other American complications came to Lafayette's mind as
he hastily composed letters of congratulation for the "Triomphe" to carry. Sharp notes of warning became mingled with
his song of jubilation. The looseness of the American confederation had often caused him anxious moments in the past, when
the states had failed to heed the demands of Congress or had
hesitated to aid one another in distress. To that unco-operative
spirit would now be added the hostility of the soldiers if they
were not properly rewarded by their country. Lafayette considered that disaffection of patriots and that confusion of authority as phases of the same problem, which could be solved
together—with his help, of course. In his "most private" letter
to Livingston he proposed a new constitution: "As public affairs have the first place with me, let me tell you that our articles of confederation ought to be revised and measures immediately taken to invigorate the Continental Union. Depend
upon it, there lies the danger for America. This last stroke is
wanting, and unless the States be strongly bound to each other
we have to fear from British, and indeed from European politics. There ought to be delegates from each state, and perhaps

[63] See n. 52 above and Fitzpatrick, XXVI, 266–67.

[64] Estaing to Lafayette, March 11, 1783, Morgan Library, Lafayette, Vol. II.

[65] Washington to Livingston, March 29, 1783, Fitzpatrick, XXVI, 267; cf. Washington to Hamilton, March 31, 1783, *ibid.*, p. 277.

some officers among them, one of whom I would be happy to be, who towards next fall would meet together and under the presidence of Gal Washington, may devise upon amendments to be proposed in the articles of confederation, units of states, etc., etc." To influence public opinion in favor of such a constitutional convention he suggested that Livingston publish the last paragraph of his letter to the president of Congress.[66] That paragraph read: "Now, Sir, our Noble Cause has prevailed, our independence is fairly settled, and American virtue enjoys its reward. No exertions, I hope, will now be wanting to strengthen the federal union. May the States be so bound to each other as will forever defy European politics. Upon that Union, their consequence, their happiness will depend. It now becomes the first wish of a heart so truly American, that no words can express its gratefull, unbounded, and eternal affection."[67] The same idea was vigorously conveyed to Washington and Greene.[68] It fell on ready ears, but circumstances were to prevent the creation of a strong American federation far beyond the few months which Lafayette thought would be sufficient "to propose whatever amendments would insure a state of union, vigor, and independence."[69]

The problem of international trade also interested Lafayette to a degree that would have surprised those who thought money matters beneath the dignity of a nobleman of the sword. Recognizing that the future relations of his native country with his adopted country depended upon their commercial ties, he urged upon his American correspondents that they exert themselves to promote trade between the two nations.[70] He had already spoken to French and American merchants in America and France on that subject. Finding them well disposed, he now promised to use his influence "in forwarding any plans that may

[66] See n. 54 above and Wharton, VI, 240.

[67] See n. 53 above and Wharton, VI, 238.

[68] See nn. 52 and 55 above.

[69] Lafayette to Greene, February 5, 1783, *loc. cit.*   [70] Cf. *ibid.*

want either mercantile connections or the protection of the French government."[71]

Lafayette also was worried about the American army. He asked Washington, "What will be its fate? I hope their country will be grateful. Should the reverse be the case, I would indeed feel very unhappy. Will part of the army be kept together? If not, I hope we won't forfeit our noble titles as officers and soldiers in the American army, so that in case of danger, we may be called upon from every quarter and reunite in the defense of a country which the army has so effectively, so heroically served."[72] He had learned that the officers of the army, dissatisfied with the promise of half-pay for life, had petitioned Congress for immediate payment of a lump sum or partial payment of back wages and retirement after the war on full pay for a fixed number of years.[73] He hoped that these demands would be met, as the good will of the army must not be lost.

For the dangers to America, the marquis felt, were not over. He distrusted the Spanish and was disturbed that by the terms of the treaty they received the Floridas from England. He foresaw that there would be trouble not only there but in the Mississippi Valley. "The people of Florida will, I hope, remove into Georgia," he wrote to Livingston.[74] "But the Spaniards will insist upon a pretended right to an extent of country all along the left shore of Mississippi. Not that they mean to occupy it, but because they are affraid of neighbours that have a spirit of liberty. I am sorry those people have the Floridas, but as we cannot help it we must endeavour to frustrate Lord Shelburne's views, which I presume are bent upon a dispute between Spain and the United States. A day will come, I hope, when Europeans will have little to do on the Northern Continent, and God grant it may even be for the happiness of mankind and the propagation of liberty." He hoped his trip to Madrid would do

[71] Lafayette to unknown, February 5, 1783, *loc. cit.*

[72] See n. 52 above and Sparks, *Correspondence of the American Revolution*, III, 548.

[73] Cf. Burnett, VII, x.

[74] See n. 54 above and Wharton, VI, 293.

something to improve the attitude of Spain toward the United States. "For ever the Spaniards will be extravagant in their territorial notions, and very jealous of the encrease of American wealth and power. But it is good policy for us to be upon friendly terms with them."

The "Triomphe" did not leave Cadiz until February 14. After a rapid passage of only thirty-six days, it brought to Philadelphia the first report of the general peace.[75] The news of the separate American negotiations had traveled to Philadelphia slowly (since no naval corvette was especially assigned to carry it). That of the general preliminaries traveled much faster and arrived only a short time afterward. That fortunate accident cut short the flurry in Congress over the separate negotiations, which some members were inclined to resent as a breach of instructions and a reflection on American honor.[76] Throughout America the end of the war was coupled with the name of Lafayette, who had first reported it.[77] Even Franklin's name was less regularly and less gratefully pronounced along with the blessed word "peace." Franklin, nevertheless, had been a better peacemaker, and Washington (as well as several others) had been a better warrior; but no man had been more conspicuous as both warrior and peacemaker than America's marquis.

Nothing detained Lafayette in Cadiz longer. He prepared to set out to join Carmichael but first wished to see the famous stronghold of Gibraltar. He and a fellow-officer, the Prince de Nassau, traveled to the rock together, only to learn that, since General Eliott, the British commandant, had not yet officially

[75] Boudinot to Washington, March 23, 1783, Burnett, VII, 93–94.

[76] *Ibid.*, pp. vii–ix and xvi; Livingston to the commissioners, March 25, 1783, Wharton, VI, 340.

[77] Cf. Boudinot to Washington, March 23, 1783, *loc. cit.*; Boudinot to Livingston, [*ca.* March 23, 1783], *New York Gazette and Weekly Mercury*, March 31, 1783, and *Boston Independent Chronicle and Universal Advertiser*, April 3, 1783; several letters of members of Congress, March 24–25, 1783, Burnett, VII, 94–105; Mercer to Weedon March 24, 1783, *Calendar of Weedon correspondence*, no. 144; Bedford to Read, March 24, 1783, and to Van Dyke, March 24, 1783, J. P. Nields, *Gunning Bedford, Junior*, etc. (n.p., n.d.), pp. 6 and 7; Huntington to Andrew Huntington, March 29, 1783, *Letters written by Ebenezer Huntington during the American Revolution* (New York, 1914), p. 104; Washington to several correspondents, March 27–31, 1783, Fitzpatrick, XXVI, 262, 267, and 275; General orders, March 29, 1783, *ibid.*, pp. 268–69.

learned of the peace, he could not permit them to enter.[78] They
returned to Cadiz, and Lafayette left immediately for Madrid.[79]
In reporting to the minister of war on the merits of the officers on
his staff, Estaing placed the *maréchal-général des logis* at their
head with this comment: "M^r le Marquis de Lafayette; his
name says all that there is to say. I permit myself as his general
only the satisfaction of calling him to the attention of the
Maréchal de Ségur, who is well aware of all the persistence I
showed in requesting such a second. I shall limit myself to repeating what the king's minister knows—that M^r le Marquis
de Lafayette has been at Cadiz, as in America, always himself.
He has incurred only necessary expenditures but those were indispensable and they have been considerable."[80]

Still wearing the uniform and sword of an American major-
general,[81] Lafayette arrived in Madrid on February 15. He first
reported to the French ambassador, the Comte de Montmorin,
and, finding him sympathetic with his plans, proceeded to confer with Carmichael.[82] Remembering that Carmichael was "the
first American I ever knew,"[83] he saw only justice in their co-
operation now to secure American recognition at Madrid. All
agreed that he should go to pay his respects to Charles III at
the country palace of the Pardo. Despite his "rebel title and
uniform" he was graciously received.[84] He found that the king
had "odd notions" regarding the American revolution, "as he
has indeed upon everything."[85] The "rebel" was amused at the
formality of Spanish court etiquette. "I saw some grandees who
seemed quite petty, especially when they were on their knees,"

[78] *Gazette de Leyde*, March 18, 1783; *Pennsylvania Gazette*, May 14, 1783.

[79] Lafayette to Jay, February 15, 1783, *Correspondence of Jay*, III, 27.

[80] AMG, Lafayette dossier 1261; AN, Marine B⁴ 210, fol. 90.

[81] *Gentleman's magazine*, LIII (1783), 268; *Pennsylvania Gazette*, June 11, 1783.

[82] Lafayette to Jay, February 15, 1783, *loc. cit.*, p. 28; to Livingston, March 2, 1783,
Wharton, VI, 268 (where, however, some editorial changes from the original in PCC,
no. 156, fols. 344–50, are to be found).

[83] Lafayette to Washington, March 2, 1783, Sparks MSS LXXXVIII, Part I, fol. 31.

[84] Lafayette to Mme de Tessé, February 17, 1783, *Mémoires*, II, 60.

[85] Lafayette to Livingston, March 2, 1783, *loc. cit.*

he reported in his best "republican" style to Adrienne's aunt Mme de Tessé, who was also somewhat of a *philosophe*, "and there was good reason for an independent nose to sniff."[86] His pleasant reception at the Pardo made him feel his duties in Madrid would not take long.

On leaving the king's presence, Lafayette sought out Floridablanca. Having everywhere made it known that he intended to take Carmichael to Paris with him unless his credentials were formally accepted by the Spanish government, he found it easy to raise the question of American affairs. As he had suspected, the Madrid court was fearful of the contagious effect that American ideas of independence might have on the Spanish colonies in America. He also discovered that Floridablanca was very ignorant of the United States. He went into considerable detail about each of the states, trying to allay the minister's fears. Floridablanca, agreeing to lay the American situation before the king, promised to call on Lafayette within two days at Madrid.[87]

While waiting for his second interview with Floridablanca, Lafayette made it his business to have Carmichael be seen with him on every occasion. He introduced him everywhere "in the most public manner as the representative of the country which he serves."[88] The French ambassador ably seconded his efforts. At the appointed time Floridablanca came to see Lafayette and the Comte de Montmorin. The Spanish minister now assured them that Spain desired only harmonious relations with the United States. Lafayette insisted that recognition must then be offered soon, for he was leaving Spain in a few days. Floridablanca, though with obvious reluctance, agreed to accept Carmichael's credentials before Lafayette left and to present him to the king as soon as Mr. Jay might be informed and should approve. Meanwhile Carmichael would be invited to a dinner which the minister was tendering to the ambassadors at Madrid.[89]

[86] Lafayette to Mme de Tessé, February 17, 1783, *loc. cit.*

[87] Lafayette to Livingston, March 2, 1783, *loc. cit.*

[88] Carmichael to Livingston, February 21, 1783, Wharton, VI, 260.

[89] Lafayette to Livingston, March 2, 1783, *loc. cit.*, pp. 268–69.

That victory having apparently been won, Lafayette broached the subject of a treaty between Spain and the United States. The boundaries of the Spanish territories in America need create no complications, Floridablanca thought, since Spain was ready to accept the limits described in the separate Anglo-American preliminaries of peace. The navigation of the Mississippi, codfish duties, and similar commercial problems proved more difficult, and Floridablanca was less yielding on those points. But he was prepared to do what he could to satisfy the Americans. Lafayette's success on all the moot issues led him for a moment to hope that Floridablanca might be willing to lend the United States some much-needed money, but the minister's answer to the first hint in that direction "put it out of my power," Lafayette reported, "to do it in any way but such as was inconsistent with the dignity of the United States."[90]

Lafayette, nevertheless, was quite satisfied and wished only to make sure that there would be no misunderstanding of what had been promised. Accordingly he asked permission to submit a written résumé of what had been said. Floridablanca at first objected, since, he said, "his word was as good as his writing,"[91] but finally consented. The minister then took his leave. There had been a little of threat and challenge on both sides, but all had gone off remarkably well. As soon as the Spanish minister was gone, the marquis wrote out an *aide-mémoire* of what had been said, taking care to give it "the best construction I could make."[92] Since he would soon visit the American Congress, he said, he wished to present an exact account of their conversation and hoped Floridablanca would approve of his report.[93]

Even before replying, Floridablanca acted in the friendly manner he had promised. The day after his conference with Lafayette, Carmichael, accompanied by the marquis, was granted an audience. When it was over, Carmichael reported that Lafa-

---

[90] *Ibid.*, p. 269.   [91] *Ibid.*

[92] Lafayette to Washington, March 2, 1783, *loc. cit.*, fol. 30.

[93] Lafayette to Floridablanca, February 19, 1783, Wharton, VI, 256.

yette "was content with my reception and personally I had no reason to be dissatisfied."[94] In the course of the conversation, the minister's "expressions of friendship for the Marquis were unbounded." Lafayette for his part "omitted no opportunity of pressing in the strongest manner" for "speedy and effectual measures to convince the States of the desire of his Catholic majesty to cultivate their amity."[95] Floridablanca assured him that he would be satisfied on all the points which they had discussed.

Only one matter proved somewhat embarrassing. As he had promised Lafayette, Floridablanca invited Carmichael to attend the dinner of the foreign ambassadors the next Saturday. Carmichael had previously told the marquis, however, that he thought he ought to have a written invitation in the customary form. Lafayette, therefore, took the minister aside and after a short whispered conversation induced him to agree to send his invitation in writing. Floridablanca also brought up the delay in presenting the American chargé to the Spanish royal family. He explained that no chargés d'affaires except those of France and Austria had hitherto been presented at court; nevertheless, Carmichael could rest assured that he would be received "in the most honorable manner," if he presented himself. On leaving the ministry, however, Carmichael expressed the opinion that, until formally presented, he ought not to go to court, and Lafayette agreed.[96]

True to his word, Floridablanca replied in a friendly fashion to Lafayette's *aide-mémoire*. He did so by a formal endorsement of the marquis' own letter, stating that Lafayette "had perfectly well understood" Spain's disposition toward the United States. Only on one point did Floridablanca demur. "Although it is his Majesty's intention to abide for the present by the limits established by the treaty of November 30, 1782, between the English and the Americans," the minister's endorsement stipulated, "yet the king intends to inform himself particularly whether it can be in any way inconvenient or prejudicial, and

[94] Carmichael to Livingston, February 21, 1783, *loc. cit.*, p. 259.
[95] *Ibid.*   [96] *Ibid.*, p. 260.

to settle that affair amicably with the United States."[97] This conditional recognition of the boundaries roused Lafayette's suspicions. Together with the French ambassador he went to see the Spanish minister again.[98] On his request for an explanation, Floridablanca stated that the condition applied only to minor details regarding which he wished to have reports from the Spanish commandants in the Mississippi area. Those details would be settled amicably, however, and would in no way affect the general acceptance of the boundary agreed upon by the Americans and the English. When asked for his word of honor on that point, he readily gave it, adding that Lafayette was free to pass on his promise to Congress. The marquis immediately added to his *aide-mémoire* a note describing this conversation.[99]

That evening, since Floridablanca had sent the written invitation which he had promised, Carmichael and Lafayette went to the ambassadors' dinner at the Pardo. Several colleagues who had informed their governments that relations between the United States and Spain appeared quite strained were obviously embarrassed to see Carmichael there. They now were in some dismay regarding the proper attitude to take toward him, since, though acknowledged by the minister of foreign affairs, he had not yet been presented to the king. The dinner passed without incident and immediately produced a good effect.[100] The representatives of several European governments soon made overtures to the American chargé and his patron. So intent was Lafayette upon preserving the dignity of the United States in European chancelleries that when the Prussian envoy asked him if Congress would be willing to make advances to his court, he answered, "The United States ought in my opinion not to make

[97] Floridablanca to Lafayette, February 22, 1783, Wharton, VI, 260–61. In the copy signed by Lafayette in PCC, no. 156, fols. 324–27, this letter follows on the same sheet of paper as the end of Lafayette's to Floridablanca (February 19, 1783, *loc. cit.*). In the English translation in PCC, no. 156, fol. 331, the word "and" between "prejudicial" and "settle" is omitted, thus changing the meaning somewhat.

[98] Lafayette to Livingston, March 2, 1783, *loc. cit.*, p. 269.

[99] Endorsement of Lafayette, February 22, 1783, following Floridablanca's letter to him of the same date; see n. 97 above.

[100] Carmichael to Livingston, March 13, 1783, Wharton, VI, 294.

but to receive advances."[101] Likewise, Carmichael took the attitude that he would extend the usual diplomatic formalities only to those who had shown a similar courtesy to him.[102] The marquis shortly took up the matter of America's boundaries with other Spanish ministers. Minister José Galvez, who was head of the department of the Indies, proved dissatisfied with the boundaries fixed by the Anglo-American agreement but sent orders to the Spanish governors to abide by them for the present and promised to send him a copy of those orders.[103]

Lafayette had thus with astonishing success completed "after a week's stay and exertions"[104] the task he had come to Madrid to perform. In fact, he had good reason to congratulate himself upon the diplomatic coup that he had executed, since he had obliged the Spanish minister to commit his government formally and officially, though he had kept the United States free from any commitments—"which it was easy for me to do in my private capacity."[105] He had sent several letters to Jay in the course of his negotiations at Madrid, so that Jay ("whose political aide de camp I have been")[106] might speedily accept or repudiate what he had done. Now, with Floridablanca's signature and duly recorded promises in his portfolio, Lafayette prepared to leave for Paris. Carmichael regretted to see him go. "It is the happiest circumstance of my life," he confessed, "that the man whose services I was instrumental in procuring to my country should be the one to whom in a great measure I owe my first public appearance at the court of Spain."[107]

Lafayette left Madrid convinced of the "sincere and steady intention" of the Spanish court to cultivate the friendship of America. "They labour under fits of territorial madness. They have an ill understood and an ill conducted pride. It is disagreeable to treat with them, and their own interest does not persuade them out of their prejudices. But tho' they had rather

[101] Lafayette to Livingston, March 2, 1783, *loc. cit.*, p. 269.

[102] Carmichael to Livingston, March 13, 1783, *loc. cit.*

[103] Lafayette to Livingston, March 2, 1783, *loc. cit.*, p. 270.

[104] Lafayette to Washington, March 2, 1783, *loc. cit.*, fol. 30.

[105] Lafayette to Livingston, March 2, 1783, *loc. cit.*, p. 269.

[106] *Ibid.*   [107] Carmichael to Livingston, February 15, 1783, *loc. cit.*, p. 260.

there was not such a thing as North America, they are truly and earnestly desirous to maintain a good harmony and live in friendship and good neighbourly union with the United States."[108] But perhaps he overestimated the friendliness of the Spanish government. It was months before the final and formal recognition of the United States was forthcoming. And the dispute over the Spanish-American boundary was to go on for years. When the American negotiators were to remind the Spanish emissaries of the promise made to Lafayette, they were to learn that "the marquis [had] misunderstood."[109]

BIBLIOGRAPHICAL NOTES

There has been no careful study of Lafayette's visit to Spain in 1782–83. Lafayette's brief account in *Mémoires* (II, 3–6) and the letters written from Brest, Cadiz, Madrid, and Bordeaux, which are published there (II, 46–69), have been the only sources that his biographers have so far exploited with any degree of care, though there are many pertinent documents in Wharton, in the published correspondence of Jay, and in contemporary journals. For the foregoing chapter several unpublished letters (particularly those of Lafayette and Roux to Poix) have been very revealing. Of some documents the versions published by Sparks, by the editor of Lafayette's *Mémoires*, and by Wharton, proved upon comparison with the originals to have been garbled. Such instances have been indicated for the most part in the footnotes, though usually, for the reader's convenience, reference has been made to the best printed texts.

In addition to the account of the negotiations with Floridablanca contained in the *Mémoires*, Lafayette inspired several others, notably those by Sparks (Sparks MSS XXXII, pp. 112–15) and Chateauneuf (*Général Lafayette*, pp. 7–8). All the sources which are derived directly or indirectly from Lafayette create the impression that he was both more peremptory and more successful than other contemporary evidence would indicate.

The only study of the relations of Lafayette and the Comtesse de Hunolstein is my *Lady-in-waiting*. I should point out that Mr. John F. Gough, of Jersey City, N.J., for reasons that seem to me unconvincing, believes that the letter of Lafayette to "Aglaée" of March 27, 1783 (*ibid.*, pp. 94–95 and 99–102; and see below, pp. 418–19) is not addressed to Mme de Hunolstein but to Mme de Lafayette.

[108] Lafayette to Livingston, March 2, 1783, *loc. cit.*, p. 270.

[109] *Journals of Congress*, XXXI, 543 (under date of August 22, 1786). Cf. "Report on negotiations with Spain," [March 18, 1792], P. L. Ford, *Writings of Thomas Jefferson* (10 vols.; New York, 1892–99), V, 465; Carmichael to Short, April 18, 1793, *American state papers, class I: foreign relations*, etc., I (Washington, 1832), 260; G. L. Rives, "Spain and the United States in 1795," *AHR*, IV (1898), 67; D. Y. Thomas, "The diplomatic struggle for the Mississippi and the southwestern boundary," *Gulf states historical magazine*, II (1903–4), 346–47.

CHAPTER XVII

Reward, Renunciation, and Maturity

I T WAS again carnival time when Lafayette crossed the Pyrenees into France. Well pleased with his political successes at Madrid, he proceeded by leisurely stages, not averse, as Admiral d'Estaing had shrewdly guessed, to spending the festival season en route.[1] Only in March did he reach Bordeaux, where Adrienne's uncle, the Maréchal de Mouchy, lived. It was his first visit there since he had "stolen" from its harbor in 1777 to lend his name to the rebel American cause.[2]

From Bordeaux the young soldier-diplomat made a full report to Livingston of his Madrid exploits.[3] Along with this account he sent copies of his *aide-mémoire* and its endorsements, reserving the original for Jay's records. The latest news in Bordeaux was that an American vessel had at last displayed the American colors in the Thames at London. Justifiably proud, Lafayette concluded his lengthy report with a reminder of the new role he wished to play in America's salvation: "The ruin of Carthage was the last sentence in every speech of a Roman patriot. Upon the same principle of an unbounded zeal for America, can I be permitted to repeat that every American patriot must wish that the federal union between states may soon receive an additional strength. Upon that intimate, eternal union, their happiness, their consequence depend."[4]

A briefer account of the Spanish enterprise was dispatched

[1] Estaing to Lafayette, March 11, 1783, Morgan Library, Lafayette, Vol. II.

[2] Gottschalk, *Lafayette comes to America*, p. 100.

[3] March 2, 1783, Wharton, VI, 268–70.

[4] An incomplete version of these sentences is to be found *ibid.*, p. 270. They are quoted here from the original in PCC, no. 156, fol. 349.

also to Washington.[5] "I hope it will meet with your approbation," the marquis wrote, "for your approbation next to your friendship is necessary to me." Taking advantage of a boat in the harbor that was leaving for Boston, he expressed to Samuel Adams and Samuel Cooper also his congratulations upon the peace, not without regret for "the hope I had of enfranchising a new state."[6]

From Bordeaux, Lafayette continued northward by easy stages. Delayed somewhat by the spring flood which washed away the bridge over the Seine at Mantes just before he was to cross it, he reached Paris on March 12.[7] In Paris he waited only long enough to receive an honor, to fulfil a duty, and to experience a chagrin—all three fitting climaxes to his brilliant American career. The honor came from the minister of war with formal notification that, peace having been made, he might now assume his rank of *maréchal-de-camp* in the French army.[8] The duty resulted from the request of a deputation of Bayonne merchants for aid in their efforts to persuade the government to dredge their harbor and free them from certain tariff restrictions. They felt entitled to his support because they hoped to get more American trade if they succeeded. Lafayette consented—all the more readily because of a report that two American vessels loaded with tobacco had left Lorient, disgusted with the complicated tariff system of France and had sailed for England. The complications arose from the fact that tobacco was one of the several "farms" or monopolies assigned by the government for a price to groups of especially designated individuals known as "farmers-general."

Lafayette took it upon himself to approach the ministers of finance and of foreign affairs[9] as the champion of American

[5] March 2, 1783, Sparks MSS LXXXVIII, Part I, fols. 30–32.

[6] March 3, 1783, NYPL, Bancroft collection, Samuel Adams papers. The "pretty long" letter to Samuel Cooper is known only from the reference to it in this letter to Adams.

[7] *Gazette de Leyde*, March 21, 1783.   [8] AMG, Lafayette dossier 1261.

[9] Lafayette to Fleury, March 19, 1783, AAE, corr. pol., É.-U., Vol. XXIII, fols. 347–48; to Vergennes, March 19, 1783, *ibid.*, fols. 345–46, and *Mémoires*, II, 69–71.

trade. He thus found himself embarked upon his first systematic conflict with a privileged class in France. He proposed to the ministers the designation of certain ports—Bayonne, Marseilles, Dunkirk, Lorient—where American merchants would receive special favors and which the French government would make a special effort to improve. "In trading with the United States," he wrote to Minister Fleury, "we shall derive a great advantage from the war, our expenditures, and the Revolution. . . . . After long reflection on the common interests and on the particular disposition of our allies, I am convinced of two truths which my duty as a citizen oblige me to submit to you. The first is that it is up to us to get almost all the American trade. The second is that by our shackles upon commerce we are in imminent danger of losing the largest share of it. . . . . Having acquired the right to reflect upon the interests of France and America, I am unhappy to think that in repelling their trade rather than attracting it, we shall help the English much more than they can help themselves." And to Vergennes he stated: "I can not repeat too often that after a great war and a beautiful peace, it would be ridiculous to lose the fruit of so much blood and treasure, and that only to please a class of people [the farmers-general] who please no one. After having taught England some lessons, let's learn the one which she is now giving us, and so direct our efforts that the Americans, finding themselves as well treated by their friends as by their enemies, will not be forced to give preference to the latter."

Lafayette thus took a new step as a liberal—one which led him from the glamorous fields of soldiery and diplomacy into the stodgy atmosphere of counting-houses and commerce. He began to oppose restrictions upon trade. It was a logical result—in fact, an integral part—of his championship of America's interests. Since Vergennes also believed that "every question of tariff is no less a political than a financial question,"[10] he was easily convinced. In fact, he had communicated with Fleury on the problem of special privilege for American traders even be-

[10] Quoted in F. L. Nussbaum, "American tobacco and French politics, 1783–1789," *Political science quarterly*, XL (1925), 497.

fore Lafayette had done so.[11] The next few years were to find
the two men in close alliance in the effort to bind the United
States to France by purse strings.

Along with the new honor Lafayette received as *maréchal-de-
camp* and the new duty he assumed as patron of American commerce came a deep chagrin. It resulted from the open scandal
that his relations with Aglaé de Hunolstein had caused. Her family wished her to be reconciled with her husband. Her mother
particularly was incensed at her behavior. Aglaé, who more easily switched her affections than did her lover, had wished to put
an end to their affair almost as soon as it had begun. She had
not persisted in ending it only because of Lafayette's obvious
unhappiness at the mere suggestion. During his long absence in
Spain, however, she had had to face her family and public gossip
alone, and, when Lafayette returned, she begged to be released.
She urged him to go away from Paris for a few days, to think
it over, and to write her.[12]

Lafayette decided to go to Chavaniac. The bad weather and
poor harvest of 1782 had brought to the peasants of Auvergne a
great alarm, which Adrienne, in his absence, had already taken
some steps to assuage.[13] Besides, his aunt, Mme de Chavaniac,
was now alone there, her sister Mlle de Motier having just died.
He thought he should bring her to Paris.[14] And so, after only a
week in the metropolis, Lafayette set out on his journeys again,
back to the Midi and to his native village, which he had not
visited since he had left it nearly ten years earlier, a lad in his
teens, to marry Adrienne de Noailles.

As the seignior of Chavaniac moved among the starving
peasantry, interviewing the local nobility and officials, distribut-

[11] *Ibid.*, p. 500.

[12] Cf. Lafayette to [Mme de Hunolstein], March 27, 1783, John Carter Brown Library,
Providence, R.I. See also Gottschalk, *Lady-in-waiting*, pp. 99–102 and 128–29.

[13] Mme de Lafayette to Chazerat (intendant of Riom), February 26, 1783, Henri
Doniol, "Une correspondance administrative sous Louis XVI: épisode de la jeunesse de
Lafayette," *Séances et travaux de l'Académie des Sciences Morales et Politiques*, CIV (1875),
49–50.

[14] Bachaumont, XXII, 276–77; Charavay, pp. 97–98 and 552; Gottschalk, *Lafayette
comes to America*, p. 24.

ing hundreds of bushels of wheat from his own granaries, appealing to Versailles for greater aid,[15] he ceased to be the absentee landlord he had so long been. The spectacle of miserable human beings coming in crowds to beg his protection wrung his heart, and he did not fail them. Local tradition long afterward recorded that when he was told that this was a good time to sell his grain he answered, "No, it is a good time to give it away."[16] And it was also long recalled (if, indeed, not invented) that when grateful peasants came to thank him for his kindnesses, bringing their pathetic gifts and falling on their knees, Lafayette rebuked a relative who commented on the humility of these vassals. "Wait three or four years and things will not be the same!" he said.[17]

Perhaps his own suffering helped the young marquis to understand the sufferings of others. After five days among the mountains around Chavaniac he was ready to make the sacrifice which Mme de Hunolstein asked. He wrote her a long letter—protesting but yielding. Since he had to choose "between love and duty," since he alone derived happiness from their love "and it is you who risk everything while I get nearly all the pleasure," he would silence his heart and do "what reason tells you and decency imposes upon me." But that he would do only for her, and not out of regard for public gossip or the wishes of her family. "As to the nonsense people tell you, I do not care to take those feeble weapons away from your family. You know yourself, and some day you will know better yet what those weapons are. But at least my heart is my own, my dear Aglaée. All that you are, all that I owe to you, justifies my love and nothing, not even you, would keep me from adoring you."[18] On that painful note ended a love whose frustration had been a partial cause of Lafayette's first departure to America to seek fame and glory. It had turned into wormwood as soon as he had

[15] Gueyffier, (subdélégué of the election of Brioude) to Chazerat, March 27, 1783, Doniol, "Correspondance administrative," pp. 60–62; Lafayette to Montaran (maître des requêtes in the ministry of finances, in charge of food supplies), March 30, 1783, AN, F¹² 1376 (folder dated 1782), and Martin, Lafayette et l'école pratique, pp. 22–23.

[16] Doniol, "Correspondance administrative," p. 47.   [17] Ibid., pp. 307–8.

[18] Lafayette to [Mme de Hunolstein], March 27, 1783, loc. cit.

won it; it now came to a clean-cut close at the moment that his fame and glory were at their highest point.

When Lafayette left Chavaniac to return to Paris once more, he left youth behind him, just as once, ten years earlier, he had left childhood behind. Aglaé, disowned by her family and exposed to more and more scandalous gossip, soon went to live in a convent.[19] Lafayette passed from conquest to conquest, winning love, adulation, and jealousy—until revolution brought devotion and death to her, failure and imprisonment to him. But with the renunciation of his boyhood love for Aglaé, with the assimilation of a new set of political and economic principles, he passed from youth to manhood. Maturity could not have come at a more auspicious moment. A new career now awaited the hero of two worlds as a leader of liberal action in his own country.

A hundred years of political thought and evolution had conspired toward that end. During the eighteenth century, French political thought passed through three stages. In the first, which lasted up to the middle of the century, the writers were generally aristocratic in point of view. They held that the way to check absolutism was to return to the nobility a goodly share of the political authority that they had had before Louis XIV had subordinated all classes within the realm to his personal domination. These writers, of whom the foremost was Montesquieu, looked to the "good old days"—to history—for the justification of their contentions. Their appeal was limited and, in fact, largely clandestine, because of an effective censorship.

That stage was succeeded in the third quarter of the century by one in which the writers were middle class in point of view. These writers, of whom the foremost were Voltaire and Rousseau, held that it was necessary to restrain not only royal absolutism, but also aristocratic and clerical privileges. They looked to the "laws of nature and of nature's god"—to Reason—for the justification of their contentions. Their appeals met with the approval of a broader section of the people.

[19] Bachaumont, XXIII, 32–33; *Mémoires inédits de Madame la Comtesse de Genlis,* etc. (10 vols.; Paris, 1825), II, 271–73; cf. Gottschalk, *Lady-in-waiting,* pp. 102–7.

Both Voltaire and Rousseau died in 1778—the very year in which the alliance of France with the United States was made. Their mantles fell on men like Condorcet and Mably, who continued to search both in history and in Reason for political axioms but who also saw in America an empirical truth—an example of Philosophy teaching by example. Because they thought more often in terms of actual conditions than in political theories and because the censorship permitted a relatively free discussion of developments in an allied country, their ideas met with a general reception among all classes of the population—including many of the clergy and the nobility.

Among the nobles who were interested in the proposals of these *philosophes* for political and social reform, very few, however, came from the court nobility until after the American Revolution. Rare examples of "officers and gentlemen" who read and even wrote books could be found. Lafayette's friend, the Chevalier de Chastellux, and Franklin's friend, the Duc de Larochefoucauld-Liancourt, were among them; but they were of an older generation and were in no sense typical even of their generation. The younger people, before the American war, looked upon any of their number—Aglaé de Hunolstein's brother, for example—as queer if he had a taste for serious literature.[20] "In the midst of our games, our dances and our plays," wrote the Comte de Ségur, after decades of revolution had convinced him that the frivolity of his youth had been ill timed, "politics dared intrude only in laughter and reveal itself only in the form of a joke."[21]

That attitude changed with the war. Lafayette was the only prominent member of the court nobility who had been permitted to "volunteer" in the American cause before the alliance. But after the alliance they went to America in large numbers with the king's army. Lafayette knew them all. They were great men—like Estaing, Rochambeau, and Chastellux—or the sons of great men—like Noailles, Ségur, and Charlus—or the

[20] *Mémoires du Lieutenant-Général Puget-Barbantane* (Paris, 1827), pp. 2–6; cf. Gottschalk, *Lady-in waiting*, pp. 5–6.

[21] Ségur, I, 42.

nephews of great men—like Lameth. Among them were some who were to become the leaders of a revolutionary France, having been converted to ideas of liberty and equality—as they themselves admitted—by their American experiences.[22] When they returned with glowing reports of what they had found overseas, America became "the sole topic of conversation" among the aristocracy.[23]

Foremost among the converts was Lafayette. His conversion had begun earlier than theirs; he was already well on the road toward the new dispensation before the others started out; he was the richest of them; and he had become the most famous. Though he was soon to discover that he could also wield the pen in defense of liberty, his path was already marked out for him. It was to use his personal influence at court upon ministers and soldiers and among the people with merchants and writers. Few could resist the fervor and assiduity of one who was at the same time the "adopted son of Washington" and the most popular man in France. Lameth's brother complained that, of the great number of Frenchmen who had gone to fight in America, he alone stole all the praise—especially of the ladies.[24] He was "the hero of two worlds." Enraptured school children listened to masters who spoke as often "of Washington and of Lafayette as of the odes of Horace and the orations of Cicero."[25] He had spent his energies, his blood, and more than 700,000 livres in the good fight.[26] "One would say that he made it a law to imitate

[22] Cf. Alexandre de Lameth, *Histoire de l'Assemblée constituante* (2 vols.; Paris, 1828), I, lxv; and Dumas, I, 61–62. See also Gottschalk, "Attitude of European officers toward Washington," pp. 22–28.

[23] Talleyrand, I, 54.   [24] *Mémoires de Lameth*, pp. 108–9.

[25] A. V. Arnault, *Souvenirs d'un sexagénaire*, ed. Auguste Dietrich (4 vols.; Paris, n.d.), I, 51; cf. Daniel Mornet, *Origines intellectuelles de la Révolution française 1715–1787* (Paris, 1933), pp. 337 and 398–99.

[26] "Observations du Général Lafayette," p. 26 n.; Jean de Bernières, "Les revenus de La Fayette et la Révolution," *Revue bleue: revue politique et littéraire*, 3d ser., XIV (1887), 381–82; Morizot, "Compte rendu sur la fortune du Gal Lafayette à differentes époques de sa vie," in Chinard, *Lafayette and Jefferson*, pp. 303–15. Morizot says that he spent 1,033,000 livres from 1777 to 1783, of which only about 300,000 livres were for purposes not directly related to America. A livre could buy then roughly about as much as an American dollar today.

General Washington in everything," commented Philip Mazzei, who knew both men.[27] And, like Washington, he refused salaries and rewards. The strain on his resources had been such that he had had to sell some of his most profitable lands, thus reducing his annual income from 146,000 livres a year to 118, 000. What was worse, he had acquired the habit of spending money in large quantities for worthy causes and was to become poorer and poorer as one great cause followed upon the heels of another.

Chateaubriand would one day say of Lafayette that his American career inspired him with "a single idea and unhappily for him, it was that of the century."[28] It was true that fixity of purpose became the young man's strength. It was in the end unfortunate for him, in the sense (which Chateaubriand probably meant) that it lifted him above the level of his fellow-nobles to make him a leader of lost causes. His American successes in the long run meant material loss and spiritual tragedy for him. In America alone was he to find compensation for both. Europe presented only a succession of temporary victories followed by resounding defeats, somewhat alleviated by the faith that truth must ultimately triumph. "He left America you know," Gouverneur Morris later wrote of him,[29] "when his education was but half finished. What he learned there he knows well, but he did not learn to be a government maker." Unfortunately, he was to be called upon time and again to make governments, and he was to fail.

After Lafayette had played a leading role in the European scene for several years, he was ready to agree with Morris that he had been only half-educated in America. "Our American

[27] *Recherches historiques et politiques sur les États-Unis de l'Amérique septentrionale* (4 vols.; Paris, 1788), IV, 117 and n.; cf. "Portrait de La Fayette par Madame de Staël," Charavay, p. 541.

[28] *Mémoires d'outre-tombe*, ed. Edward Biré (6 vols.; Paris, 1899), VI, 385; an earlier edition quoted by Charavay (pp. 548–49) makes Chateaubriand say "happily for him."

[29] Morris to Washington, January 22, 1790, Gouverneur Morris, *A diary of the French Revolution*, ed. B. C. Davenport (2 vols.; Boston, 1939), I, 377.

Revolution," he then confessed,[30] "had left my mind as it were in a state of maidenhead. It was not acquainted with the ways of man as it is now. I have fought the same battles for the same cause with the same spirit and success at the head of the right angels against the wrong ones. But the scene of the one action was in Heaven, the other in Hell." A short year later he might have been willing to add that, though the roads to both heaven and hell were paved with the same good intentions, the path through heaven had proved easier to find than the path through hell—and probably because there had been a Washington and a Franklin to show the way through the one and no one to chart his confused course through the other.

In America, at any rate, Lafayette had not failed. He remained the triumphant champion of liberty, the shining symbol of the French alliance that had made victory possible. "It is no trifling compliment," wrote one of the officers of the American army,[31] "to say that, next to the Commander-in-Chief and the intrepid Greene, no general stood higher in the public favour or more constantly commanded the admiration of the army than La Fayette." John Adams, indeed, thought that he had acquired "too much of popularity in our own country." He discovered in the young idol "an unbounded ambition which it concerns us much to watch." For, he added, "I see in that youth the seeds of mischief to our country if we do not take care. He was taken early in our service and placed in an high command, in which he has behaved well, but he has gained more applause than human nature at twenty-five can bear." The marquis might live another fifty years; and the Francophobe Adams dreaded that, within ten, he would have come "by order of succession" to the command of the American army and at the same time have risen high in the French army, perhaps even into the ministry. "This mongrel character of French patriot and American patriot cannot exist long," he feared, "and if

[30] Lafayette to Short, November 16, 1791, LC, William Short papers.
[31] Garden, III, 201.

hereafter it should be seriously the politicks of the French court
to break our union, imagination cannot conceive a more proper
instrument for the purpose than the Marquis." And yet even
Adams had to admit that the object of his fears "is an amiable
nobleman and has great merit," that "he is now very active,
everlastingly busy, ardent to distinguish himself every way, especially to increase his merit toward America."[32]

Adams was right in guessing that Lafayette would live "these
fifty years." In fact he lived for fifty-one years after Adams
thus gave vent to his apprehensions. But Adams might have
spared himself his torment. Lafayette would use his great reputation, his "mongrel character of French patriot and American
patriot," not in an effort to make America French but to make
France American. Adams' suspicion of France blinded him to
the course of events in that country. Things soon happened
there that were to make ideas and not swords the better weapons; and the arsenal of Lafayette's ideas was America.

Lafayette long afterward said to the brother of Napoleon
Bonaparte that in the American Revolution "the world's greatest concerns were decided by a few skirmishes between patrols."[33] In that half-truth lay at least one striking fact: The
skirmishes in America provided dissatisfied Frenchmen of the
next decade with a concrete example of "a new nation conceived
in liberty and dedicated to the proposition that all men are created equal," and with a young leader whose loyalties and personal ambitions led him to strive for the realization of those
ideals in his own country. Two prerequisites for a successful
revolution in France or elsewhere—a program and leadership—
were, if not created, at least developed to maturity in the
"skirmishes between patrols" in America. The French Revolution might have come without Washington, Franklin, Adams,
Greene, Jefferson, Laurens, Hamilton, McHenry, and other
friends of "America's marquis." But it did come at the time it
came and it did take the form it took largely because of them.

[32] Adams to Warren, April 16, 1783, *Warren-Adams letters*, II, 213–14.

[33] "Mes rapports avec le premier consul," *Mémoires*, V, 167.

And the channel of their influence, the chief bridge in the communication of their spirit to France, was furnished by Lafayette. Apparently well educated by them for his new role, he appeared on the French scene, marked as a natural leader, just at the moment when nebulous hypotheses were ready to be translated into plans of action.

BIBLIOGRAPHICAL NOTES

For a discussion of the letter of Lafayette to "Aglaé," see Gottschalk, *Lady-in-waiting*, pp. vii and viii, and above, p. 413. Doniol's article on Lafayette's part in the Auvergne famine of 1783 is based on documents in the departmental archives of Puy-de-Dôme. Mornet's *Origines intellectuelles de la Révolution française* is the best available study of French public opinion before 1789. Charavay (pp. 538–50) has brought together from the memoirs of Lafayette's contemporaries a number of excerpts giving their opinions of him.

APPENDIX I

Some Legends and Traditions

Wherever anecdotes about Lafayette can be confirmed by acceptable historical evidence, they have been included in the text of this book if they belong in the period of time which it covers. Several stories that lend praiseworthy republican proclivities to the French aristocrat[1] quite clearly relate to the years following the American Revolution and have therefore been reserved for a forthcoming volume. For the years covered in the present volume, however, there are many tales of which no historical confirmation has been found.

Among the legends that have sprung up around Lafayette are several which couple his name with some American lady. One of the most elaborate traditions persists in Delaware. It runs to the effect that the ardent and lonesome marquis fell desperately in love with the beautiful Mary Vining and became a rival of Anthony Wayne for her affections.[2] A long correspondence is supposed to have been exchanged between them until her death. None of these letters seem to have survived, however; nor is there any reference to her in the numerous extant letters of Lafayette and Wayne to each other; nor is any mention of their rivalry made in the scores of memoirs written by the men and women who knew Lafayette during his American years. If he knew Mary Vining at all—which is quite possible—it is highly unlikely that he spent with her any large part of his hurried passages through Delaware or even of his less hurried sojourns in Philadelphia.

More credible than the tradition about Mary Vining is the anecdote regarding Margaret Sheaffe of Boston, who in 1779 married John R. Livingston. Lafayette is supposed to have said to her fiancé before the wedding: "Were I not a married man, I'd try to cut you out."[3] There is nothing improbable in this story. Indeed, such a bit of gallantry would have been altogether in keeping with Lafayette's character. If there were any contemporary evidence that he knew Margaret and John in 1779, it would be tempting to accept it as a fact.

Lafayette is also supposed to have visited Mary Bowen, sister of Jabez

[1] Cf. *Mémoires*, III, 196–97, 200, and 221–22; VI, 3–5.

[2] R. W. Griswold, *The Republican court or American society in the days of Washington* (New York, 1855), p. 21 n.; Elizabeth Montgomery, *Reminiscences of Wilmington in familiar village tales, ancient and new* (Philadelphia, 1851), p. 151; Mrs. Henry G. Banning, "Miss Vining, a Revolutionary belle," *American historical register*, II (1895), 1190–1205; J. H. Preston, *A gentleman rebel; the exploits of Anthony Wayne* (New York, 1930), pp. 106, 108, and 221; H. E. Wildes, *Anthony Wayne* (New York, 1941), pp. 179–80.

[3] S. A. Drake, *Old landmarks and historical personages of Boston* (Boston, 1873), p. 97; Catharina V. R. Bonney, *A legacy of historical gleanings* (2 vols.; Albany, 1875), I, 271.

427

Bowen, deputy-governor of Rhode Island, and to have maintained a long correspondence with her.[4] Lafayette undoubtedly knew Miss Bowen. This tradition of a fairly long friendship, however, seems to be due to a confusion of Lafayette with his friend Comte Mathieu Dumas. In 1824 when neither French nobleman was any longer young, Lafayette visited Rhode Island again. He saw Mary Bowen, who had long since married and was then a widow. "I found her face changed a little but her affection always the same," he wrote Dumas.[5] She asked Lafayette to tell Dumas that she still guarded carefully some papers that the count had left with her in 1781. Since Dumas spent a much longer period of time in Rhode Island than did Lafayette, he would appear to be the one who knew "the pretty miss of fifteen"[6] more intimately. Apparently, however, neither man corresponded with her, or she would not have had to wait until her old friend's visit in 1824 to tell Dumas that she still had his papers.

Another anecdote relates that when a young American officer on returning from France to America called on Mme de Lafayette for her messages to her husband, her small son said to him, "Faites mon amour à mon papa Fayette, et à mon papa Washington."[7] This episode is supposed to have taken place in 1781; and it could not have taken place later since Lafayette returned to Paris in January, 1782. As George Washington Lafayette, Adrienne's only son, was barely two years old in December, 1781, the story sounds apocryphal.

Another legend would have Lafayette sliding down the hills of Newburgh, New York, on oxsleds in the company of dashing American officers and Newburgh's prettiest girls.[8] Lafayette, however, seems never to have visited Newburgh until 1824. Though several writers have loyally claimed that honor for the town when it was Washington's headquarters,[9] Lafayette had left America before Washington went there in 1782.

Several doubtful traditions deal with the Virginia campaign. James McHenry's nephew is responsible for the belief that, fearful of Lafayette's "youthful ardor," Washington placed near him "one whom he knew to be a prudent adviser."[10] Another "authority" assigns the same function to An-

---

[4] Elizabeth F. Ellet, *Women of the American Revolution* (3 vols.; New York, 1850), II, 293.

[5] Lafayette to Dumas, September 21, 1824, Morgan Library, Lafayette vol., p. 38.

[6] *Ibid.*

[7] Cf. *An authentic biography of General Lafayette* (Philadelphia, 1824), pp. 33–34.

[8] Thurlow Weed, "Lafayette's last visit to America," *Galaxy*, XVI (1873), 76–77.

[9] New Windsor (pseud.), "Replies: Lafayette's knowledge of the Washington headquarters," *Magazine of American history*, XI (1884), 82; W. J. Roe, "A notable neighborhood," *Americana*, IV (1909), 583 and 585.

[10] Steiner, p. 29. Cf. L. D. Ingersoll, *History of the war department of the United States* (Washington, 1880), p. 423; F. J. Brown, "A sketch of the life of Dr. James McHenry," *Publications of the Maryland Historical Society*, No. 10 (Baltimore, 1877), pp. 12–13; General J. W. de Peyster, "Anthony Wayne, third general-in-chief of the United States Army," reprinted from the *United service*, XIII (1886), 4–5, 28–30.

thony Wayne as well as to McHenry.[11] There is no doubt that McHenry did use his very real influence with Lafayette to moderate the marquis' ardor.[12] On the other hand it would appear that it was Lafayette who was called upon to dampen Wayne's.[13] Moreover, neither Wayne nor McHenry joined Lafayette until June, 1781[14]—"in time," as McHenry put it, "to close his chapter of marches";[15] and both expected to join Greene as soon as expedient.[16] It would seem that, if Washington had felt that he ought to send inferior officers to Virginia to keep a watchful eye upon a young man whose independent judgment was bad, he was extraordinarily remiss in appointing the young man in the first place and then in not seeing to it that the officers reached their posts in time and with the intention of staying there. The documents, however, make very clear that Washington had every confidence in his young lieutenant's ability[17] and sent no one to "dry-nurse" him.

In Maryland they tell the story of how Aquila Deaver put Lafayette on his shoulders and carried him to safety from a scow stuck on a submerged rock in the Susquehanna River.[18] But the authority for that story seems to be no other than Aquila Deaver himself—and in the days when Deaver had become rather fond of his jug.[19] There is nothing in the story, however, which is in itself incredible. In Virginia they say that Lafayette's men accidentally burned one of the buildings belonging to William and Mary College.[20] It appears indubitable from two documents in the William and Mary papers[21] that the president's house was destroyed by some French troops. There is no evidence, however, that these troops were under Lafayette's orders. In fact, since the documents are dated June, 1782, it seems highly unlikely that Lafayette was anywhere in the neighborhood at the time.

Of all these anecdotes the one which has gained perhaps the widest credence is that of the quarrel between Steuben and Lafayette on the day of Cornwallis' surrender. Steuben's division, the story goes, was in the trenches when the first intimation of Cornwallis' proposal to surrender was received.[22] When Lafayette came up with his division to take his turn in the trenches, the old

[11] De Peyster in the *United service*, XIII, 28–30; and in "Anthony Wayne," *Magazine of American history*, XV (1886), 132–33.

[12] See above, p. 253.

[13] *Ibid.*, n. 32.

[14] McHenry to Lee, June 9, 1781, Kite, *Sidelight on history*, p. 17.

[15] See above, p. 253, n. 32.

[16] See above, pp. 253 and 274.   [17] See above, p. 270.

[18] See above, pp. 208 and 215; Shriver, p. 26.

[19] See Preston, *History of Harford County*, p. 141; cf. Shriver, p. 33.

[20] "Supplementary documents . . . . concerning the four forms of the oldest building of William and Mary College," *William and Mary College quarterly*, X (1930), 86.

[21] Folder 13A. I am indebted to E. G. Swem, librarian of William and Mary College, for this information.

[22] This statement in itself is false (see above, p. 324 and n. 64).

Prussian refused to be relieved, stating that to the soldiers who were on duty when the negotiations began belonged the honor of planting their flags on the enemy's parapets. Lafayette immediately galloped to headquarters, according to this tale, and appealed to Washington, who, on consulting Rochambeau, decided that Steuben was right.[23]

There is no immediately contemporary evidence to confirm this story. The several diaries of the Yorktown campaign say nothing of a dispute. Colonel Butler's journal states simply: "The troops in the trenches being entitled to the honor of closing the siege, we therefore remained unrelieved in the trenches."[24] The alleged dispute appears first to have been recorded by Colonel North, Steuben's aide-de-camp, sometime after Steuben's death in 1794.[25] North seems to have disliked Lafayette.[26] It was probably he who retold the story in 1818 under the pseudonym of "One who was in the trenches."[27] The story appeared again in 1859 on the authority of General T. S. Jesup, who said he had learned it from Major William Croghan, who had been on Steuben's staff, and from Colonel Richard Anderson, who had been on Lafayette's staff.[28]

The story thus seems to have the support of several contemporaries, even if no immediate record of it is available. Yet it is incredible. Lafayette's turn in the trenches did not come after Steuben's. The three major-generals succeeded one another in the order of their seniority: Lincoln, Lafayette, Steuben. It was Lincoln who would have relieved Steuben on October 18, if his tour of the trenches had not been countermanded by Washington's "after orders."[29] Lafayette's division did not again mount the trenches until October 19.[30] If North did not invent the story out of whole cloth, he was at least mistaken as to the parties to the dispute.[31] Lafayette in any case was probably not involved. Those who say he was were probably misled by North's positive statement (or statements) to that effect. For all the apparently independent sources seem to be derived from his testimony alone—except, perhaps, General Jesup's story, which at best is secondhand.

[23] Cf. Kapp, p. 458; Palmer, p. 292; Sargent, p. 482.

[24] *Historical magazine*, VIII (1864), 110.

[25] Quoted in Kapp, p. 458; cf. *ibid.*, p. 627. No one since Kapp seems to have been able to discover this pamphlet. An account, which was apparently very similar, was prepared by North in 1814 and is published in the *Magazine of American history*, VIII (1882), 187–99, and in the *German-American historical review*, XXIX (1929), 188–206.

[26] Cf. Kapp, p. 629.

[27] *New York National advocate*, 1818, quoted in Niles, p. 371.

[28] "Denny's journal," pp. 486–87.

[29] See above, p. 324; General orders, October 17, 1781, Fitzpatrick, XXIII, 234; After orders, October 18, 1781, *ibid.*, p. 238.

[30] General orders, October 18, 1781, *ibid.*, p. 238.

[31] Cf. Colonel J. W. Wright, "Some notes on the Continental Army," *William and Mary College quarterly*, 2d ser., XIII (1933), 96.

APPENDIX II

"The Boy Cannot Escape Me"

In the part of Lafayette's *Mémoires* that is called by their editor "Manuscript No. 1" (probably written between 1800 and 1814), Lafayette speaks of an intercepted letter of Cornwallis. That letter was written at the beginning of the British pursuit of Lafayette in the Virginia campaign. So sure was the English commander of capturing his young opponent that, according to Lafayette, he wrote: "The boy cannot escape me."[1]

I have searched carefully for such a sentence in the several available collections of Cornwallis' correspondence[2] but have not been able to find it, though the collections do contain the text of several intercepted letters. The words closest to the alleged quotation are a phrase in a letter of Sir Henry Clinton to Lord George Germain reporting that, according to Cornwallis' latest dispatches, "La Fayette could not escape him."[3] This brief declaration was apparently a conclusion drawn from a longer and less explicit statement by Cornwallis regarding his plans.[4] Nowhere in their official correspondence does either British general seem to have had the bad taste to refer to their opponent as "the boy." Though generals of twenty-four were rare even in the days of hereditary military classes, they were not so rare that Lafayette was unique. Witness Turenne and Condé. Cornwallis' attitude toward Lafayette seems to have been consistently respectful.

The words "the boy cannot escape me" appear to have originated with David Ramsay, the historian of South Carolina.[5] "Lord Cornwallis," Ramsay wrote, "exulting in the prospect of success, which he thought to be heightened by the youth of his opponent, incautiously wrote to Great Britain 'that the boy could not escape him.'" Unless Ramsay found some letter of Cornwallis which is unknown to me, he derived that phrase from the *Political magazine* of June, 1782.[6] His words are exactly the same as those of Clinton which are

---

[1] *Mémoires*, I, 272 (Amer. ed., p. 264).

[2] Among others: "State papers laid before the House of Peers relating to the loss of Lord Cornwallis's army at Yorktown," *Political magazine, and parliamentary, naval, military and literary journal*, June 1782; Sir Henry Clinton, *Observations on some parts of the answer of Earl Cornwallis to Sir Henry Clinton's narrative* (London, 1783); Stevens, *Clinton-Cornwallis controversy;* and Ross, *Correspondence of Cornwallis.*

[3] June 9, 1781, *Political magazine*, June, 1782, p. 345. On May 31, Clinton had written to Eden (Stevens, *Facsimiles*, VII, no. 748), "I fear he will escape."

[4] Cornwallis to Clinton, May 26, 1781, Stevens, *Clinton-Cornwallis controversy*, I, 488.

[5] *The history of the revolution of South Carolina from a British province to an independent state* (2 vols.; Trenton, 1785), II, 314.

[6] See n. 3 above.

quoted there, except for the substitution of "the boy" for "La Fayette." Ramsay attributed them to Cornwallis, though they were the words of Clinton reporting the attitude of Cornwallis.

From Ramsay other writers derived their information. Henry Lee, one of the most frequently exploited sources of knowledge of the Virginia campaign, indicates that he took the sentence from Ramsay.[7] William Gordon and John Marshall, who wrote their accounts of the Virginia campaign before Lee but after Ramsay, do not indicate their source for the sentence, though they quoted it.[8] There seems to be no other source than Ramsay that they could have used, since other probable sources do not give the phrase.

Lafayette, composing part of his *Mémoires* under the consulate of Napoleon Bonaparte, studied Gordon, Marshall, and Ramsay carefully.[9] He probably borrowed the phrase from them. He could not have taken it from Philip Mazzei's *Recherches historiques et politiques sur les États-Unis*,[10] (which he probably also knew) because there the sentence is correctly translated ("Lafayette ne pouvoit échapper") and correctly ascribed to Clinton.

The phrase "the boy" occurs in a somewhat different context in an unpublished letter of Colonel Aaron Ogden, written shortly after Lafayette's death. "His Lordship [Cornwallis]," Ogden wrote, "in the pride of his heart wrote home 'that he would catch the boy.' "[11] It would seem that Ogden was quoting from memory words which he had picked up somewhere. If he is an independent source, then Ramsay, and therefore the others, certainly misquoted Cornwallis, even though they all agree that His Lordship called Lafayette "the boy." The absence of that phrase from the collected letters of Clinton and Cornwallis leads to the conclusion that Ogden, as well as Lafayette, was misled by Ramsay—though probably indirectly, since, by the time Ogden wrote, the sentence had become part of the national tradition. It is to Ramsay's credit (and at the same time it would seem to be a confession of guilt) that he did not repeat the sentence in his later *History of the American Revolution*, though it would have appeared to belong there more logically than in his *History of the revolution of South Carolina*.

[7] *Memoirs of the war*, II, 198.

[8] William Gordon, *History of the rise, progress, and establishment of the independence of the United States of America* (3 vols.; New York, 1789), III, 207; John Marshall, *Life of George Washington*, etc. (5 vols.; Philadelphia, 1804–7), IV, 432. Cf. W. A. Foran, "John Marshall as a historian," *AHR*, XLIII (1937), 51–64.

[9] Cf. *Mémoires*, I, 67 (Amer. ed., p. 69). "Observations sur quelques parties de l'histoire Américaine par un ami du Gal Lafayette" (cf. p. 142 above) consists of comments on and criticisms of several American books, including Gordon, Marshall, and a second work by Ramsay, *The history of the American Revolution* (2 vols; Philadelphia, 1789). In this later work by Ramsay, it should be pointed out, the disputed sentence cannot be found (cf. II, 256–58). It is possible, therefore, that Lafayette was not familiar with Ramsay's earlier volumes and derived this sentence from Gordon and Marshall rather than from Ramsay directly.

[10] II, 218.   [11] Ogden to unknown, May 6, 1835, Jackson Collection.

APPENDIX III

The Masons Again

It is part of the Masonic tradition that Lafayette, together with Washington, Governor Nelson, and John Marshall, attended a meeting of Lodge No. 9 at Yorktown shortly after the capture of Cornwallis.[1] I have been unable to find any contemporary evidence for that belief, but it is not incredible.

There is another story, less persistent in Masonic literature, that Lafayette was initiated in "the Temple" at New Windsor, New York.[2] If this were so, it would probably have occurred in the winter of 1781, when Lafayette for a few weeks lived at New Windsor. Evidence for such an event is likewise missing. Moreover, it conflicts with the earlier claims of Morristown and Valley Forge to the honor of having been the scene of his initiation.[3]

No American town, however, has a good claim. Lafayette was a Mason before he came to the United States. The circumstances of his initiation are still clothed in mystery, but there can be no doubt of his having been a member in 1775.[4] Mr. R. Baker Harris, librarian of the Supreme Council 33°, Washington, D.C., has kindly sent me reproductions of pages from a contemporary document entitled *Planche à tracer de la cérémonie de l'inauguration de la Loge de Saint Jean, regulièrement constituée à l'Orient de Paris, sous le titre distinctif de la Candeur.* This document lists among the "Chers Frères Visiteurs" the "Marquis de la Fayette." The circumstances, Mr. Harris assures me, were such as to make it necessary for a visitor to be a Mason. This inauguration took place on December 25, 1775. From Mr. Harris likewise I have received a reproduction of the *Tableau des frères qui composent la Loge de S. Jean . . . . de la Candeur . . . . à l'époque du premier jour du premier mois de l'an de la véritable lumière 5776* (i.e., March 1, 1776). Lafayette's name is not among them. Hence he must have been a member of some other lodge. Mr. Harris' effort to discover whether it was a Metz lodge made up largely of army officers produced no clear answer. Lafayette's youth in 1775, when he was only eight-

[1] Cf. C. H. Claudy, *Washington's home and fraternal life* ("Honor to George Washington," published under the direction of the George Washington Bicentennial Commission, pamphlet No. 14, Washington, [1932]), pp. 174 and 177; E. B. Delzell, "Lafayette," *Grand Lodge bulletin, Grand Lodge of Iowa, A.F. and A.M.*, XXXI (1930), 743; Sidney Hayden, *Washington and his Masonic compeers* (New York, 1867), p. 78; P. A. Roth, *Masonry in the formation of our government, 1761–1799* (Milwaukee, 1927), p. 98 n.

[2] E. M. Ruttenber and L. H. Clark, *History of Orange County, New York* (Philadelphia, 1881), p. 226.

[3] See Gottschalk, *Lafayette joins the American army*, pp. 337–38

[4] Cf. *ibid.*, p. 337, where I was doubtful. Since that book was published the additional evidence discussed below has come to my attention.

433

een, would seem to indicate that he was initiated in an officer's lodge, since otherwise he would have been too young for initiation. Moreover, among the "Chers Frères Visiteurs" at the inauguration of the Loge de la Candeur are to be found the "Comte de La Meth" and the "Prince de Poix," also officers in the Army of the East, whose headquarters were at Metz (as well as several other friends, acquaintances, and relatives of Lafayette like La Marck, Coigny, Fronsac, Hunolstein, the Marquis de La Rivière, Rochambeau, Shuvalov, and the Marquis de Ségur).[5] The *Planche à tracer* is confirmed by a statement made by Lafayette in 1825 in reply to his welcome by the Grand Lodge of Tennessee.[6] "He had, he said, been long a member of the order, having been initiated, young as he was, even before he entered the service of our country in the Revolutionary War."

The most probable date of Lafayette's initiation into the Masonic Order thus appears to be 1775. Despite the efforts of pro-Masonic and anti-Masonic historians to prove the influence (good or bad, as the case may be) of Freemasonry on Lafayette's future career,[7] there is no testimony to show that it had any significance whatsoever until 1782.

[5] Mr. Harris' document seems to be the source of a description of the meeting of December 25, 1775, in two old histories of the Masons: Georg Kloss, *Geschichte der Freimaurerei in Frankreich (1725–1830)* (2 vols.; Darmstadt, 1852–53), I, 207; and G. J. F. Findel, *History of Freemasonry from its origins down to the present day* (London, 1869; translated from the German, 2 vols.; Leipzig, 1861–62), p. 226. It is possible, of course, that Findel borrowed his description from Kloss.

[6] *Proceedings of the Grand Lodge of Tennessee*, May 4, 1825, p. 135; C. S. Plumb, *Lafayette and his contacts with American Freemasonry* (reprinted from the *Proceedings of the Grand Lodge of Ohio* [1934]), pp. 22–25; Lebey, I, 48. For a copy of the *Proceedings of the Grand Lodge of Tennessee* I am indebted to Mr. W. P. Gardner.

[7] A list of their works is given in Gottschalk, *Lafayette joins the American army*, p. 337, n. 4. To this list should be added Gaston Martin, *La Franc-maçonnerie française et la préparation de la Révolution* (Paris, 1926), p. 50, V. B. Voorhis, "Lafayette, citizen and Mason of two countries," *Transactions of the American Lodge of Research, Free and Accepted Masons*, II (1934–36), 25–43 and 309–37, and the works referred to in this Appendix.

INDEX

(Names in italics indicate bibliographical data.)

THE CLOSE OF THE AMERICAN REVOLUTION

INDEX

447

La Touche, 375

Latouche (i.e., Louis-René-Madeline Lavassor, Vicomte de Latouche-Tréville), 73 and n., 74 and n., 77 n., 79, 80 n., 96, 212

Laurens, Henry, 3 n., 26, 27, 31 n., 47, 175, 330, 331 and n., 354 and n., 359, 364, 365, 373 n., 376 n.; *Correspondence of*, 331; *"Letters from Lafayette to,"* 354 n., 359 n., 373 n., 376 n.

Laurens, John, 79 n., 167–69, 171, 173, 175–76, 178, 180–83, 186, 211 and n., 257, 308, 310, 316, 320, 322, 325, 424–25

Lauzun, Armand-Louis Gontaut Biron, Duc de, 152, 186, 331, 332, 333; Legion of, 227, 234, 285; *Mémoires de*, 152 n., 373 n.; *"Narrative of,"* 373 n.

Laval-Montmorency, Marquis de, 163

Lawson, Robert, 229 n., 234 n., 239, 240, 24 , 252, 263, 266

Lear, Tobias, 135 n., 136 n.

Lebanon, Connecticut, 102 and n.

Lebey, André, 368 n., 369 n., 434 n.

Le Brigant, 361

Lee, Arthur, 27, 29, 44, 380

Lee, Henry ("Lighthorse Harry"), 121, 125, 148, 149, 432; *Memoirs of*, 142, 188, 248 n., 272, 319 n., 322 n., 326 n., 432 n.

Lee, Major [Henry?], 326 n.

Lee, Richard Henry, 29, 47, 206 n.; *letters of*, 29 n., 206 n., 244 n.; *Memoirs of*, 29 n.

Lee, Thomas Sim, 196, 197 and n., 200 n., 201 n., 213 and n., 214 n., 217 n., 219 and n., 234 and n., 244 n., 247 n., 258 n., 271 n., 276 n., 278 n., 280–81 nn., 283 n., 293–94 nn., 295, 321 n., 333 n., 429 n.

Leland, W. G., 85 n.

Le Plessix, 375

Leray de Chaumont. *See* Chaumont, Leray de

Lescure, M. de, 152 n., 348 n., 358 n.

Leslie, Alexander, 240, 264, 266 n.

Létombe (French consul in Boston), 342–44

"Letters of Lafayette," 196 n.

Lewis, George Washington, 345 n.

Libbie, C. F., catalogue, 286 n., 294 n., 296 n., 298 n.

Liberalism, ix, 27, 51, 52, 54, 128, 174, 183–85, 287, 327, 367, 369, 402, 416, 419

Liberty, 9, 19, 31, 52, 60, 86, 94, 95, 147, 183, 184, 220, 271, 359, 405, 421–24

Liberty Pole Tavern, 125

Library: British Museum, x, 78 n.; *Alderman*, x; *John Carter Brown*, x, 417 n.; *University of Chicago*, x, 38 n., 294 n. (*see also* Morizot, *papers* of); *Clements*, x, 152 n., 192 n., 211 n., 220 n., 230 n., 242 n., 244 n., 252 n.; *of Congress*, x, 9 n., 18 n., 31 n., 47 n., 72 n., 98 n., 136 n., 222 n., 257 n., 269 n., 274 n., 312 n., 337 n., 358–59 nn., 366–67 nn., 370 n., 377 n., 380 n., 385 n., 394 n., 399–400 nn., 423 n. (*see also* Congress, *papers* of; Rochambeau, *letter book* of; Hamilton, Alexander, *papers* of; Washington, *papers* of; Holker, *papers* of); *Harvard College*, x, 8 n., 55 (*see also* Sparks, *manuscripts*); *Huntington*, x, 58 n., 85 n., 167 n., 239 n., 385 n.; *Illinois State Historical*, 325 n.; *Pierpont Morgan*, x, 101 n., 232 n., 247 n., 252 n., 258 n., 269 n., 276–78 nn., 294 n., 297 n., 319 n., 337 n., 351 n., 375 n., 403 n., 414 n., 428 n.; *New York Public*, x, 124 n., 186 n., 192 n., 200 n., 243 n., 245, 258 n., 273 n., 274 n., 283 n., 298 n., 339 n., 344 n., 345 n., 356 n., 358 n., 370 n., 380 n., 383 n., 385 n., 390 n., 415 n.; *University of Pennsylvania*, x, 65 n.; *University of Rochester*, x, 15 n., 67 n., 375 n.; *Supreme Council 33°*, x, 433; *Virginia State*, 211 n.; *William and Mary College*, x, 429 n.; *Yale University* x, 87 n., 191 n. *See also* Archives; Bibliothèque; Society, historical

Light Camp, 122, 144, 153, 154

Light Division, 110, 121 and n., 122–25, 130, 141, 146, 148–50, 153–58, 170, 189, 190, 212, 316, 317, 319, 323–24, 358

Light Horse Corps, 121, 125

Lincoln, Benjamin, 56, 89, 301, 302, 305, 313, 315, 316, 324, 325, 326 and n., 339 n., 366, 430